A MORE ABUNDANT LIFE

New Deal Artists and Public Art in New Mexico

Jacqueline Hoefer

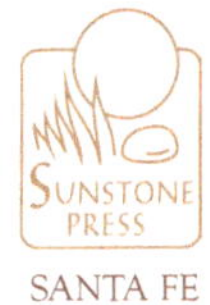

SANTA FE

On the front cover: *The Old Cuba Road*, William Penhallow Henderson.
On the back cover clockwise from upper left: *Dear Dancers*, Pablita Velarde; *Biology*, Raymond Jonson; *Cheyenne War Dance (Hoop)*, Paul (Chief Flying Eagle) Goodbear; *Indian Village*, William Lumpkins; *Winter Mass,* Gene Kloss; *A Woman Whose Baby is Dead*, Patrocinio Barela.

Sunstone books may be purchased for educational, business, or sales promotional use. For information please write: Special Markets Department, Sunstone Press, P.O. Box 2321, Santa Fe, New Mexico 87504-2321.

Printed on acid-free paper ∞

Library of Congress Cataloging-in-Publication Data:

Hoefer, Jacqueline.
A more abundant life: New Deal artists and public art in New Mexico / Jacqueline Hoefer.
p. cm.
Includes bibliographical references and index.
ISBN: 978-0-86534-305-4 (hardcover)– ISBN: 978-0-86534-371-9 (pbk)
1. Art, American—New Mexico—20th century. 2. Federal Art Project.
3. New Deal, 1933–1939. I. Title.

SUNSTONE PRESS Post Office Box 2321 Santa Fe, NM 87504-2321/USA
(505) 988-4418/orders only (800) 243-5644 FAX (505) 988-1025
WWW.SUNSTONEPRESS.COM

Dedicated to the memory of Jacqueline Hoefer
who loved art and who loved New Mexico

If I were asked to state the great objective which Church and State are both demanding for the sake of every man and woman and child in this country, I would say that that great objective is "a more abundant life."

–Franklin Delano Roosevelt
Address to the Federal Council of Churches of Christ, December 6, 1933

Contents

Preface

This book is about the experience of artists in New Mexico who participated in the New Deal art programs and the works they produced, many of which still enhance towns and villages all over New Mexico.

The first New Deal programs were developed in 1933, early in Franklin Roosevelt's presidency, in response to an economic crisis that gripped New Mexico as well as the entire nation. The hard times that lasted almost to the end of the decade have come to be called the Great Depression. In a brief introduction, the historian Marc Simmons describes the special circumstances of the Great Depression in New Mexico. He gives us an economic and political context in which to understand the desperate need for jobs and money faced by New Mexicans, artists as well as workers and farmers.

In the first section, "The New Deal for Artists in New Mexico," my intention is to describe how the art programs worked on a local level. Talented New Mexicans, not outside specialists, came forward to organize and supervise the art programs, and over a hundred local artists signed onto the government payroll. In state-sponsored interviews in 1964 and in 1992, artists and administrators were asked about their New Deal experience. Their responses are the basis of my interpretation. They tell us in their own words a great deal about what they actually did as participants, about their relationship with their co-workers, and also, how they felt about their part in the program.

The main section which follows, "Pictures, Pots, Murals, Weavings and Carvings: The Work of New Deal Artists in the Towns and Villages of New Mexico," offers a photographic record of works that can still be seen in schools and post offices and courthouses. They are, however, but a selection. During the almost ten years of federal programs, the artists of New Mexico produced over a thousand works of art. Almost nine hundred pieces are still preserved, though not always in accessible public places. The works here presented were chosen because they are fairly accessible and may lead the viewer to seek them out. Of equal if not greater importance, they show the quality and diversity of artwork presented to the state by the federal programs and as such have become part of an important historical record.

Finally, in the last section, "The Artist's Voice," I have presented excerpts from Kathryn A. Flynn's interviews with three artists: Pablita Velarde, Eliseo Rodriguez and Gene Kloss, Indian, Hispanic, and Anglo, respectively. They talk at length about their New Deal experiences and reveal something of the culture of which they were a part. They also express the enthusiasm of artists who saw the art programs as an opportunity for work that was more than employment and for community participation in which the dignity and social value of art were recognized.

The Great Depression in New Mexico

There was a sour joke among New Mexicans in the 1930s that since living poor was so common in their state, the collapse of the national economy went unnoticed for the first several years. The unhappy reality was that no one escaped the pain that wracked the country. Prolonged drought and unprecedented dust storms had ravaged dry-land farming in the American Southwest. Within five years of the 1929 crash, the state's largest employer, the Santa Fe Railroad, had reduced its local work force by more than half. Mining, another major industry, deeply cut production. At the height of the Depression nearly half the working population of New Mexico was out of work.

In 1930 Hispanics numbered sixty percent of New Mexico's population. Spanish as much as English was heard in the halls of the State Legislature and on city streets. A small but energetic Hispanic middle class flourished in the larger towns. In rural areas, though, and in the villages, conditions were generally bleak. Much of the public grazing land that had been the foundation of traditional village life had been lost to private ownership. What remained showed the scars of over-grazing and erosion. Many of the men had to find work as day-laborers or travel seasonally to sheep herding jobs in Wyoming or to the beet fields of Colorado. Almost eighty percent of the farming population was on the relief rolls even before the Depression.

New Mexico's relatively large Indian population also found itself in pinched circumstances at the beginning of the decade. Like their Hispanic neighbors, they depended heavily on subsistence farming. In the face of poor markets, it was hard going. Even so, they had some advantages. Legal recognition and protection of old reservation boundaries enabled them to enjoy a larger land base. Further, the tight structure of tribal life, particularly among the Pueblos, allowed those communities to resist more effectively threats posed by outside social and economic upheaval.

Franklin Delano Roosevelt, Democrat, assumed the presidency on March 4, 1933. He had been swept into office by his plan for reform and recovery. His pledge of "a New Deal to aid the forgotten man" lifted the spirit and hopes of the public. Quickly he launched a comprehensive federal effort to relieve unemployment and rehabilitate the national economy. His strategy was to funnel dollars from Washington into state-run programs, which would offer, he believed, the best way to restart local economies.

New Mexico garnered some of the greatest dividends from the new government largess. New Mexico certainly needed help, but it was political determination, perhaps, as much as need that brought New Deal programs here. Clyde Tingley, an eccentric man, who often declared that his aim in life was not to get rich but to be re-elected, was mayor of Albuquerque when the Depression began, and in 1934 he won the office of governor on the Democratic ticket.

Tingley was a strong supporter of Roosevelt, and that helped him gain direct access to the White House and to heads of New Deal agencies. He was also tireless. He made trip after trip by train to Washington to seek federal dollars for New Mexico. He was able to tap into such relief projects as the Works Progress Administration and the Civilian Conservation Corps. His success brought jobs and new construction across the state from Bosque del Apache in the south to the mountain villages of the Sangre de Cristos.

New Deal money, it turned out, was allocated in programs that helped almost everybody, big towns as well as villages, farmers as well as construction workers, small businesses as well as larger employers.

It also changed social policy in regard to major segments of the New Mexican population. In Spanish-speaking villages, the government introduced what we may call an Hispanic New Deal. Its aim was to stimulate small-scale farming and revive traditional arts and crafts. The hope was to restore economic self-sufficiency and in so doing sustain local culture.

The same goal underlay programs for the Pueblos and other tribes, but tribal programs were administered, as they always had been, through the Bureau of Indian Affairs. Its policy had been that of forced assimilation. Encouraged by New Deal leadership to respect local institutions, the Bureau abandoned their long-standing policy in favor of programs that protected tribal identity. The consequence of this new respect for local institutions was especially important to New Mexico where to some extent it helped preserve community life among both Hispanics and Indians.

Not all government funding, however, went to these large groups. There was also, one might say, a New Deal for artists. By the 1930s, Taos, Santa Fe and Albuquerque had significant artist populations. Like farmers and workers generally, they faced a disappearing market. Nobody had money to buy paintings or sculpture or even beautiful pots. And there were no pick-up jobs to pay the rent. Fortunately, New Deal planners who offered help to farmers and factory workers also understood the need to help artists. They too were essential to sustain the spirit and traditions of the community. In light of such recognition, the New Deal developed programs to help painters, sculptors, potters, indeed, artists of all kinds.

Funding for these New Deal programs continued until the end of the decade, for some even into the war years. The war itself ended the crisis in unemployment. It also reshaped social and economic patterns in ways quite beyond anything New Deal planners had anticipated. Whether these new patterns reinforced or simply bypassed the ambitious social goals of the New Deal planners, in regard to Hispanic villages, for instance, is difficult to estimate. The short-term success of the programs, however, was immediate.

They gave people jobs and put money in their pockets. For many this meant money to buy food. In the following chapters artists express their gratitude for the help given them. I would speculate that such feelings were common in the towns and villages of New Mexico.

–Marc Simmons, Ph.D.

The New Deal for Artists in New Mexico

It's very difficult to make a living out of painting. . . .Why the artist paints I don't know. It's just like why a person preaches, you know. They just do it.

–Jozef Bakos, Santa Fe painter

The New Deal inspiration for funding art came from President Franklin Delano Roosevelt's friend George Biddle, an artist who had studied with Diego Rivera in Mexico. Biddle understood the social importance of the Mexican muralists Rivera, Orozco and Siquieros. In painting the life of ordinary people as beautiful and worthy of notice, they expressed the ideals of the Mexican Revolution. He persuaded Roosevelt that in a time of economic trauma American artists could do likewise by painting murals that inspired confidence in American life and history. Indeed, the popular Regionalist painters Thomas Hart Benton, Grant Wood and John Steward Curry, were painting local American scenes that, quite coincidentally, underlined the social themes envisioned by Biddle.

New Deal planners set about almost immediately to employ artists to paint pictures of everyday America. The first Federal program, the Public Works of Art Project, started in December, 1933, at the very beginning of Roosevelt's first term, and ended six months later. Two programs under the Department of the Treasury quickly followed: The Section of Painting and Sculpture began in late 1934; the Treasury Relief Art Project in 1935. A fourth program, the Federal Art Program under the WPA, in some ways the most significant, also began in 1935 and was the last to close, in the early 1940s. For almost ten years, until the war effort took precedence, the New Deal funded public art.

The artistic largess New Deal programs brought to New Mexico was extraordinary. Deservedly so, one might argue. Less than one month after the first program began, New Mexicans were organized and ready to go to work. In early January, 1934, the Albuquerque Journal announced that public buildings in New Mexico, including the Albuquerque city hall, "will be beautified with Federal money."

Almost a hundred artists and craftsmen were assigned to local projects throughout the state. Such a rush of painting and potting and carving must have aroused public curiosity, even astonishment. If there were doubts, they were probably momentary. Many of the artists as well as the people who ran the program were local and well known—Gerald Cassidy, William Penhallow Henderson, Fremont Ellis, Olive Rush, Gene Kloss, Russell Vernon Hunter, John Gaw Meem, among others—and the results were almost immediate.

When the first program ended, less than six months later, New Mexican communities had received 292 works of art, not including the work of Indian craftsmen or works sent to a national exhibit in Washington. Public libraries, courthouses, post offices, state and county buildings had been, as the Journal promised, "beautified," some by easel painting, some by murals, some by decorative objects. Every public high school in towns with a population over 1,000 as well as many smaller communities had received original works of art.

Never before had the Federal government funded art on such a scale. The goals and procedures of the four major programs were somewhat different, as was evident in the New Mexican experience, but underlying each was the idea that art mattered, and that artists were contributing members of the community.

Shortly before he died at the age of ninety, the Santa Fe artist William Lumpkins was asked about his recollection of the Depression in New Mexico and his feelings about being a WPA artist. "Everybody in Taos was on the WPA," he said. "We thought it was heaven on earth." His exuberant response gives us some idea what it was like, as he put it, "to be paid to paint."

Fortunately, like William Lumpkins, many New Deal artists in New Mexico had an opportunity to speak for themselves. They were interviewed in 1964 by Sylvia Loomis for the Archives of American Art. Much later, in the early 1990s, Kathryn A. Flynn conducted additional interviews. She talked with artists, with local people who ran the New Deal programs, and with old friends who remembered the times and knew the artists personally.

What these interviews offer is the personal experience of artists and, in a few instances, of administrators who participated in the New Deal art programs. Their interpretation of that experience and the art they produced in response is what this book is chiefly about.

The first New Deal program, the Public Works of Art Project, was commonly referred to as PWAP. This ugly sounding acronym had as its high aesthetic purpose to employ professional artists to decorate public buildings and parks throughout the country. The preferred subject matter was, as George Biddle had proposed, to paint pictures of everyday America.

PWAP was an entirely new idea and immensely ambitious. It was fortunate in its leadership. Edward Bruce, the National Director in Washington, was multitalented. Lawyer, business man and professional painter, Bruce was dedicated to the New Deal idea of creating a public art in which people could discover something of themselves and the life around them. As they looked at the walls of their post offices and courthouses and schools, they would see "the American scene in all its phases." Except for these general directions and the need for some kind of accountability, Bruce did not interfere with local choices. It was up to regional committees to select artists and supervise employment. The artist himself had complete freedom in choosing subject and style.

The administrative structure was fairly simple. Sixteen regional districts were set up, each of which had local representation. New Mexico along with Arizona was Region 13.

New Mexico had a rich source of talent to offer Region 13. Early in the century, the extraordinary physical beauty of the state began to attract a large number of talented and well-trained artists from all over. They could live cheaply and enjoy the hospitality of a village culture. The towns were small. In 1930, Taos had around 2,000 people; Santa Fe, 11,000; Albuquerque, the largest, about 27,000. Artists knew each other, and many were closely connected to their local communities, influenced, perhaps, as was all of New Mexico, by the strong communal bonds enjoyed by Indians and Hispanics. Distances were not great. Artists in Taos and Santa Fe did not have daily contacts—it was a four hour trip between Taos and Santa Fe—but they were certainly aware of what neighboring artists were doing.

New Mexico offered, in addition, a long tradition of native arts and crafts. Local artists of exceptional quality—Indian weavers, painters and pot makers, Hispanic carvers and furniture makers—had prepared people to think of art as part of daily life, a way even of making a living. The locals might not buy much, but they regarded art as an acceptable activity.

Some applauded it. When the Public Works of Art Project was announced, leading citizens stepped forward to help organize and stayed on to become steadfast supporters. Senator Bronson Cutting and the architect John Gaw Meem, whose architectural passion was to preserve indigenous styles and culture, were on the Regional Committee. The local administrators they helped select were intellectual and artistic leaders in New Mexico: Jesse Nusbaum, a distinguished anthropologist who had done major projects all over the state, was the director; Kenneth Chapman, also an anthropologist and well known locally, was secretary.

From the time he came to New Mexico from Colorado, early in the century, Jesse Nusbaum's talents led him to become acquainted with artists throughout the state. He taught at the State Normal School in Las Vegas, worked on the original survey at Mesa Verde National Park and later became its first archeological supervisor. His first job in Santa Fe was to rehabilitate the Palace of the Governors. He contributed to the design of the Fine Arts Museum and in 1930 became the first director of the Laboratory of Anthropology.

He was an excellent choice for regional director, though not a willing one: "I did everything possible to get out of it," he said, "archeology not art was my field." But Senator Cutting persuaded him: "I'm asking you to accept it, but if you won't . . . then I'll simply tell the artists in Taos and Santa Fe and elsewhere . . . that they haven't the project because you wouldn't accept the directorship."

Nusbaum did agree to "generally look after it" on the condition that he have a field coordinator. That job went to Gustave Baumann. Baumann was a noted wood-block artist who seemed to know every artist in New Mexico. He got paid a salary and transportation and went all over the state to talk with artists about how the work was going and, also, to ask local people as well as artists to suggest public buildings that might be decorated.

As Nusbaum explains it, artists were evaluated and paid according to their skills and experience. Class A was the "upper class, . . . the best known artists, like Walter Ufer, Victor Higgins. . . . There were a few who didn't come in because they didn't need it, like Blumenschein. But the others were all anxious to get in on it, Kenneth Adams, the whole group."

They were the professionals who worked in traditional fine arts media, frescoes, oil paintings, watercolors, etchings, sculpture. It was their talents and experience the Project was primarily intended to utilize, both for their own benefit and for the public decoration they were asked to do. Nusbaum's recollection is that they were paid about two dollars an hour for twenty hours a week. They had to furnish their own material except for large projects that required expensive canvas.

Others, less experienced, less skilled, were in Class B. They made $27.50 a week for twenty hours work. A third Class C group were craftsmen and laborers. As Nusbaum explained, "It was a relief measure . . . any person could get in if he was an artist and he asked."

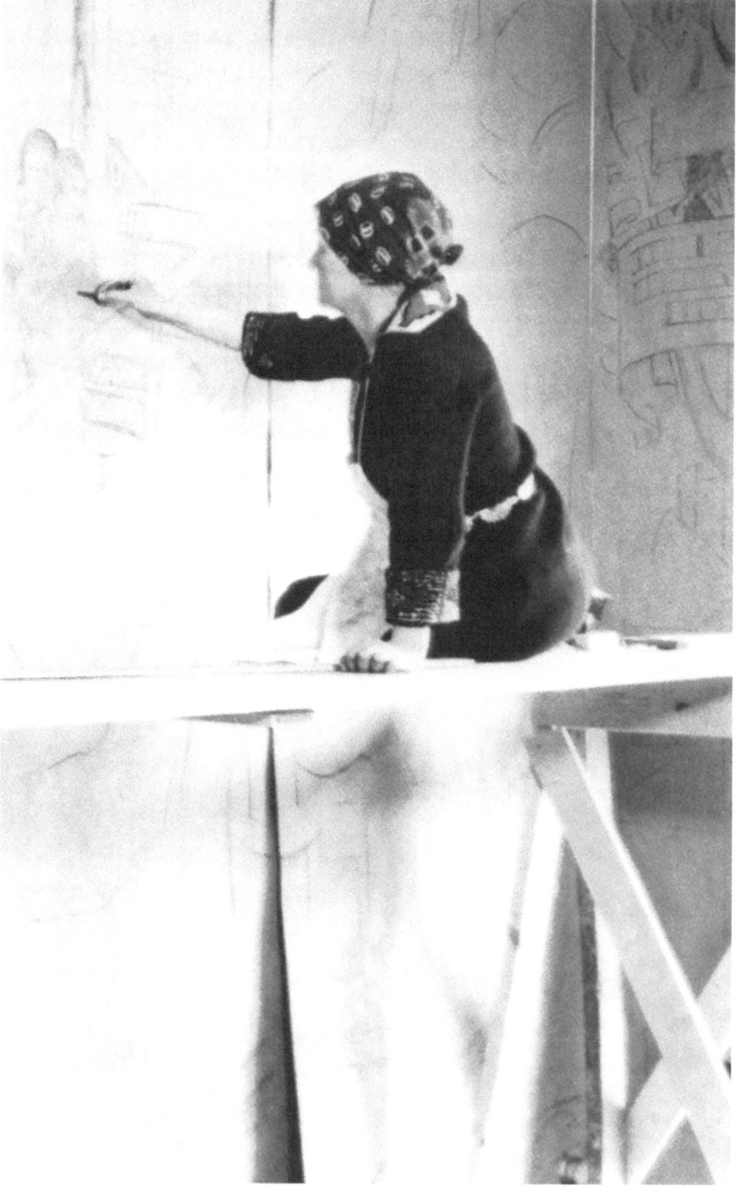
Olive Rush working on a fresco mural in the stairwell of the Santa Fe Public Library.

Putting weavers, wood carvers and pottery makers along with laborers in the Class C group might indicate a lack of regard for their skills. Yet they were enthusiastic producers, and their work was sent off to Washington to be exhibited in museums along with easel painting and sculpture. The laborers who helped the artists were also appreciated. The painter Olive Rush praises the skill of the man who prepared the fresco plaster for her: "Every day he put on the plaster ready for me to paint. And it was marked out, this very exact amount that I would be able to paint that one day." She recog-nized the job was important to him. "I think it was something he needed to do," she says, "and he did it beautifully."

Since the Public Works Art Project derived in part from George Biddle's enthusiasm for the Mexican muralists, it is not surprising that murals became a major genre for the Project. They could be seen easily, even by a casual observer, and they could accommodate social and regional themes that required scale. From a practical point of view, they were ideal for filling large, sometimes ill-shaped public spaces.

A few artists, Lloyd Moylan, Emil Bisttram and Dorothy Stewart, were directly acquainted with Rivera and the Mexican muralists, but for the most part, the artists who worked on murals were self-taught. Emil Bisttram, who had studied with Rivera and had done frescoes with him in Mexico, tells how they learned the technique:

> I was very anxious to do some [frescoes] here and have the opportunity to work on a large scale. And the other men were anxious too. None of them had ever done any of it. We all learned, some from books, some from me, as to how this was done.

The Project required that artists first submit a black and white sketch to the regional director, then a cartoon, and finally a full scale black and white drawing before starting on the mural itself. The picture design had to fit an allotted public space, sometimes above elevator doors, on stairwells, around windows and hallways. Later, of course, the artists themselves had to work in these difficult spaces. While doing murals for the domed entrance of the biology building at the State Agricultural College, Las Cruces, Olive Rush had to work from a rickety ceiling scaffolding while students, it would seem, strolled in and out.

In spite of difficulties, artists were eager to participate. "The surprising thing about the whole project," Jesse Nusbaum reports, "was as soon as we got started . . . the number that wanted to be in it."

Many of the murals and the locations for them, Nusbaum tells us, were proposed by the artists themselves. In Taos, the "Fresco Quartet," as they came to be called, Emil Bisttram, Ward Lockwood, Bert Phillips and Victor Higgins, "went and got the project in the [old] Taos County Courthouse." All did not go smoothly Jesse Nusbaum admits: "They decided they'd do it as a guild and would choose lots to see who would do certain pictures. . . . The only thing was that one fellow insisted he should have the space just behind the back of the judge." Apparently, the problem was worked out because the mural was completed and is still to be seen.

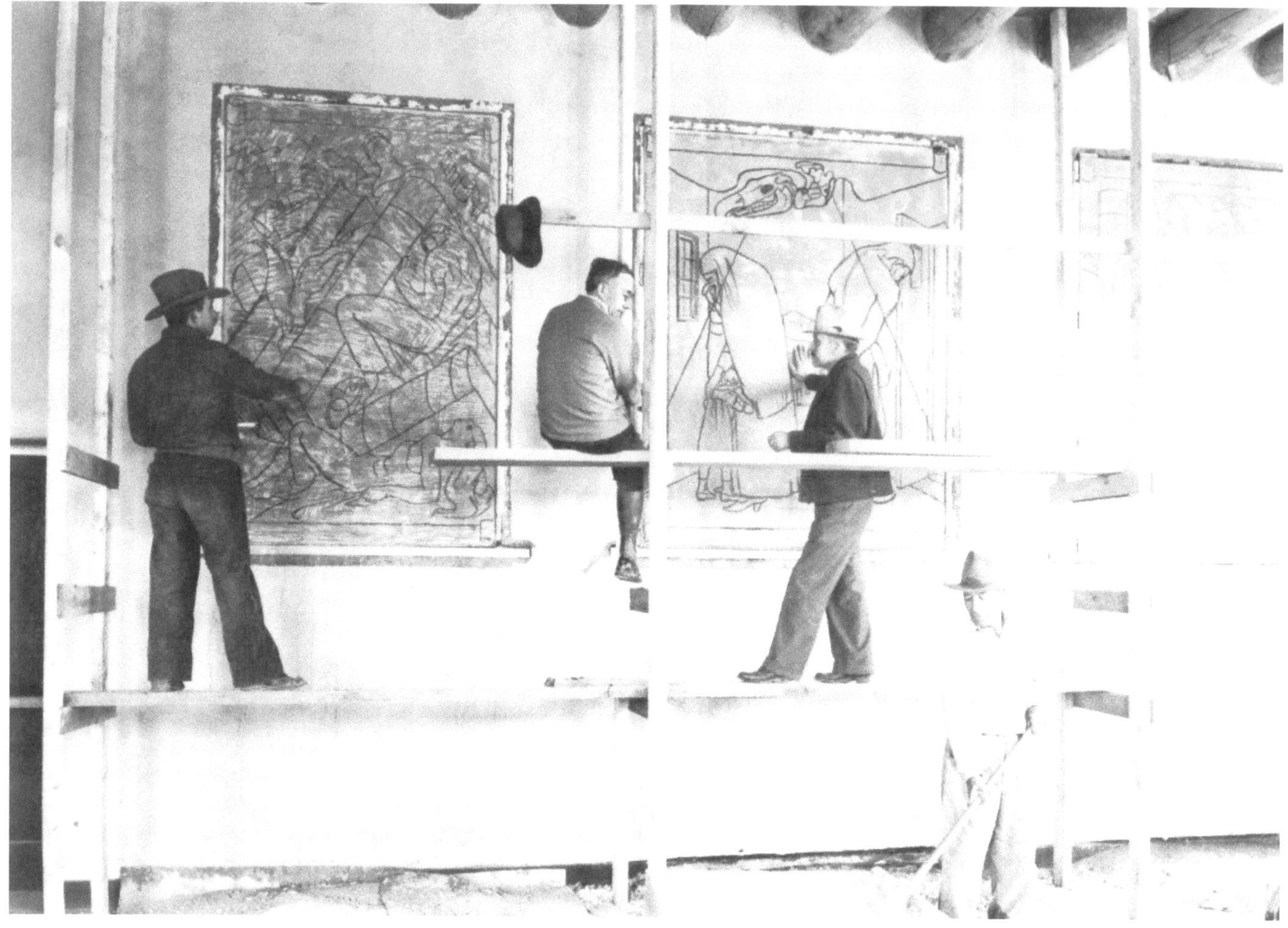

Three unidentified members of the "Fresco Quartet" working on the murals in the old Taos Courthouse.

William Penhallow Henderson, Nusbaum reports, proposed murals for the United States Court House in Santa Fe: "Those paintings . . . as you go down the hall, that was his project." Olive Rush suggested frescoes "would be a nice thing" for the Public Library in Santa Fe. And they were glad, Nusbaum says, "because there was no cost connected to it." Theodore Van Soelen, a member of the National Academy, wanted to do something in the courthouse in Silver City. They too were delighted. He did two big murals, and when they were finished, they had "a big to-do about it."

The art that came out of the Project, whether it be mural, easel painting, etching, whatever the genre, could go in any government building, but it had to be accepted by the local authorities. "It was up to the people," Nusbaum explained, "to have an interest." As Nusbaum's stories attest, they did take an interest. Buck Dunton, he tells us, did beautiful animal pictures. He did one of an elk, and Judge Neblett "had to have that elk in his chambers up there at the Federal Building. So he got that." There were several works in the Supreme Court Building, and the Justices came up to see them. "They were sorry," Nusbaum says, "they didn't get there earlier because they wanted more. They wanted to decorate."

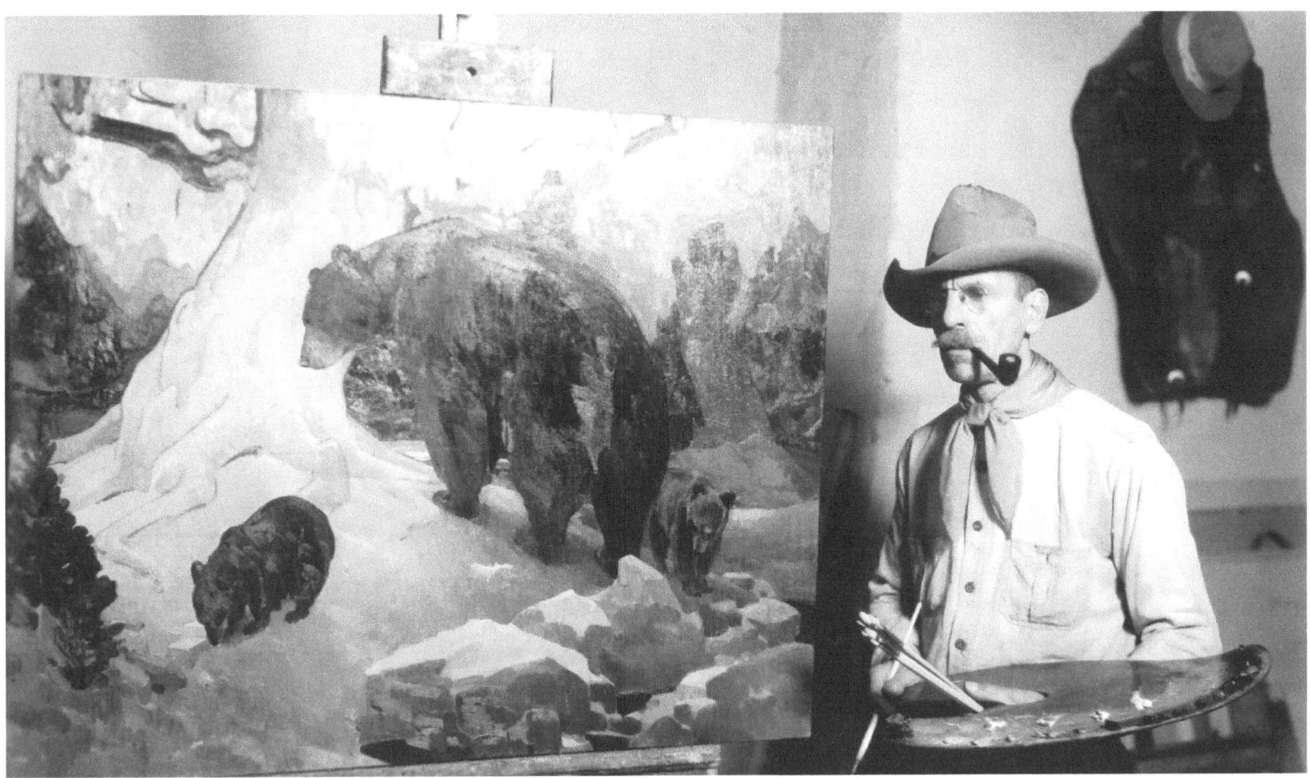

W. Herbert (Buck) Dunton was born in 1878 in Augusta, Maine and died in 1936 in Taos, New Mexico. He came west in 1896 and hunted bear and worked as a cowboy in the summer. Later, he went back east to study, but settled permanently in Taos in 1914. One of the founders of the Taos Society of Artists. His mature work was noted for its animal imagery, and in 1934 his painting of a bear, *November in the Sangre de Cristos,* for the Public Works of Art Project was selected by President Roosevelt for the White House. WPA Photo Collection #5387, New Mexico State Records and Archives, Santa Fe.

The "widest spread of any work we had," Nusbaum reports, was that of the Taos artist Gene Kloss. As a student at the University of California, Gene Kloss bought a two-dollar book, How to Make an Etching, went home, and working in her mother's kitchen, made her first plate. The "how to" book was instruction enough to launch her on a distinguished career. She first came to Taos on vacation in 1925. Inventive and free-spirited, she brought her small etching press, a sack of concrete, and set up the press on a stump in the woods and made her etchings.

By the time the Project came along, she was producing "beautiful little prints" in a more conventional studio. "We ordered those by the hundreds," Nusbaum says. "Each one was supposed to have a little brass tab on it showing it was from the Public Works of Art Project. . . . They went to schools all over the state wherever they expressed an interest. The University of Albuquerque [University of New Mexico] got some."

Jesse Nusbaum was full of praise for the artists, and especially for Gerald Cassidy, "one of the fellows that worked hardest." Cassidy made two sketches, one of Chaco Canyon and one of Canyon de Chelly. The original sketch of Canyon de Chelly was sent to the director's office of the National Park Service. Unfortunately, Cassidy's story ended tragically. He was working in winter, Nusbaum tells us, in an old empty store building:

> He had a big canvas to get started the way he does. He worked with a fire in there, and he had to dope it, the canvas, to stretch it out and get it ready. It was cold weather and they kept the building tight, and he inhaled too much of the fumes. . . . He didn't last long after that.

In his opinion, Gerald Cassidy was a hero in the art program: "he literally gave his life," Nusbaum says, "to the work he was so anxious to get started." If there were shirkers in the program, Nusbaum doesn't mention them.

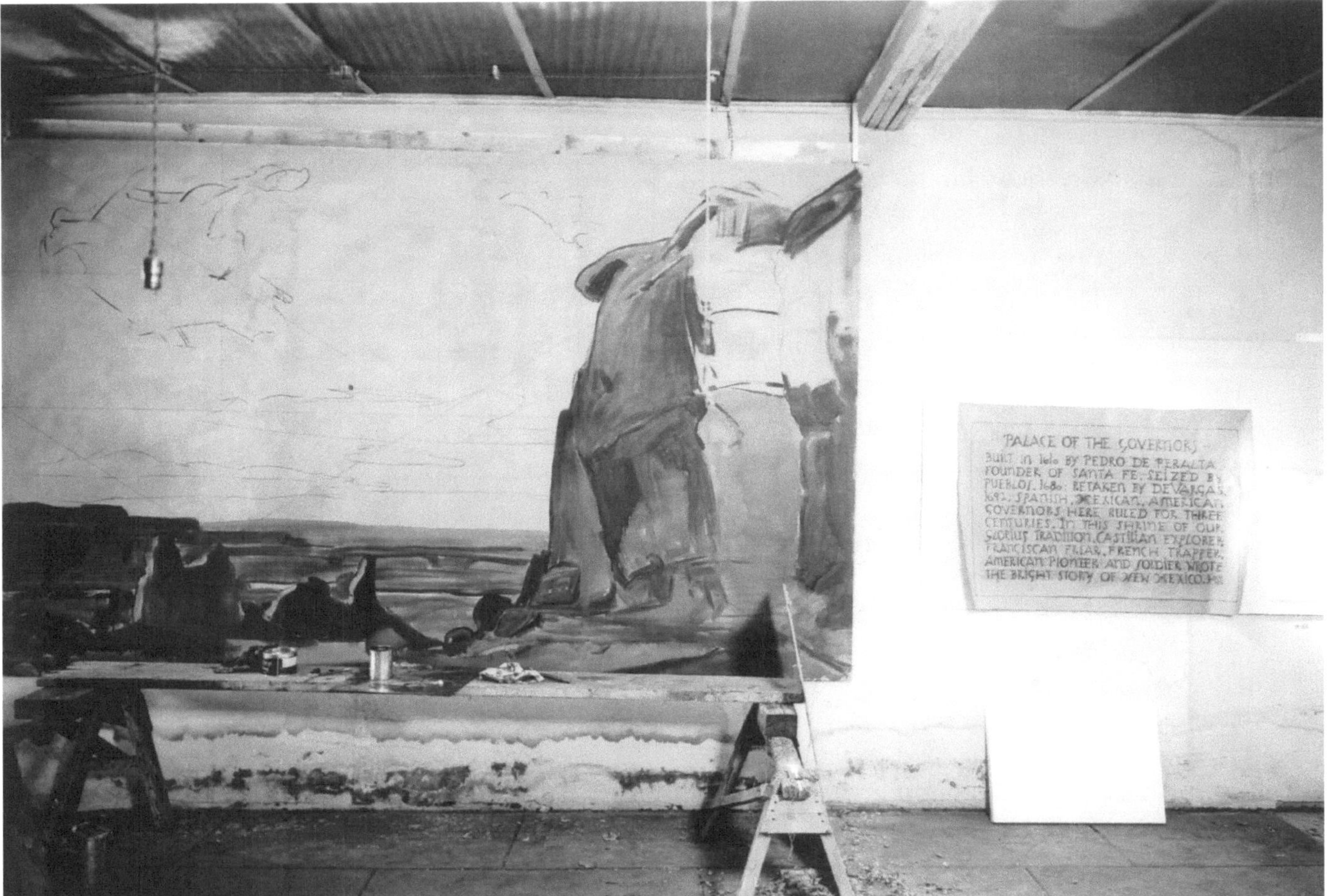

A large mural was planned for the United States Court House in Santa Fe and was begun by Gerald Cassidy, the first local artist to be chosen by the Public Works Art Project. Cassidy died shortly after he began working on it. William Penhallow Henderson took over the project and completed the courthouse murals. WPA Photo Collection #5383, New Mexico State Records and Archives, Santa Fe.

Datus Myers, a Santa Fe artist, was field coordinator for the Indian Division. His job was to visit the Pueblos to enlist the Indians in the government program and to organize and supervise production at the Santa Fe Indian School where the work was done. His thoughtful report shows him to be as admiring of Indian artists as Jesse Nusbaum was of the Project as a whole.

The Indian Division worked in four areas, mural painting, watercolors, pottery and blanket weaving. The potters and blanket makers, he tells us, worked with little supervision from him. Among those participating were the famous Pueblo potter Maria Martinez, her husband Julian, and Apache painter-sculptor Allan Houser.

Julian and Maria Martinez, San Ildefonso Pueblo, Photograph by Wyatt Davis, Museum of New Mexico #4591.

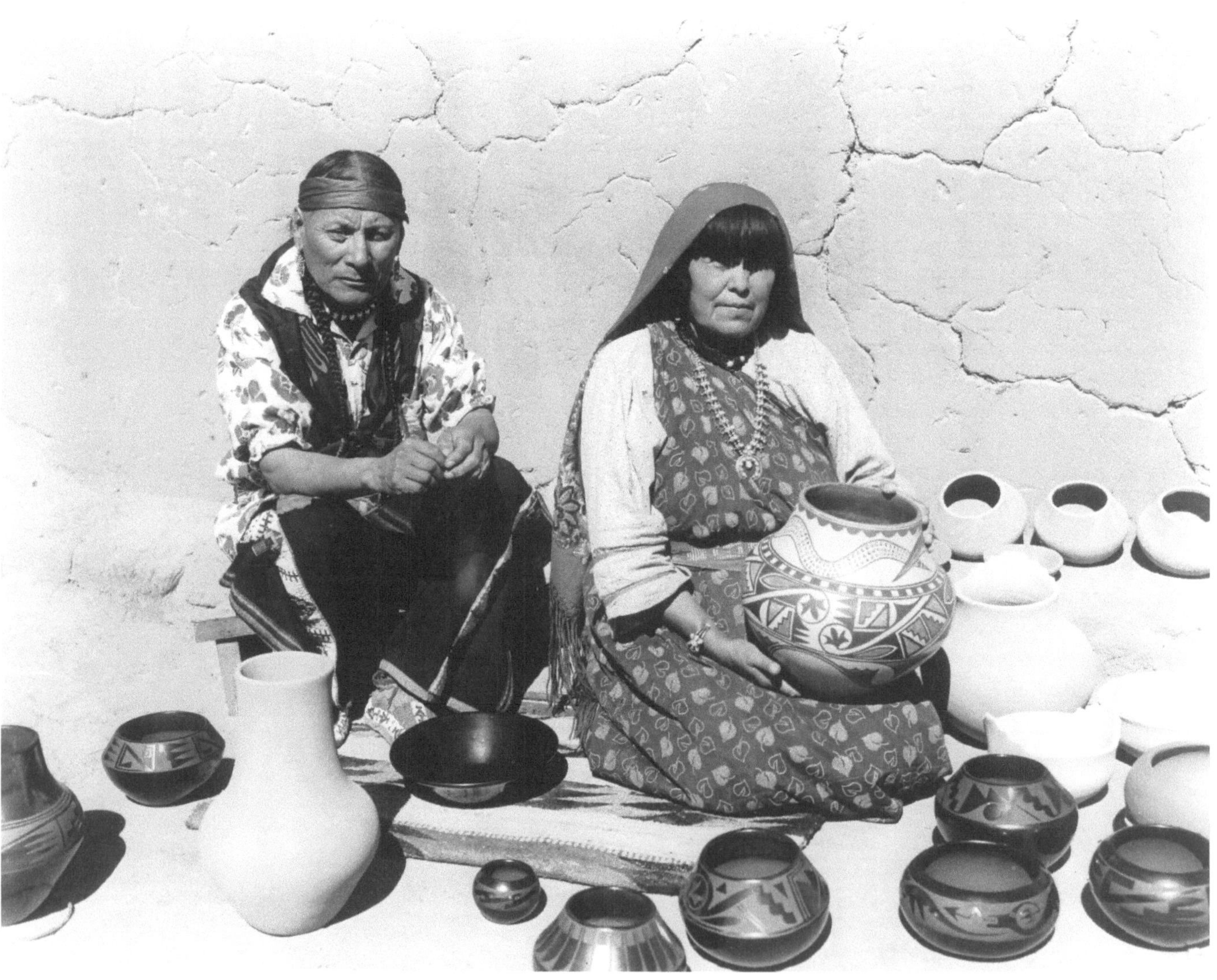

The Indians had been making beautiful pots and blankets for centuries. They were exceptional artist-craftsmen. They were also, Myers discovers, brilliant muralists and watercolorists. He describes their working methods:

> I asked the Indians about making sketches, and they all said they would rather not because they knew what they were going to do, and as soon as a panel was ready, they would begin drawing on it. They prepare their panels with the correct tone of the background. . . . Once the design has been decided upon, the edges are drawn in quite carefully so that there will be no retouching later.

He offers the example of Velino Herrera, an experienced watercolorist. Herrera would spend several days mixing his colors, Myers tells us, "in a five-and-ten-cent store gem pan, the kind of pan whites used for baking muffins." When he got them just right, he would thin them with turpentine and start to paint: "very slowly and carefully with a rather small brush, keeping his areas very flat. . . . He would finish as he went along, always taking care to keep his edges clean and sharp. . . . He never scrubbed, as we sometimes do, because that would create unevenness."

Herrera was equally skilled and meticulous in making murals. He used masonite panels four by eight feet, prepared with the background color he wished to use:

> He would spend several hours without lifting pencil or brush, but during that time he was thinking. After this concentration he would begin drawing in his design with either charcoal or pencil. This work would probably take two days, at the end of which he would have a beautiful drawing . . . perfectly fitting the space with no visible construction lines or measurements.

Maria Antonia (Tonita) Pena, also an experienced artist, worked in the same exacting way. She would begin with figures on the extreme left of a panel four feet high and eight feet long, adding one figure at a time. When she completed the last figure on the extreme right, Myers tells us, she would have achieved "a perfect unit of design and organization."

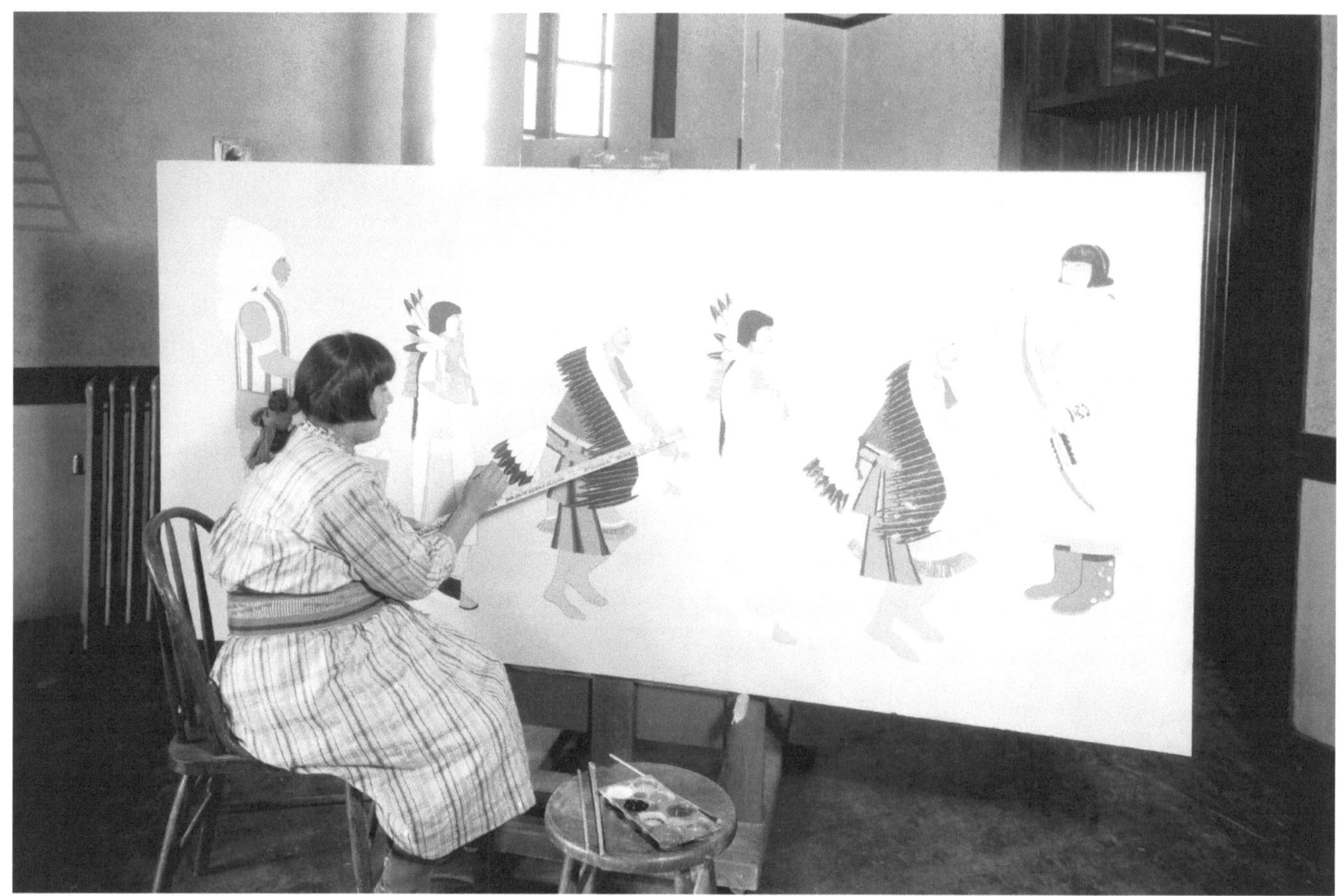

Maria Antonia Pena (Quah Ah) was born in 1893 in San Idlefonso Pueblo, New Mexico and died 1949 in Cochiti Pueblo, New Mexico. She attended the Santa Fe Indian School where she studied art under Dorothy Dunn. She was the first to reject the tradition that women paint only on pottery and won independent recognition as a painter. Photograph by T. Harmon Parkhurst, Museum of New Mexico #73945.

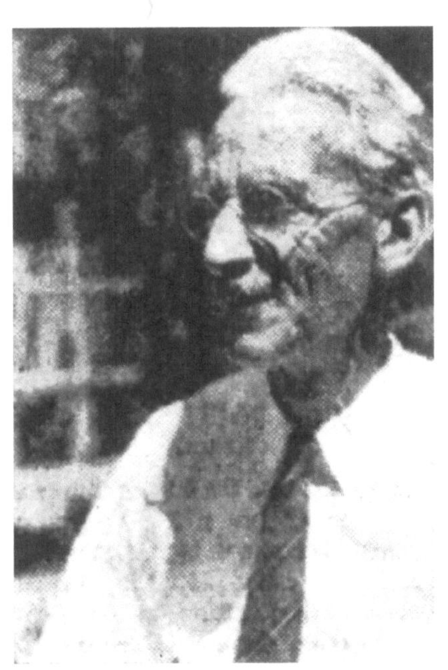

Datus E. Myers

Datus Myers must have been a good supervisor. He was surely a respectful one. He wanted the artists to be free to work in their own tradition: "whatever they did," he said, "should be one hundred percent Indian." Of the very young group, between fourteen and seventeen, he judged Pablita Velarde and Andy Tsihnajinne, as outstanding. And he was right. They turned out to be among the leading Indian artists of their generation.

In Myers' opinion, Indian participation was helpful to his Anglo colleagues as well. It gave them an opportunity to work alongside Indians and to learn their way of working. Indeed, he compared their talents and found the Indians in many respects superior: "[Their] whole design is visualized to the smallest detail and colors before drawing a line. I doubt if this is possible for any white man."

When PWAP ended, after only six months, in June 1934, Region 13, which included Arizona, had produced a miraculous number of art works. Twenty-six murals had been installed in public spaces. The murals brought something new and highly visible to the American Southwest, but there was also a rich production of traditional genres, less dramatic but important in introducing original art to the community: 103 paintings, 79 watercolors, 41 sketches, 270 etchings, 200 lithographs, 2 pieces of sculpture, 20 carvings, 200 Indian design studies. In addition, the Indian Division produced 13 murals, 46 watercolors, 12 blankets, and 62 pots.

In New Mexico alone, according to Nusbaum, 97 artists were on the payroll. Their salary for six months' work and almost a thousand pieces of art came to $39,600. By any standard one might use, the taxpayers got their money's worth.

PWAP's final celebration was a large exhibit in Washington showing works from all parts of the country. Region 13 had much to offer. Among its finest contributions in Jesse Nusbaum's view was the work of the Cordova woodcarver Jose Dolores Lopez. His best carving, Lopez believed, was of the Garden of Eden with Adam and Eve beside the tree, and he wanted the President to see it. He drove down himself in an old car to deliver it to the Park Service. And word came back that the President and his wife did see it. "I never saw a man more pleased in my life," Nusbaum tells us.

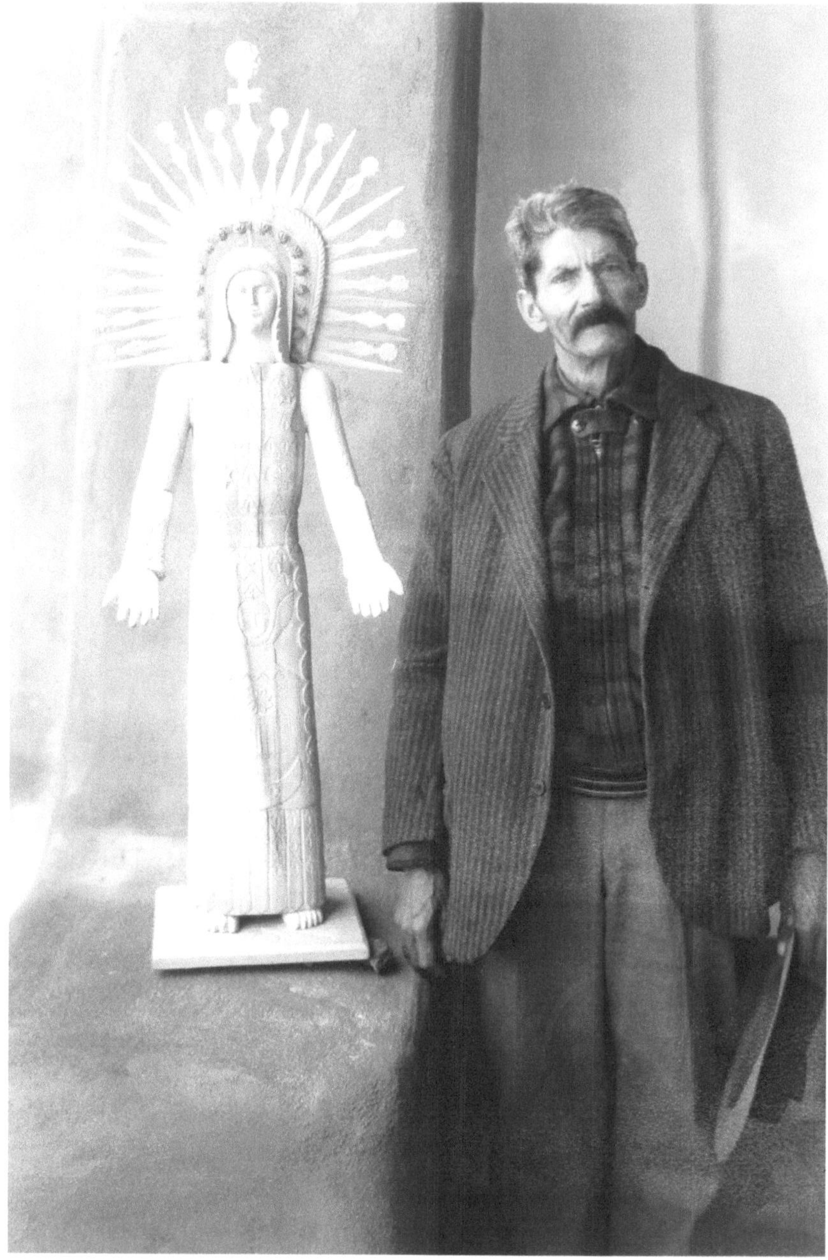

Jose Delores Lopez was born in 1868 in Cordova, New Mexico and died there in 1937. He was a farmer and carpenter and had a reputation as a maker of furniture which he sold or gave as presents to his friends. Not until the last decade of his life did he begin the carvings for which he is famous. Photograph by T. Harmon Parkhurst, Museum of New Mexico #94470.

The second major art relief program was organized by the Department of the Treasury. Begun in late 1934, the Treasury Section of Painting and Sculpture became known simply as the Section. Edward Bruce, who led the first Federal art program, was called on again to become national director. Jesse Nusbaum continued as director of Region 13.

The aim of the Section was quite different from PWAP. It was intended to employ professional artists to produce murals only for Federal buildings. The selection committee was national, based in

Washington, not local. They made their selections from artists' sketches. Their choices were sometimes for particular sites but not necessarily. They might hold work they liked in reserve for new projects. The funds were to come from the construction budget of Federal buildings, as much as one percent, but not more. To include money for art in a Federal building project was a new idea, and like much that began with the New Deal, it changed our thinking. Art in public buildings became an accepted part of architectural planning.

The Section offered New Mexican artists the opportunity to continue working in the mural tradition that they had begun so successfully with PWAP. Their intention was, as before, to express the life and spirit of the region. Theodore Van Soelen took photographs of sandhills and carried bear grass back to his studio so he could represent an authentic buffalo range for the Portales Post Office. Boris Deutsch painted Indian ceremonial dancers for Hot Springs (now named Truth or Consequences) in a decorative style imitative of native painting. Kenneth Adams, like Van Soelen, copied local vegetation in his landscape "Mountains and Yucca" for Deming.

But the Section was open only to the best and most experienced professionals. New Mexico was fortunate to enjoy the talents of artists like Van Soelen, Deutsch and Adams. They had studied at professional academies and in Europe before settling in New Mexico, and their reputations were established, at least on the local scene. For artists who were on relief and could not offer such credentials, in the summer of 1935, the Treasury introduced another program, the Treasury Relief Art Project, known as TRAP.

As in the earlier Federal programs, TRAP was headed by people sympathetic to artists and to the problems of artistic production. Olin Dows was chosen national director. Dows was a professional painter and friend of Edward Bruce; he had worked with Bruce from the very start of PWAP. Jesse Nusbaum, who like Dows had worked hard and enthusiastically in the earlier programs, consented to act as regional director but without pay.

In spite of its comically ominous acronym, TRAP was a humane and artistically useful program. Ninety percent of the artists were from relief rolls, many of them novice artists. They were paid salaries and the cost of materials. A major goal was to help needy artists, but quality continued to be an important consideration. A portion of the budget, between ten and twenty-five percent, was set aside for difficult projects like large murals. For those projects, master artists could be hired and put in charge.

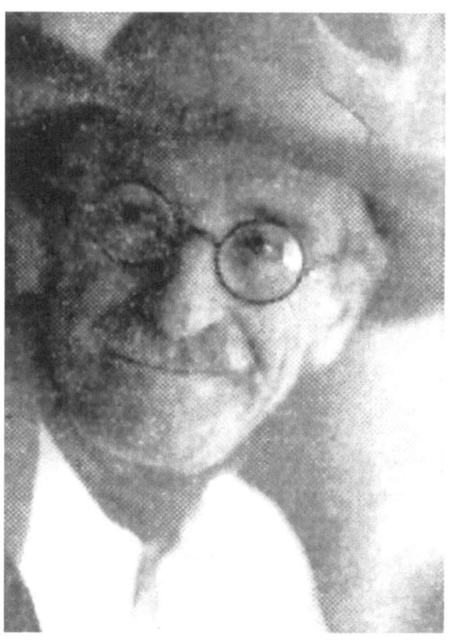

William Penhallow Henderson

Unlike the Section, TRAP produced work in a variety of genres, easel paintings, posters, portraits, sculpture and decorative objects. But murals depicting local history and local landscapes remained the principal genre for decorating the large, blank walls of otherwise unadorned public buildings. In New Mexico certainly, people liked the drama they represented of everyday life, and so did the local critics.

Among the most popular were the Santa Fe United States Court House murals William Penhallow Henderson had begun earlier under the Public Works of Art Program. Henderson had come with his wife, the poet Alice Corbin, to Santa Fe in 1916 for his wife's health, and had found in the distinctive contours and high colors of the Southwest an immense beauty. He chose as subjects of his six murals, not robed figures holding the scales of justice, but famous local sites. "Gorgeous New Mexican landscapes," comments the local newspaper, "brought right into the Courthouse." Henderson himself brags: "After all it is best out here," he says, " so why not use it?"

Joseph Fleck's Raton murals were received with equal enthusiasm. Fleck was born in Austria-Hungary, studied art in Vienna, and came to Kansas City, Missouri, to work as a designer in a stained-glass factory owned by Tiffany. Attracted by an exhibit of Taos painters in a local Kansas City gallery, he came to Taos in 1924. Trained in history painting and portraiture, he was responsive to the local scene.

Designed originally to fit around the postmaster's door, Fleck's Butterfield Mail shows Taos Indians, Raton miners, a scout delivering mail, against the Raton landscape. A second mural, Unloading Mail at Raton, depicted mail delivery in the 1930s. Both show local history, but their significance in the opinion of the Raton Daily Range was much larger: "New Mexico Post Offices will have probably the best

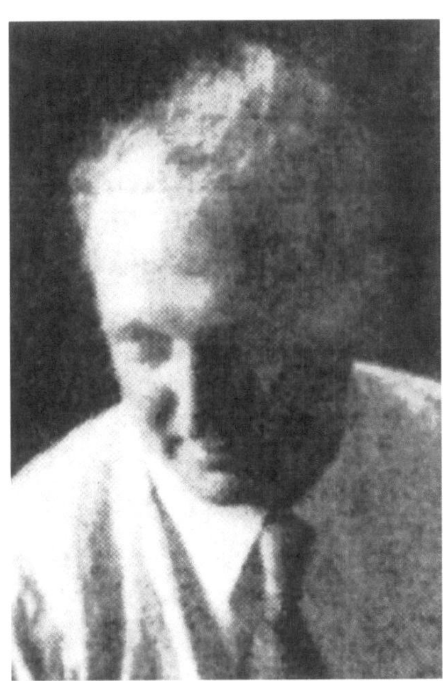

Joseph Fleck

murals of any of the post offices throughout the nation, because New Mexico has the best artists, and it is difficult to find paintings of their equal."

Not all local evaluations were as glowing. Emil Bisttram, who had come to Taos from New York as a Guggenheim Fellow, described himself as an "abstractionist and non-objectivist" and spoke with some scorn about the "old-timers who were making a very good living painting . . . Indians." Nonetheless, he was eager to participate in the first Federal art program as a muralist, and he must have been on good terms with his colleagues because later they chose him as their supervisor for the Northern New Mexico TRAP program.

Bisttram was a candid observer. In his opinion, the government asked too much and paid too little. To fill their TRAP quota, one painting a week, artists, he says, "were going . . . in their piles of discarded paintings and sending some of those." Bisttram was sympathetic: "If an artist didn't paint that week, I didn't say a word." What he objected to most was Washington's insistence on using local subject matter if at all possible. When he was asked to go down to Ranger, Texas, and talk to the Chamber of Commerce and the Lion's Club, he was indignant: "Well, what do they know about art? So they wanted the mural to have something to do with potash and potato fields."

He did do a mural in Ranger, Texas, "where the rangers were," but vowed never to do another one. "It doesn't raise them one iota," he declared, "from the level that they have always been on."

Emil Bisttram's complaint about lowbrow taste and local scenery was not a common one. Almost to a person the artists interviewed for the Archives of American Art were enthusiastic. Gene Kloss, whose etchings Jesse Nusbaum was pleased to report were the "widest spread" over the entire state, thought regional subjects were particularly appropriate for a state that embraced Anglo, Indian and Hispanic cultures. Many artists, like Henderson, found the local scenery a source of inspiration. Whatever the problems, the Federal programs offered a steady source of income, and for that they were grateful. "Well, I guess," Jozef Bakos said, "every time you eat you feel happier."

The fourth and most inclusive of the art relief programs evolved under the direction of a newly formed agency, the Works Progress Administration, conveniently shortened to WPA. Begun in May, 1935, chiefly as an agency to build dams, public shelters, roads, sewer systems, even outhouses, the WPA was quickly expanded to include programs for the visual arts, music, theatre, writing, and architectural history.

The visual arts program under the WPA was called the Federal Art Program, FAP. Burdened like the earlier programs with an acronym that belied its mission, it ran side by side with the Treasury programs. But its emphasis was not on decorating public buildings, although such decoration was fortunately the result of many WPA projects. The primary concern was to put artists to work, and if at all possible, in jobs that matched their talents. There was also a strong interest in developing art programs that would benefit the entire community.

As before, the directors were themselves art professionals, well qualified by sympathy and experience to lead a totally new kind of arts program. Holger Cahill, a distinguished art collector and folklorist, was the national head. Donald Baer, an artist and effective administrator much admired by artists who worked with him, was the director of Region 5, a five-state territory that included New Mexico.

Russell Vernon Hunter was state director for New Mexico. Hunter was a professional artist, trained at the Art Institute in Chicago, but he had lived most of his life in the Panhandle Plains and he understood the deep local significance of the American themes the Federal government wished to show. In the first Treasury program, he had painted murals for the De Baca County Courthouse in Fort Sumner, depicting the history of eastern New Mexico and the people who had settled the territory. The local papers praised the scenes as "vast," the figures "authentic," all in all a work that " Fort Sumner will cherish . . . and thousands will visit there to see."

Hunter was a teacher as well as an artist, dedicated to the rich artistic and cultural heritage of New Mexico. His talents were ideal for the WPA. It was a hard job, he didn't get paid much, but according to his widow Virginia Ewing, it was "the high point of his life . . . the

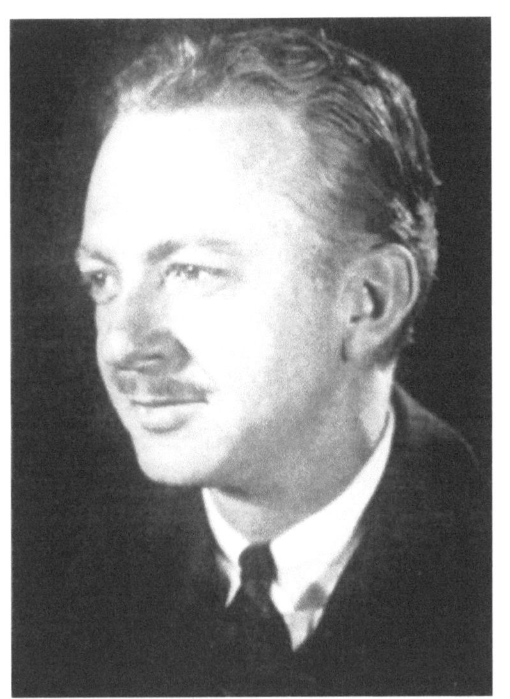

Russell Vernon Hunter

most challenging and exciting job he had ever had." He was one of only two directors who stayed on until the program closed in 1943, and nobody worked harder to make it a success.

Russell Vernon Hunter's job was to devise projects the community was willing to pay for and find local sites suitable to receive the work, whether it be painting, sculpture, mural or decorative object. Only then could he assign artists to the job. Unlike the Treasury programs, the WPA artist had to be certified as receiving a subsidy from the Welfare Department. Only if a project required special skills could Hunter bypass Welfare and hire directly.

After he found a sponsor, located a site, bought materials, and assigned artists, Hunter would appoint a local county supervisor to keep track of the job. In Bernalillo County, Hunter appointed Roland Dickey, fresh out of the University of New Mexico, to supervise between 15 and 20 artists.

Dickey gives a good account of what he did. His job was to make contracts with artists, collect time slips, record hours, and do progress evaluations. It was tough, Dickey says, telling people they weren't doing a good job. Most often, Hunter took that responsibility. Dickey's wages reached $95 a month. Only one supervisor did better at $100. He recalls that wages began at $66. "No bonanza," he says, "and yet people were grateful to have something on which they could live." He himself worked out a system whereby he could eat on fifty cents a day. Most of the time, he claims, he managed to do that.

Like Hunter, Dickey was enthusiastic about the program. "There was a great deal of remarkable talent," he says, "We had sculptors and painters, . . . a Negro boy who was going to the University, a very talented sculptor, . . . Paul Goodbear, a Cheyenne whose Indian name was Flying Eagle, a very talented boy and very astute in terms of taking an opportunity. We had, of course, many people of Spanish descent and what we call Anglos."

In emphasizing need more than professional credentials, the WPA art program opened the way for talented young people like those Roland

Dickey describes. But for many highly skilled, established artists the welfare certification was not a deterrent. Under Hunter's leadership, they were offered significant and often unusual artistic opportunities.

Those who had experience painting murals or who showed talent were offered an opportunity to work in this highly visible medium. The subjects often reached back to local history. Loren Mozley painted the Indian rebellion against the Spanish in 1680 for the old Federal courthouse at 421 Gold, S.W., in Albuquerque. Raymond Jonson did two large symbolic paintings, Art and Science, for Eastern New Mexico University. Lloyd Moylan painted three murals for Las Vegas that began with the mythic Garden of Eden and confidently worked its way forward to end with the history of New Mexico. Murals such as these, large in scale and local ambition, were done in schools and post offices and courthouses all over the state, many in towns that had never seen a painting.

Murals were deservedly a favored genre of the earlier Federal programs. But Hunter was disposed to try out new ways of working. He had heard about silk screen printing to produce multiple copies. It had not yet been introduced in New Mexico, and he assigned a talented engraver, Louie Ewing, to learn about it.

Ewing and the painter Eliseo Jose Rodriguez took three days to make their first print. They had no squeegee to draw the paint across the screen. None had been invented so they made their own out of an auto tire. It gummed up. Then they tried a ready-made squeegee used for window cleaning, but the oil paint melted the rubber. Finally, a manufacturer helped them out and made a composition squeegee that would hold up.

"I was the first in on that," Ewing says. Learning about silk screen, it turned out, led to more work. The Laboratory of Anthropology wanted drawings of Indian blankets to be made and reproduced for museums. Ewing made the drawings and, using the silk screen process, reproduced them in two steps, many fewer than required by the engraving process. The project took about a year, but it gave him his start. "I could break away from the WPA," he says, "and have my own business."

At the time of the WPA job offer, Hunter was the director of a vocational school in Puerta de Luna, a Spanish village near Fort Sumner. His admiration for Spanish Colonial arts and crafts was deeply held, and he had encouraged the local people to revive their traditional arts of furniture making, weaving and carving. As WPA director, he dedicated two of the most innovative projects to preserving that tradition.

The first and, from all reports, the most beautiful, was the Albuquerque Little Theater building. John Gaw Meem was the architect. Hunter himself designed pieces of furniture, using traditional Spanish Colonial patterns. Craftsmen who had developed their skills under the federally sponsored National Youth Administration built the furniture. A noted Hispanic tin worker, Ildeberto "Eddie" Delgado, designed and made huge tin lighting fixtures as well as other tin objects. The Women's Project made cushions and pillows and a stage curtain using the traditional colcha stitch. It was, Virginia Ewing declared, "the gem of the state," a beautiful and wonderfully executed project, much admired by the community and celebrated by a gala opening.

Eldeberto "Eddie" Delgado in his studio

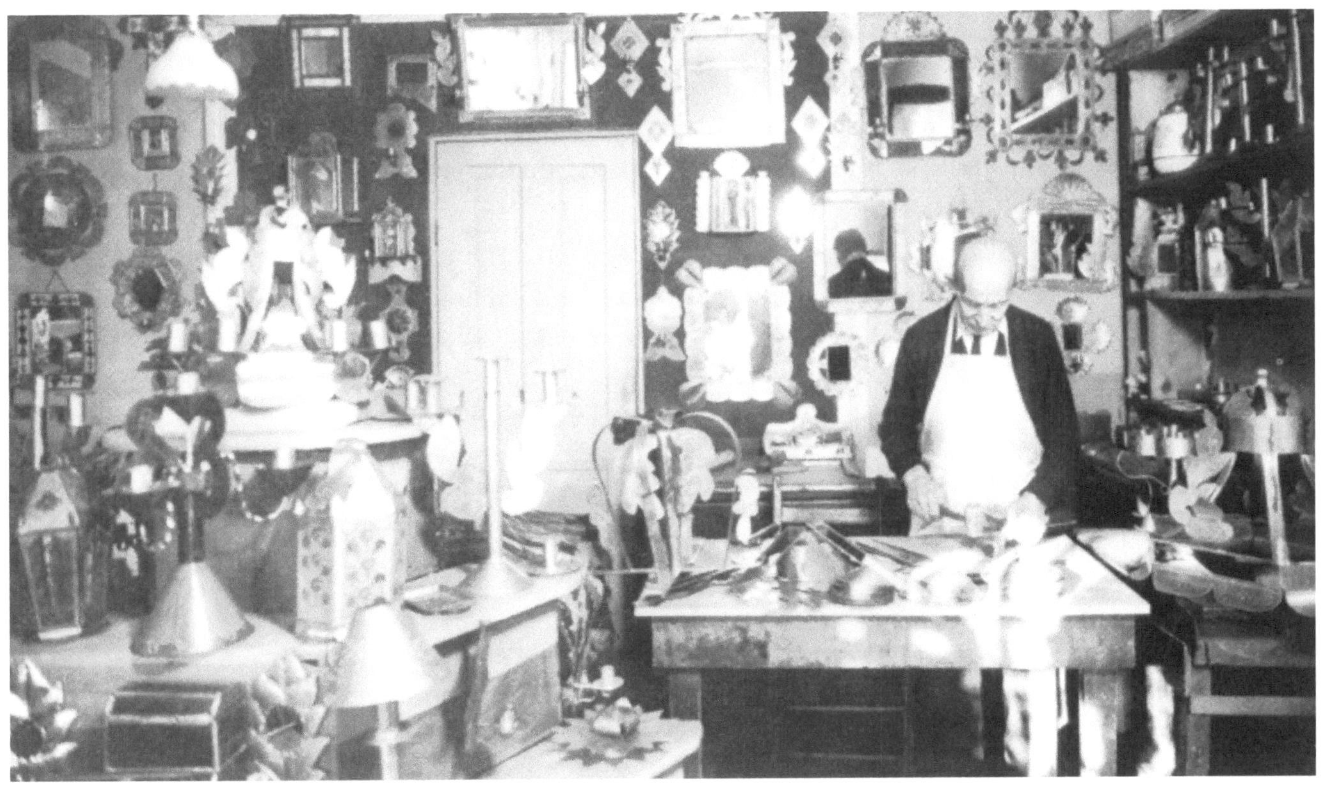

The second large-scale project was the Portfolio of Spanish Colonial Design in New Mexico, a project as ambitious in its way as the Little Theater project. The intention was to make a pictorial record of the work of the Santeros, the Hispanic artist-craftsmen whose carvings of saints, missal stands and altar pieces decorated mission churches. It was also to be New Mexico's contribution to the Index of American Design, a national project.

The artist chiefly responsible for creating this record was E. Boyd. Boyd had studied painting at the Philadelphia Academy of Fine Arts and the Grande Chaumière in Paris. She came to New Mexico in 1929 and immediately became interested in the Santero tradition. Her WPA job was to go out to the churches and make watercolor copies of the Santero carvings.

It was not an easy task. The doors of village churches were almost always locked. And anybody from outside the village, she discovered, was not welcome. Boyd asked Archbishop Gerken of Santa Fe to help her. He was, she says, the first to take a serious interest in the history of the region and in the Santeros. He gave her a letter of introduction, a kind of "Open Sesame" for church doors. She would show the letter to the custodian, and he would take it to the storekeeper:

> He would read aloud, and they would say yes, yes, yes, it really is from the archbishop. And then they would assign an old woman or a child to sit in an unheated church—it happened to be winter and quite cold—and watch me for hours on end while I sat there doing little renderings in watercolor.

She remembers a church in Santa Cruz that had a large iron stove. It got cold in the dank, closed church, but the stove was never lighted during the week. "It got so cold," she reports, "I would go outside and jump up and down in the sun for a few minutes, and go back inside."

The Portfolio plan was that each watercolor rendering be done to scale as nearly as possible, and that a history of each item be provided.

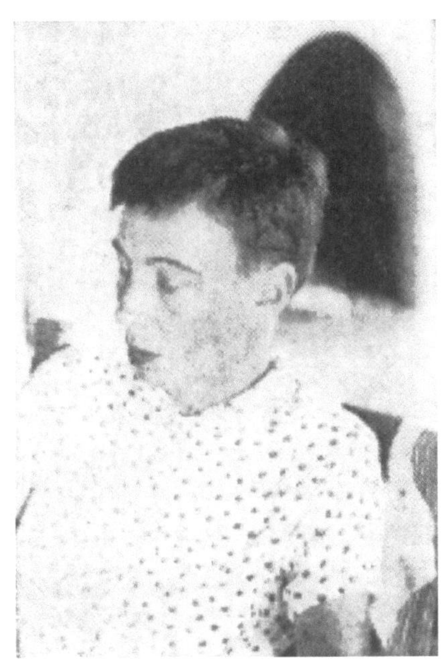

E. Boyd

Unfortunately, there was very little history available. About all Boyd could do was to provide measurements, location and ownership.

After Boyd prepared the original drawings, the plan was to produce an edition of two hundred copies. But there was no money for printing so the copies had to be made by hand. The process was fraught with difficulties. The first step was to reproduce Boyd's watercolor renderings on a wood or a linoleum block. This was done by Manville Chapman. The blocks were then used to reproduce two hundred copies of each rendering. In the final and surely the most chancy step, two hundred complete sets of the renderings were sent to WPA artists of varying abilities around the state; each was given a little box of watercolors and asked to fill in the colors.

Creative artists, Boyd points out, do not like to copy other people's work. Even if willing, the colorists had never seen the originals and were not working with the watercolor brand that Boyd herself had used. Worse, although many artists were employed, in keeping with WPA goals, their skills varied. There was, she says kindly, "a great discrepancy between the neatness and efficiency with which they filled in the area of color and ran over the line."

Charles Barrows, a professional artist on the project, was less charitable: "old ladies who should have been sewing on buttons" were coloring wood blocks. "There was so much lousy work," Barrows says, "that Vernon came out to see me and practically begged me to do it all over so at least it would be presentable. We probably had more than ten percent who should not have been on the project at all."

Unexpectedly, a small amount of money was found to print an introductory text by E. Boyd. There were problems there too. Levi J. Whiteman at Clovis was doing the job in handset type on very large pages. But he didn't have enough type to go very far. He could only set about a half a page a day. To move things along, Roland Dickey, the Bernalillo supervisor, went over to Clovis and set type himself.

In the end, Washington rejected the uneven coloring of the "old ladies who should have been sewing on buttons." The Portfolio was not accepted for the Index of American Design. But from a New Mexican point of view, it fulfilled its mission. Almost two hundred workers had participated in an art project. Mr. Whiteman finally managed to turn out a handsomely printed introductory text. Most important, perhaps, E. Boyd's beautiful renderings offered, as far as possible, an historically accurate record of Santero art. Two hundred copies of the Portfolio were produced and distributed to libraries and museums in New Mexico, treasured pieces still.

The primary mission of the WPA was to employ as many artists as possible, but there was also an obligation to engage the larger community. From their inception, the New Deal art programs were intended to speak to the American people. The art that decorated the walls of public buildings showed images that celebrated their everyday lives and their common history. In the last and in many ways the most ambitious of the Federal programs, the WPA took up the theme of community not only by offering works of art but by providing a place, an art center, where local people could gather and share the artistic experience being offered.

The community art center project was ideally suited to engage the talents that Russell Vernon Hunter brought to the WPA. He had mobilized artists and craftsmen to create the Albuquerque Little Theater. In spite of the difficulties of the Portfolio project, he had supported E. Boyd's valiant efforts until the final copies were completed. Both projects depended to some extent on community support. The art center project offered an opportunity in which community support was central to success.

The challenge was significant. Under Hunter's direction, the WPA set up art centers not in the towns where most of the artists lived and showed their work, but in the outlying communities of Gallup, Melrose, Las Vegas and Roswell. We know the most about Roswell because shortly after it opened in 1938, Hunter sent Roland Dickey, the young supervisor of Bernalillo County, to be director.

Dickey was not only a good reporter, he was as enthusiastic about Roswell as he had been about Bernalillo. He felt he was lucky right off. The woman who operated the Center Gallery had been the

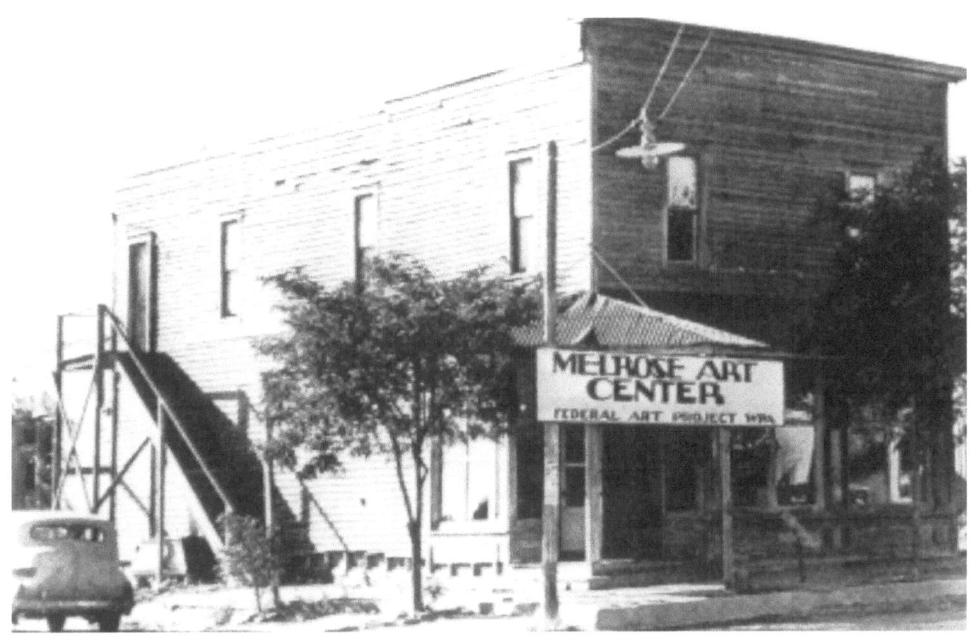

Melrose Art Center

telephone switchboard operator. She not only knew everybody in Roswell, Dickey says, but she knew their telephone numbers. And their family histories. Even so, there were uneasy moments. When he met the Board for the first time, he discovered that to a person they were the elders of the town. "Every one of those people," he says, "had snow white hair." Dickey's job was to introduce them to art, especially modern art. A challenging task for a young man just out of college.

Nevertheless, the Center thrived. The first director had scolded people for not responding to art he considered important. Dickey was more diplomatic. He gave a public lecture once a week, offered afternoon and evening classes in painting, sculpture, design. Washington sent through marvelous exhibits: a Kuniyoshi show (Kuniyoshi was himself a WPA artist); Currier and Ives prints; original drawings, including a drawing by Ingres.

The greatest draw, however, were local shows. Once a week, the townspeople brought in their own collections, coins, clocks, antiques, whatever. The first year, Dickey tells us, they got twice the population of Roswell into the gallery.

Part of the Roswell success must be attributed to the commitment of the town itself. The centers in Melrose and Las Vegas and Gallup

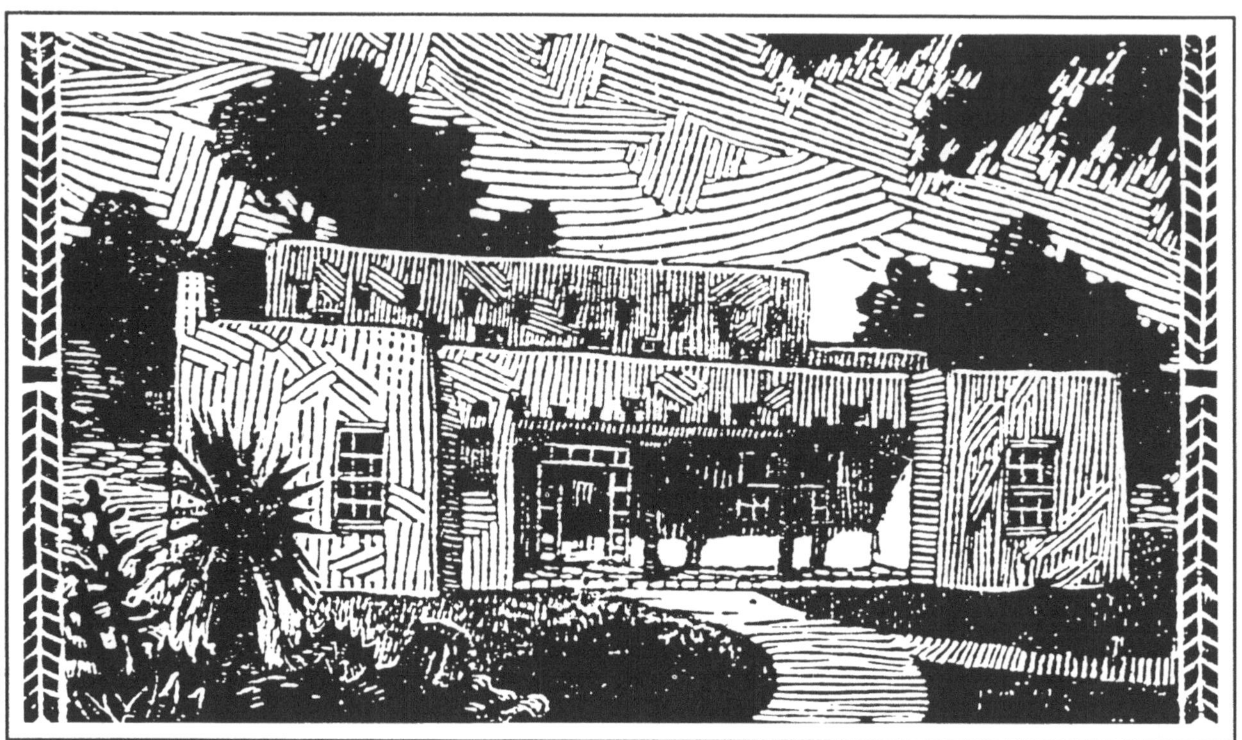

Roswell Museum and Art Center, a woodcut by Manville Chapman created at its opening in 1937.

were all old buildings. But the Roswell Center was built by WPA labor on city land. The city owned the building, and the city council paid for utilities.

The building was done in Spanish Colonial style, and Hunter was the genius planner. Roland Dickey describes what he could do:

> Vernon had a very remarkable talent, and this was the ability to visualize real things before they happened. He could sit down and draw an entire room or a building or a mural or pieces of furniture as it was going to look. . . . He would do something very exciting, very beautiful. And then he had the ability to give artists and craftsmen something to work with that was real enough so that they could achieve this.

In this effortless way, Dickey tells us, Hunter planned the interior of the Roswell Center: there was a stage that would also work for lectures, stage curtains embroidered in colcha stitch that "knocked your eyes out," tall gilded candlesticks on either side of the stage, a carved lectern copied from a church design. The ladies' powder room was done in a mid-nineteenth century version of Spanish colonial, the walls painted to imitate embroidery, the mirror framed in a handcrafted tin work. It was "a gorgeous piece," Dickey says, "a perfect kind of thing."

The Roswell Art Center combined the WPA ideals of offering employment and, at the same time, creating something beautiful to be enjoyed by all. It survives and continues to hold its place as one of the finest small museums in the country.

Not all community projects fared so well. The art centers at Melrose, Las Vegas and Gallup closed at the end of the project. Except for Eddie Delgado's wall sconces, the Albuquerque Little Theater's fresco was destroyed and the building stripped of its beautiful furnishings.

The Albuquerque Little Theater as it originally appeared with a mural/fresco called "Los Moros" by Dorothy Stewart.

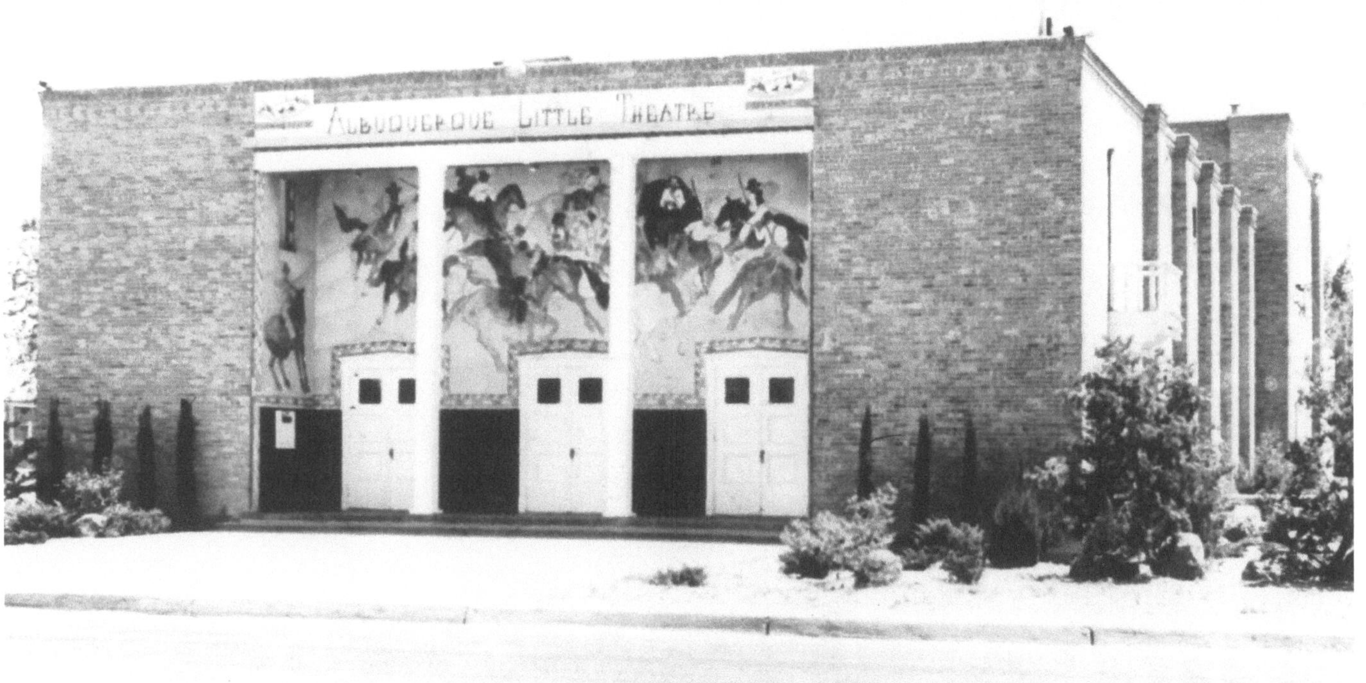

As for individual works, some were lost, some simply taken. Jozef Bakos says of a favorite WPA painting at the State Capitol, "I just loved that watercolor. Then later somebody told me they had it in their home, and I said, well, you have no right to have that painting. I hope it comes back to the public, whoever has it." But as Roland Dickey reasonably points out, the art works were public property; there were no strong legal protections; and most places were not inclined to take such responsibilities. The story goes, he says, that one county treasurer disliked the WPA paintings so much he burned them in the incinerator. Roland Dickey seems to forgive him: "He probably thought this was radical modern art."

The WPA art program ended in 1943, the last of the Federal programs to shut down. For almost ten years artists in New Mexico had been paid by Federal agencies. They had produced a prodigious amount of work: fifty-five murals, over a thousand individual pieces, and as the photographic record in this book attests, a significant portion is still on the walls of public buildings, in museum collections and libraries throughout the state.

For the public who had received rich and often beautiful interpretations of the Southwest and for the artists who made these works, the New Deal art programs in New Mexico had fulfilled their mission. They had offered the "more abundant life" that Roosevelt wished for all Americans. For the first time art became for many part of their everyday life. Gene Kloss, whose "beautiful little prints" were in numerous school rooms, was confident of local response: "People in outlying places who had never seen anything had murals in their post offices and received some easel pictures or prints to hang in their schools and in public buildings. I think it is one thing that started a public interest in art."

Even the Taos painter Emil Bisttram, who was testy about local taste, conceded that the program "made art okay for everybody." Before the Depression, he says, "only the moneyed people came to this town, like the Rockefellers and the Vanderbilts and the Morgans . . . and they would be entertained by the artists, and that was the big stunt here and in Santa Fe. . . . And that was the market. . . . Well now, this project awakened the lay public to it rather than the so-called cultured group, the moneyed group. So in that way it did help."

The programs that "made art okay for everybody" also helped the artist through a bad time. The Santa Fe painter Jozef Bakos, a professional artist, trained at the Albright Gallery Art School, recognized that some people "who were selling shoe laces became all of a sudden artists." Even so, he says of the WPA, "I think it was a godsend." Charles Barrows, an accomplished watercolorist who had helped out on the Portfolio project, was grateful to be free to paint: "I did more in those few years, probably, than I could have done in two or three times that long." And also to be free of artistic restraints: "There were no restrictions at all," he says, "I think it was a very good idea, and I think it should have been continued."

For Louie Ewing, the engraver who learned silk screening, the WPA program offered "a wonderful chance, from getting out of art school to make a transition to professional, and besides making it possible to eat." Ina Sizer Cassidy says her husband, Gerald, "thought it a fine recognition for the artists . . . [he] felt honored by the assignment." William Lumpkins' praise was unequivocal: "In those days you hoped you might peddle a painting–the WPA made us feel like we were part of America."

Many New Deal artists, especially those who came to New Mexico in the nineteen tens and twenties, were professionals and continued their careers after the Federal programs ended. Will Shuster, William Lumpkins, Olive Rush, Gene Kloss, Louie Ewing, William Penhallow Henderson, among many others, went on to develop important reputations in the New Mexico art community.

But there were also artists who had no formal training and who could not even think of making a living from their art. It was outside the boundaries of their daily lives, something extra they could do only in their spare time, if at all. The Federal art programs gave them their chance.

Among them, none was more talented than Patrocinio Barela, the genius woodcarver from the village of Canõn, near Taos. He could neither read nor write. His first government relief job was working as a teamster. But Barela had already discovered his talent as a woodcarver and had managed to sell a few carvings to shops in Taos. The WPA office manager saw them, and after looking at more of his work in the small shed where he worked, she told him to give up hauling dirt and "do the carving" for the arts program.

Patrocinio Barela, Photograph Courtesy of the Museum of New Mexico, Negative #19576.

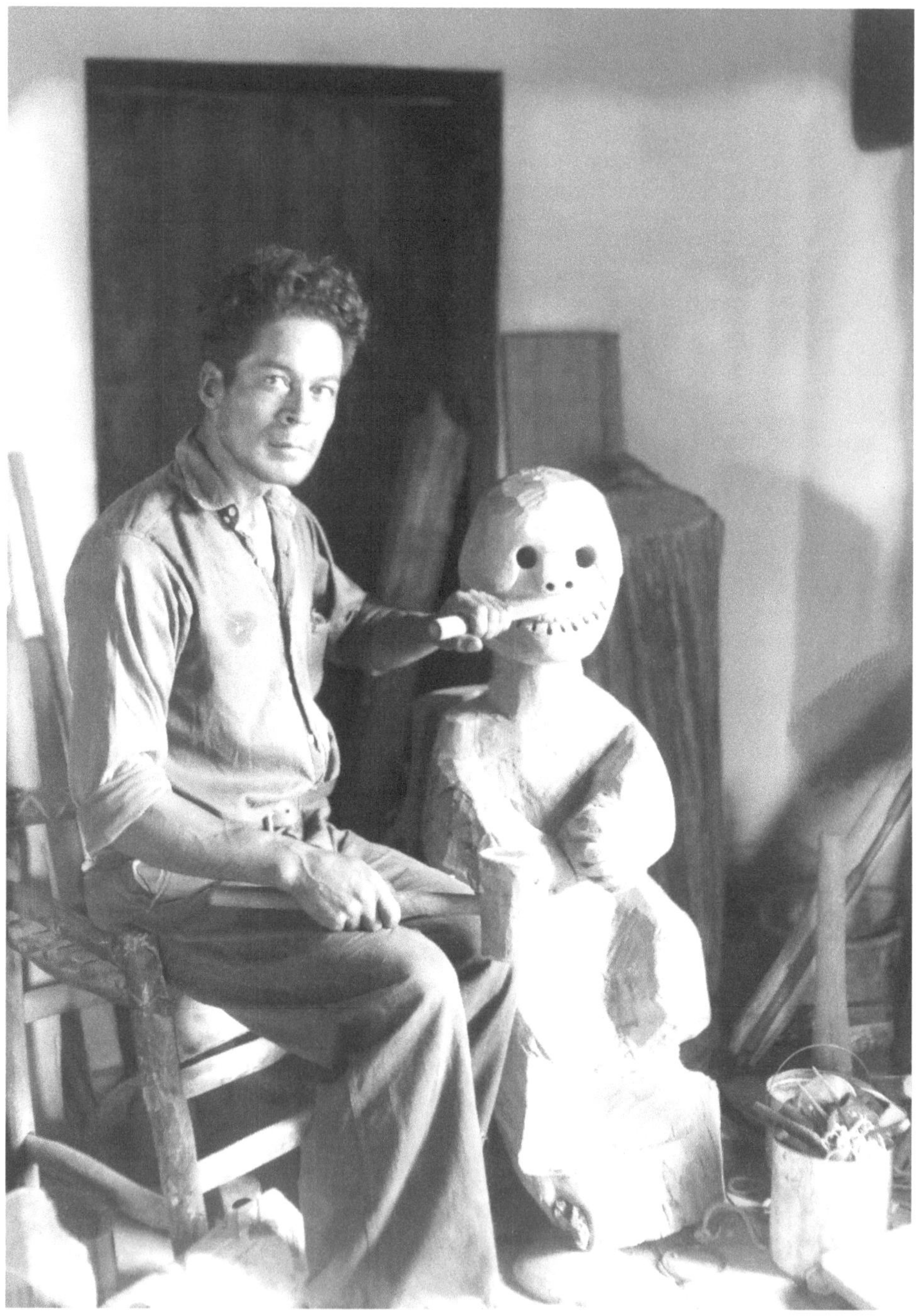

His story is worth telling, not only because he turned out to be so exceptional an art-ist, but also because without help from the WPA program, he most likely would not have had the time or money to produce a significant body of work.

He was born in 1900 (the date is not certain) in Arizona. His mother died when he was very young. His father was an itinerant laborer and herb healer. "My father," Barela says, "he do for his own. . . . He cure lots of people with wild weeds." After the mother's death, he took Patrocinio and his brother with him wherever he could find work, in lumber camps and sheep camps, picking potatoes on farms.

During their travels through the Southwest, he did not send his sons to school, and since his own religious practices were unorthodox—he was said to engage in occult rituals—he offered no traditional church. Their life apart from settled communities was not, as his son remembers it, a bad time. "Old man," Barela says, "I come from him. Owe him more than I can ever pay."

But when they came to live in New Mexico, his father married a woman who did not want Patrocinio, and at the age of eleven, although he could not speak or read English, he left home. Early in his travels, he injured his arm hopping a train. A well-meaning policeman picked him up in Denver and took him to the juvenile detention home. Not a bad place, it turned out. He was offered medical care and eventually sent to board with a black family, who helped him learn English and, also, something about the mysteries of the English-speaking world.

On his own, he worked on farms, railroads, in coal mines and steel mills, and then, in 1930, he returned to New Mexico "to get quainted." He settled in Canõn, married, and continued to make his living, as he always had, as an itinerant laborer.

But he also made a huge discovery. A friend asked him to come to his house: "Let's see, he say, if you can fix this santo, San Antonio." A lady had promised to buy the figure: "He say, if I get twenty dollars, I give it to you five." Barela did fix it. "I worked it easy," he says, "with a pocket knife." That night he went home and carved a head from a cedar log. It was a policeman, he told his children, and would watch over them. Was he remembering, we might ask, the kindly policeman who helped him in Denver?

He didn't get paid the five dollars his friend had promised, but it gave him an idea: "I don't say to him—just myself, thinkin' and thinkin' and thinkin,' so I started easy. I make a little Santa Rita . . . with one pocket knife and one single chisel. And that's the way I started."

At first, he carved saint figures, but even traditional images did not sell well enough to make a living. "My friends," he told his friend Russell Vernon Hunter, "they say, those works of yours, those carvings. . . . Can't eat, can't sit on, can't use. Why not make things to use. They laugh at me." His wife, according to Virginia Ewing, felt more strongly. She burned the carvings that brought in no money for her and their three children. He had to keep on as a casual laborer. "Sometimes," he says, "I make twenty-five cents a week. . . . If I have good luck."

The New Deal alleviated the family's desperate poverty. Barela had horses and a wagon, and he got work hauling dirt for the Emergency Relief Administration. But he had persisted in carving in his off-hours and had put a few pieces in Albino Birch's store in Taos. When Ruth Fish, the office manager of the Taos WPA, saw them, she asked about the carver.

"So they call for me," Barela remembers, "and the lady told me, "When you quitting, you don't go home. You wait for me by the church, and I want to talk to you." When he took Ruth Fish to his house and showed her his work, she said simply: "Well, Pat, I can't do it tomorrow, but the day after tomorrow . . . I can make papers so you can do the carving and let the horses rest."

After about three weeks, Barela recalls, they sent for him: "They give me a great big envelope with the papers, and they told me, every day you work eight hours and make a cross in one of these squares, because I tell them, I don't read, I don't write, and they say, you just make a cross in one of these squares." He was accepted as a WPA artist, and Russell Vernon Hunter, who had always been disposed to assist Hispanic artists, helped him.

Hunter's admiration for his work and for Barela himself was immediate and steadfast. He was the one, his wife Virginia Ewing says, Hunter talked about the most. Without any prompting from the Taos art community, Hunter appreciated the beauty and originality of Barela's art. "Certainly the meaning and intent of this work could never be construed as anything other than Patrocinio's own," he says. "Call him a natural, a primitive, a true original or what you will, with the power to philosophize what life has brought him."

He tells us in Barela's own words of what carving meant to him: "My head," Barela says, "he is often felt to be in three or four pieces, although he looks to be only one." What he wanted to do, he could say very clearly: "to carve a bulto to show the life of man." First man is born "all by himself." Then comes number two, a son, "only half the man he should be." Then, number three, the grown man. Number two and three make "the complete man." The complete man is like the tree by his side, "large and strong in life, full of happiness and hope." Then, the old man, "tiresome and weak," "nothing left but bare branches."

His carvings were so personal, Hunter speculates, that it may well have been difficult for him to part with them at all. His inspiration was everyday life, his family, his travels as an itinerant worker, the beautiful, natural things he brought into his workshop. He admired the swirls and delicate cuts of a beaver stump. "They are better carvers than man," he said. "If God sent beavers to school, they beat us all."

Barela became the star of the WPA Art Program in New Mexico. Among the hundreds of art pieces exhibited in the Museum of Modern Art in 1936, his was the only work reviewed. His picture appeared in Time Magazine. Prestigious art dealers wanted to handle his work. Russell Vernon Hunter was anxious about Barela's response to these big city types. But Barela himself was loyal to the Program that had brought respect for his work and enough money to live. He refused to sell to tourists, although he produced many more pieces than the Program required of him: "This belongs to the Art Project [Program]," he would say. "When the Project [Program] finish, then I will find a way to make a living."

He worked for the Federal Art Program until 1943. "I was," he says, "just about the last one they shut me down." By then he had a reputation and could sell some things, although not enough to support his family. He would still have to go out and pick potatoes or work on a ranch. But he was not ambitious for money. What he wanted, Hunter tells us, was food, a room to work in, a house to keep out the cold. He continued carving until his death in a fire that started late at night in his workshop in 1964.

He explained one of his carvings to Russell Vernon Hunter. The carving in the round has three sides, each revealed as one turns the sculpture. On the first side, he is crouching by a tree, "Before idea come, I got my head. But no use, just sitting, dreaming." On the second side, "a notion comes from the air." The third side is "where I planted the future for me, which has been the art I discover. I put my right hand to my head, surprised. I stand on my own feet."

In simple and unpretentious language, Barela has described the experience of creating a work of art. The support offered by the Federal art programs enabled Barela and many other New Mexican artists to repeat that exhilarating experience many times, and in so doing, enrich their lives and ours.

The factual sources on New Deal art programs are two unpublished essays: "The New Deal Was a Great Deal: Federal Patronage and Mural Painting in New Mexico, 1933 to 1943," by Sandra DeEmilio; and "A Road Map to New Deal Funded Programs" by Kathryn A. Flynn.

Artists' commentaries are taken from two sources: interviews conducted by Sylvia Loomis for the Archives of American Art, 1964: Jozef and Teresa Bakos, Charles Barrows, Emil Bisttram, E. Boyd, Ina Sizer Cassidy, Roland Dickey, Louie Ewing, Virginia Hunter Ewing, Gene Kloss, Jesse L. Nussbaum, Olive Rush, Eugenie Shonnard, Will Shuster; and interviews conducted by Kathryn A. Flynn, Executive Director, National New Deal Preservation Association Incorporated: William Lumpkins, Eliseo Rodriguez, Pablita Velarde.

The sources of Barela's story are an unpublished essay, "Concerning Patrocinio Barela," by his friend and mentor, Russell Vernon Hunter; and an interview conducted in Barela's home, Canõn, New Mexico, July, 1964, by Sylvia Loomis for the Archives of American Art.

Pictures, Pots, Murals, Weavings and Carvings

The Work of New Deal Artists in the Towns and Villages of New Mexico

New Deal painters in New Mexico, almost without exception, took as their subject matter familiar sights: a desert landscape, an Hispanic village in the Sangre de Cristos, an Indian ceremonial dance, aspens turning in the Jemez Mountains, the blue door of an adobe house. Artist-craftsmen adapted the traditional shapes and designs they had always used to make pots and rugs and carvings. Taken together, as the following selection of their work shows, they offer a visual portrait of life and times in New Mexico in the 1930s.

An appropriate response in view of the federal government's recommendation that New Deal art show images local people could identify with. I would suggest, though, that the look of New Mexican life would have been the artist's material regardless of federal guidelines. Artists began coming to New Mexico in the late nineteenth century. They came from every part of the country, from Maine to California, and a few from Europe. Some because their doctors advised them to. The high, dry mountain air was ideal for tuberculosis patients, and they came in hope of recovery.

Chiefly, though, it was the spectacular shapes and colors of the New Mexican landscape that brought them. They had never seen anything like it, and they painted it again and again. The St. Louis artist Oscar Berninghaus was so dazzled that he managed to have a chair tied to the top of a railroad car and ride across the state sketching panoramic vistas. Such enthusiasm may seem excessive, even comically dangerous, but it expresses what was often felt.

Once here, they found the work of artists who for hundreds of years had shaped the historical and artistic imagination of the peoples of New Mexico. Mimbres pots, it is estimated, were made over a thousand years ago. Indian peoples reach back to prehistory. The creativity of native populations has been interrupted many times by wars and mysterious disappearances, but it has persisted and been revived in contemporary adaptations. More recently, since the seventeenth century, Hispanic village communities have created their own tradition of household decorations, furniture, carvings, domestic and church architecture. These indigenous communities, as profoundly as mountains and deserts, have influenced the daily life of New Mexico and, consequently, the artist's vision.

Kenneth Adams Born, 1897, Topeka, Kansas; died, 1966, Albuquerque, New Mexico. Studied at Art Institute, Chicago; Art Students League, New York, and in Europe. Followed his teacher Andrew Dasburg to Taos. Artist-in-residence at the University of New Mexico in 1933, an association that continued until he retired as Professor Emeritus in 1963. Under the Treasury Relief Art Project, his salary was $42.50 a week, more than he could make as a teacher at the University of New Mexico.

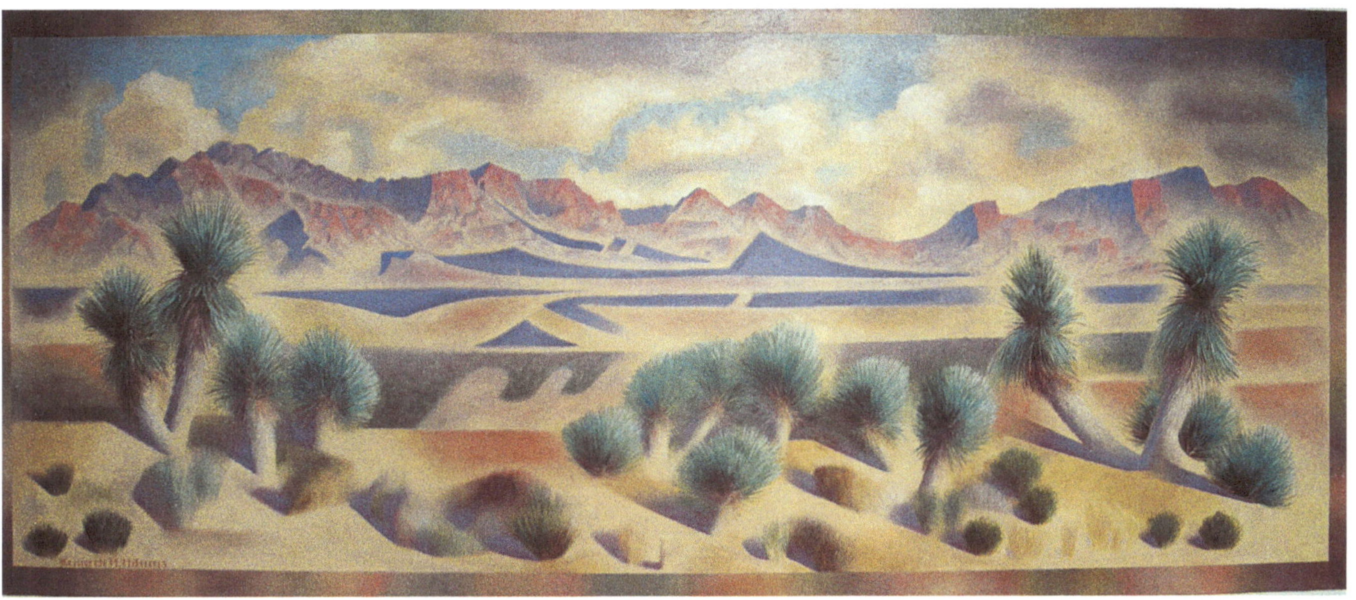

Mountains and Yucca, Kenneth Adams, mural, U.S. Post Office, Deming. Photograph by Robert Orosco.

Jozef Bakos Born, 1891, Buffalo, New York; died, 1977, Santa Fe, New Mexico. Studied at Albright Art School, Buffalo, New York, and in Europe. Came to Santa Fe in 1921. "Artists just started coming in about that time," he recalls in the Archive interview. "John Sloan was just about a year before me, and Randall Davey. Will Henderson was here, and I met Andrew Dasburg here. Paul Bourne, a nationally known artist, and Nordfeldt were here, and all of them just preceded me, and at the same time Shuster came, Willard Nash, Mruk or Murk—it was spelled both ways. It was due to him that I came out here. He was in the Forest Service and came originally from Buffalo. And then Fremont Ellis. So I organized Cinco Pintores about that time. Gus Baumann was here. It was very alive, and much more than Taos because we were called moderns—we wouldn't be called that now—because more academic painters were in Taos. [To be a painter] was always a struggle for existence. . . . I did carpenter work and Shuster did iron work and then we'd paint."

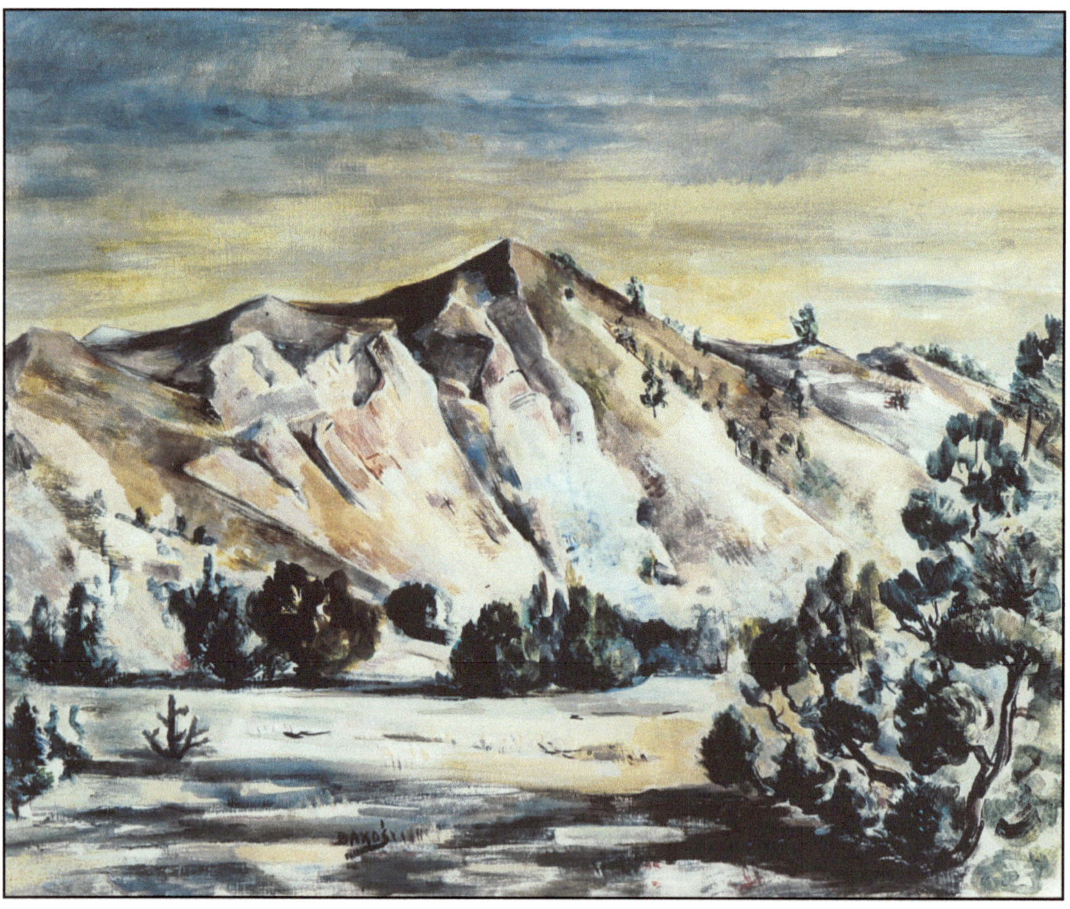

Hill Near Chama, Jozef Bakos, painting, New Mexico Institute of Mining and Technology Library, Socorro.

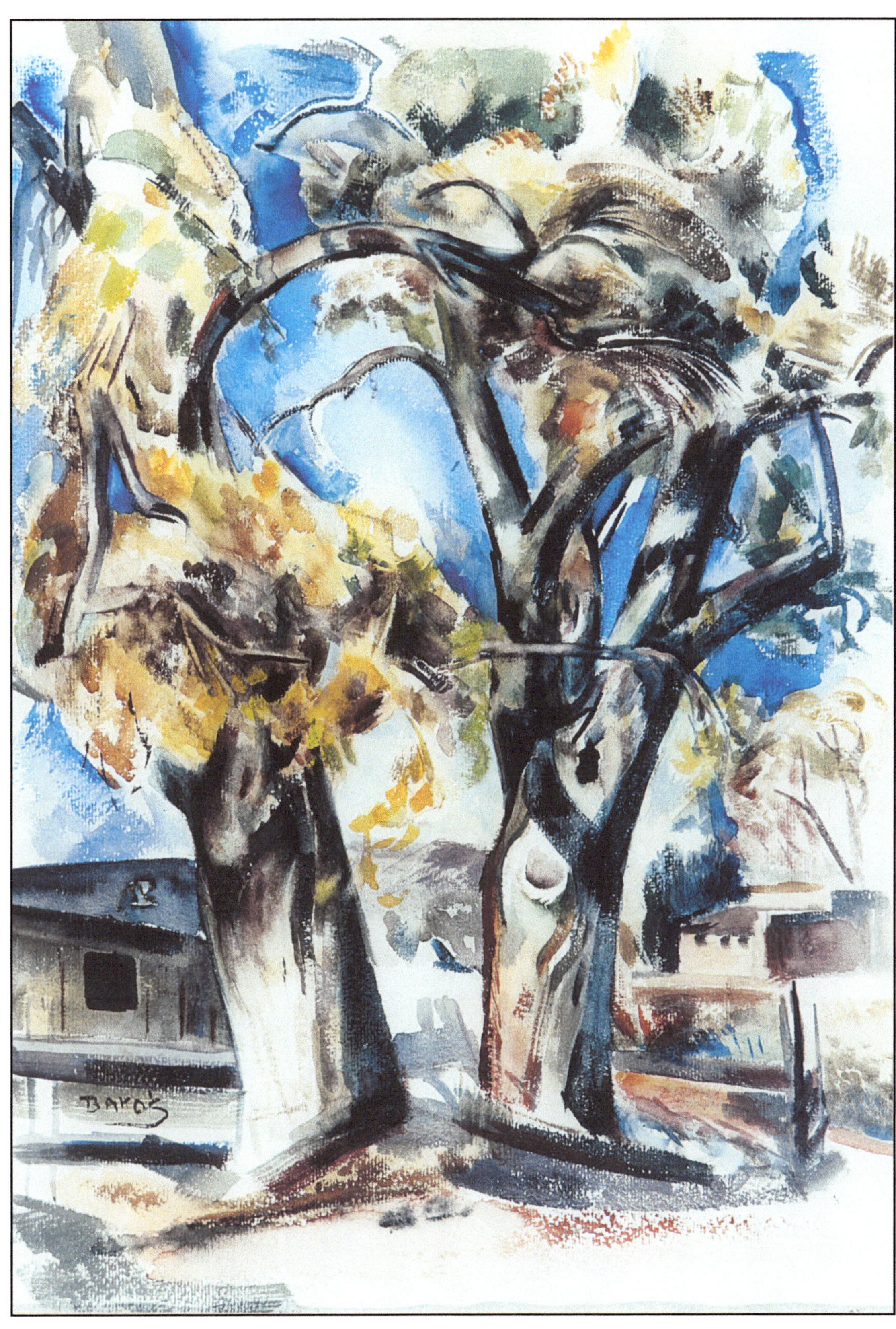

Cottonwoods, Jozef Bakos, painting, McKinley County Courthouse, Gallup.

Patrocinio Barela Born, 1900, Bisbee, Arizona; died, 1964, Canon, New Mexico. Self-taught. Shortly after settling in Canon near Taos in the early 1930s, he discovered that he had a talent, indeed a passion, for woodcarving. He began work for the WPA as a teamster hauling dirt. Fortunately, an office worker in Taos saw his carvings and arranged for him to "give the horses a rest" and join the Art Project. He became, in Virginia Ewing's words, "the star of the Project." His work was sent to exhibitions in Washington, D.C. and New York. Of the WPA works displayed at the Museum of Modern Art, 1936, only his was reviewed. He earned his living as a laborer his entire life.

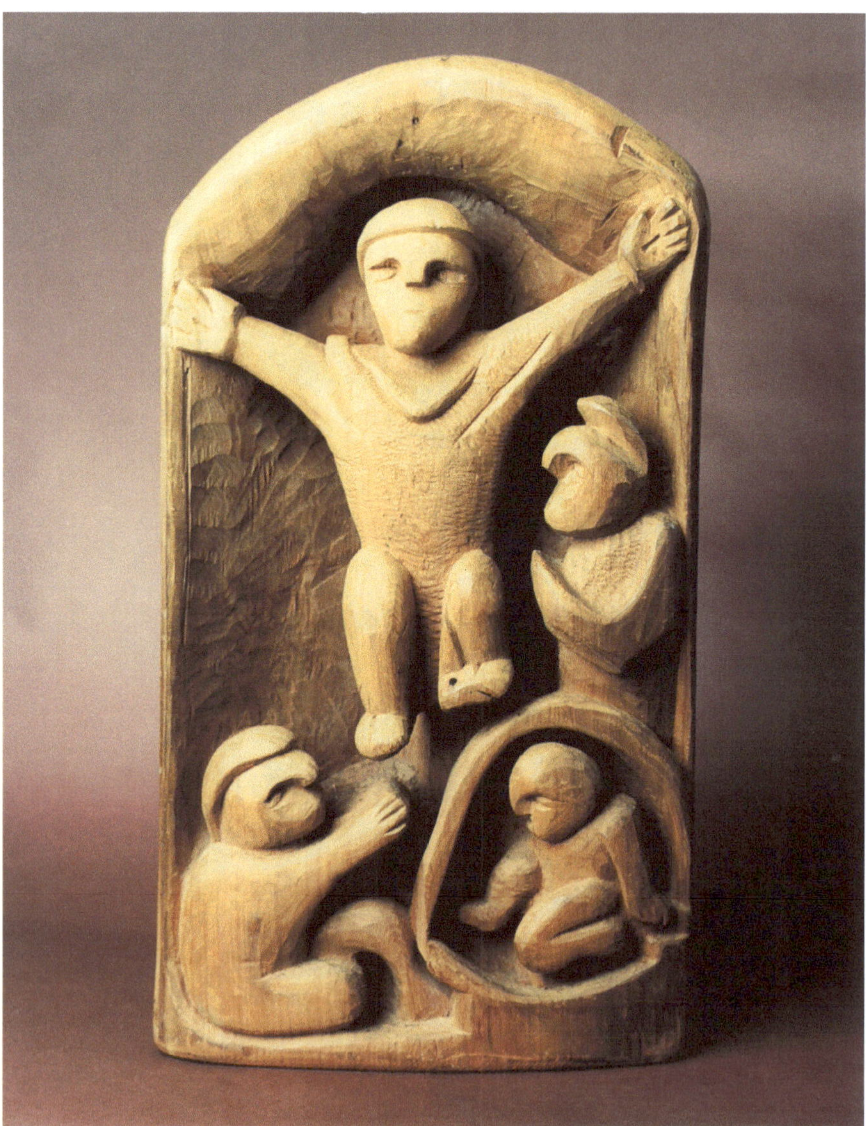

The Resurrection, Patrocinio Barela, carving, Museum of International Folk Art, Santa Fe.

A Woman Whose Baby Is Dead, Patrocinio Barela, carving, Harwood Museum, Taos. Photograph by Megan Bowers.

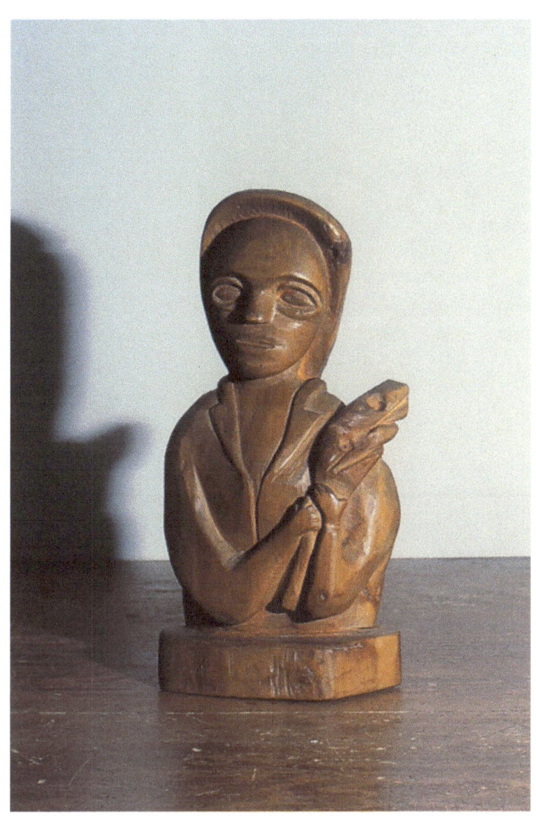

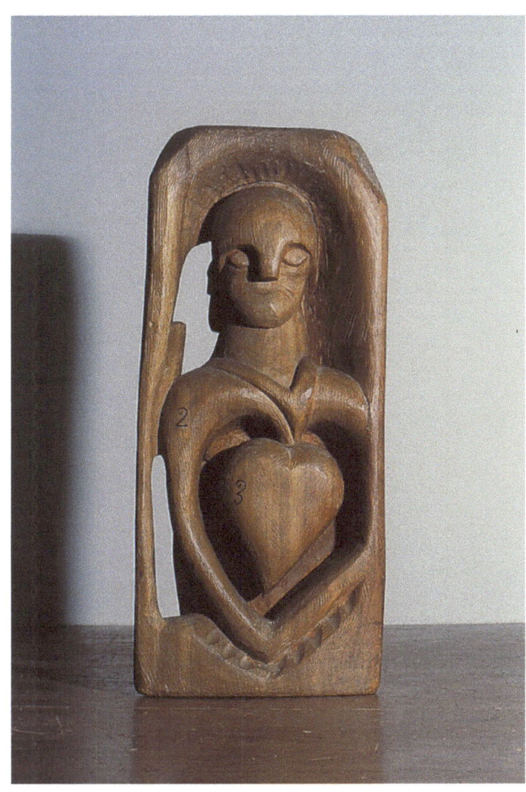

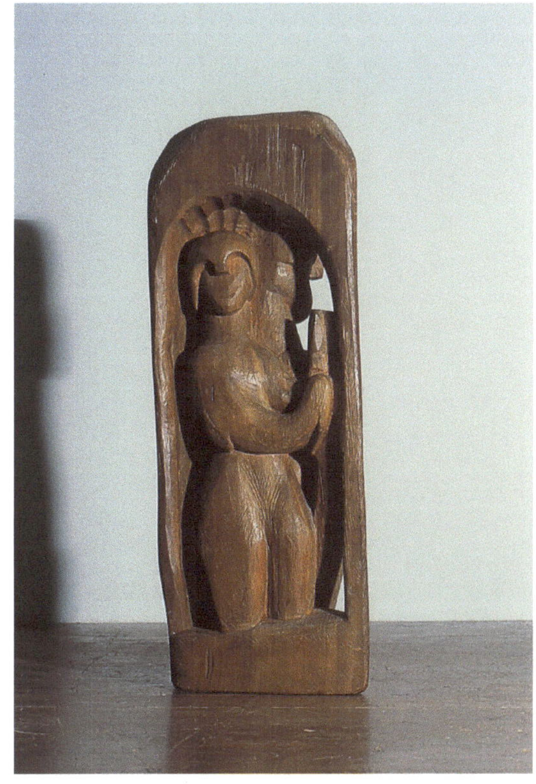

El Fiel, Patrocinio Barela, carving, Harwood Museum, Taos. Photograph by Megan Bowers. (two veiws)

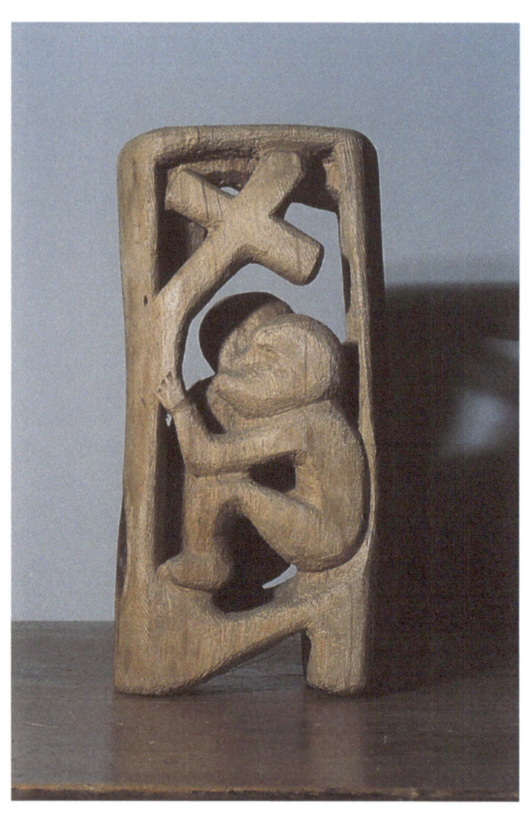

El Santo Job, Patrocinio Barela, carving, Harwood Museum, Taos. Photograph by Megan Bowers. (two views)

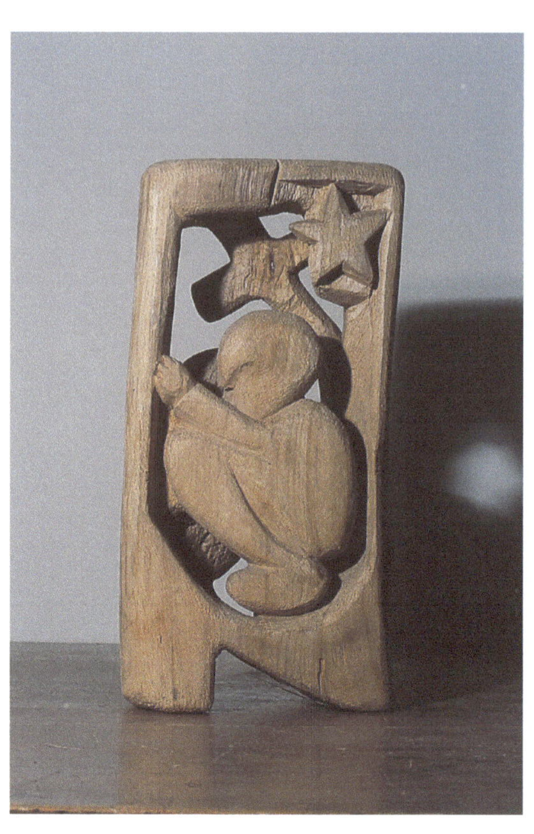

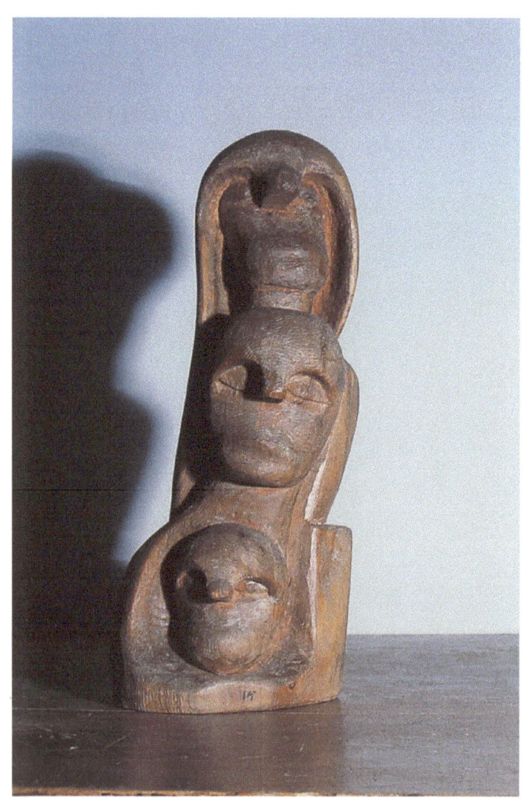

Hope, or The Four Stages Of Man, Patrocinio Barela, carving, Harwood Museum, Taos. Photograph by Megan Bowers. (two views)

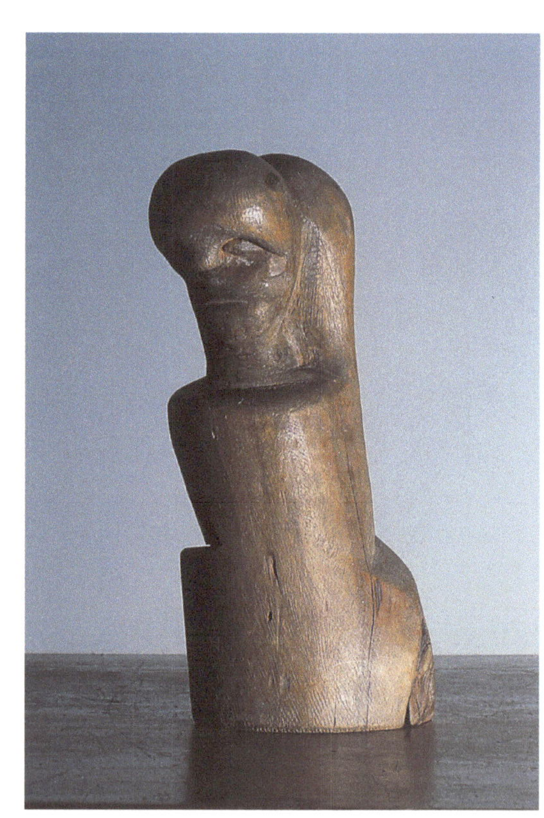

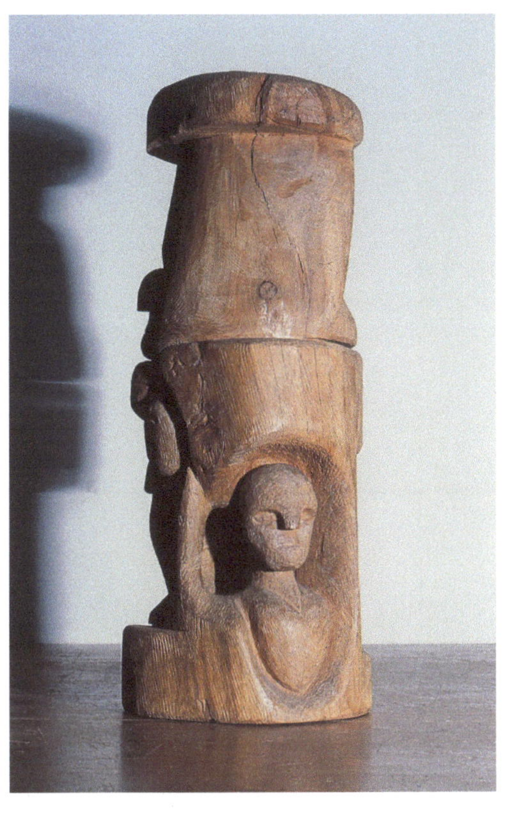

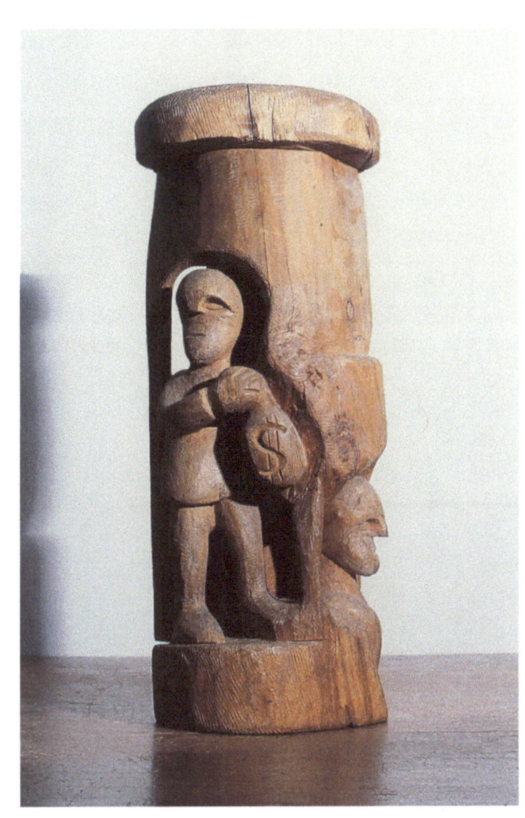

Untitled, Patrocinio Barela, carving, Harwood Museum, Taos. Photograph by Megan Bowers. (two views)

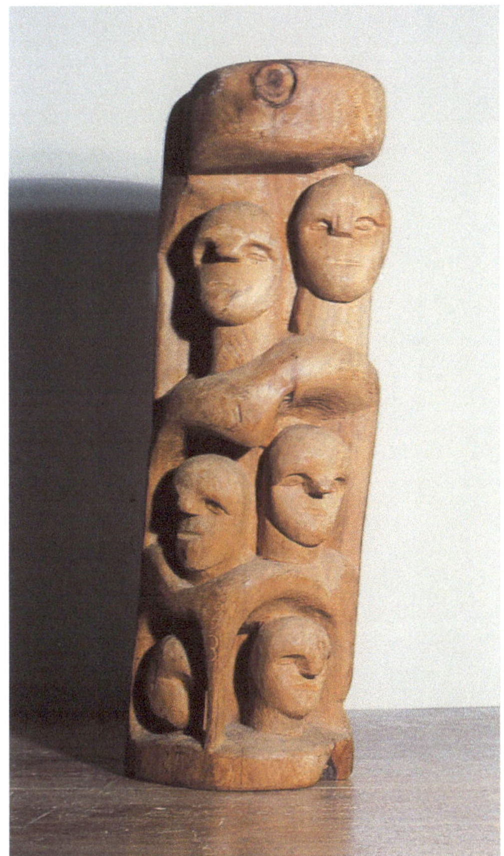

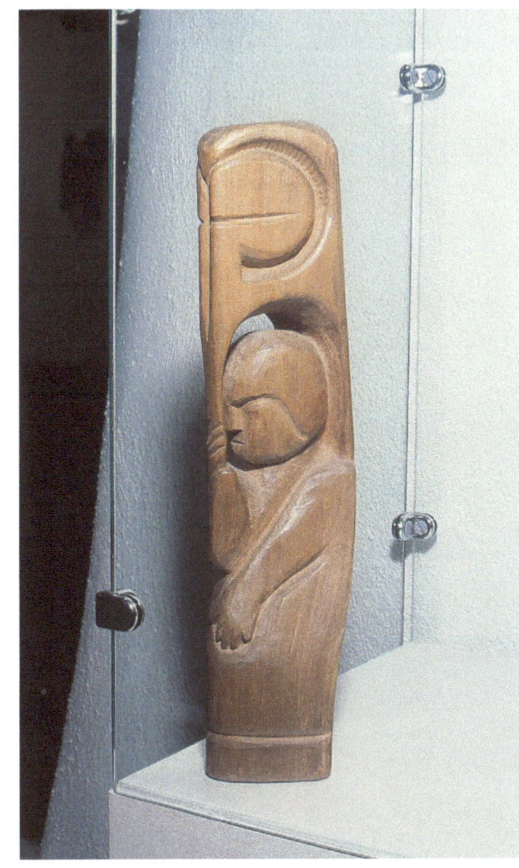

Heavy Thinker, Patrocinio Barela, carving, Harwood Museum, Taos. (left) Photograph by Megan Bowers.

Untitled, Patrocinio Barela, carving, Harwood Museum, Taos. (right) Photograph by Megan Bowers

Wayne Eric Barger Born, 1909; died, 1952. Lived in Albuquerque, New Mexico, noted as a watercolorist. For the New Deal, created copies of military insignia displayed on traveling tours.

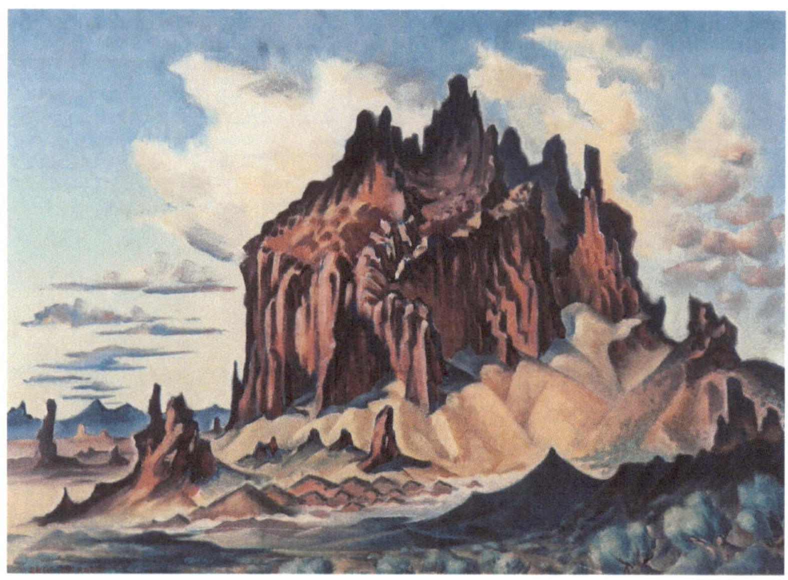

Shiprock, Wayne Eric Barger, painting, Octavia Fellin Public Library, Gallup.

Howard Barton Born, 1907, Evansville, Indiana; died, 1992. Studied at the University of New Mexico with Raymond Jonson and with Loren Mozley in Taos.

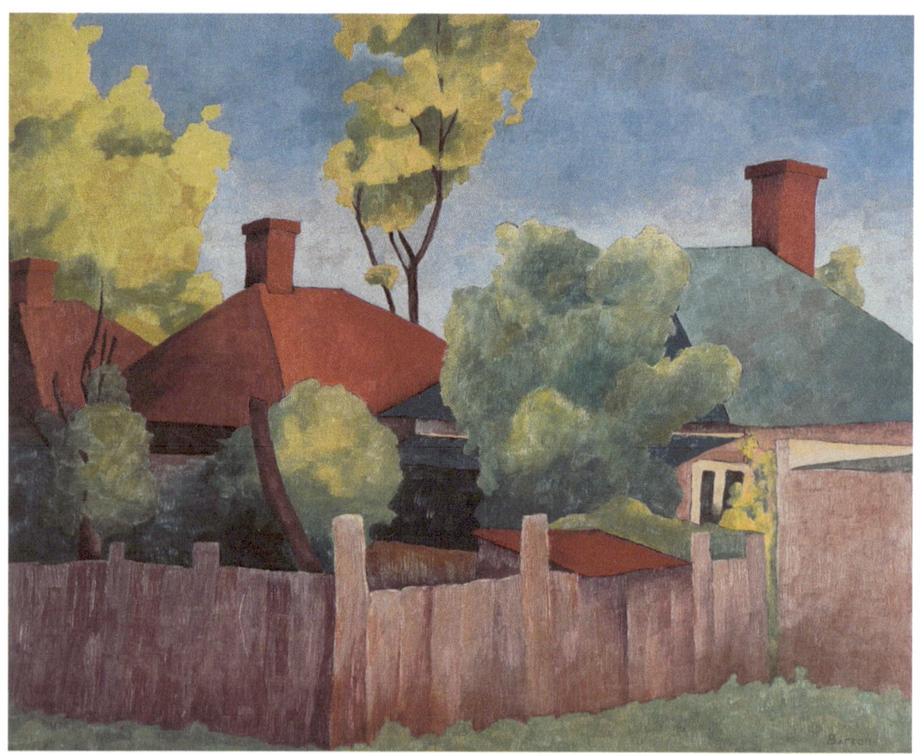

South Second, Howard Barton, painting, University of New Mexico Fine Arts Museum, Albuquerque.

Harrison Begay Born, 1917, White Cone, Arizona. Graduated from the Santa Fe Indian School in 1939; attended Black Mountain College, North Carolina; Phoenix Junior College, Arizona. Became a full-time artist whose work is exhibited internationally.

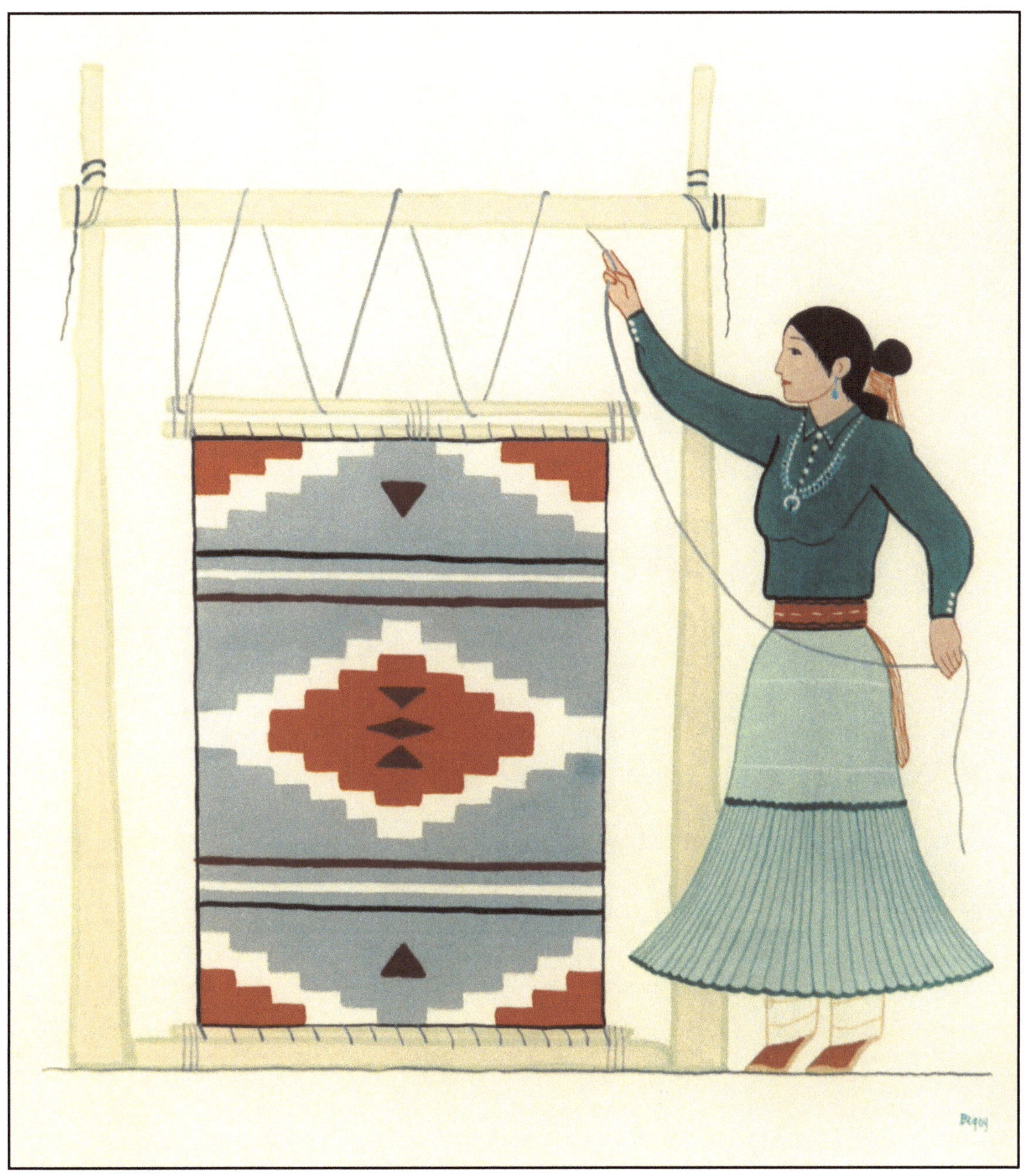

Navajo Rug and Weaver, Harrison Begay, painting, Octavia Fellin Public Library, Gallup.

Charles Berninghaus Born, 1905, St. Louis, Missouri; died, 1988, Taos, New Mexico. Studied at St. Louis School of Fine Arts, Art Institute of Chicago, and Art Students League, New York. Moved to Taos in his late teens with his family. Like his father Oscar Berninghaus, became a painter of western landscapes and still life.

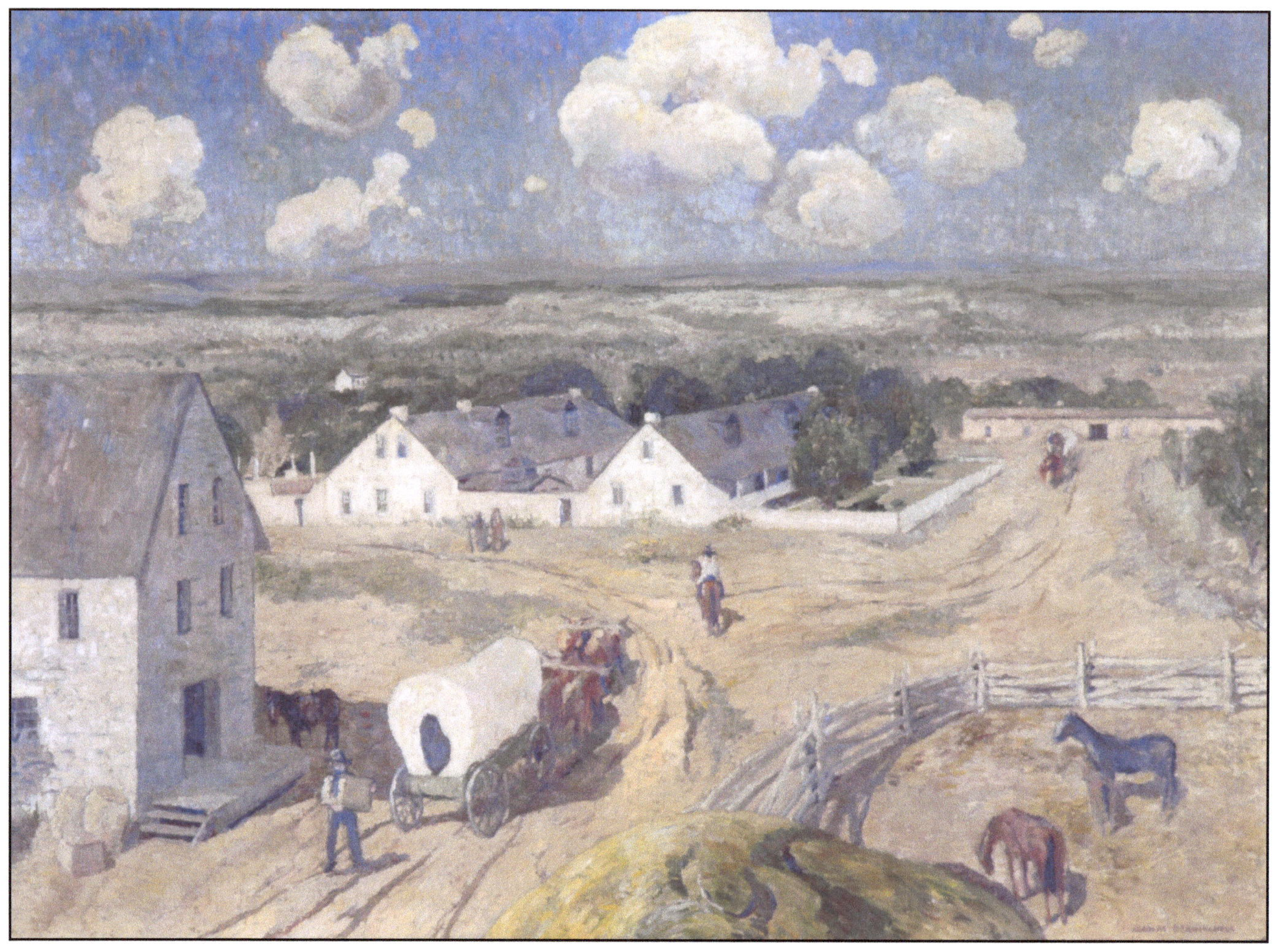

Old Maxwell House, Charles Berninghaus, mural size painting, Arthur Johnson Public Library, Raton.

Oscar Berninghaus Born, 1874, St. Louis, Missouri; died, 1952, Taos, New Mexico. Studied at St. Louis School of Fine Arts. Enthralled with the American southwest, became a founding member of Taos Society of Artists in 1912. Moved to Taos permanently in 1925. A skilled lithographer, illustrator and painter, liked to work outdoors, observing his favored western subjects directly.

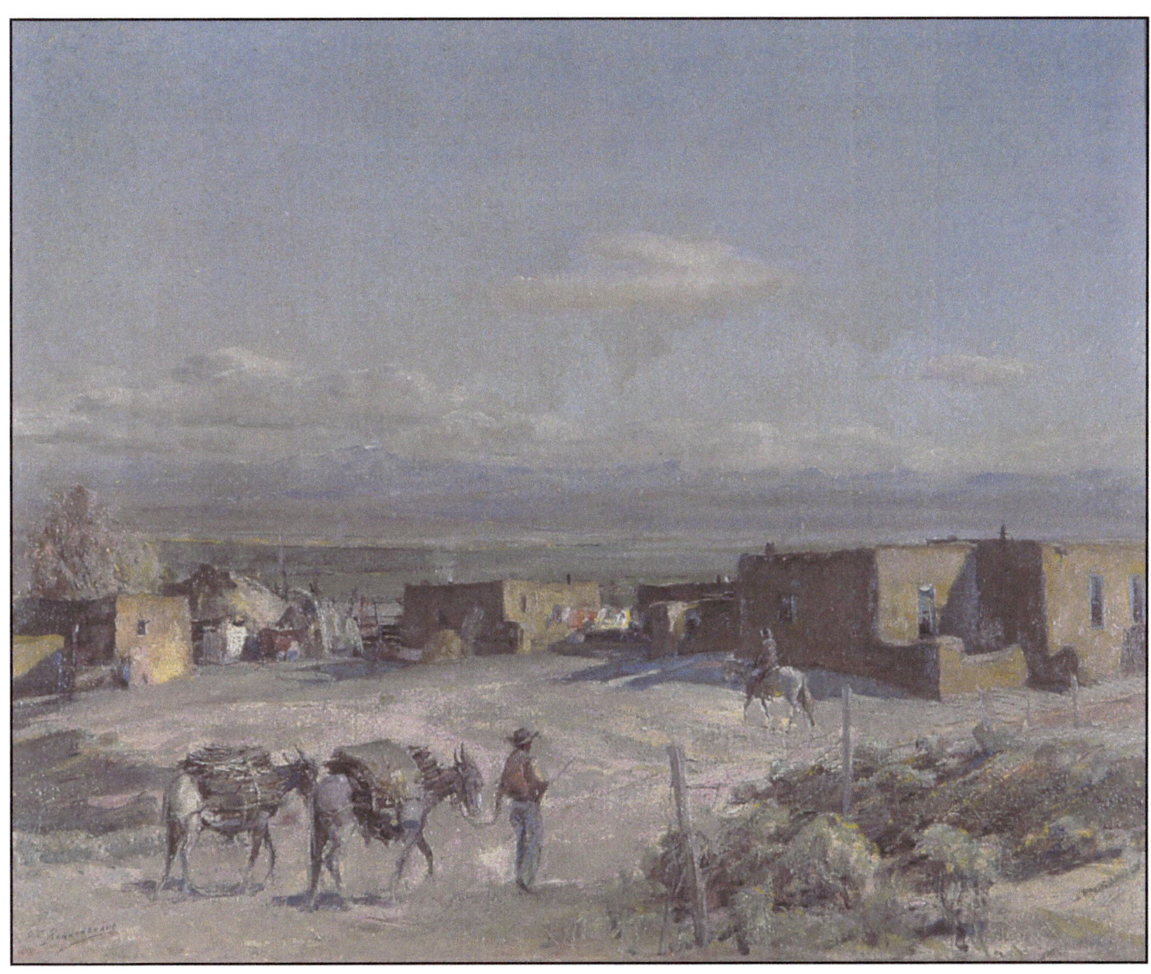

Taos Scene, Oscar Berninghaus, painting, City Hall, Raton.

Emil Bisttram Born, 1895, Hungary; died, 1976, Taos, New Mexico. Moved to New York in 1906. Studied at National Academy of Design, Cooper Union, Art Students League. Traveled to New Mexico in 1930, then to Mexico to study fresco technique with Diego Rivera. Founded the Bisttram School of Fine Arts; became the first teacher of modern art in Taos. Chosen by fellow artists to supervise the Treasury Relief Art Project (TRAP). His job was to collect paintings to be sent to Washington. One of the "Fresco Quartet" who created frescoes for the Taos County Courthouse. He painted three: Aspiration, Reconciliation, and Transgression. (See Fresco Quartet.) His major New Deal mural was for the Department of Justice, Washington, D.C.

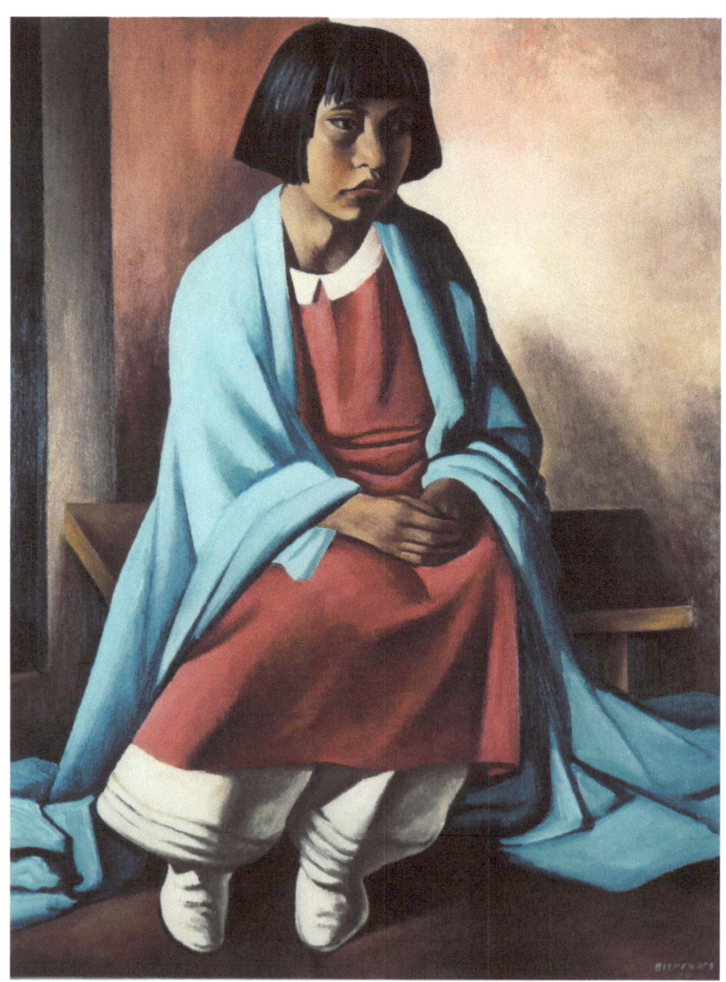

Juanita, Emil Bisttram, painting, Albuquerque Museum, Albuquerque. (above)

Old Hunter, Emil Bisttram, painting, Albuquerque Museum, Albuquerque. (below)

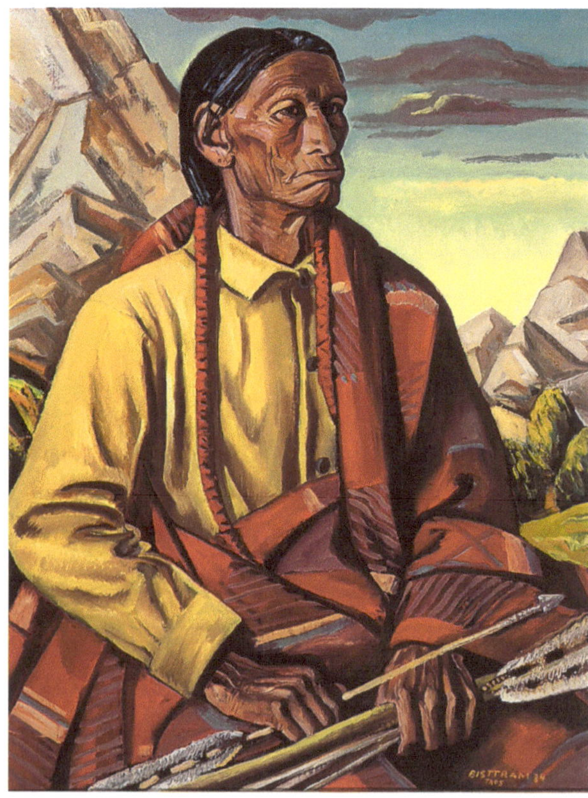

La Verne Nelson Black Born, 1887, Viola, Wisconsin; died, 1938, Chicago, Illinois. Studied at Chicago Academy of Fine Arts. Did artwork for newspapers in Chicago and New York City before moving his family west, first to Taos, then to Phoenix, Arizona.

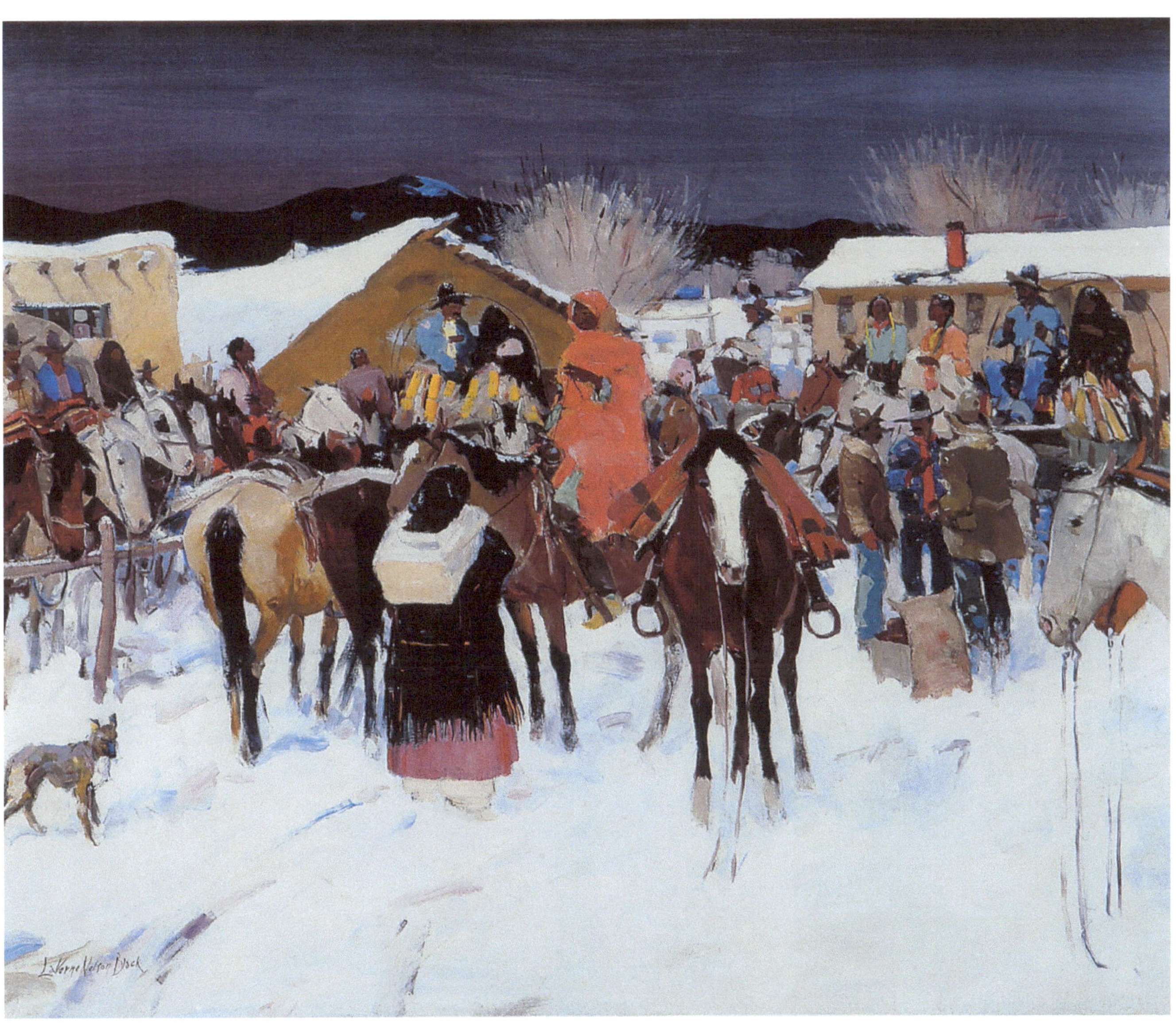

The Jicarilla Apache Trading Post, La Verne Nelson Black, painting, Carlsbad Municipal Museum and Art Center, Carlsbad.

E. Boyd Born, 1903, Philadelphia, Pennsylvania; died, 1974, Santa Fe. Studied at Academy of Fine Arts, Philadelphia; Grande Chaumiére, Paris. Came to live in New Mexico in 1930. Studied the Santero tradition of painting and sculpture; became an authority on Spanish Colonial art. Russell Vernon Hunter, state director of the WPA Federal Art Program, asked E. Boyd to document the Santo carvings in mission churches. She traveled throughout the state to make literal watercolor renderings of church artifacts. They became the basis of the Portfolio of Spanish Colonial Design in New Mexico. Manville Chapman created woodblocks for each of her renderings. Numerous individuals, identified as "copyists," then supplied the coloring as directed. (Sets are in the Branigan Public Library, Las Cruces; the Santa Fe Public Library, Santa Fe; the New Mexico State Library, Santa Fe; the Roswell Art Center, Roswell; and other sites.) E. Boyd said: "We agreed . . . to start making a series of literal renderings of the santos . . . which would give some idea of the original color better than black and white photographs."

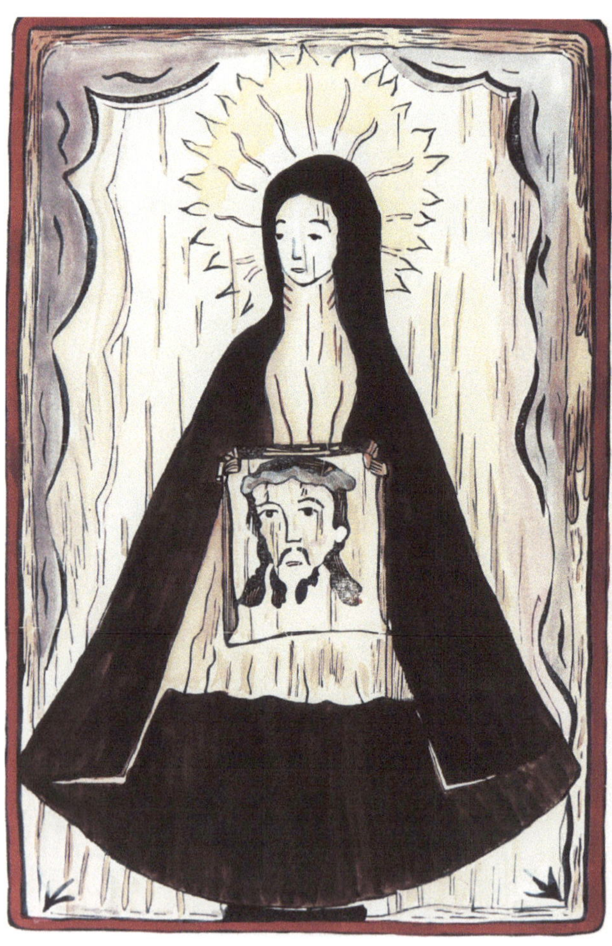

Santo, E. Boyd, woodblock, Plate 20, Portfolio of Spanish Colonial Design in New Mexico, Branigan Library, Las Cruces.

Santo, E. Boyd, woodblock, Plate 31, Portfolio of Spanish Colonial Design in New Mexico, Branigan Library, Las Cruces.

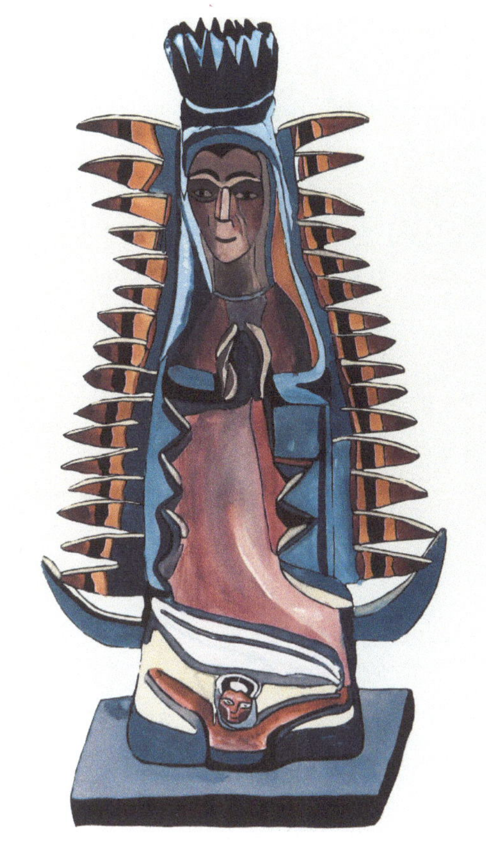

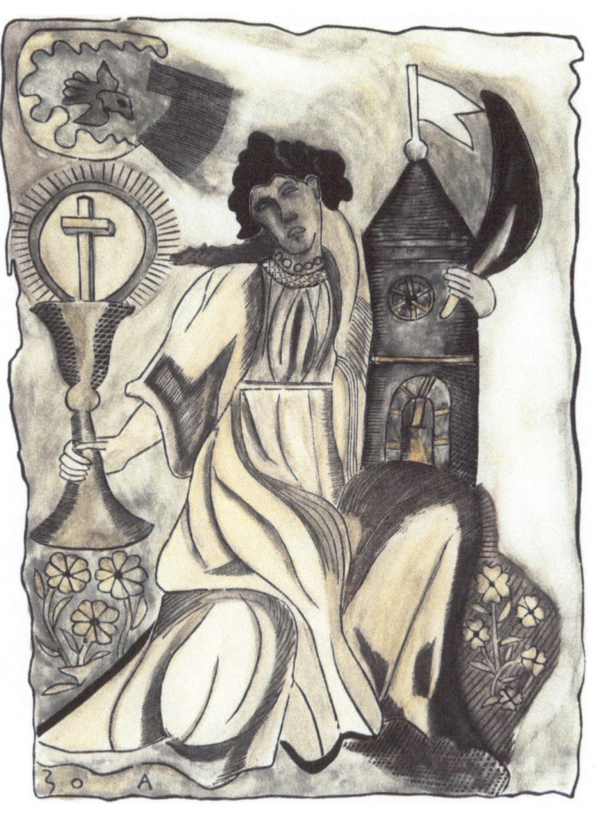

Santo, E.Boyd, woodblock, Plate 41, Portfolio of Spanish Colonial Design in New Mexico, Branigan Library, Las Cruces.

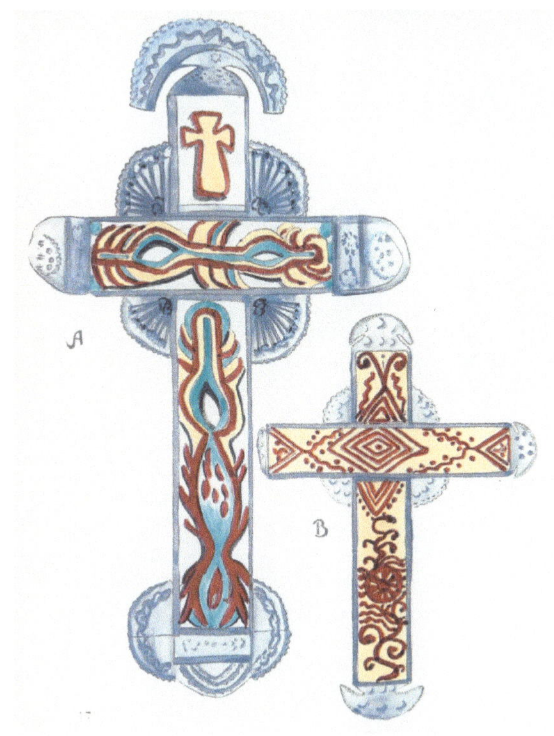

Crosses, E. Boyd, woodblock, Plate 47, Portfolio of Spanish Colonial Design in New Mexico, Branigan Library, Las Cruces.

Pedro Lopez Cervantez Born, 1914, Wilcox, Arizona; died, 1987, Clovis, New Mexico. His parents, of Mexican Indian and Spanish heritage, moved to Texico, New Mexico, when he was still very young. Studied art at Eastern New Mexico University, Portales; and later, after serving in the army, at Hill and Canyon School of the Arts, Santa Fe. He worked as an apprentice to Russell Vernon Hunter on the historical murals in the De Baca County Courthouse, Fort Sumner, New Mexico.

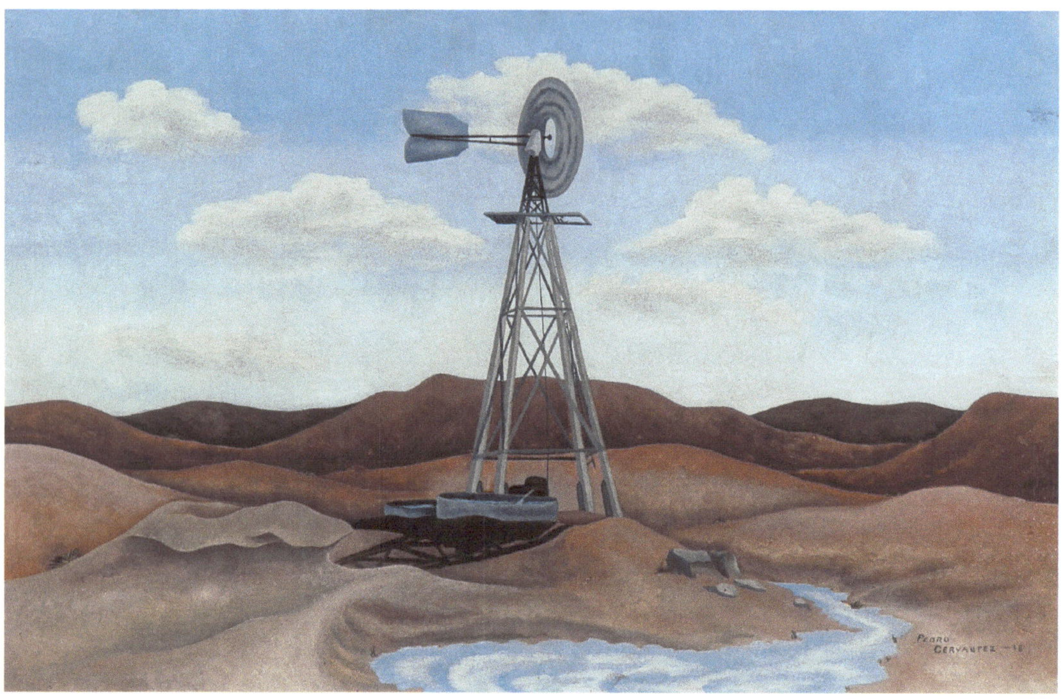

The Windmill, Pedro Cervantez, painting, Melrose High School Library, Melrose.

Manville Chapman Born, 1903, Raton, New Mexico; died 1978, California. Studied at the Art Institute of Chicago. Participated in a variety of New Deal art projects: made woodcuts for the Portfolio of Spanish Colonial Design in New Mexico and for the Roswell Museum; taught WPA artists in Raton; painted murals showing scenes of early Raton. The Raton Range reported his search for authentic local material: "Mr. Chapman is anxious to obtain all the old photographs for use in the panels. Purely scenic photographs will be of no use to him, but any pictures of old buildings, pictures of old trails, . . . old railroad engines or scenes, old customs and photographs of persons showing the general type of that time. . . ."

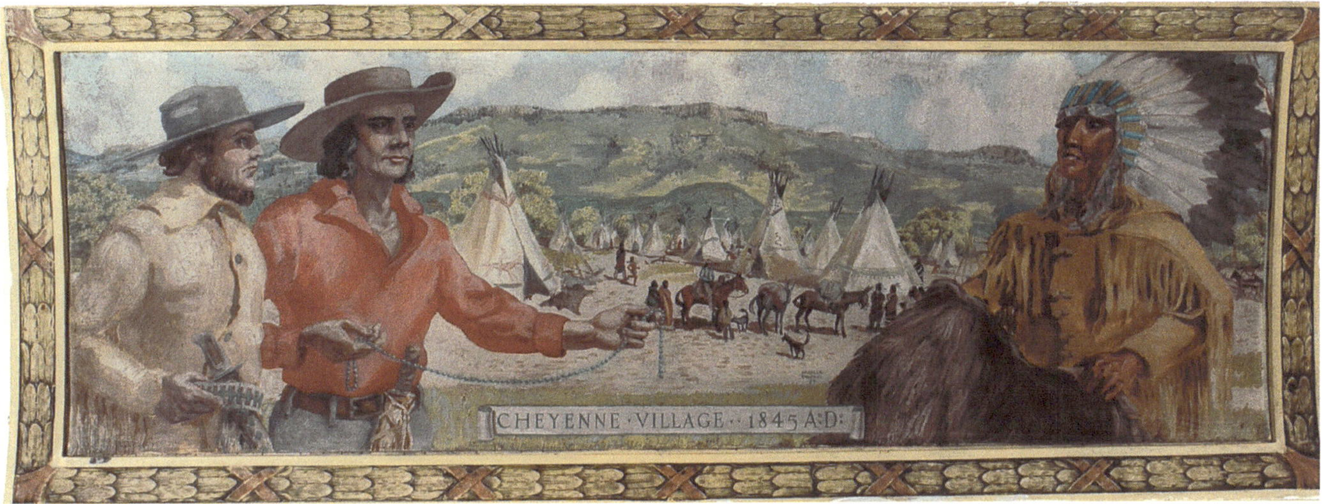

Cheyenne Village, 1845, Manville Chapman, mural, Shuler Theater, Raton.

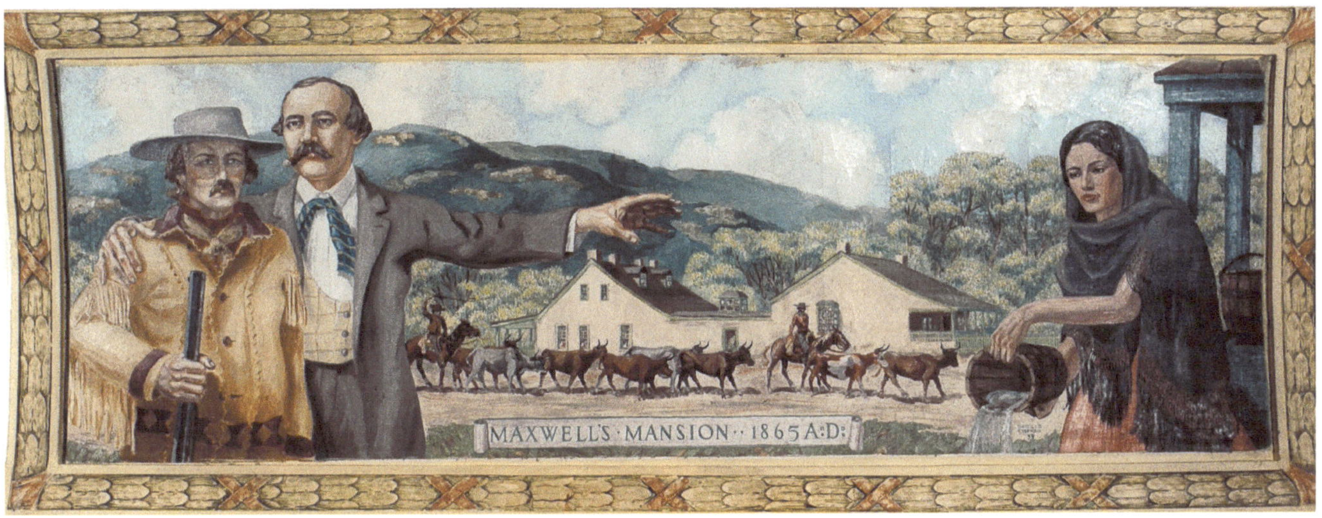

Maxwell's Mansion, 1865, Manville Chapman, mural, Shuler Theater, Raton.

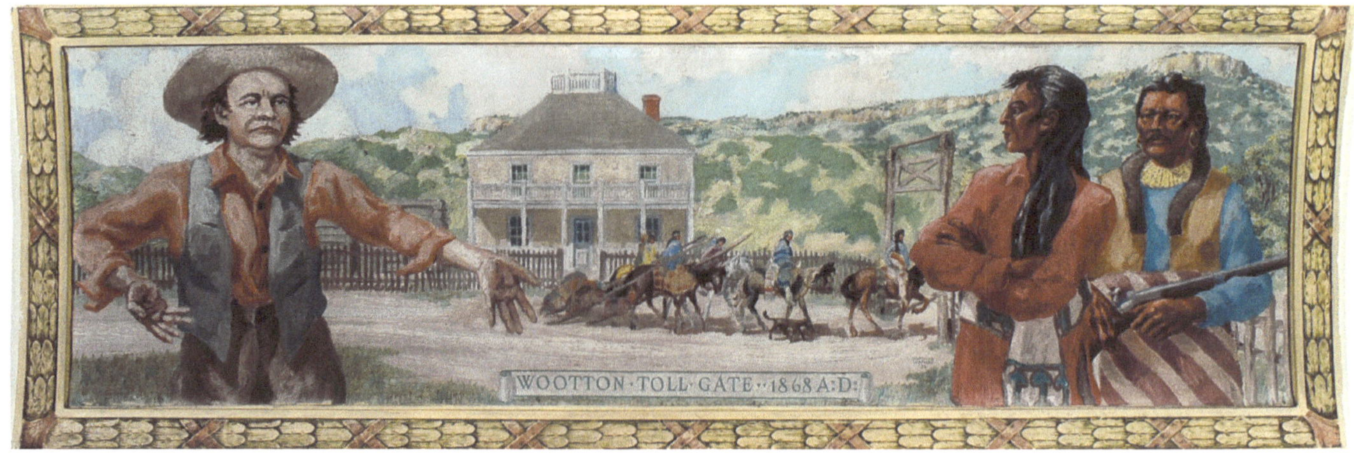

Wooten Toll Gate, 1868, Manville Chapman, mural, Shuler Theater, Raton.

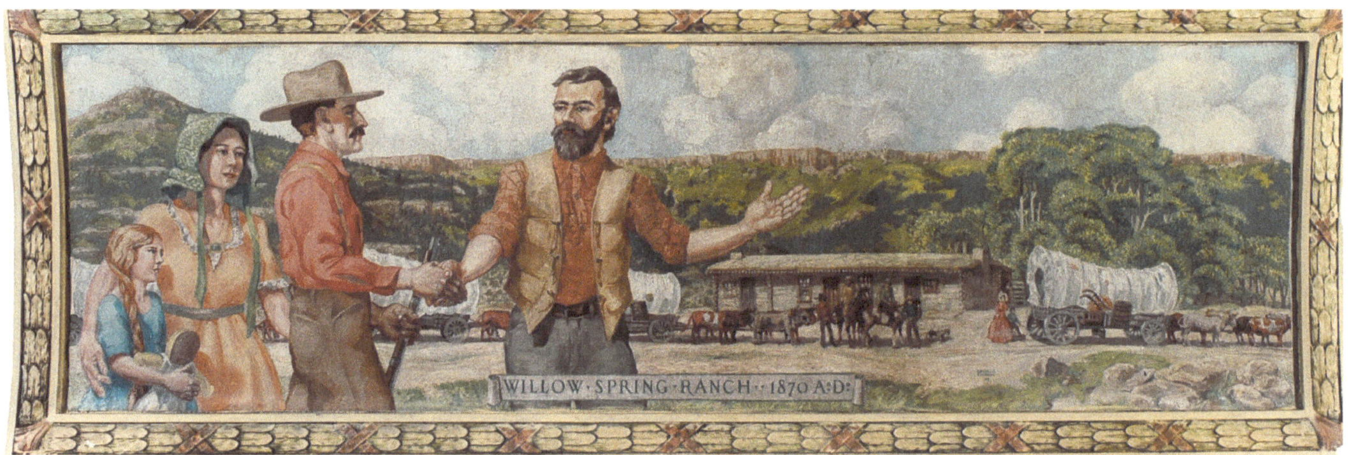

Willow Spring Ranch, 1870, Manville Chapman, mural, Shuler Theater, Raton.

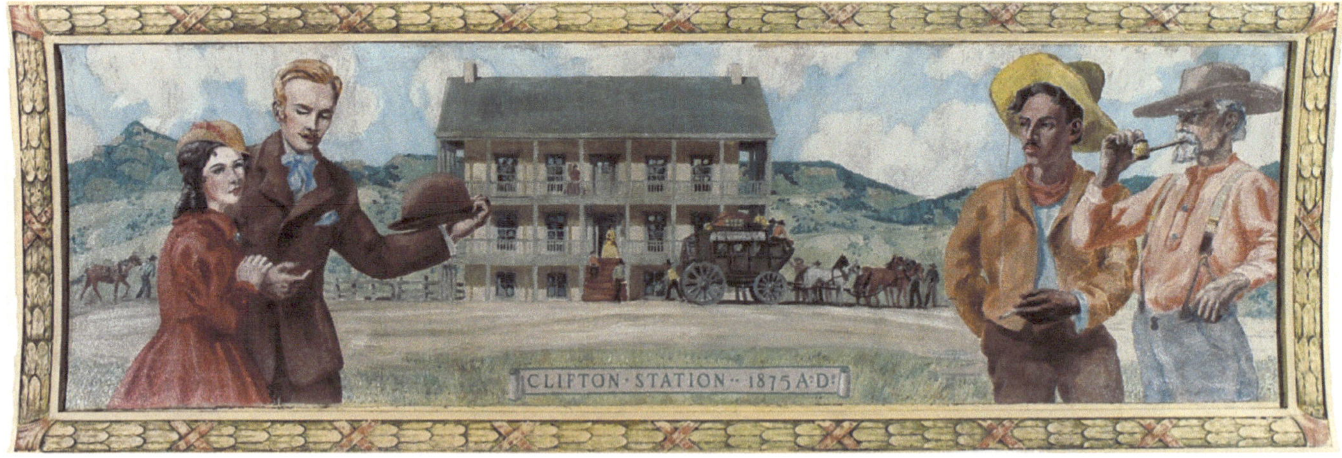

Clifton Station, 1875, Manville Chapman, mural, Shuler Theater, Raton.

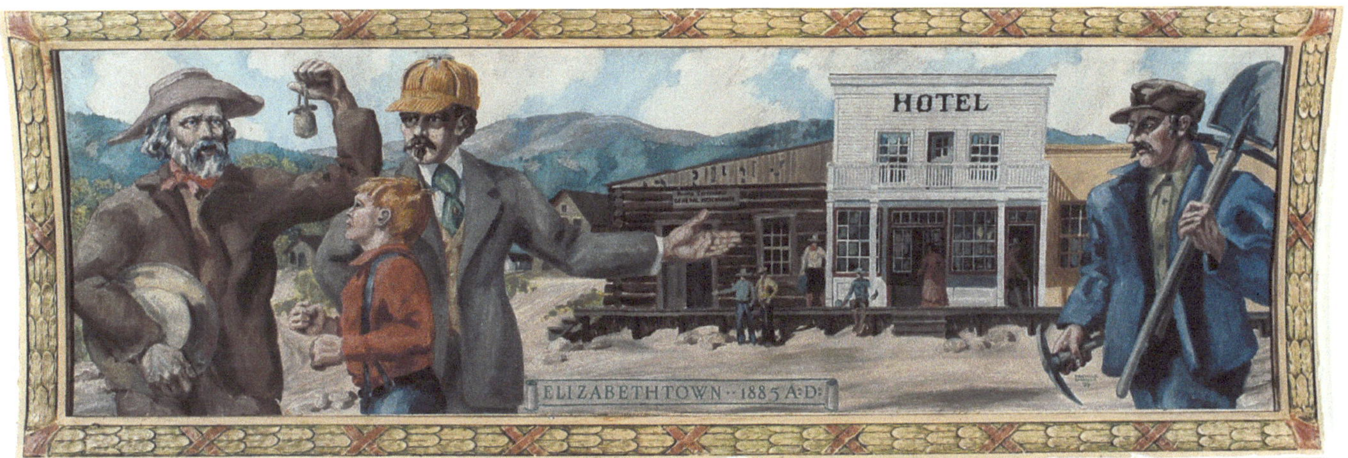

Elizabethtown, 1885, Manville Chapman, mural, Shuler Theater, Raton.

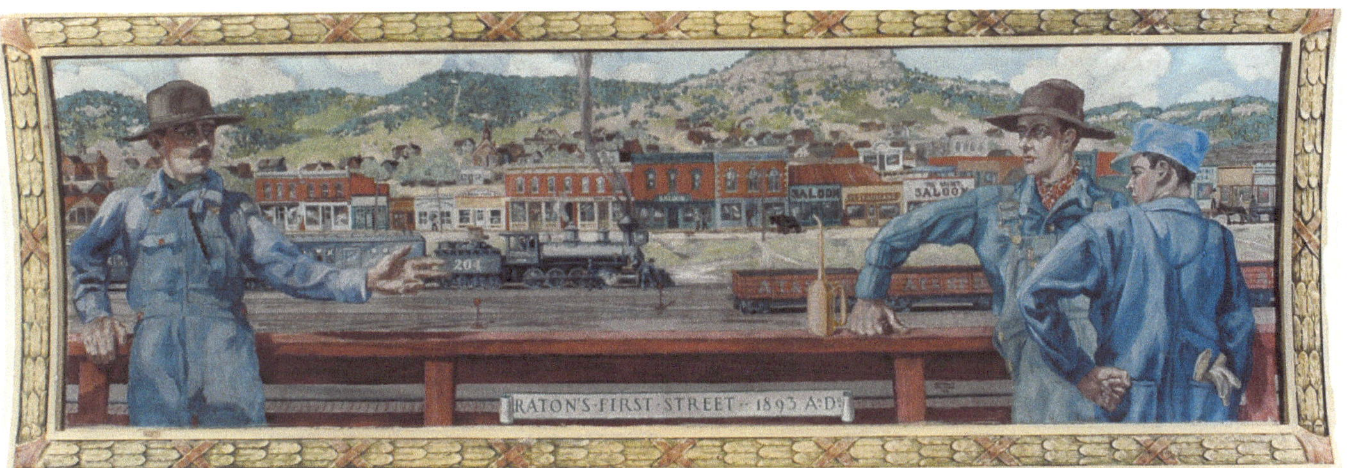

Raton's First Street, 1893, Manville Chapman, mural, Shuler Theater, Raton.

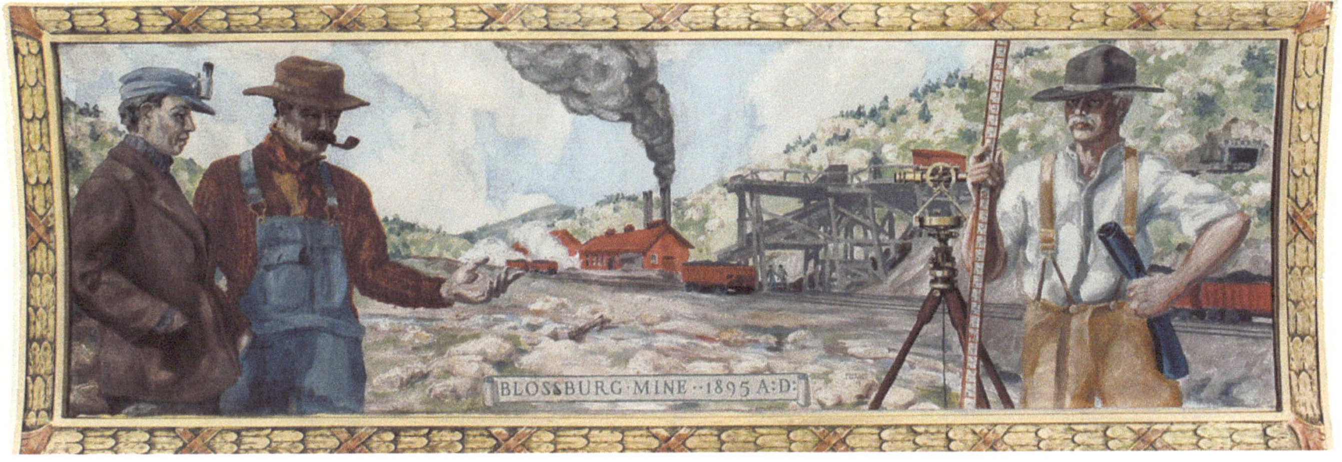

Blossburg Mine, 1895, Manville Chapman, mural, Shuler Theater, Raton.

Ruth Connely produced Twelve Examples of Navajo Weaving in a limited edition of 100 copies under the New Mexico Relief Administration. She produced the images from drawings cut on linoleum blocks as part of the Public Works of Art Project, Thirteenth Regional Committee. The project was undertaken to provide colored prints for use by the United States Indian Service in encouraging a revival of the older designs in Navajo weaving as a part of its broad program in Indian Arts and Crafts.

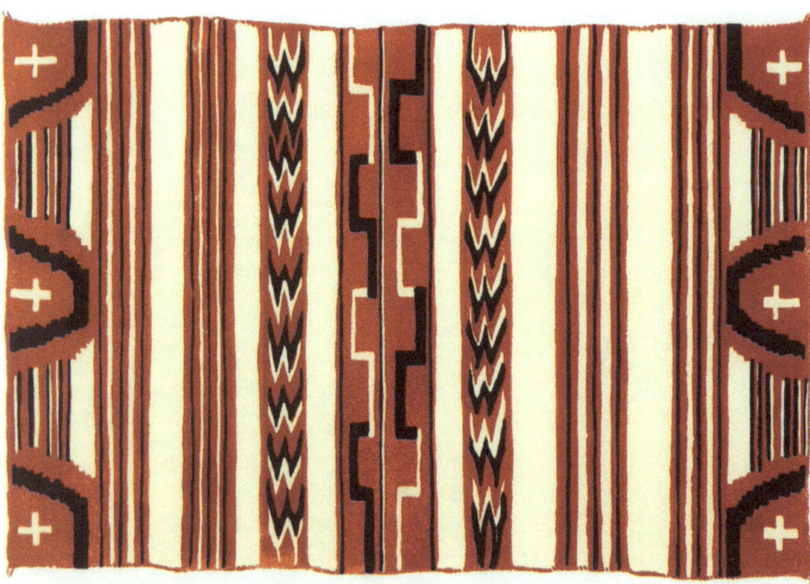

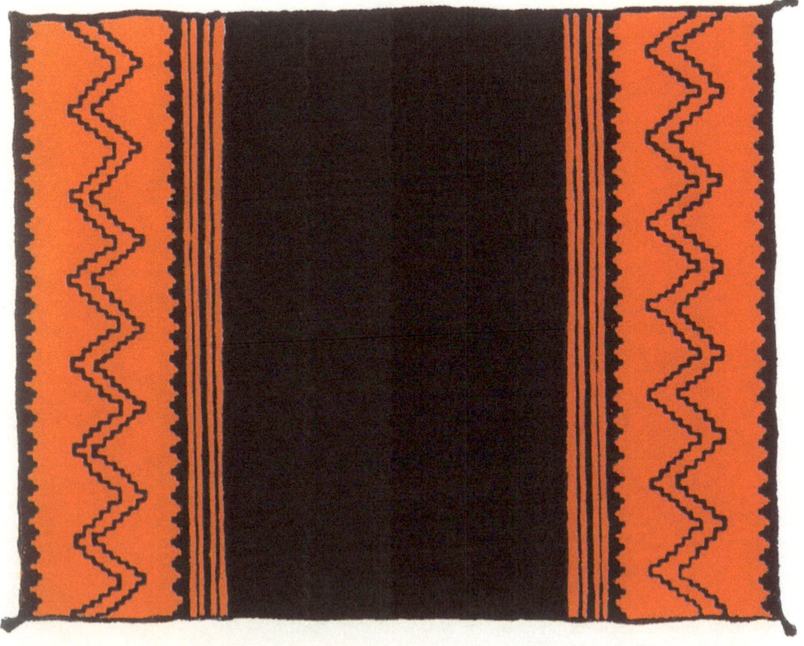

Navajo Weaving #2, (above) #3 (right) #4 (bottom)
Ruth Connely, linoleum block print,
Museum of Indian Arts and Culture, Santa Fe.
Photograph by Blair Clark.

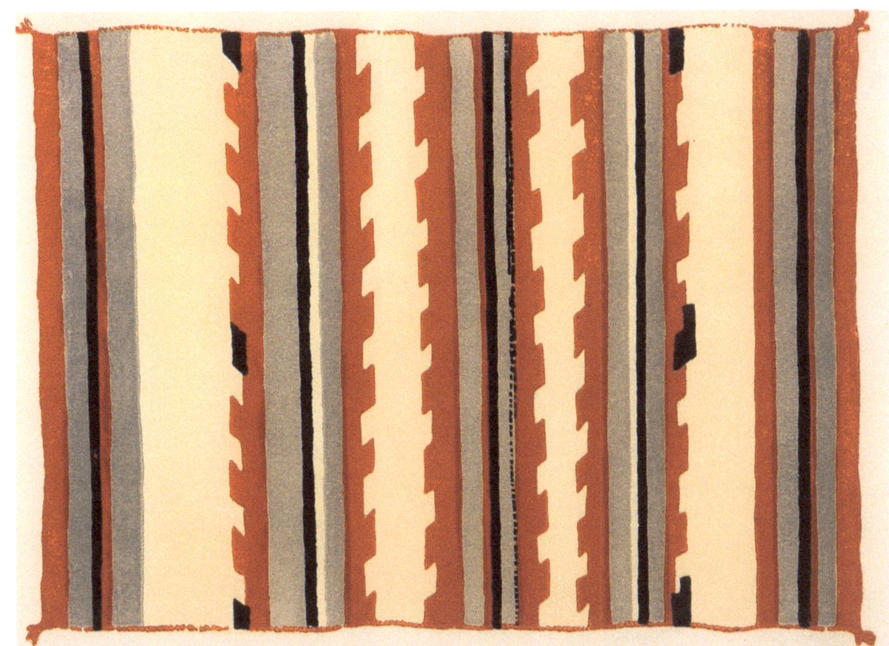

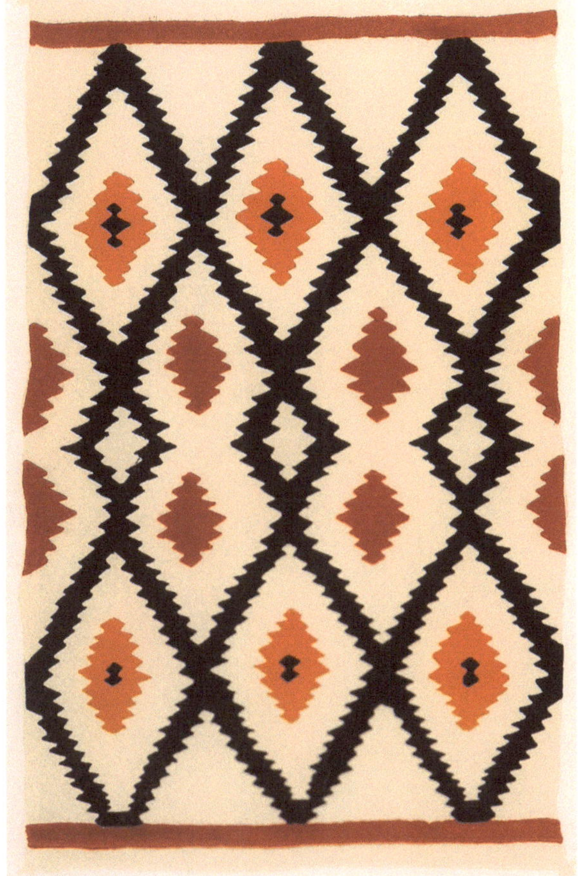

Navajo Weaving #9 (above), #11 (left), #12 (below),
Ruth Connely, linoleum block print,
Museum of Indian Arts and Culture, Santa Fe.
Photograph by Blair Clark.

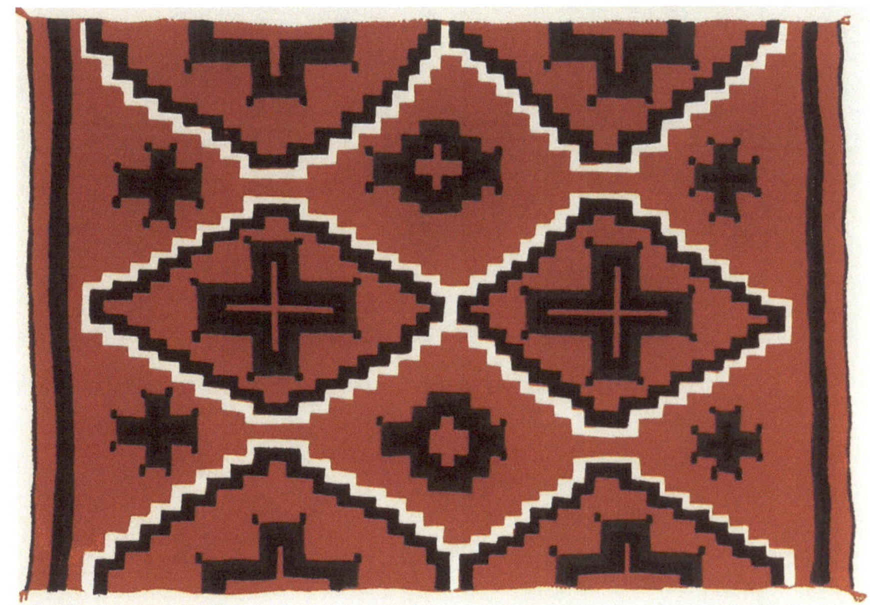

Regina Tatum Cooke Born, 1902, Corsicana, Texas; died, 1988, Taos, New Mexico. Studied art at Colorado College; exhibited at the Denver Art Museum. Moved to Taos in 1933. Founded the Taos Art Association, the Taos Little Theater, and started the Taos municipal school's art collection. WPA activities: easel paintings; work on the Portfolio of Spanish Colonial Design; dioramas, now in the Museum of Fine Arts, Santa Fe.

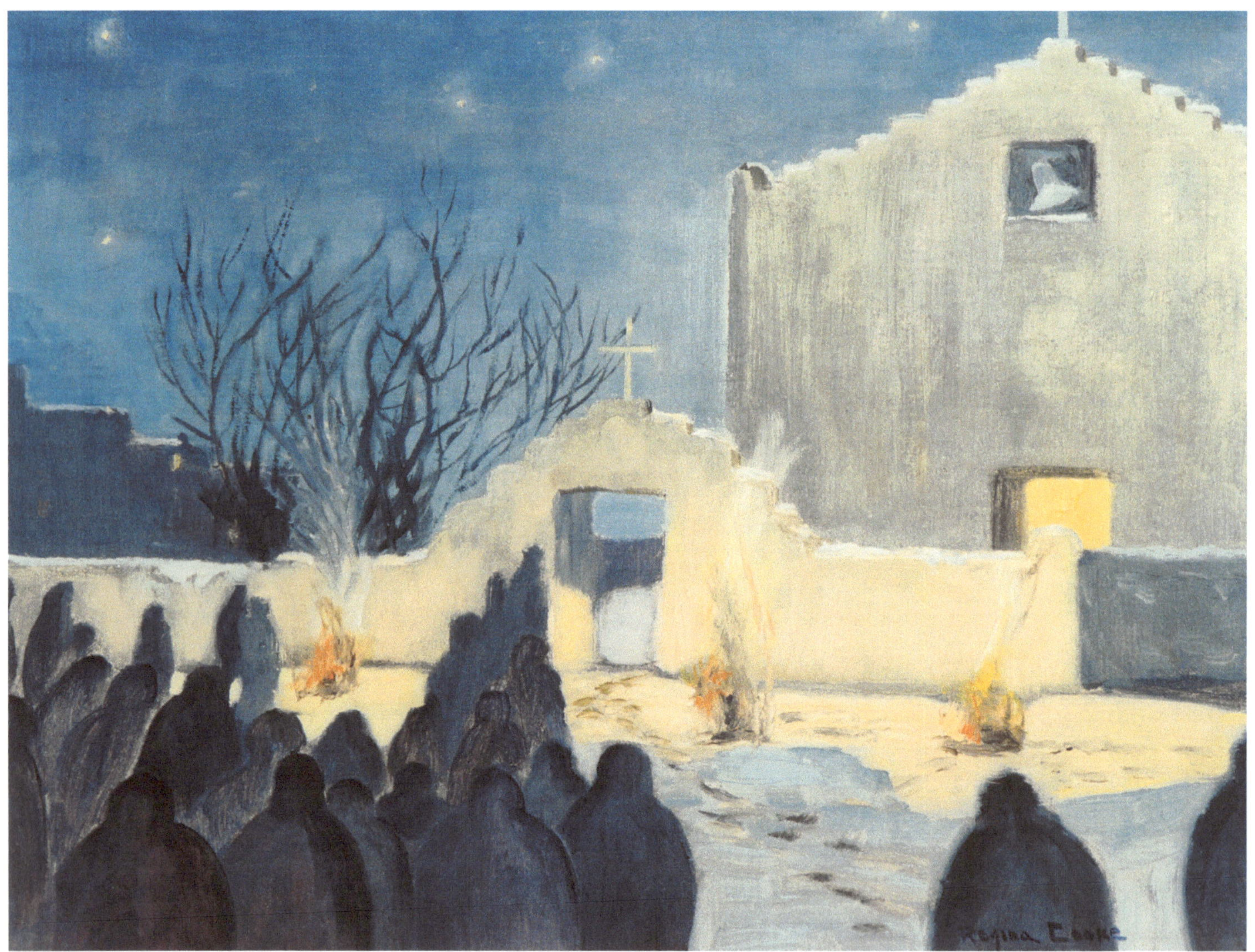

Christmas Eve, Regina Tatum Cooke, painting, Clayton High School, Clayton.

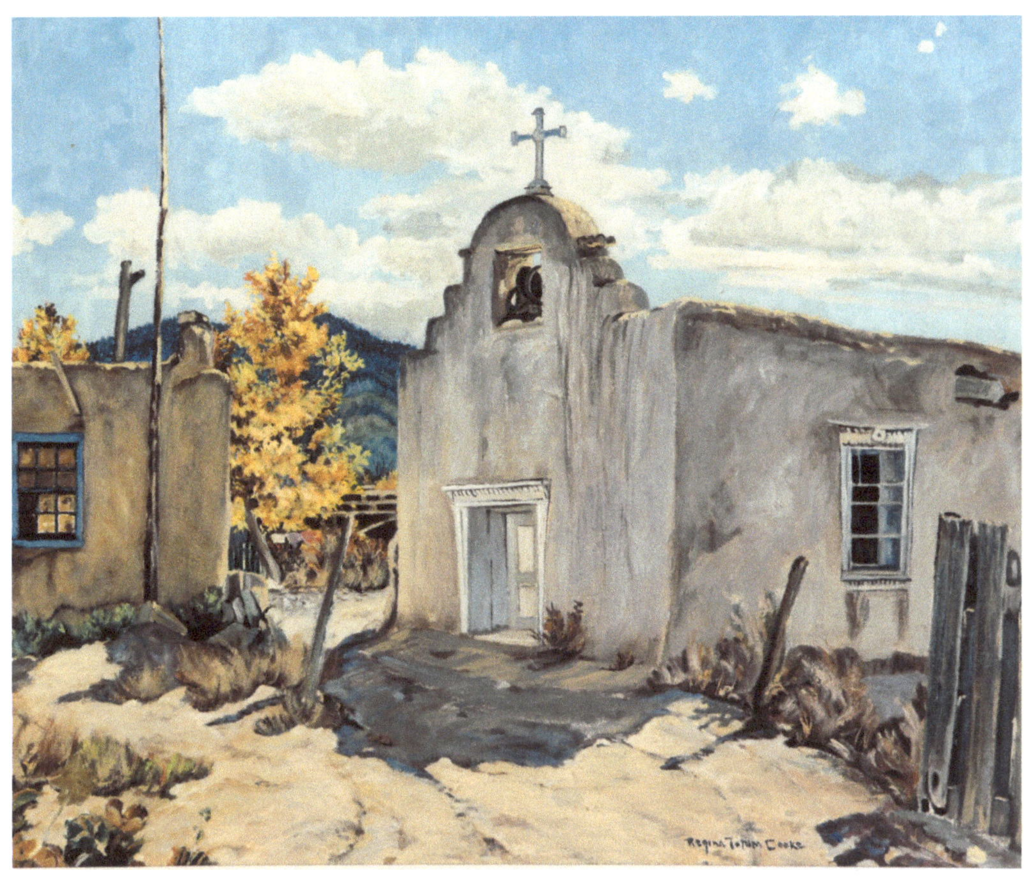

Taos Chapel, Regina Tatum Cooke, painting, Melrose High School Library, Melrose.

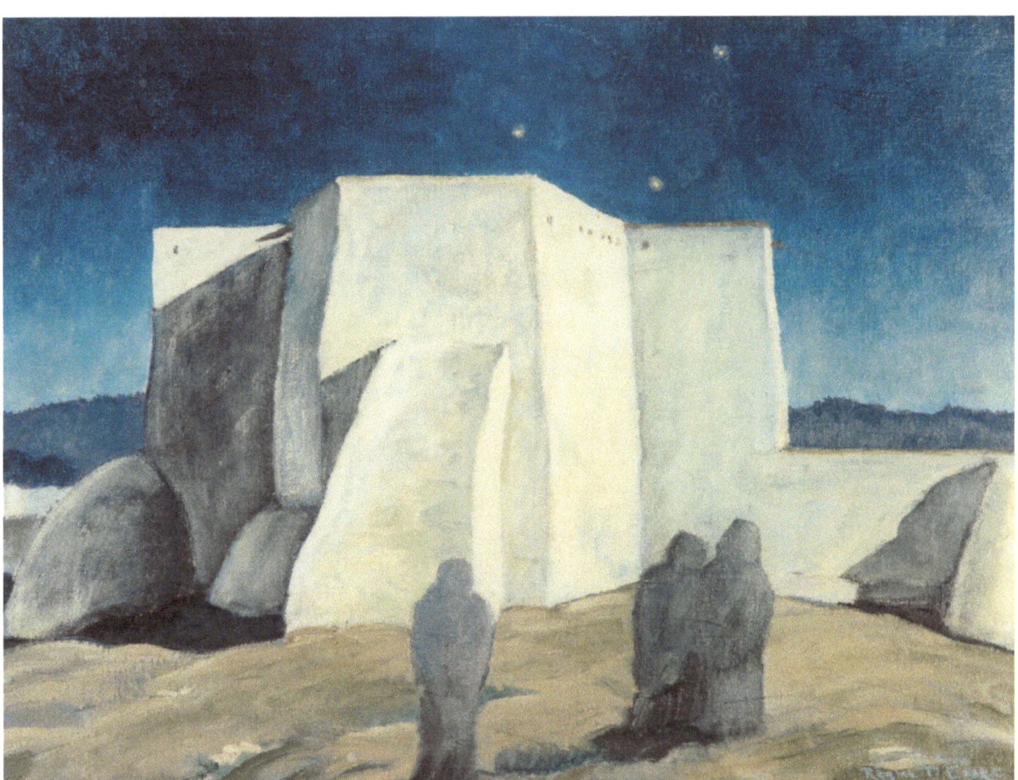

Ranchos de Taos Church, Regina Tatum Cooke, painting, Arthur Johnson Memorial Library, Raton.

Ildeberto "Eddie" Delgado Born, 1883, Santa Fe, New Mexico; died, 1973, Santa Fe, New Mexico. The Delgado family were noted Santa Fe tinsmiths for many generations. Eddie Delgado carried on the tradition and was an outstanding contributor. Among his WPA contributions were light fixtures and decorative objects, still preserved, for the Albuquerque Little Theater and the National Park Service Regional Office, Santa Fe.

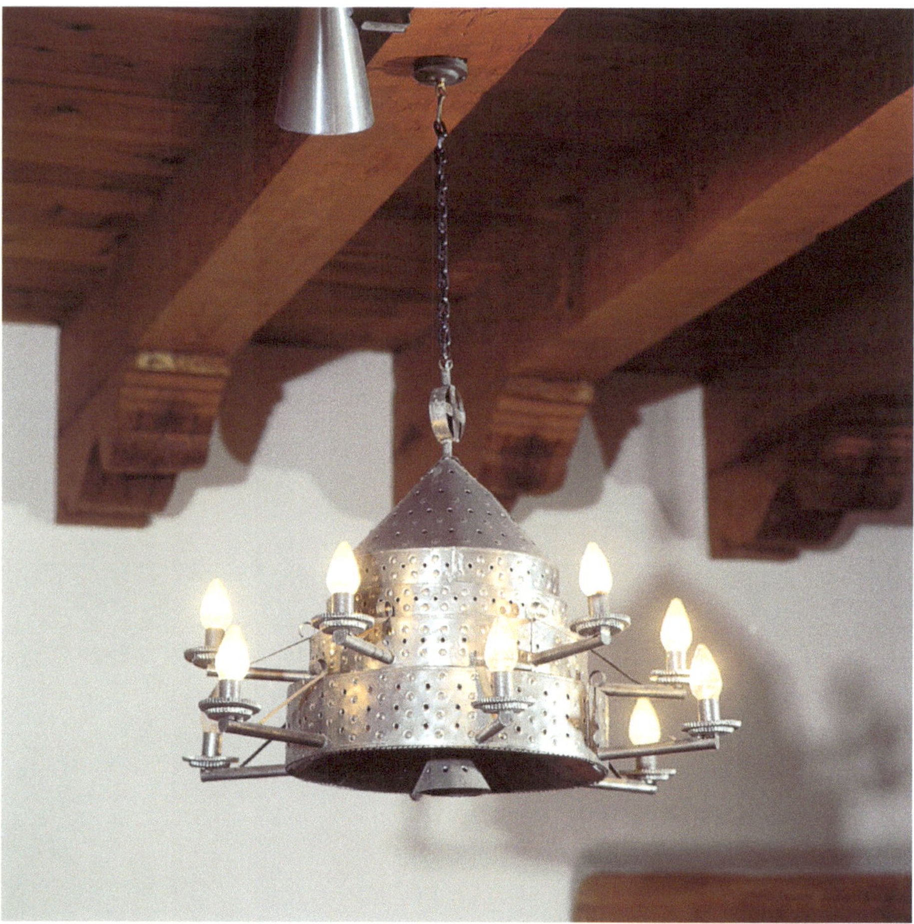

Light Fixtures, Eddie Delgado, tinwork, National Park Service Regional Office, Santa Fe.

Fremont Ellis Born, 1897, Virginia City, Montana; died, 1985, Santa Fe, New Mexico. Studied briefly at the Art Students League. In the early 1920s gave up his profession as optometrist, moved to Santa Fe, became the youngest of a group calling itself Los Cinco Pintores. Included Josef Bakos, Walter Mruk, Willard Nash and Will Shuster; their aim, to create local interest in contemporary art.

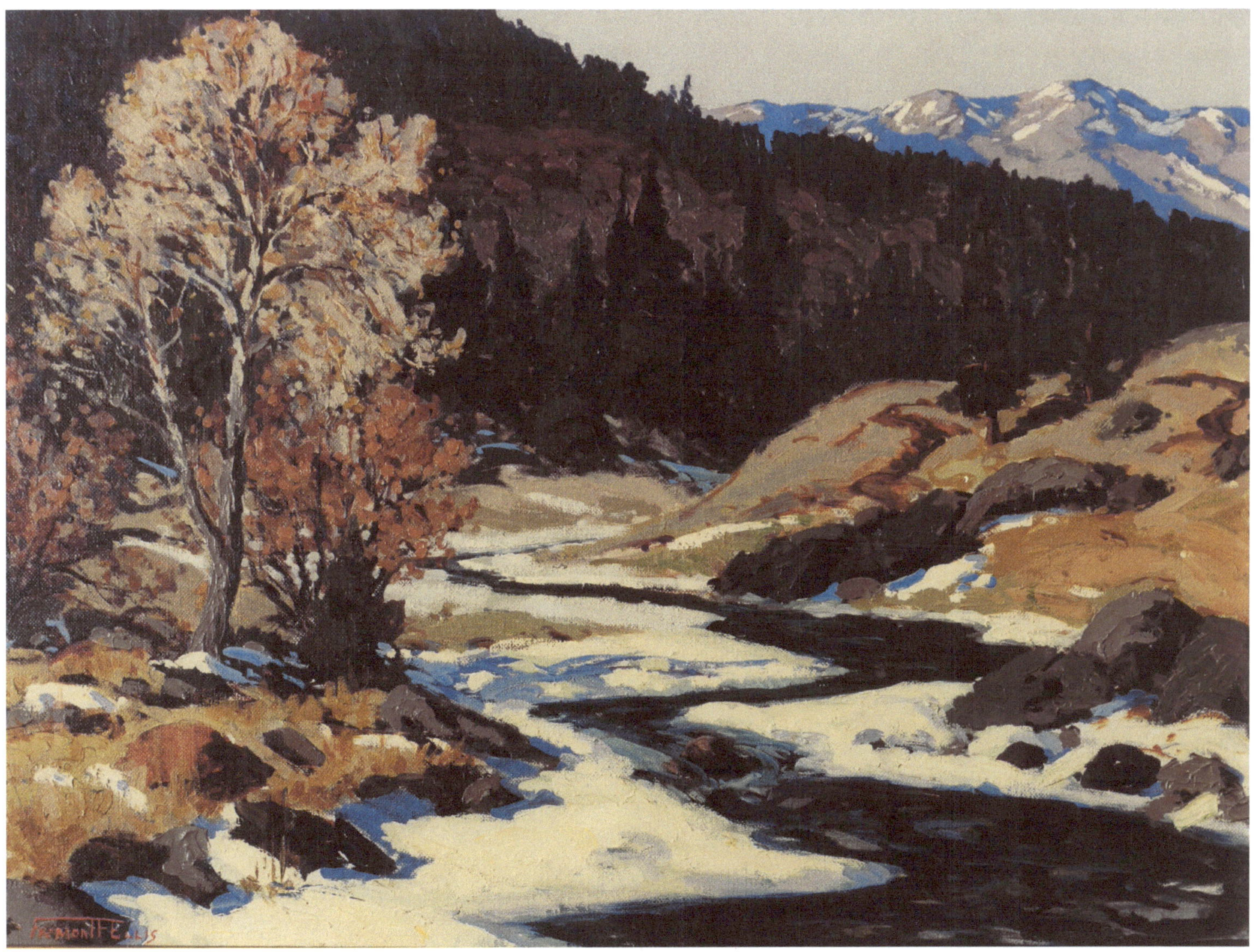

Winter Scene, Fremont Ellis, painting, Carrie Tingley Hospital, Albuquerque.

Louie Ewing Born, 1908, Pocatello, Idaho; died, 1983, Santa Fe, New Mexico. Trained as a commercial artist in California. Came to Santa Fe in 1935 to teach crafts and print making, but after only a short while "everything ran out," he says, "and there weren't any more jobs." Worked as a WPA engraver for the Index of American Design. "Vernon Hunter delegated me as an experimental artist," he recalls. "I was at home base and he could talk to me about new things that came in, like mosaic and silk screen, that was just starting out then, and I was one of the first to experiment with silk screen." He was commissioned by the Laboratory of Anthropology to make copies of 15 of their finest Navajo rugs. Assisted by Eliseo Rodriguez, he first made paintings of the rugs, then reproduced them in a series of 200 silkscreen prints. They are in the Laboratory collection, Santa Fe, and at the Branigan Public Library, as well as other sites.

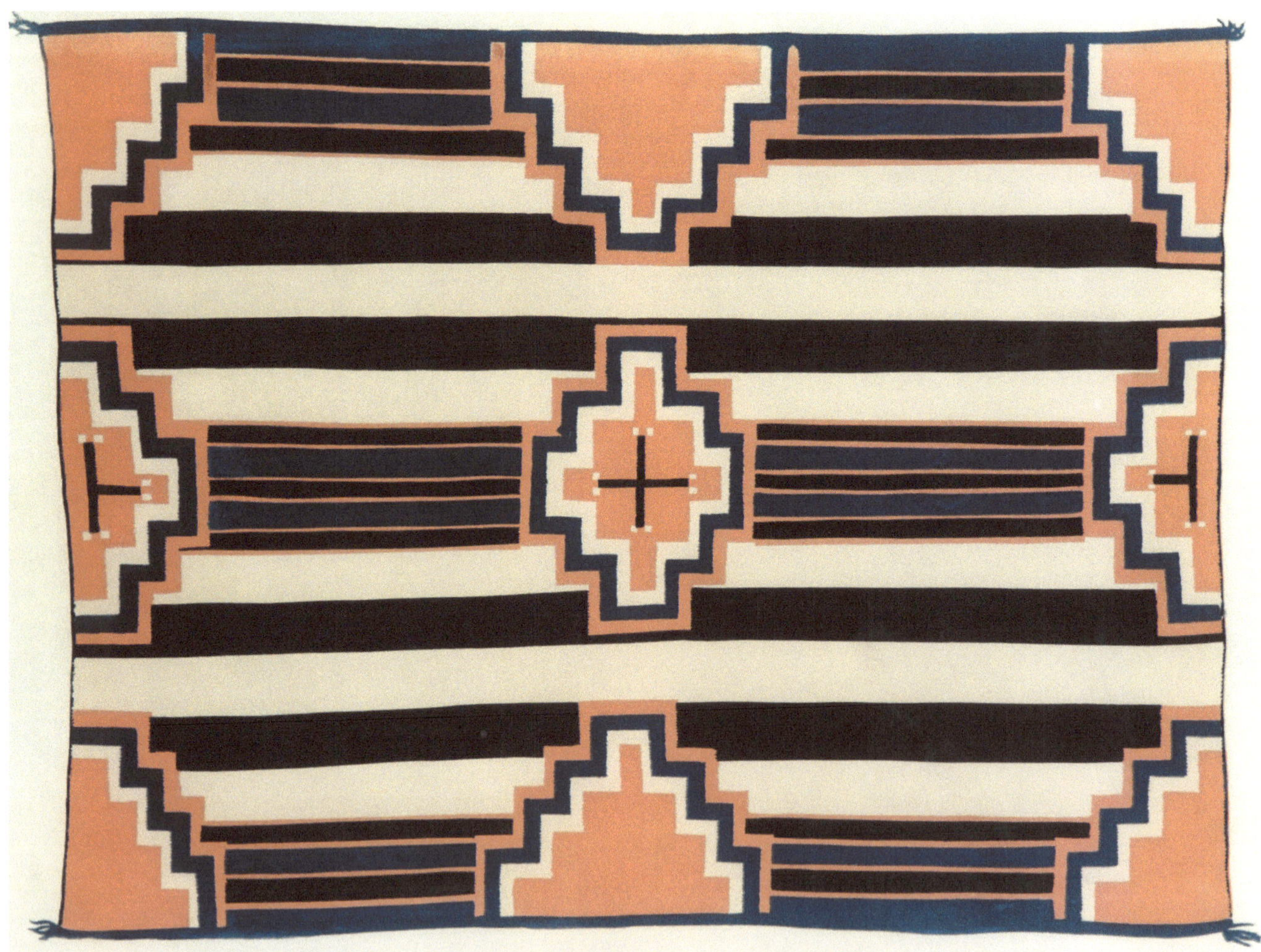

Navajo Rug, Plate #7, Louie Ewing, silkscreen print, Laboratory of Anthropology, Santa Fe.

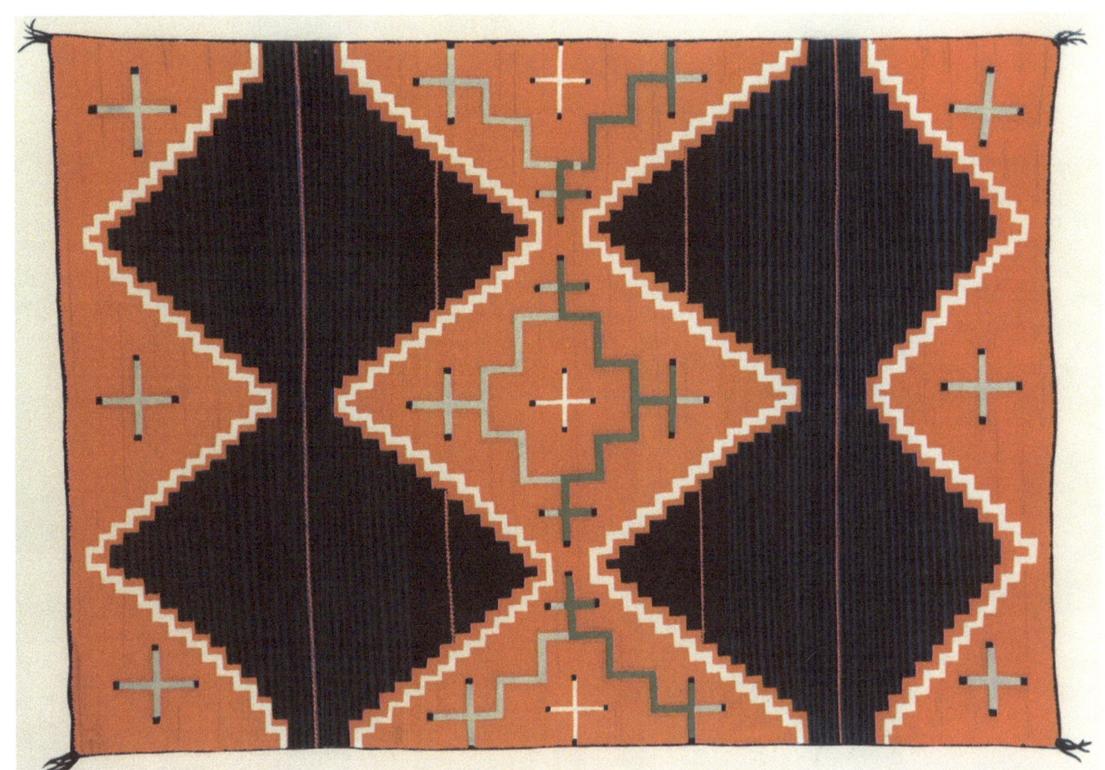

Navajo Rug, Plate #8, Louie Ewing, silkscreen print, Laboratory of Anthropology, Santa Fe.

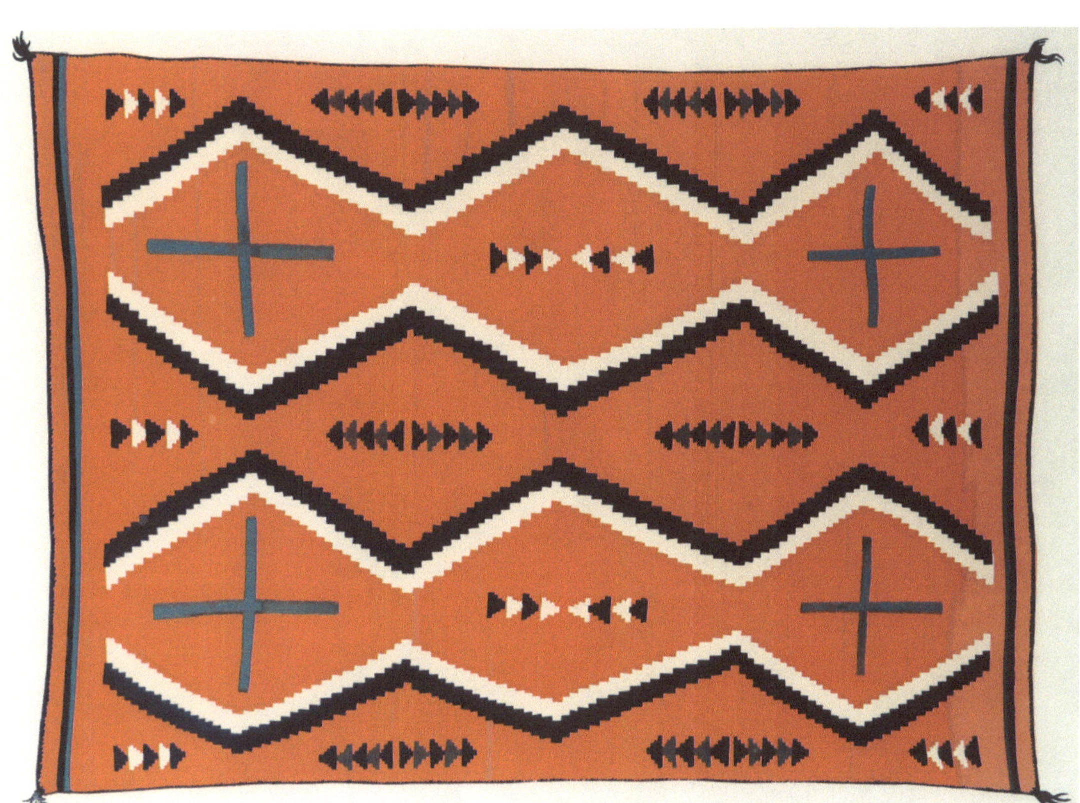

Navajo Rug, Plate #11, Louie Ewing, silkscreen print, Laboratory of Anthropology, Santa Fe.

Joseph Fleck Born, 1893, Vienna, Austria; died, 1977, Pleasanton, California. Studied at the Royal Academy of Art, Vienna; Royal Graphic Institute, Vienna. Came to U.S. in 1922. Became chief designer for Tiffany and Co., Kansas City, Missouri. Moved to Taos in 1925 after seeing an exhibition of Taos painters. Lived and painted in Taos for many years. Dean of Fine Arts, University of Missouri, Kansas City, 1942-46.

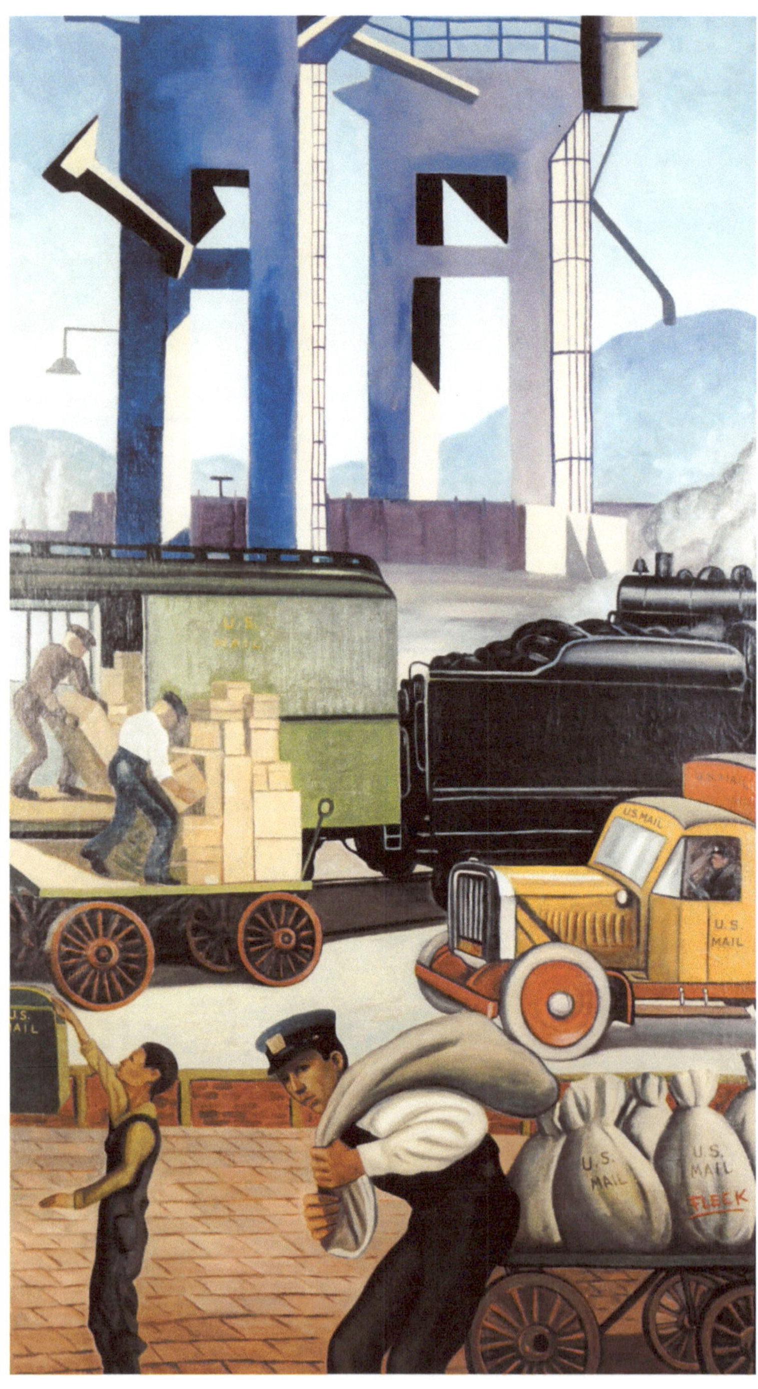

Unloading Mail at Raton, Joseph Fleck, mural, U.S. Post Office, Raton.

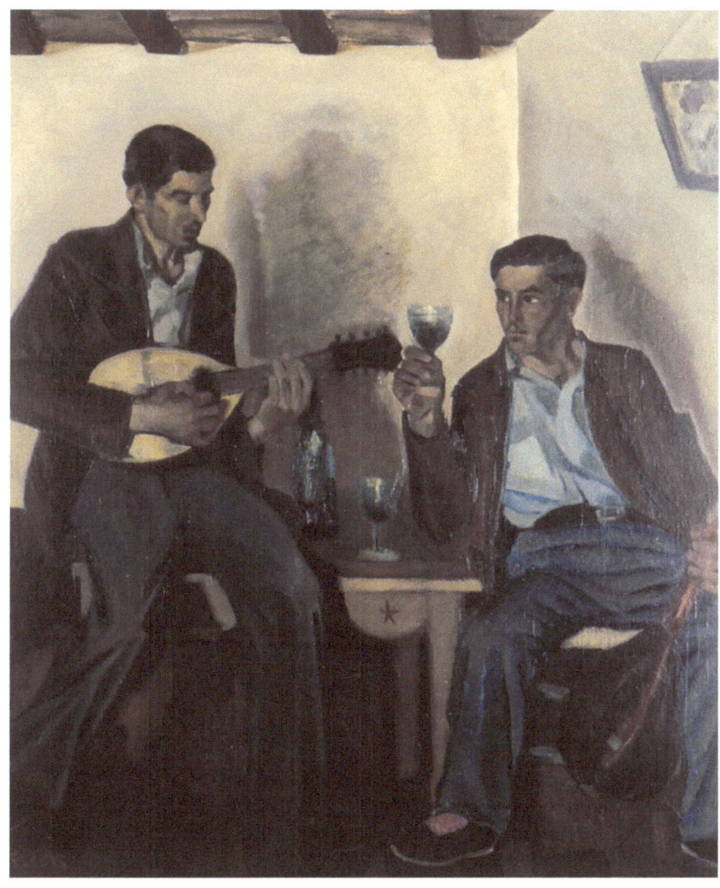

Leisure Hour, Joseph Fleck, painting,
National Park Service Regional Office, Santa Fe.

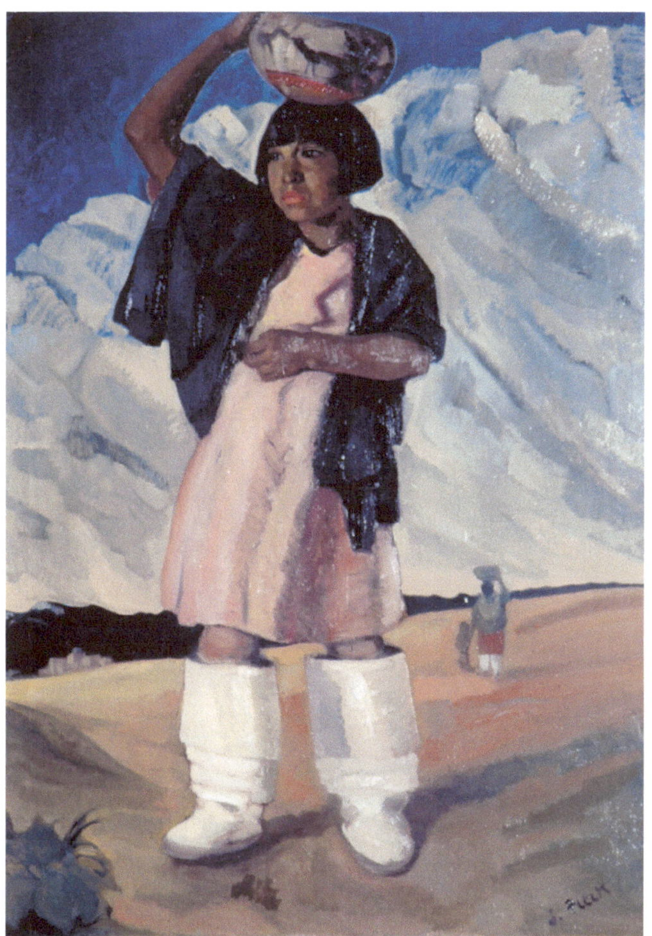

Westwind, Joseph Fleck, painting,
Octavia Fellin Public Library, Gallup.

Fresco Quartet: Emil Bisttram, 1895-1976; Victor Higgins, 1884-1949:Ward Lockwood, 1894-1963; Bert Phillips, 1868-1956. Ten frescoes on the upper walls of the main room of the old Taos County Courthouse. Inscribed in both Spanish and English. The project took three months to complete and the artists were reported to have been paid $56.00 a month.

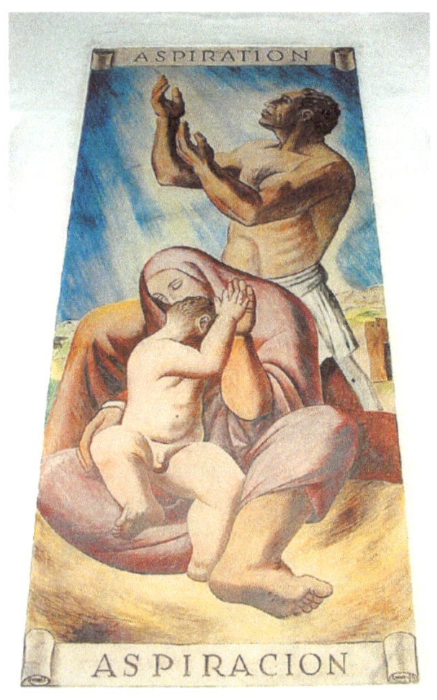

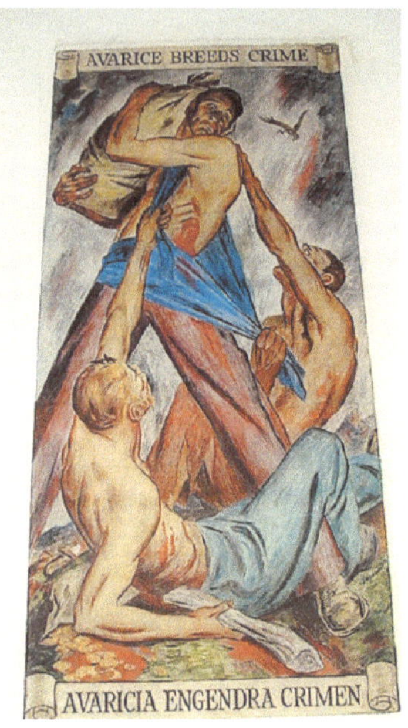

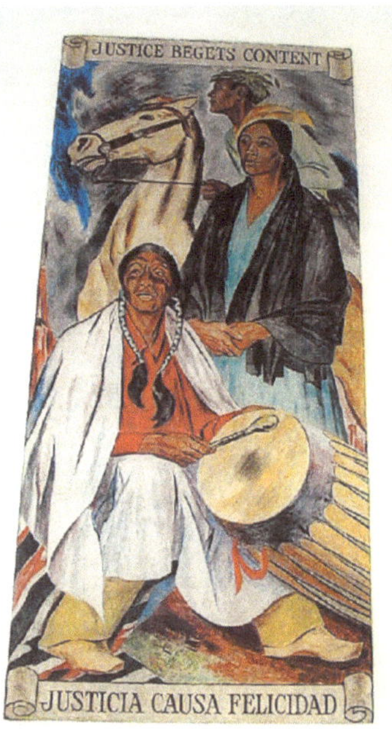

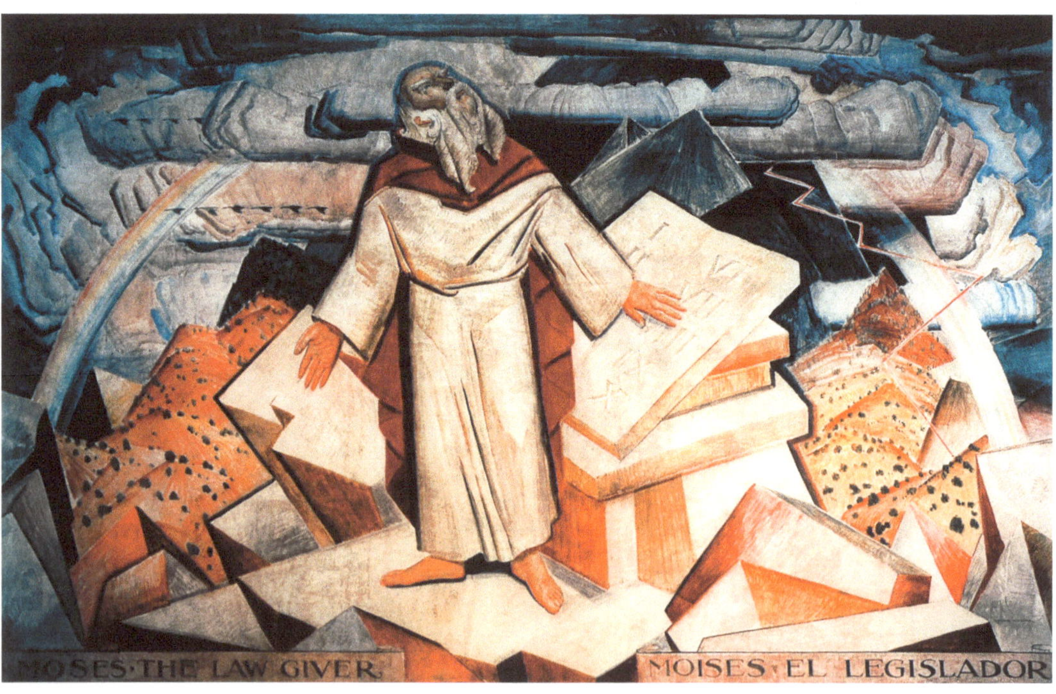

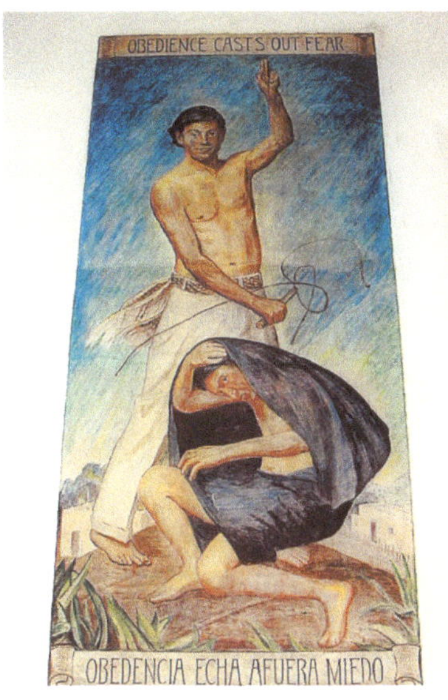

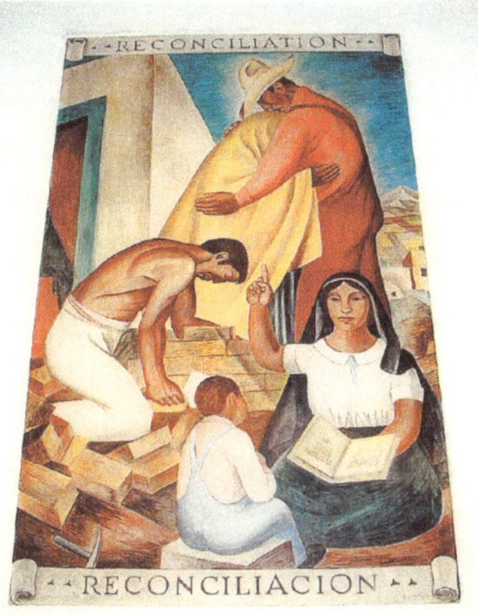

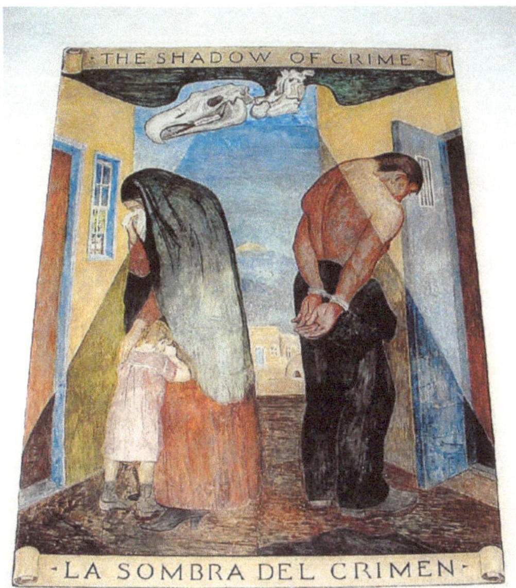

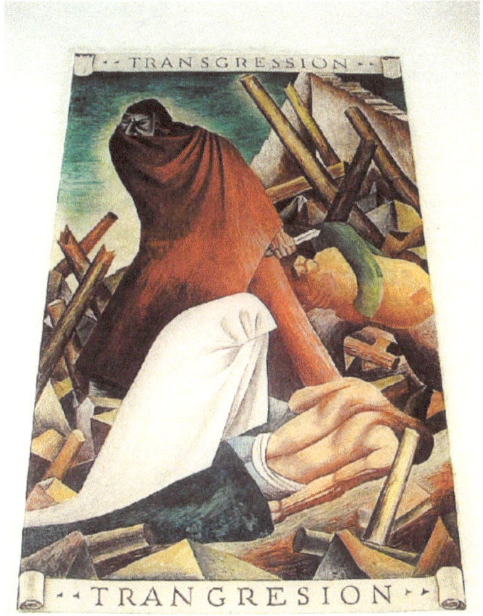

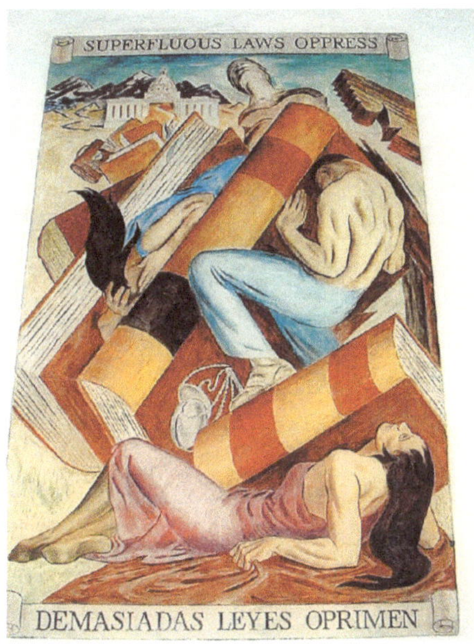

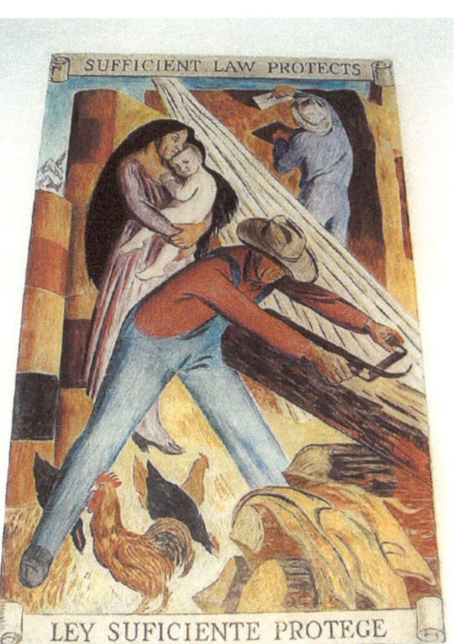

Above, clockwise, from top left
Obedience Casts Out Fear, Obedencia Echa Afuera Miedo, Ward Lockwood.
Reconciliation, Reconciliacion, Emil Bisttram.
The Shadow of Crime, La Sombra Del Crimen, Bert Phillips.
Sufficient Law Protects, Ley Suficiente Protege, Bert Phillips.
Superfluous Laws Oppress, Demasiadas Leyes Oprimen, Ward Lockwood.
Transgression, Trangresion, Emil Bisttram.

Previous page, clockwise, from top left
Aspiration, Aspiracion, Emil Bisttram.
Avarice Breeds Crime, Avaricia Engendra Crimen, Ward Lockwood.
Justice Begets Content, Justicia Causa Felicidad, Ward Lockwood.
Moses the Lawgiver, Moises El Legislador, Victor Higgins.

Paul (Chief Flying Eagle) Goodbear Born, 1913, Fay, Oklahoma; died, 1954, Chicago, Illinois. Studied art at the University of New Mexico. A Cheyenne, he became an educator interested in all tribes. Restored prehistoric murals at Coronado State Park Museum near Bernalillo. Roland Dickey, WPA Supervisor, Bernalillo, remembers him: "There was an Indian boy who was also going to the university, a painter, Paul Goodbear, a Cheyenne whose Indian name was Chief Flying Eagle, a very talented boy and very astute in terms of . . . taking an opportunity."

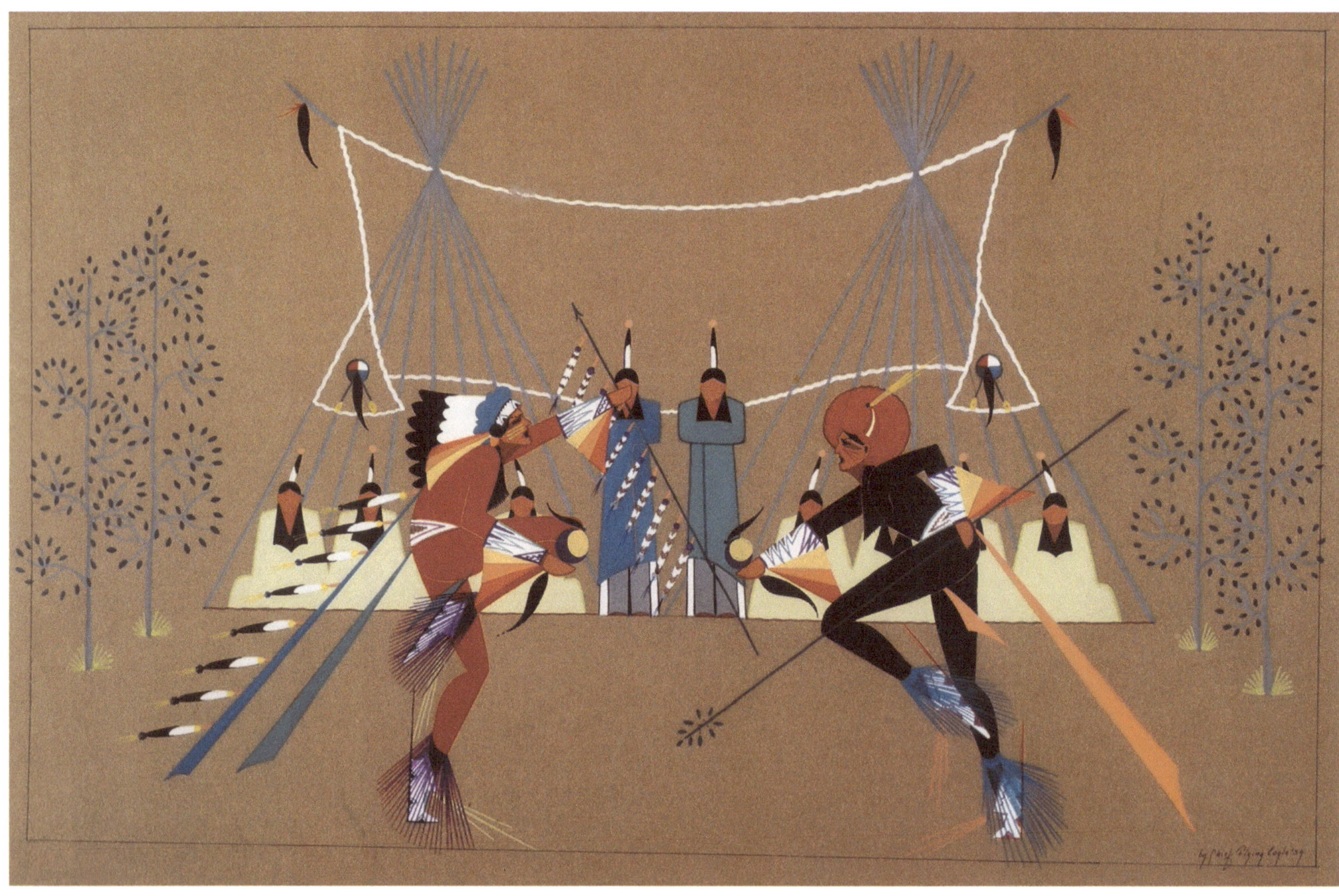

Animal Dance, Paul (Chief Flying Eagle) Goodbear, painting,
Museum of Indian Arts and Culture, Santa Fe. Photograph by Blair Clark. (14238/13)

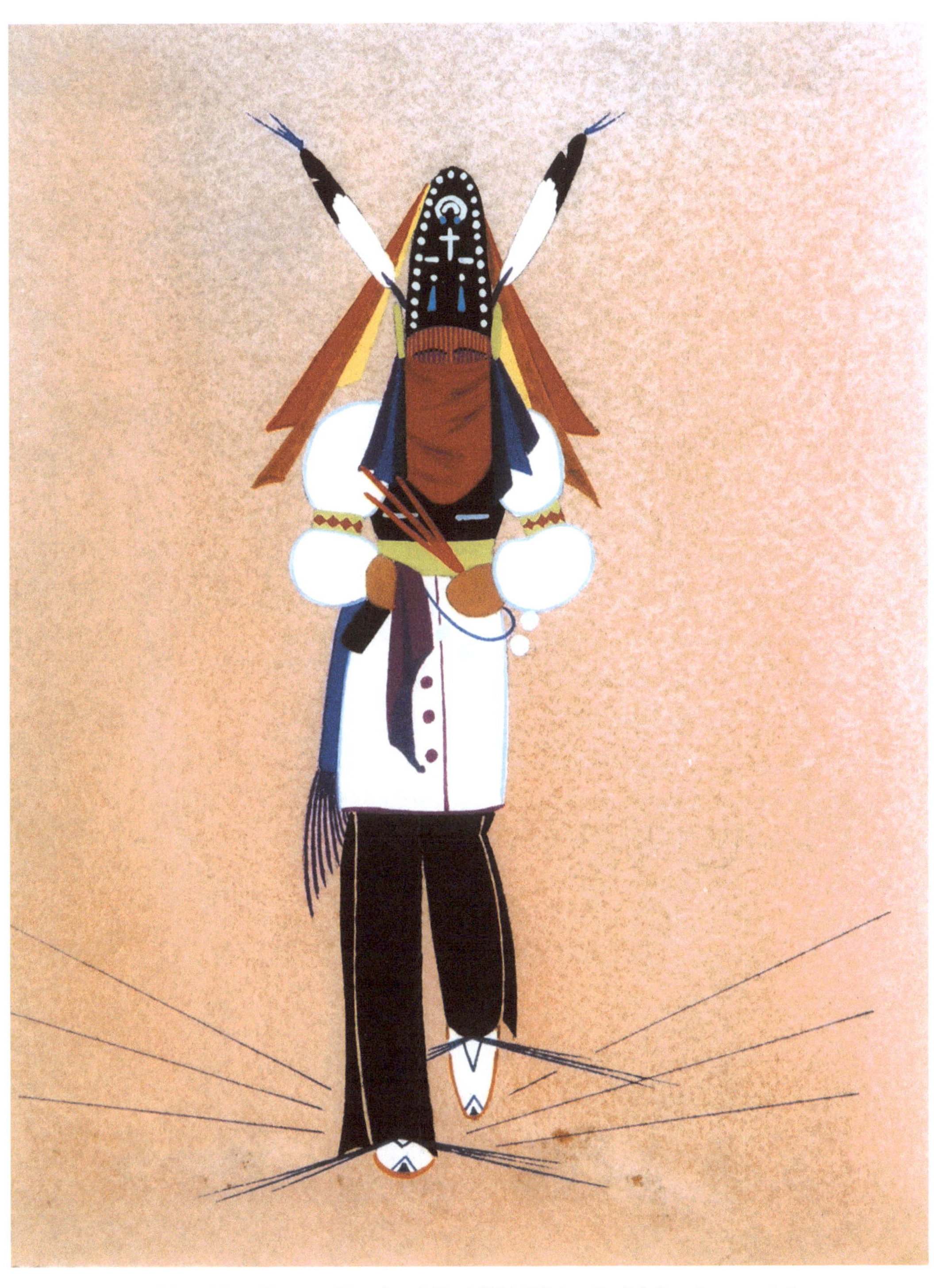

Matachinas Dancer (San Juan), Paul (Chief Flying Eagle) Goodbear, painting,
Museum of Indian Arts and Culture, Santa Fe.
Photograph by Blair Clark. (24086/13)

Cheyenne War Dance (Hoop), Paul (Chief Flying Eagle) Goodbear, painting, Museum of Indian Arts and Culture, Santa Fe. Photograph by Blair Clark. (24087/13)

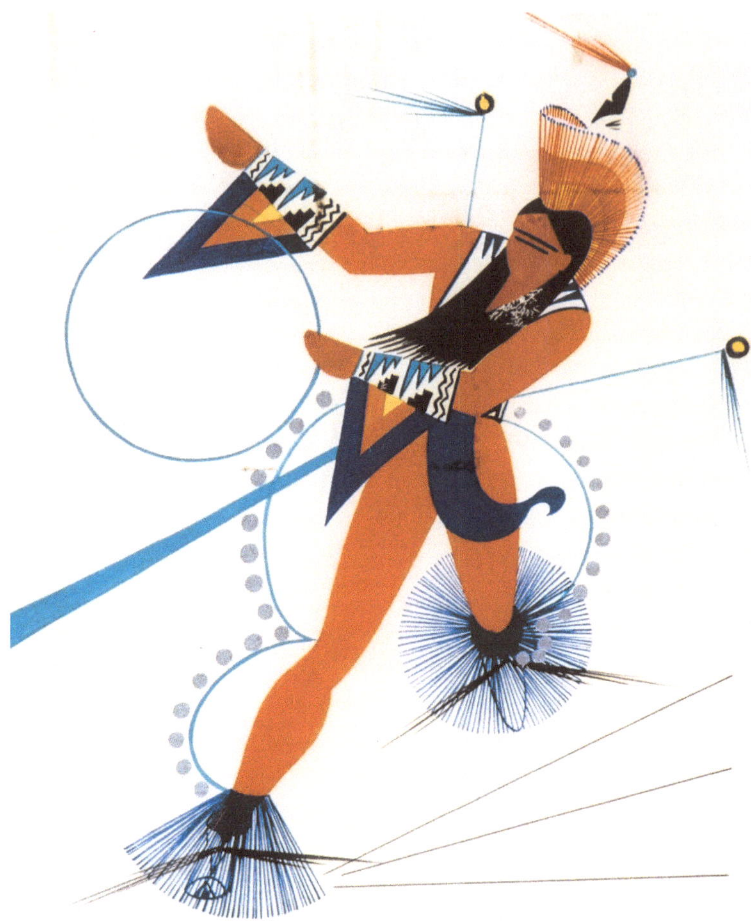

Cheyenne Arrow Ceremony (Modern), Paul (Chief Flying Eagle) Goodbear, painting, Museum of Indian Arts and Culture, Santa Fe. Photograph by Blair Clark. (24128/13)

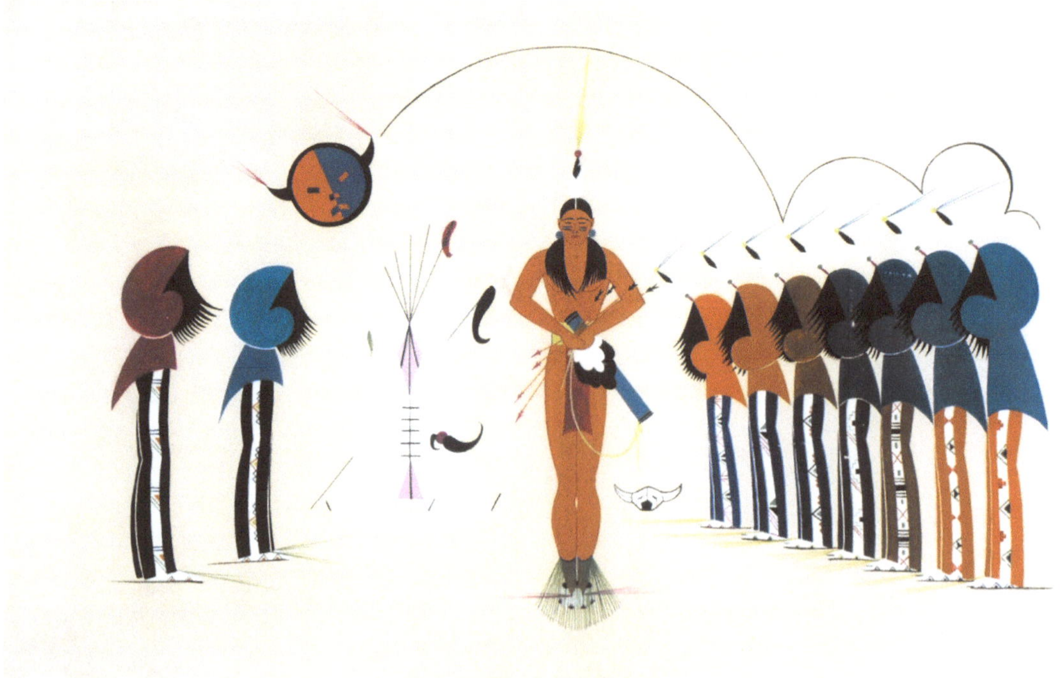

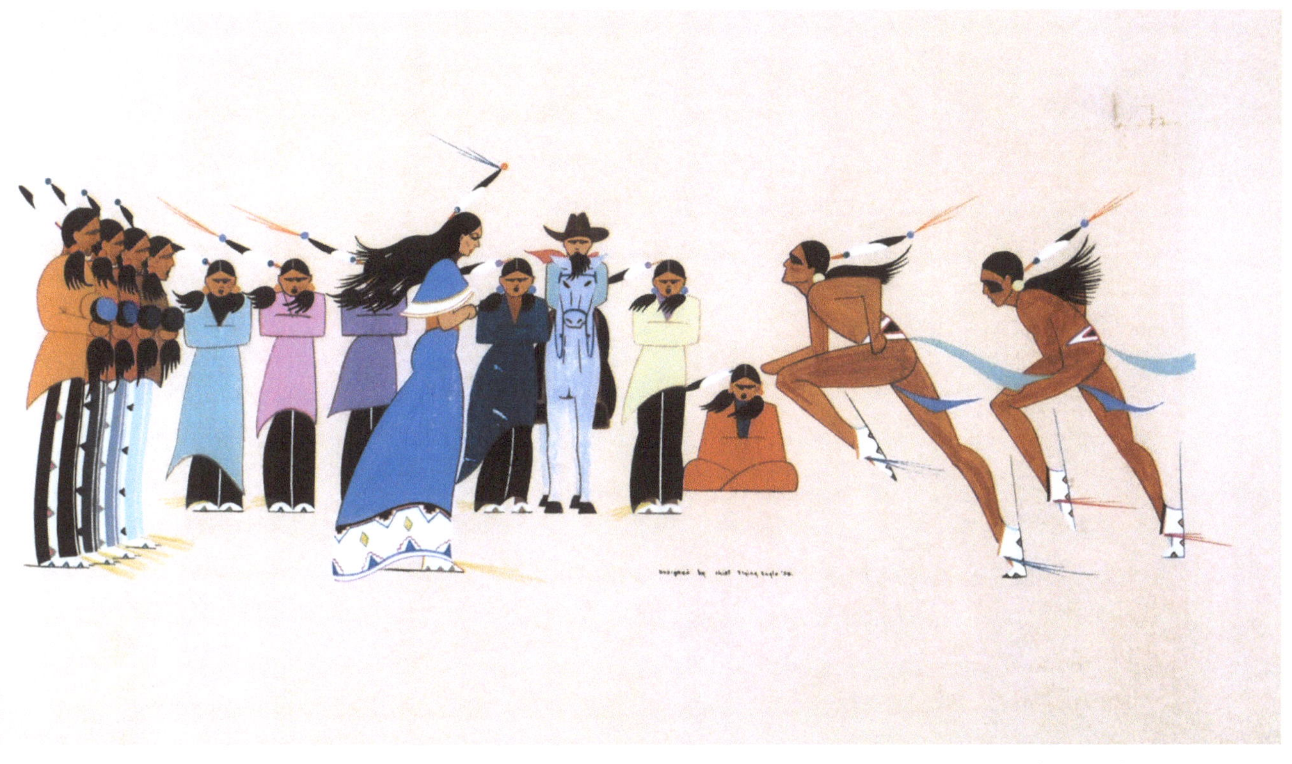

Cheyenne Animal Dance, Paul (Chief Flying Eagle) Goodbear, painting, Museum of Indian Arts and Culture, Santa Fe. Photograph by Blair Clark. (24129/13)

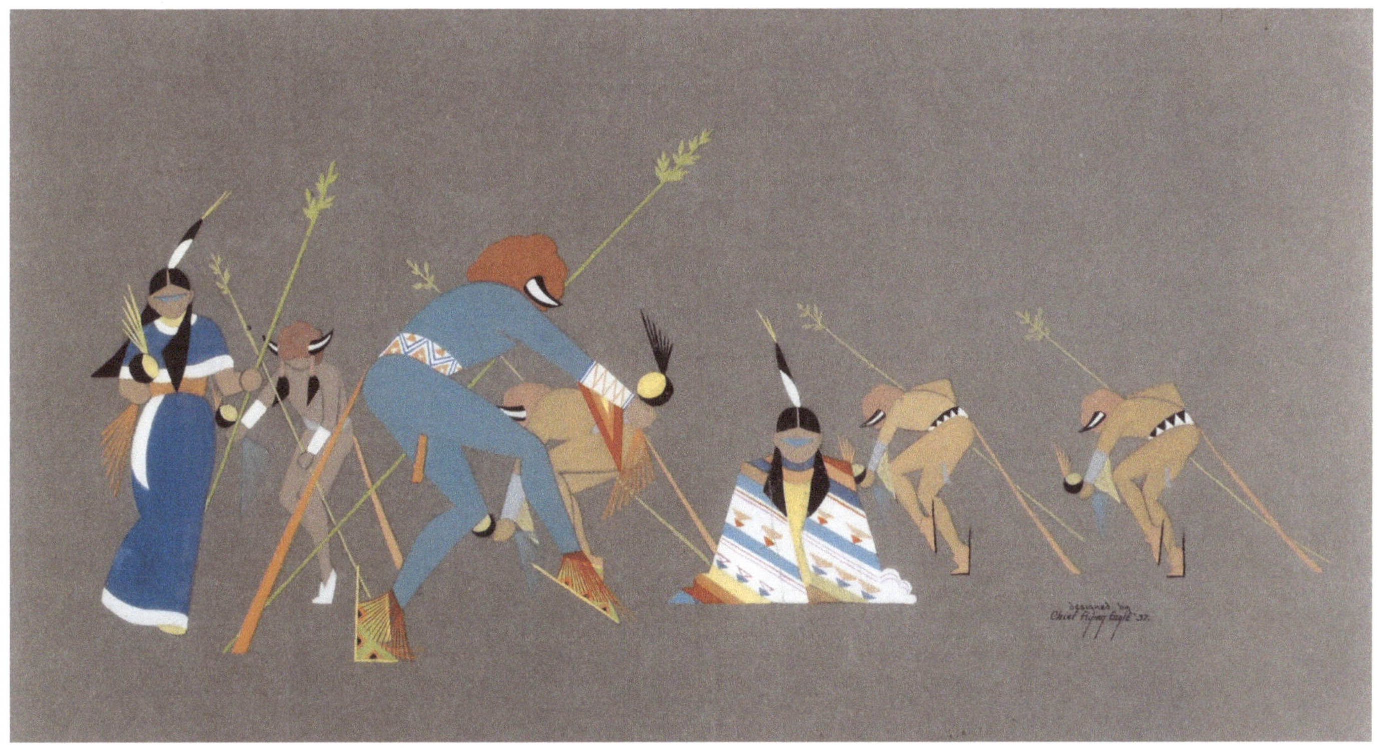

Five Buffalo Dancers, Paul (Chief Flying Eagle) Goodbear, painting, Museum of Indian Arts and Culture, Santa Fe. Photograph by Blair Clark. (24130/13)

A. L. Groll Born, 1866, New York City; died, 1952, New York City. Studied at the Royal Academy, Antwerp; also in London and in Munich. Moved west early in the century. Among the first to paint high deserts and sky.

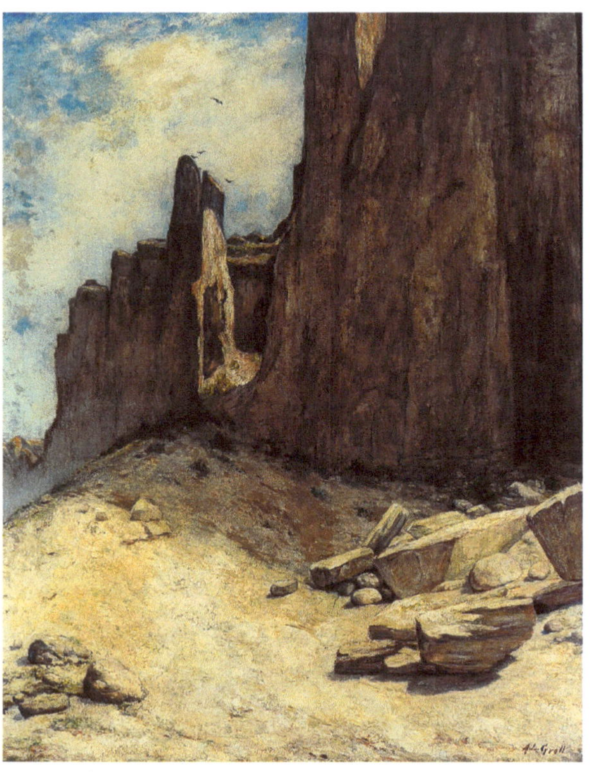

Enchanted Mesa, A. L. Groll, painting, Octavia Fellin Public Library, Gallup.

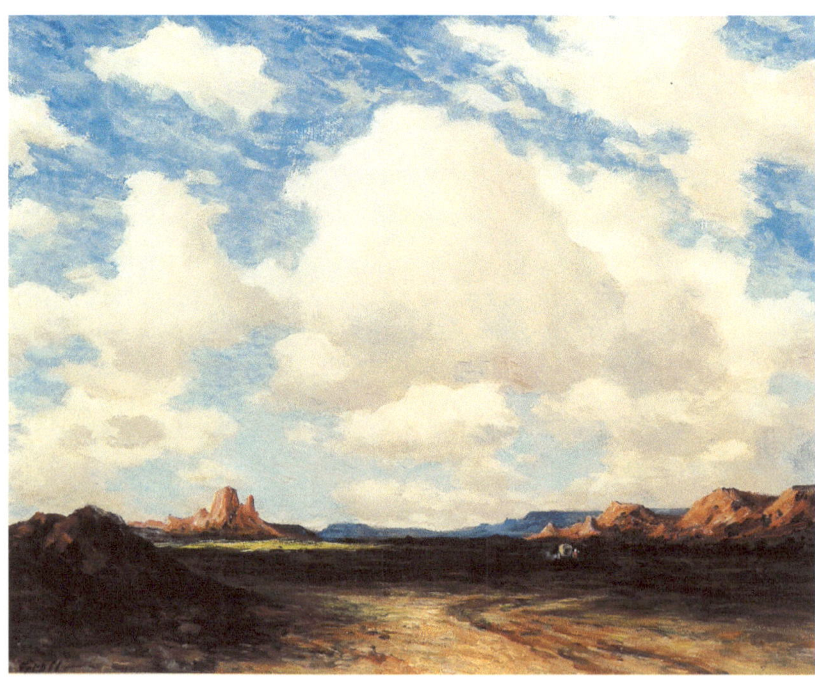

Under Western Skies, A. L. Groll, painting, Octavia Fellin Public Library, Gallup.

Lela Gutierrez Born, 1895, Santa Clara Pueblo, New Mexico; died 1969. Both Lela Gutierrez and her husband Van were innovative potters during the 1910 to mid-1950 time period.

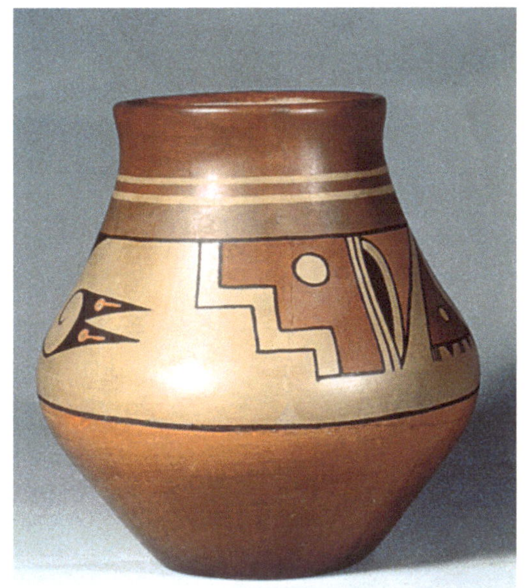

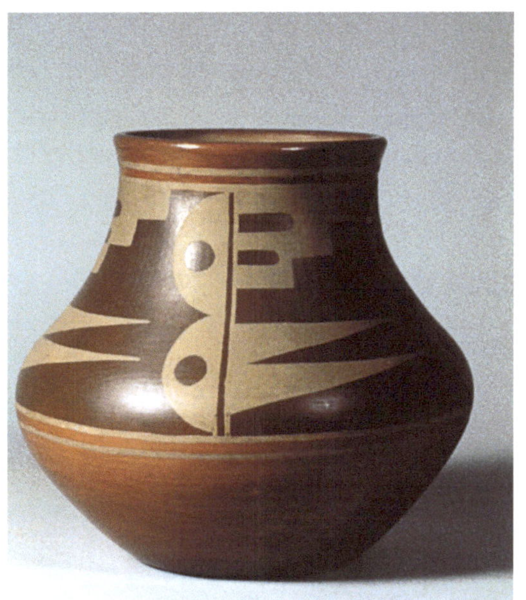

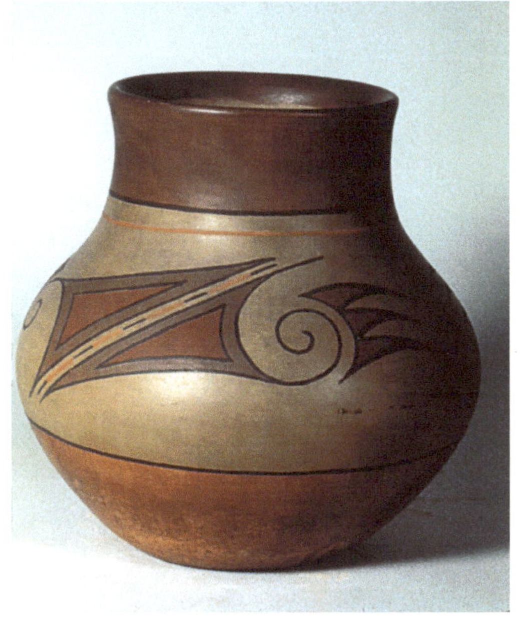

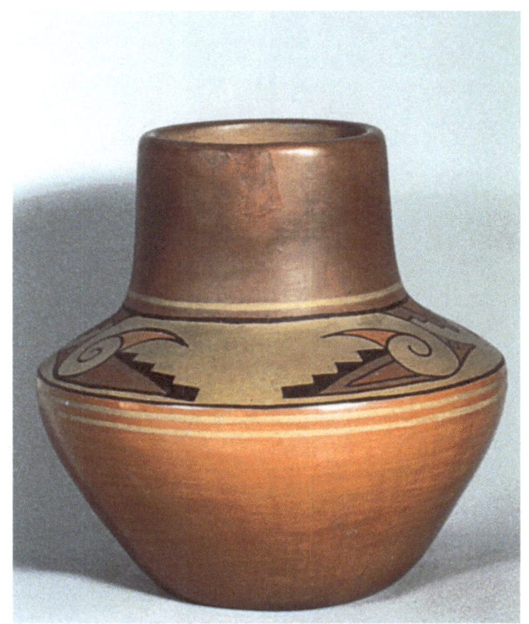

Clockwise, from top left.
Polychrome Jar, Lela Gutierrez, pottery, National Park Service, Santa Fe. (C13849, SWRO 296).
Polychrome Jar, Lela Gutierrez, pottery, National Park Service, Santa Fe. (C13855, SWRO 299).
Santa Clara Ceramic Jar, Lela Gutierrez, pottery, National Park Service, Santa Fe. (C13844, SWRO 295).
Polychrome Jar, Lela Gutierrez, pottery, National Park Service, Santa Fe. (C13840, SWRO 294).
All Photographs courtesy of the National Park Service

William Penhallow Henderson Born, 1877, Medford, Massachusetts; died, 1943, Santa Fe, New Mexico. Studied at Massachusetts Normal, Boston Museum of Fine Arts, and in Europe. Taught at the Chicago Academy of Fine Arts. Came to Santa Fe in 1916. Best known for his oils and pastels. Also did murals, furniture, stage design, innovative architectural projects. Completed six murals in the United States Court House in Santa Fe, a project originally assigned to Gerald Cassidy who died shortly after he had begun the project.

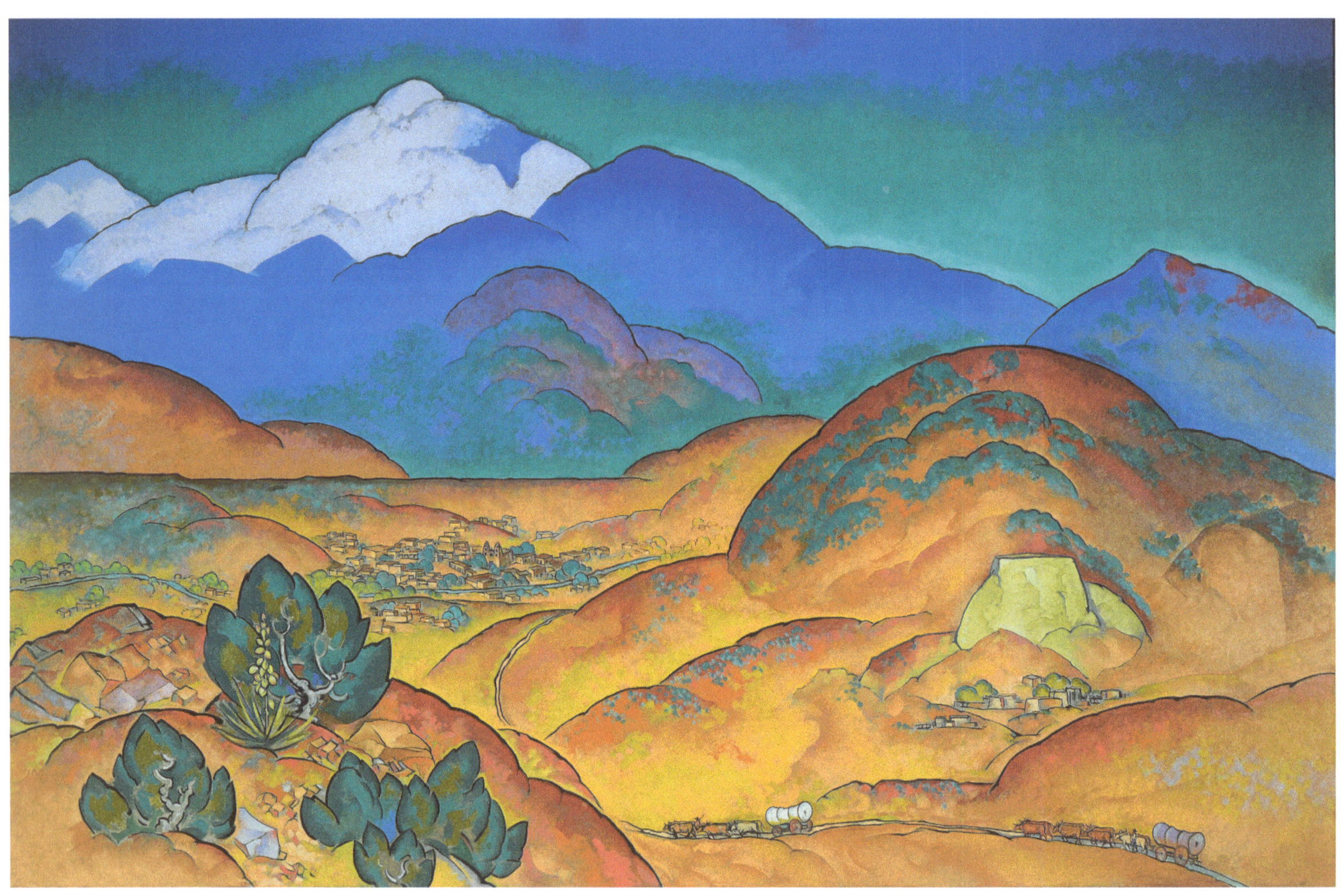

Old Santa Fe Trail, William Penhallow Henderson, mural, United States Court House, Santa Fe.

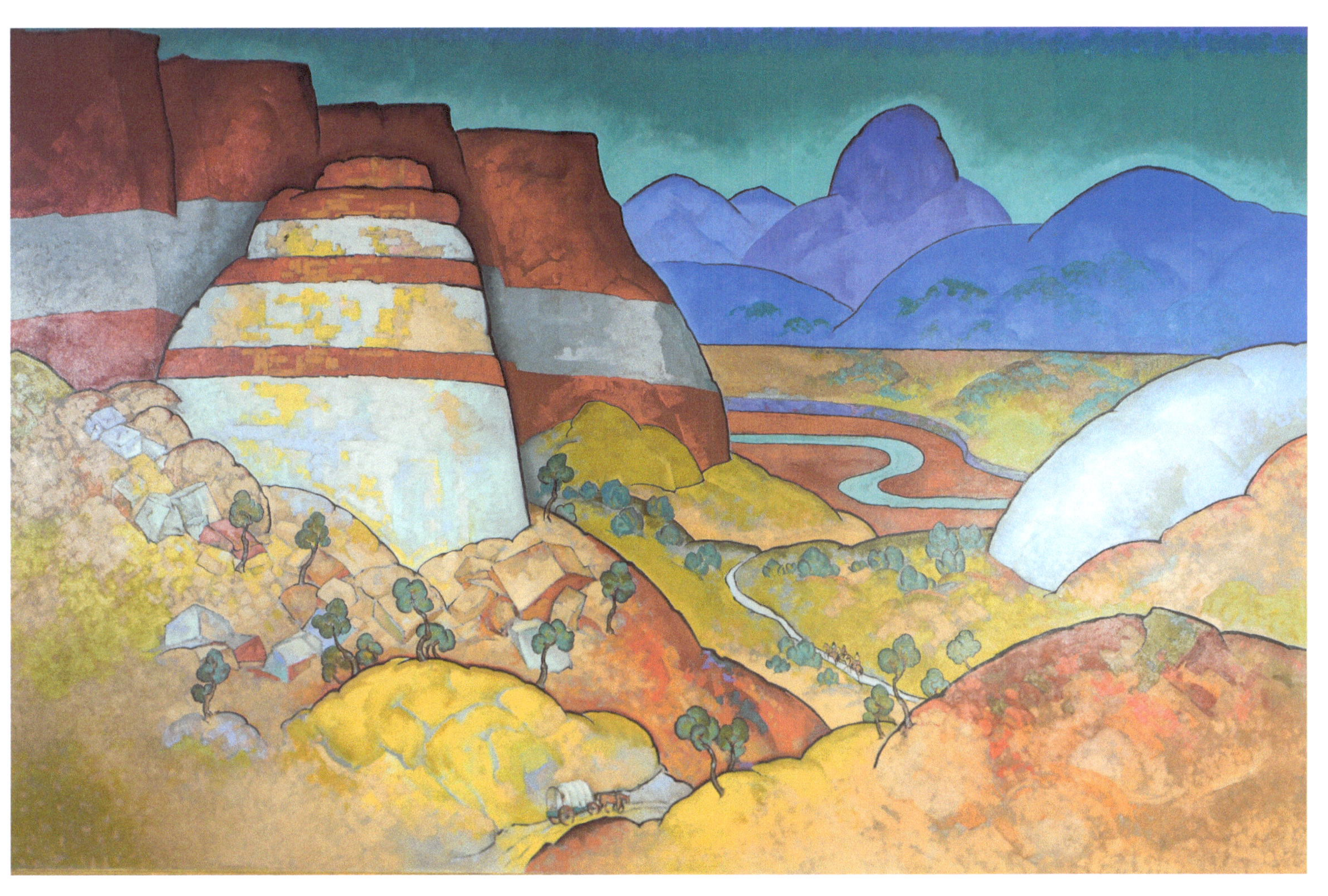

The Old Cuba Road, William Penhallow Henderson, mural, United States Court House, Santa Fe.

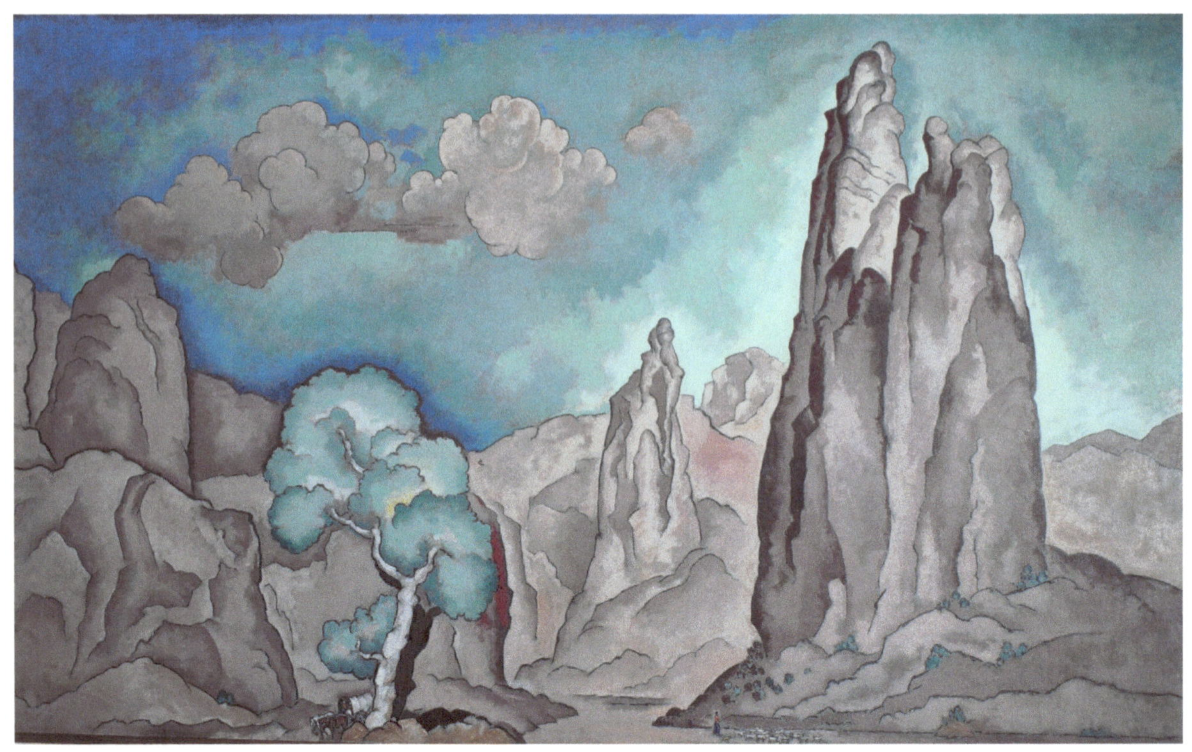

Monument Rock, William Penhallow Henderson, Canyon de Chelly, mural, United States Court House, Santa Fe.

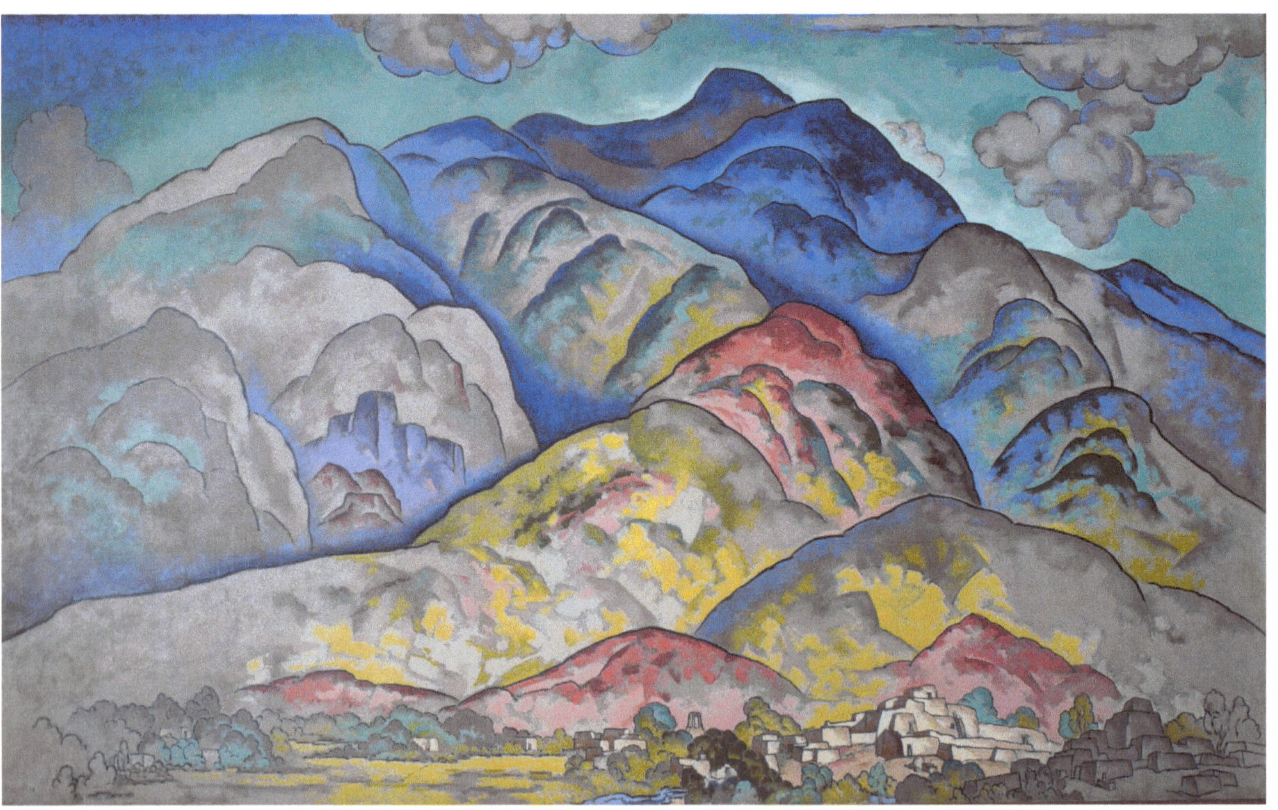

Taos Mountains, William Penhallow Henderson, mural, United States Court House, Santa Fe.

Cabezon Puerco Valley, William Penhallow Henderson, mural, United States Court House, Santa Fe.

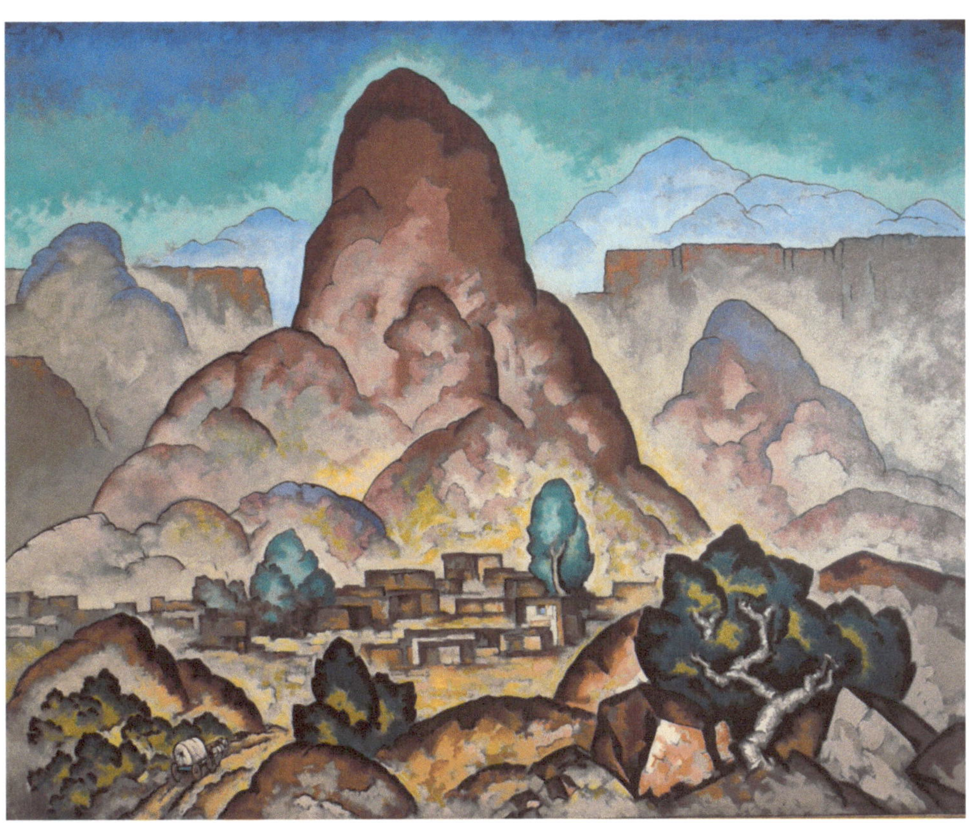

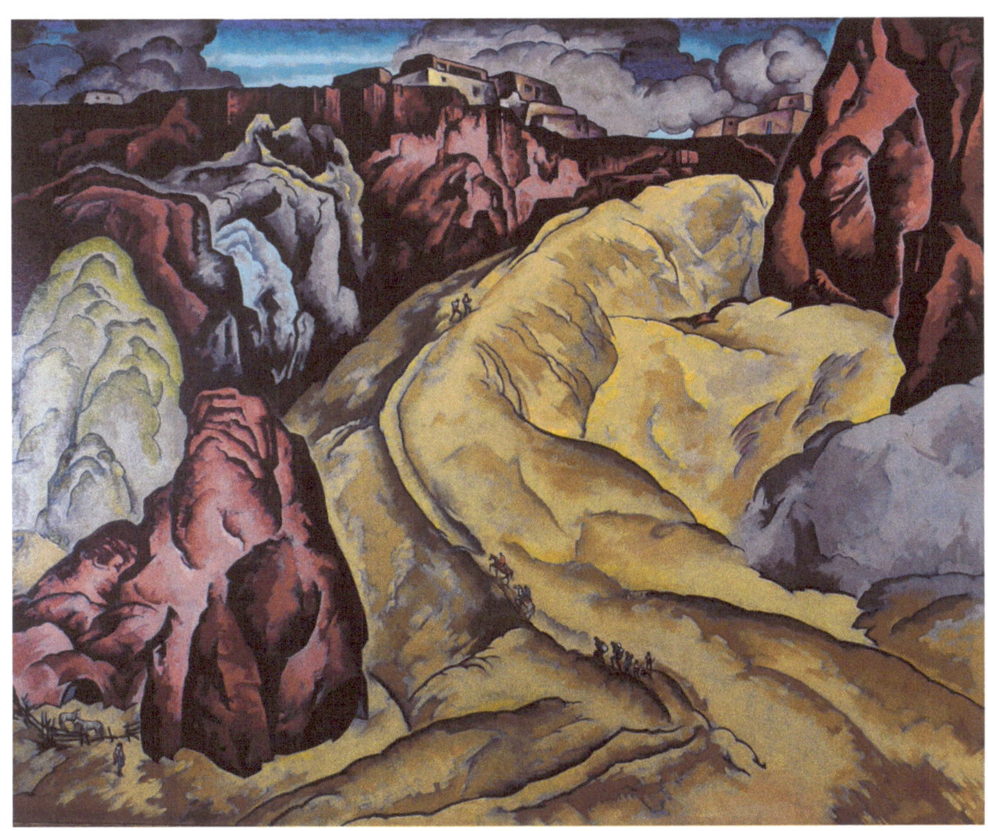

Sand Trail up Acoma Valley, William Penhallow Henderson, mural, United States Court House, Santa Fe.

Ernest Martin Hennings Born, 1886, Pennsgrove, New Jersey; died, 1956, Taos, New Mexico. Studied at the Art Institute, Chicago, and in Europe. Came to Taos in the early 1920s.

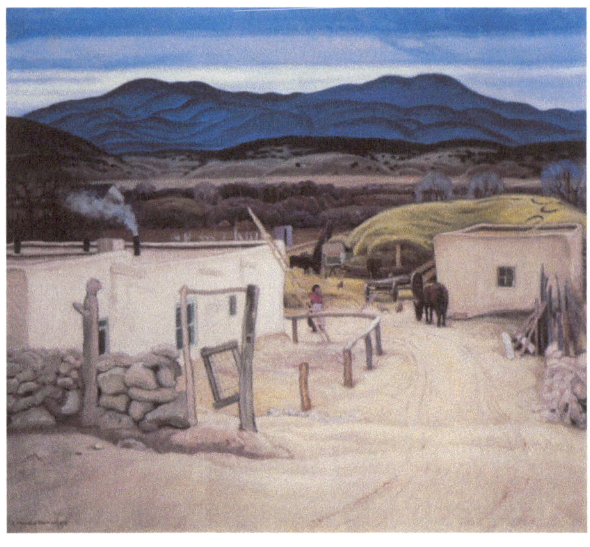

Across the Valley, Ernest Martin Hennings, painting, Dexter Public Schools, Dexter.

Velino Shije Herrera Born, 1902, Zia Pueblo, New Mexico; died, 1973, Albuquerque, New Mexico. In 1917 he began helping Dr. Edgar Hewett with restorations at the School of American Research. Credits his work there as the start of an art career. Became an accomplished painter and watercolorist, worked and taught at the Indian School in Albuquerque. Participated in New Deal art projects: reproduced ancient kiva murals found at Kuaua near Bernalillo; did mural size paintings for the Santa Fe Indian School; joined other Native Americans to create murals for the Department of the Interior.

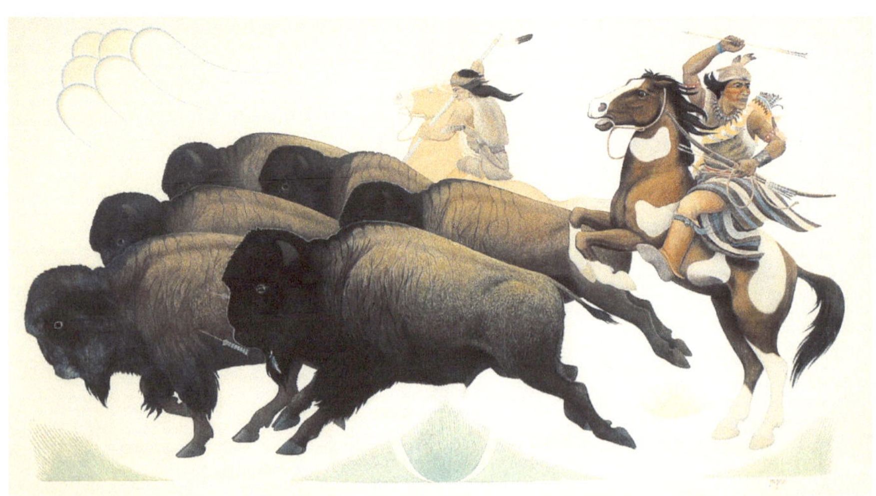

Buffalo Hunt, Velino Shije Herrera, mural size painting, Santa Fe Indian School, Santa Fe.

Victor Higgins Born, 1884, Shelbyville, Indiana; died, 1949, Taos, New Mexico. Studied at the Chicago Art Institute, the Chicago Academy of Fine Arts, and in Europe. Came to Taos in 1914. Joined the Taos Society of Artists in 1917 and in 1923 founded the Harwood Foundation with Louise Harwood and Bert Phillips. Painted Moses the Lawgiver, one of the frescoes in the old Taos Courthouse. (See Fresco Quartet.)

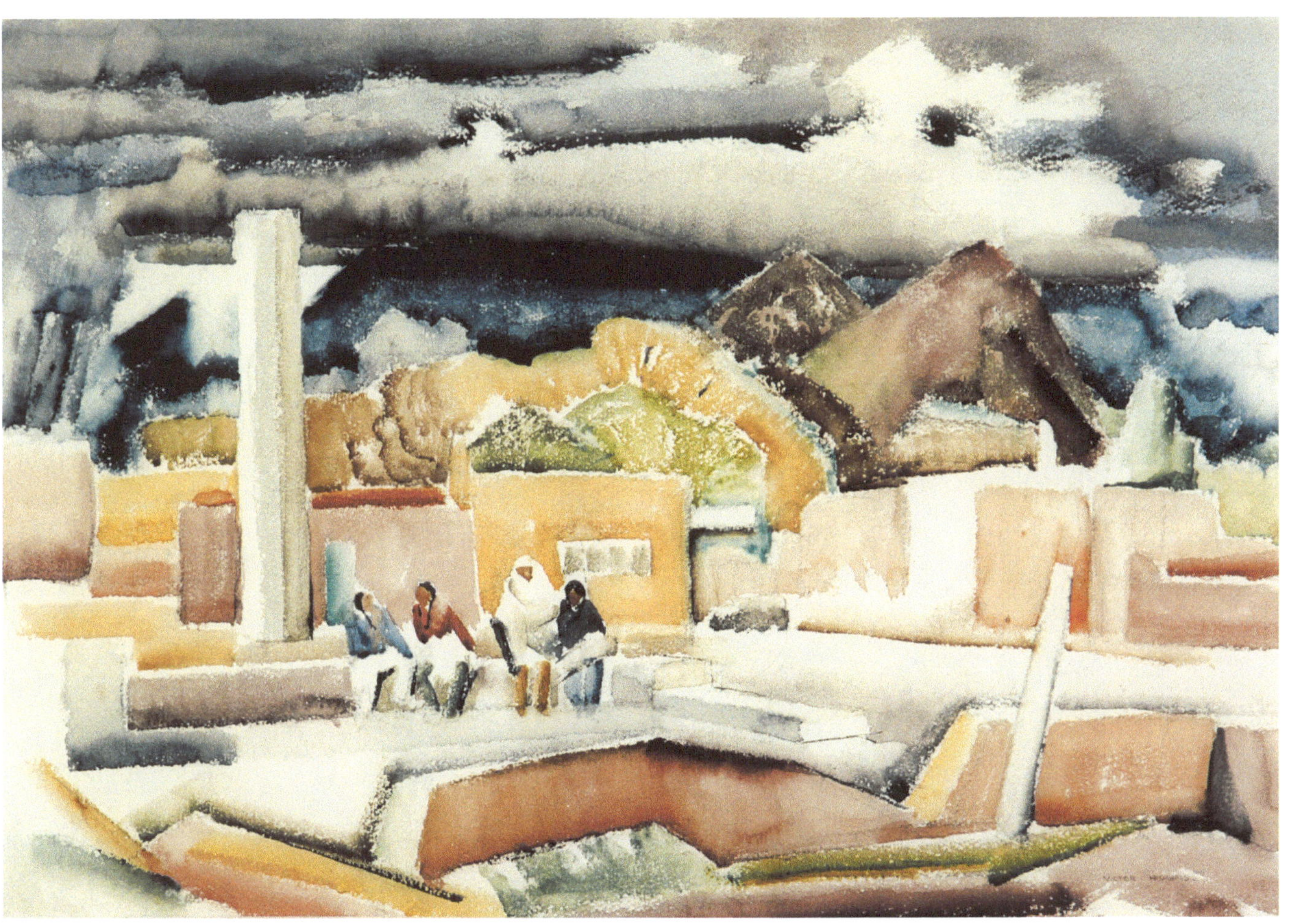

Landscape, painting, National Park Service Regional Office, Santa Fe.

Nils Hogner Born, 1893, Whiteville, Massachusetts; died, 1970, New York. Studied at Boston School of Painting and at Rhodes Academy, Denmark. Came to New Mexico in the early 1920s. Ran a trading post in western New Mexico. Taught at the University of New Mexico in the early 1930s.

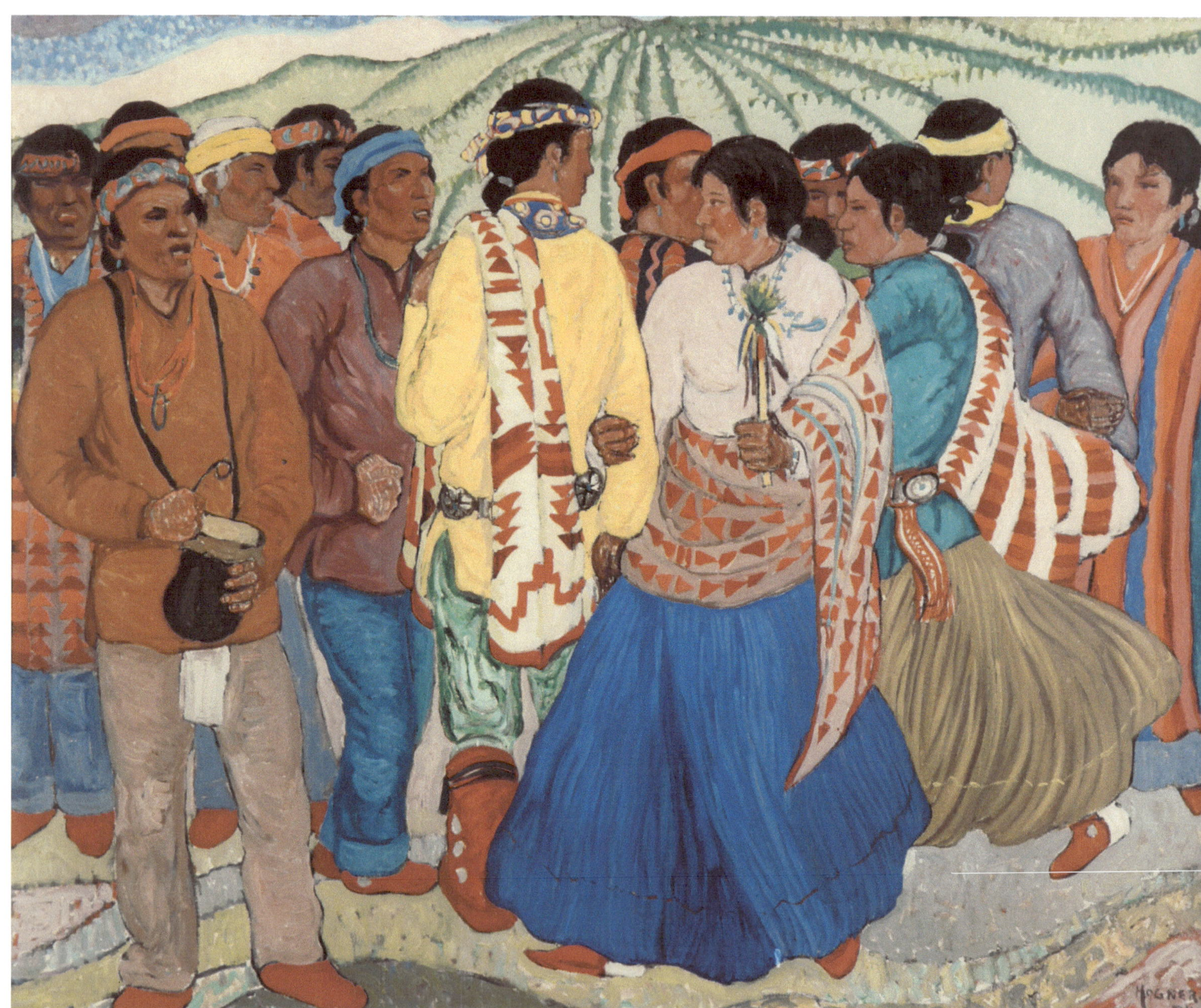

Untitled, Nils Hogner, painting, Eastern New Mexico University, Portales.

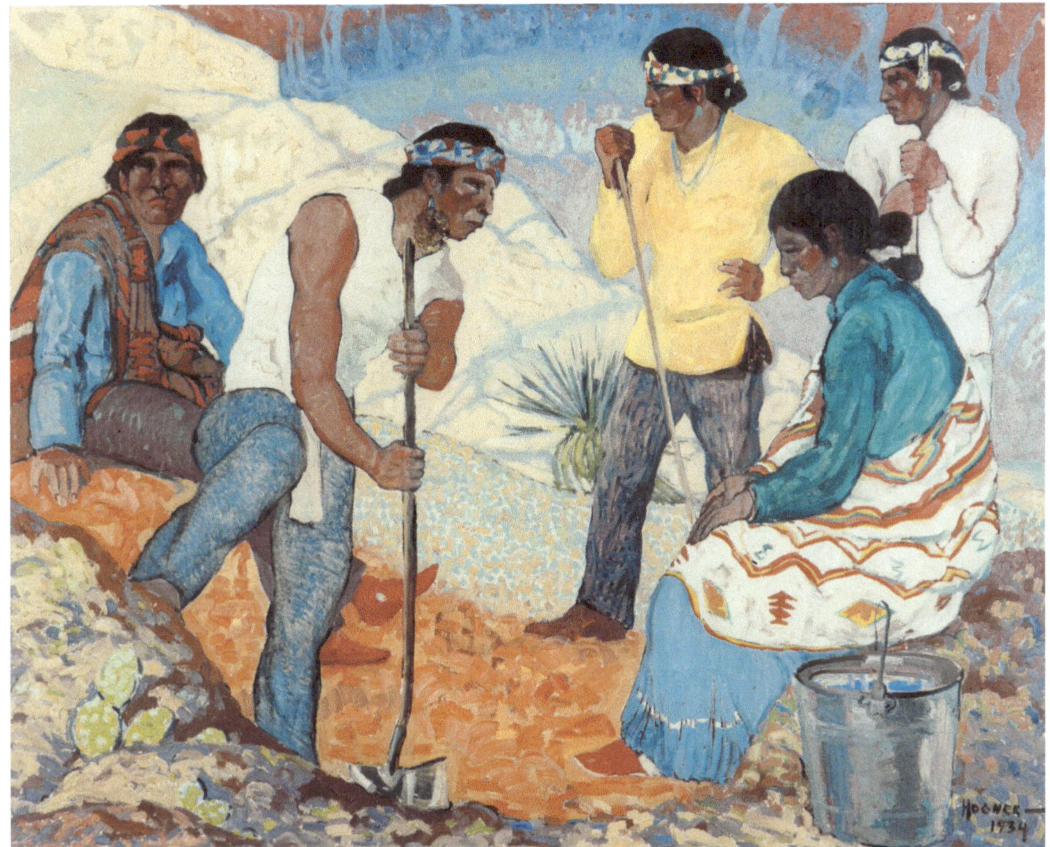

Untitled, Nils Hogner, painting, Eastern New Mexico University, Portales.

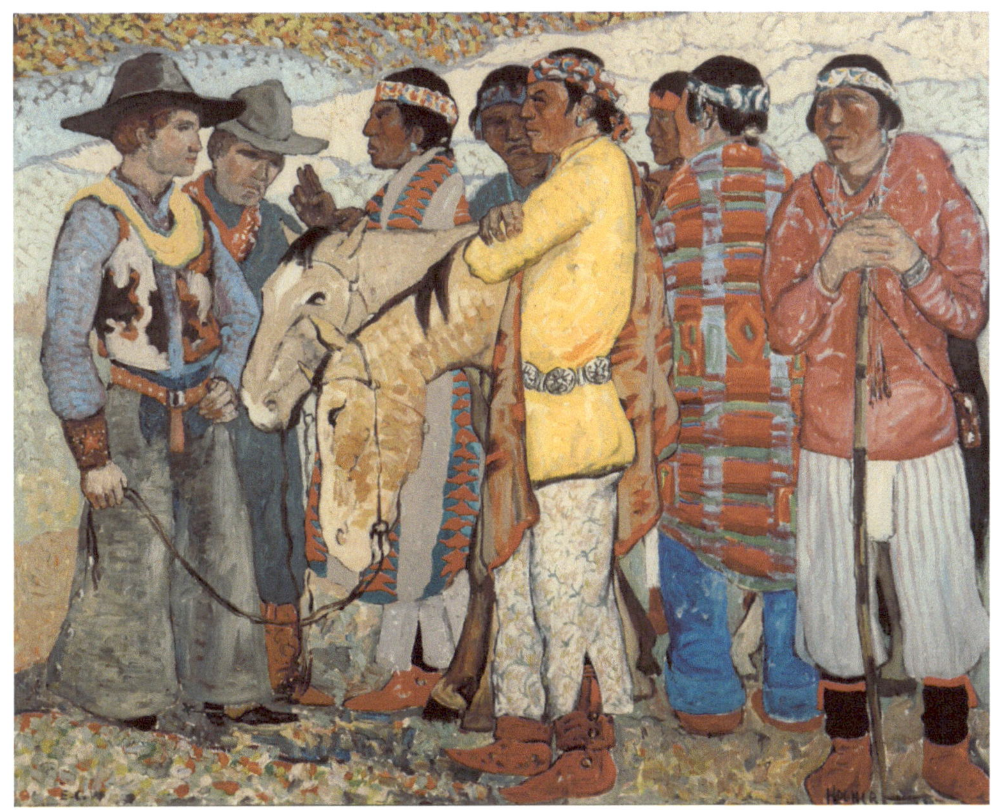

Untitled, Nils Hogner, painting, Eastern New Mexico University, Portales.

Allan Houser Born, 1914, Apache, Oklahoma; died, 1994, Santa Fe, New Mexico. Attended Chilocco Indian School. Worked on the family farm, helped his father haul rock for WPA road building. In 1936 left the farm to study at the Santa Fe Indian School under Dorothy Dunn. In 1937 represented in the National Exhibition of American Art, New York; first one-man show at the Museum of New Mexico. New Deal painting included joining with other native Americans to create two of a series of murals in the Department of the Interior, Washington, D.C. In 1962 began teaching at the new Institute of American Indian Art, Santa Fe. Among his many honors, the nation's highest art award, the National Medal of Honor.

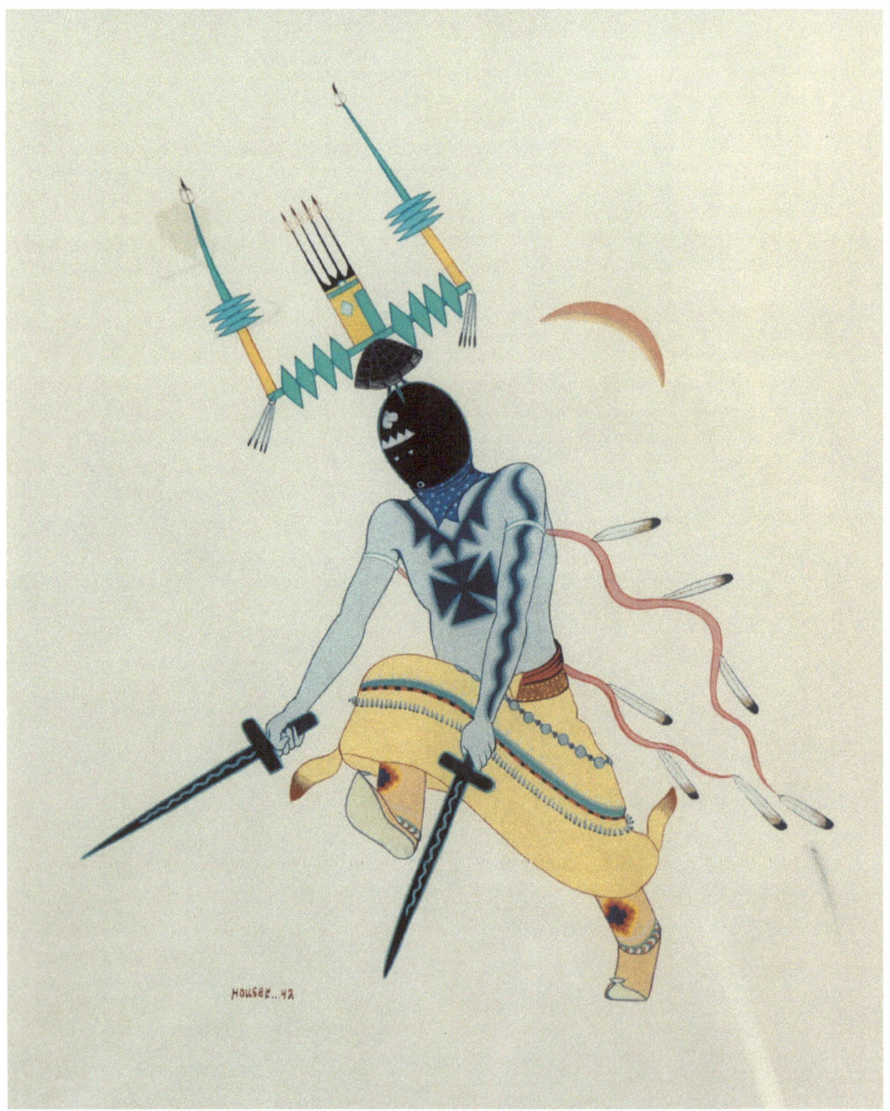

Apache Devil Dance, Allan Houser, painting, Octavia Fellin Public Library, Gallup.

Odon Hullenkremer Born, 1888, Hungary; died, 1978, Santa Fe, New Mexico. Moved to U.S. in 1912, then to Santa Fe in 1933. In addition to WPA paintings, worked on the Portfolio of Spanish Colonial Design in New Mexico. After the war, set aside painting to devote full time to humanitarian activities.

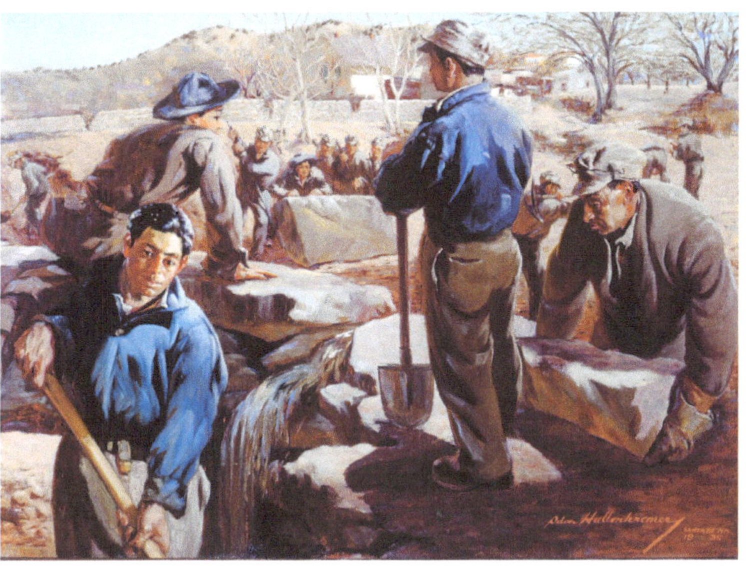

Convicts Mining, Odon Hullenkremer, painting, Carrie Tingley Hospital, Albuquerque.

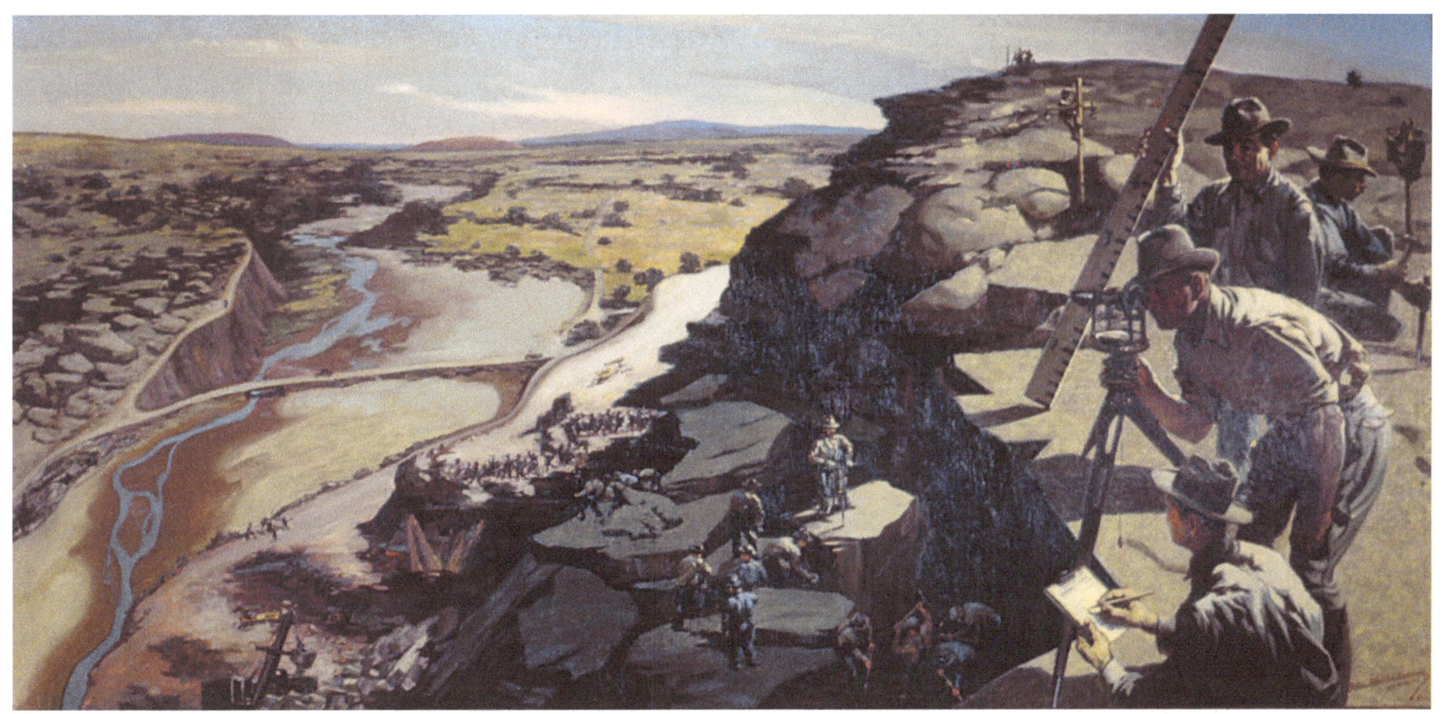

Conchas Dam Construction, Odon Hullenkremer, mural size painting, Conchas Dam Visitor Center, Conchas Dam.

Russell Vernon Hunter Born, 1900, Hallsville, Illinois; died, 1955, Santa Fe, New Mexico. Grew up in eastern New Mexico. Studied at the Art Institute of Chicago. Painted historical murals called The Last Frontier in the De Baca County Courthouse for first federal art project, assisted by Pedro Cervantez. Commenting on the murals, the Evening News Journal, June 3, 1935, reported: "They tell the story of the passing of the frontier, of the settling of a strip of territory in the southwest, between the XIT Ranch and Pecos River. . . . Fort Sumner established in the sixties [1860s] a few miles from the site of the present town, and the adventures of Billy the Kid." In 1935 became State Director of the WPA Federal Art Program.

The Last Frontier, Russell Vernon Hunter, mural, De Baca County Courthouse, Fort Sumner.

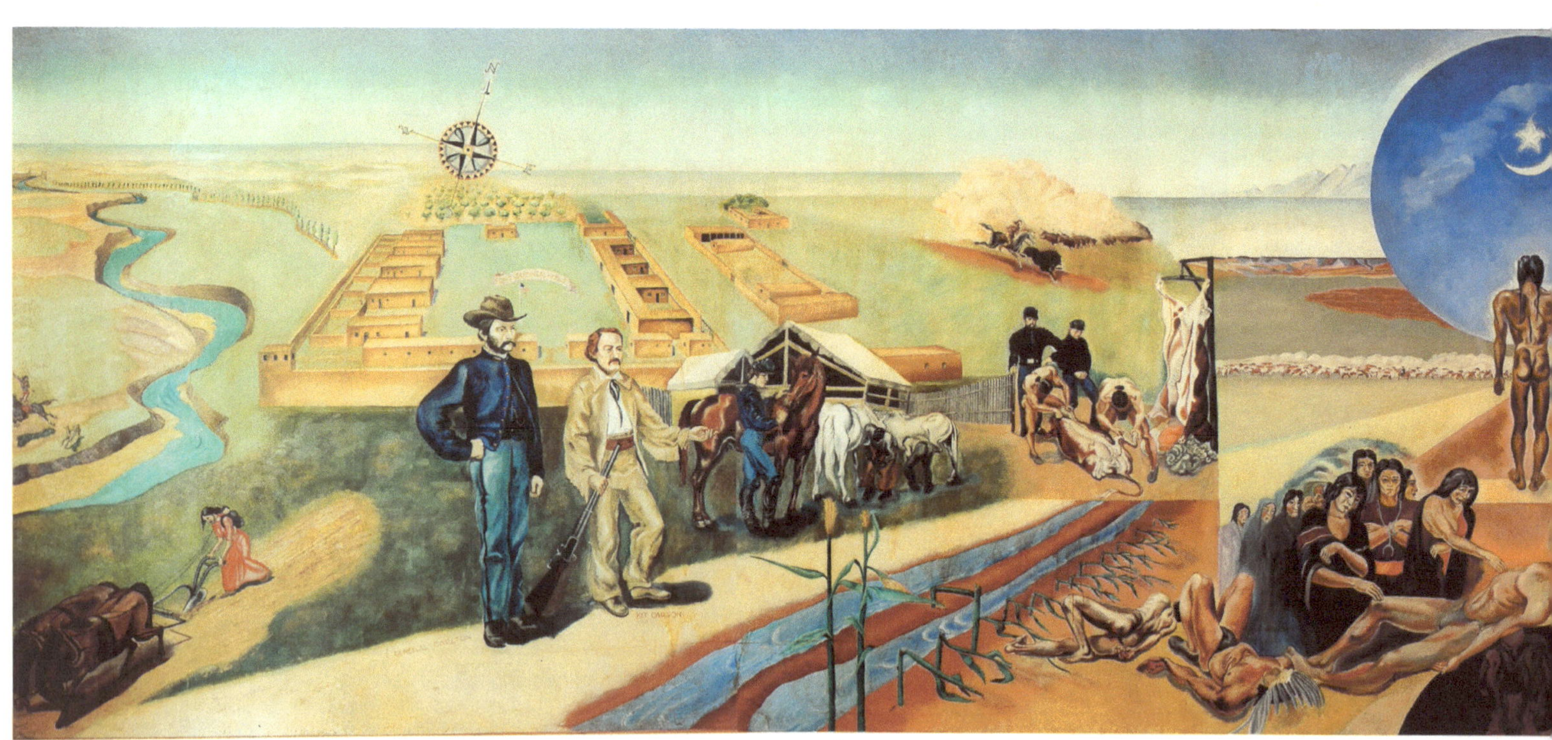

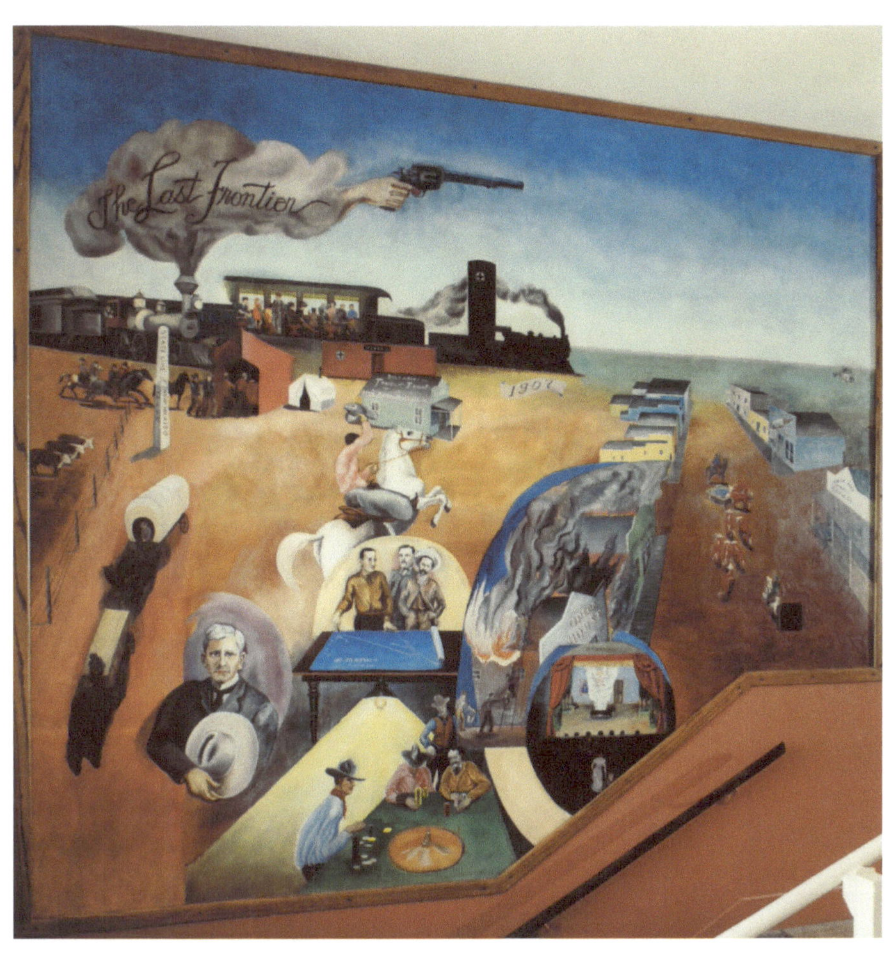
The Last Frontier
1907

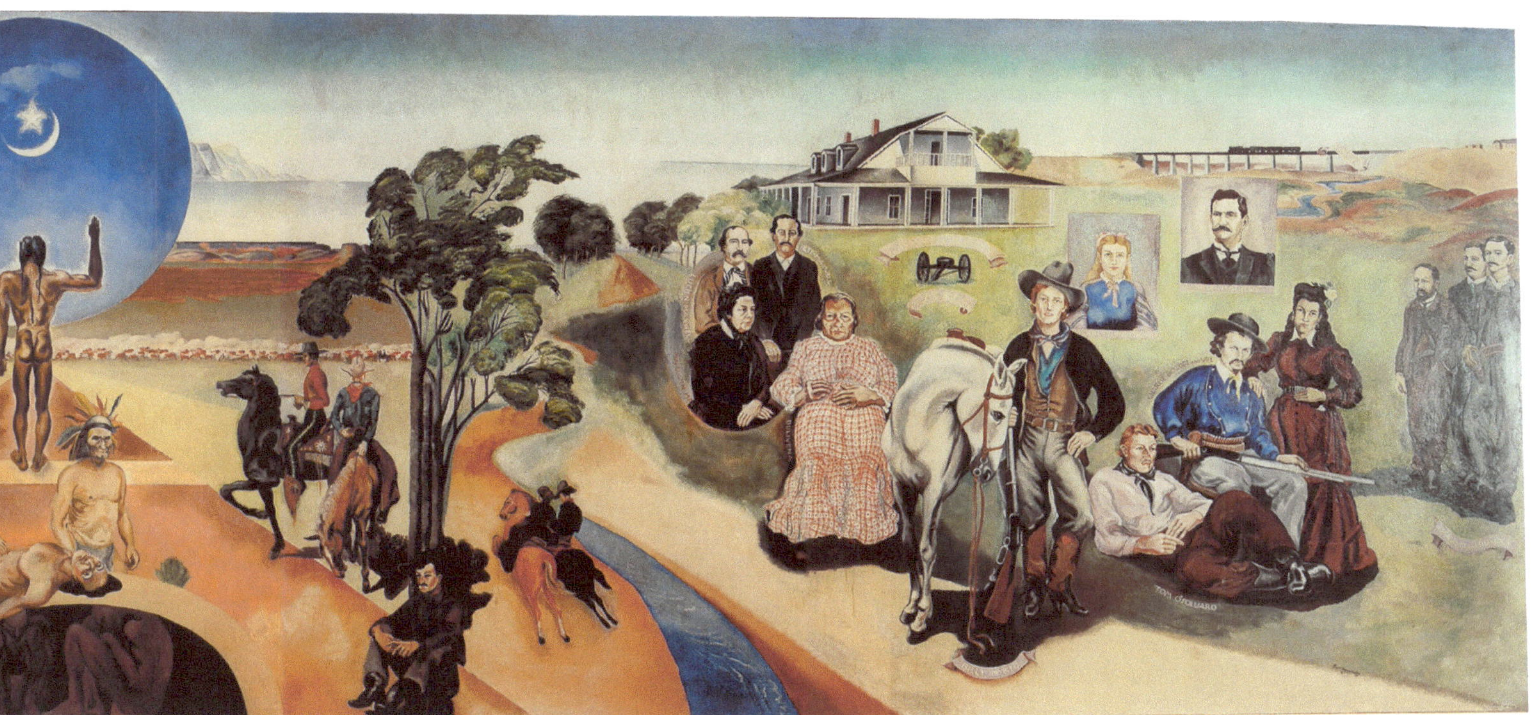

Peter Hurd Born, 1904, Roswell, New Mexico; died, 1984, Albuquerque, New Mexico. Studied at the Pennsylvania Academy of Fine Arts. Lithographer as well as painter, noted for western subjects. In describing one of the frescoes in the Lincoln National Forest Service Building (formerly the U.S. Post Office) in Alamogordo, the Alamogordo News, 1941, describes: " . . . a beautiful scene of trees and flowers with Peter Hurd's own home at Picacho in the foreground. . . . The life-sized woman is the picture of Miss Edna Imhoff, teacher in schools at Rebenton and the child picking flowers is Della Joiner, daughter of the postmaster at Hondo. At the right of the entrance is an old Mexican shepherd praying for rain."

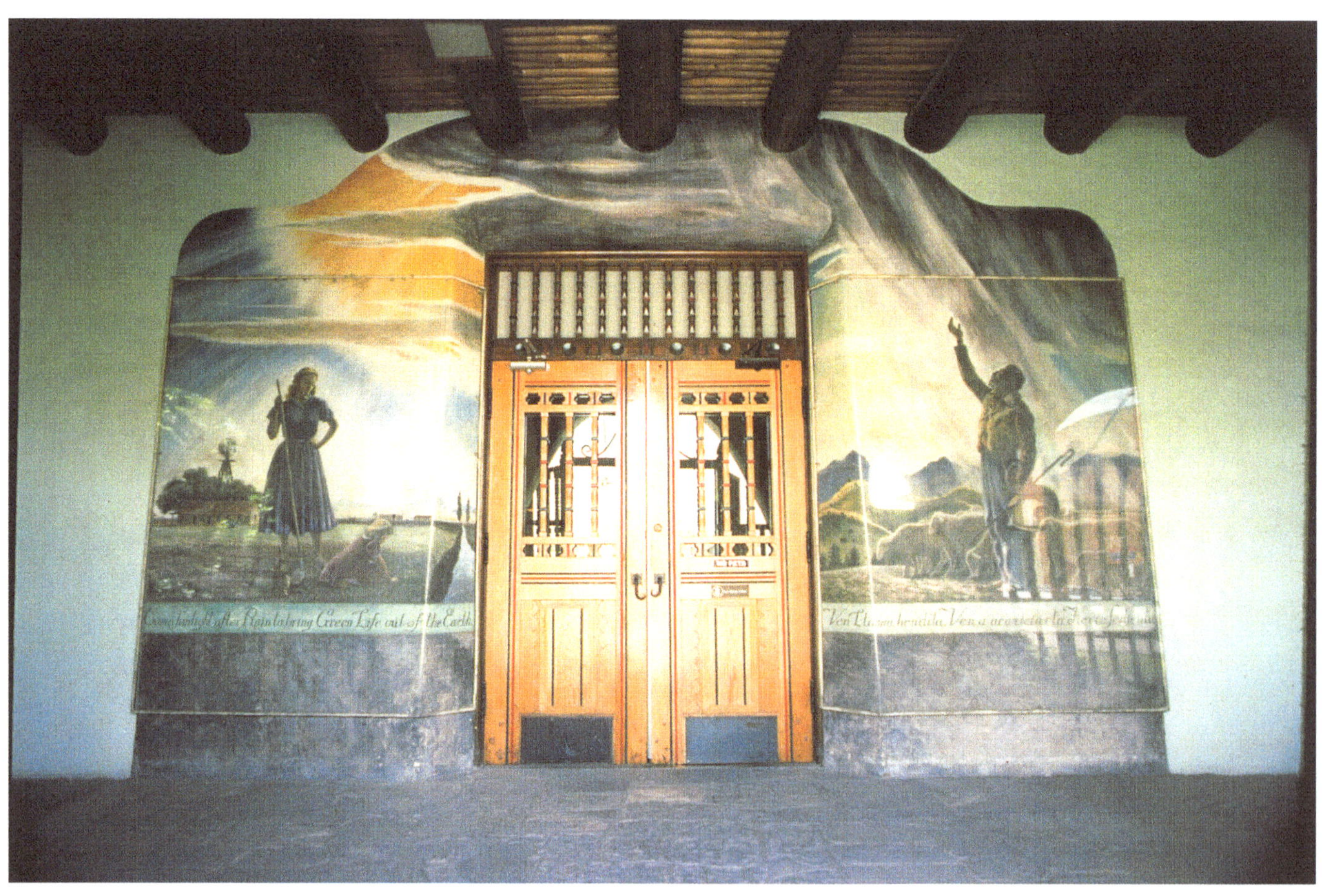

Come sunlight after rain to bring green life out of the earth,
Peter Hurd, fresco,
Lincoln National Forest Service Building, Alamogordo.

Come blessed rain, come caress the thirsty land,
Peter Hurd, fresco,
Lincoln National Forest Service Building, Alamogordo.

John Jellico Born, 1914, Koehler, New Mexico. Studied at Art Institute of Pittsburgh and in New York. Taught at the Art Institute of Pittsburgh, later became director of the Colorado Institute of Art.

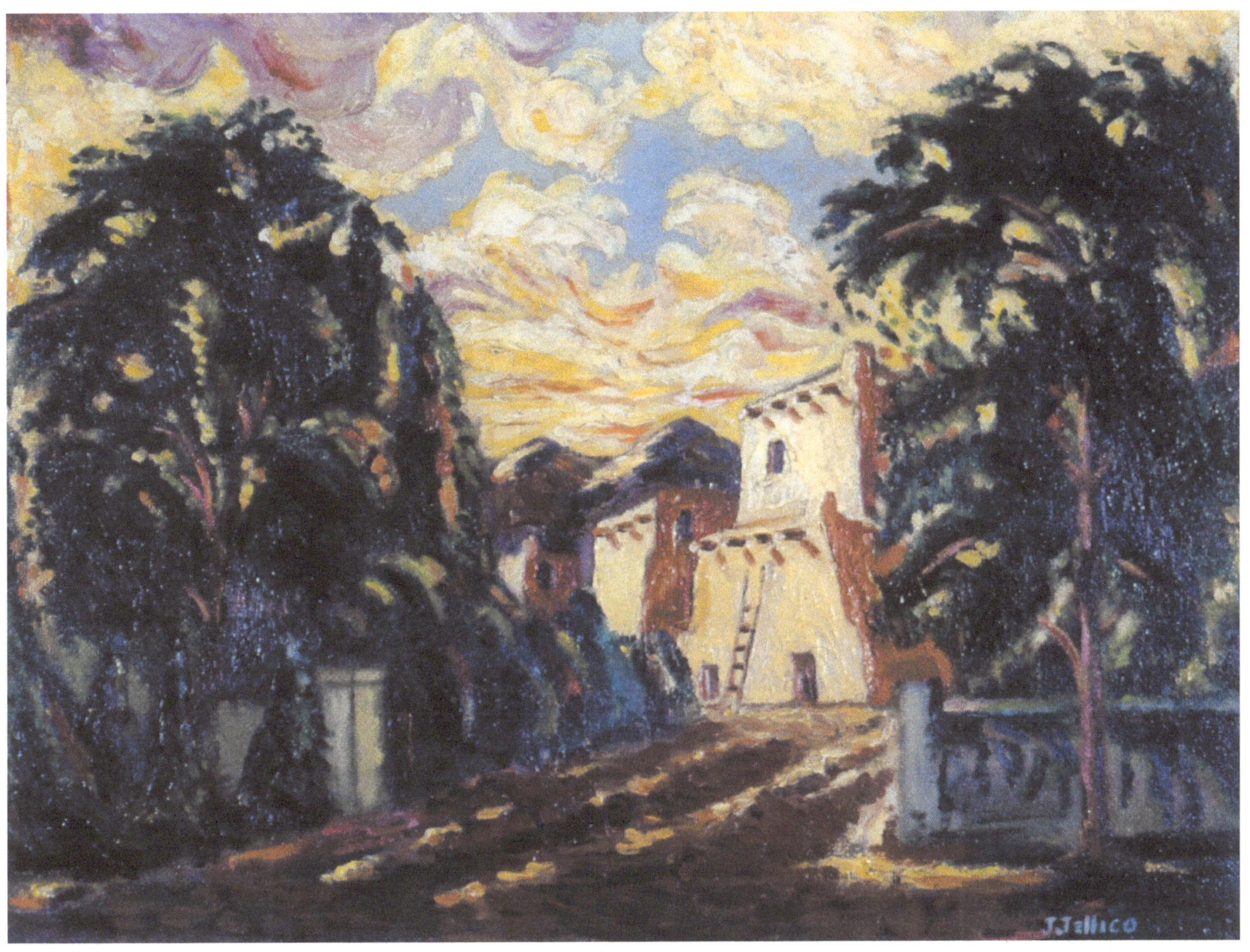

Two Story House, John Jellico, painting, Arthur Johnson Memorial Library, Raton.

D. Paul Jones Born, date unknown, in Maryland; died, 1998, Arizona. Studied art in Maryland. Served in World War I after which he went west and lived among the Indians of New Mexico. In 1921, he enrolled in the Broadmore Art Academy in Colorado Springs. Later became a teacher there. In 1933 moved to Alcalde, New Mexico, and shared a studio with his artist friend Lloyd Moylan. Worked on New Deal art programs: Portfolio of Spanish Colonial Design in New Mexico, murals and easel paintings.

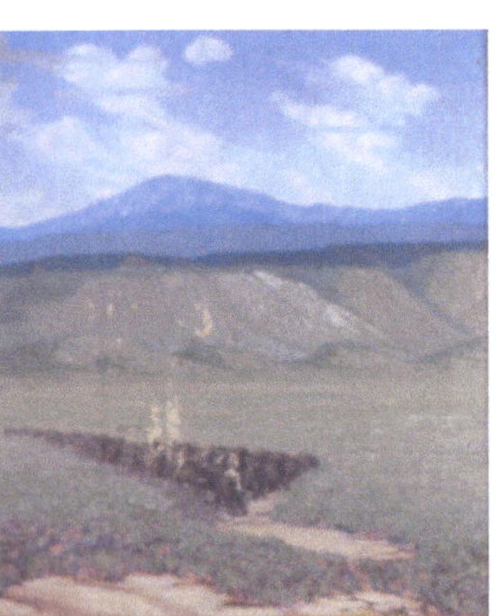
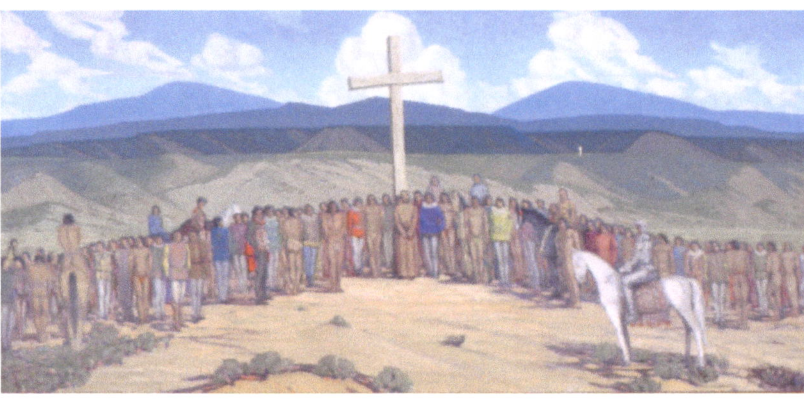
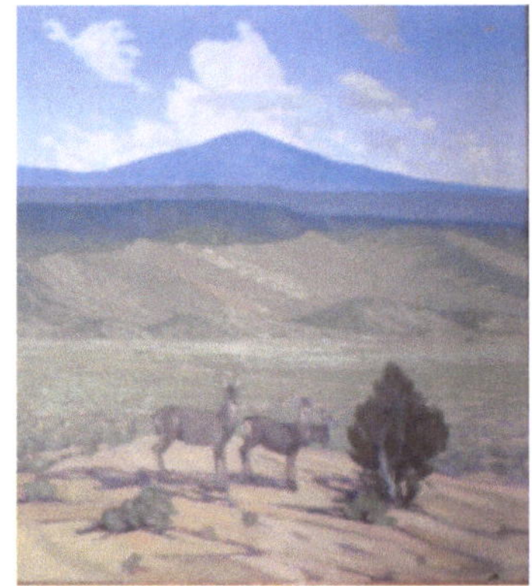

The Founding of San Juan, the First Capitol of New Spain, D. Paul Jones, triptych, Northern New Mexico Community College, El Rito.

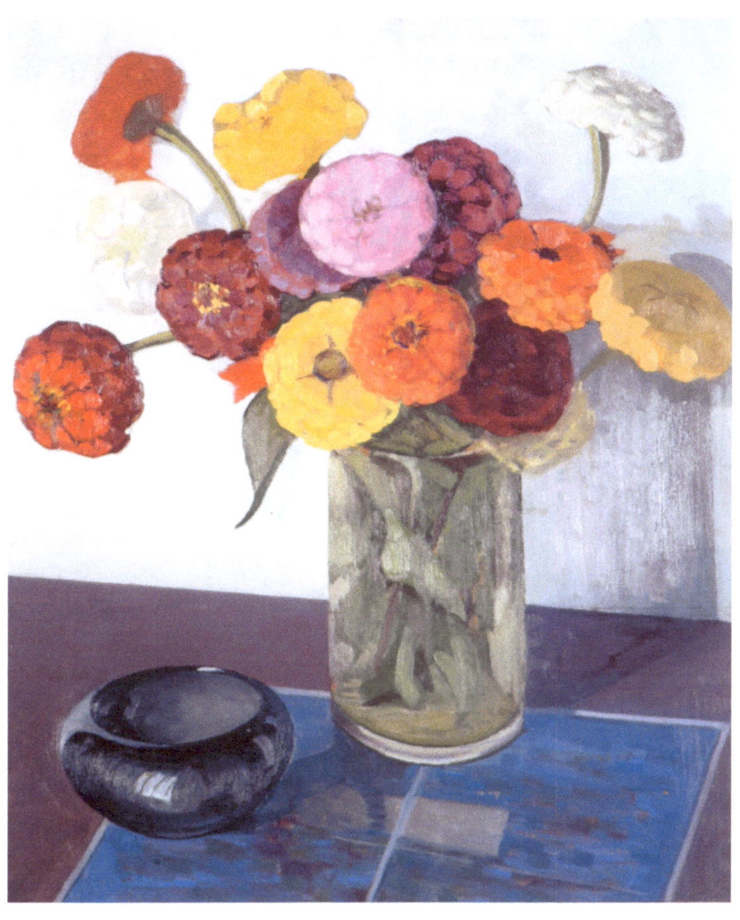

Zinnias, D. Paul Jones, painting,
Clayton High School, Clayton.

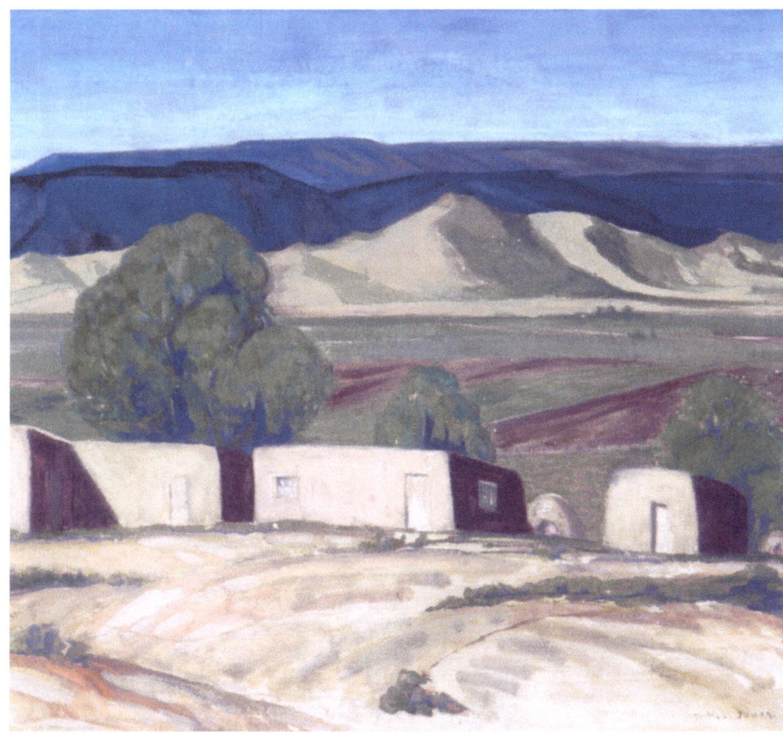

Spring Landscape, D. Paul Jones, painting,
McKinley County Courthouse, Gallup.

Raymond Jonson Born, 1891, Chariton, Iowa; died, 1982, Albuquerque, New Mexico. Studied at Portland Art Museum School, Chicago Institute of Art and Chicago Academy of Arts. Came to Santa Fe in 1924. Later, in the early fifties, became a teacher at the University of New Mexico. Influenced by theater design and Bauhaus concepts, he was throughout his career an advocate for modern art. In his Technical Notes (1933), Johnson wrote: " Each composition is the result of a definite concept of color harmony in relation to the form and design. I think of them as symphonic compositions consistent with my medium and honest to the highest ideal I stand for."

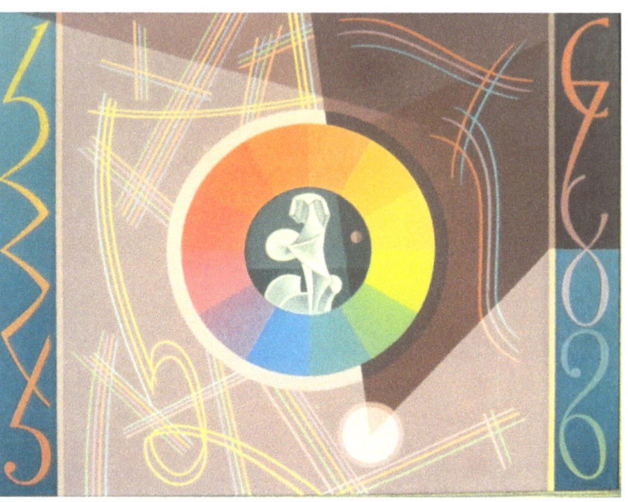

Mathematics, Raymond Jonson, painting, Raymond Jonson Museum, Albuquerque. Photograph #1905 courtesy of the Museum.

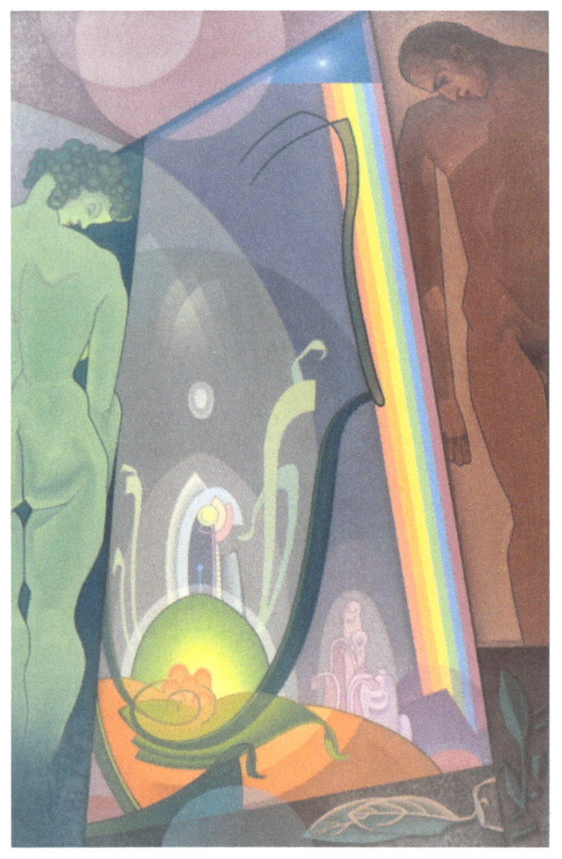

Biology, Raymond Jonson, painting, Raymond Jonson Museum, Albuquerque. Photograph #1906 courtesy of the Museum.

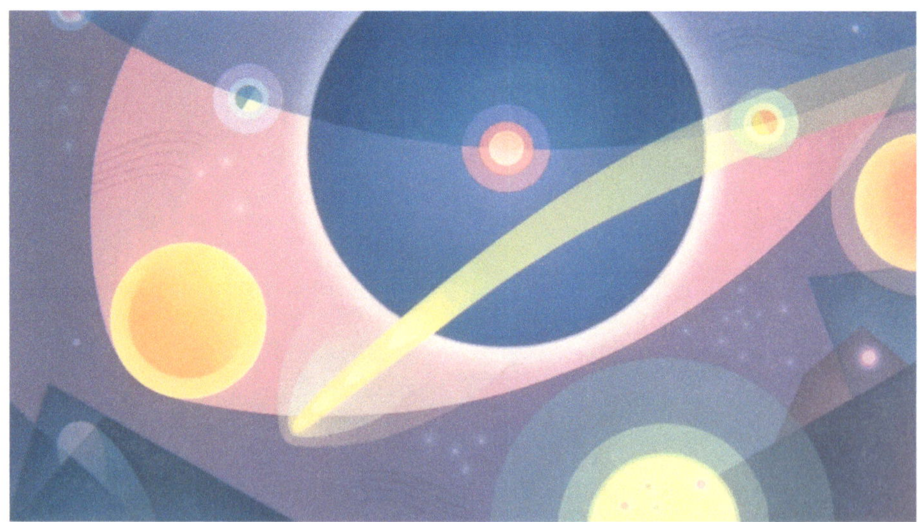

Astronomy, Raymond Jonson, painting, Raymond Jonson Museum, Albuquerque. Photograph #1907 courtesy of the Museum.

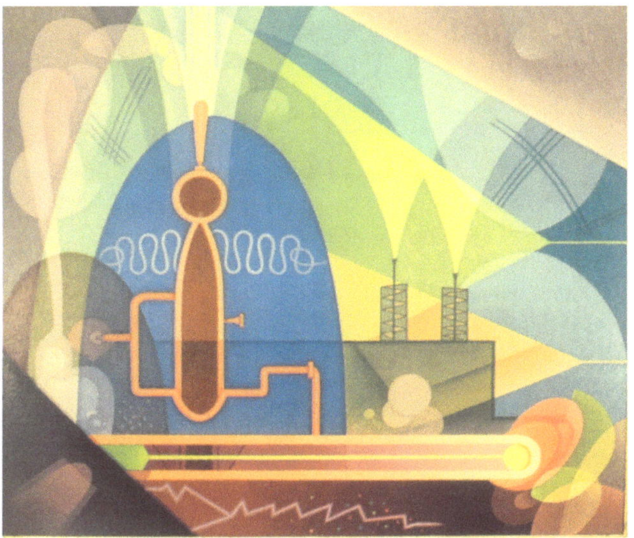

Engineering, Raymond Jonson, painting, Raymond Jonson Museum, Albuquerque. Photograph #1908 courtesy of the Museum.

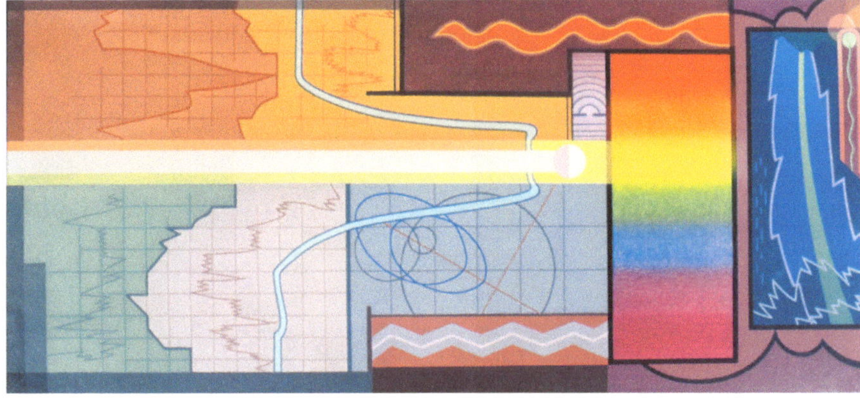

Physics, Raymond Jonson, painting, Raymond Jonson Museum, Albuquerque. Photograph #1909 courtesy of the Museum.

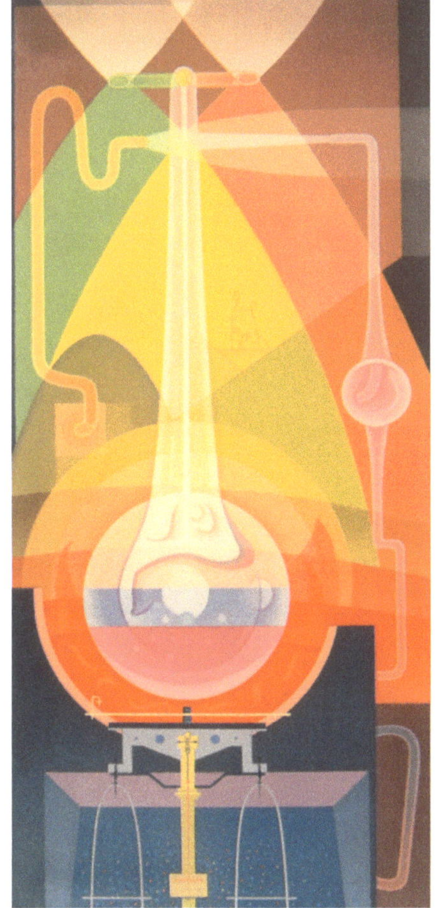

Chemistry, Raymond Jonson, painting, Raymond Jonson Museum, Albuquerque. Photograph #1910 courtesy of the Museum.

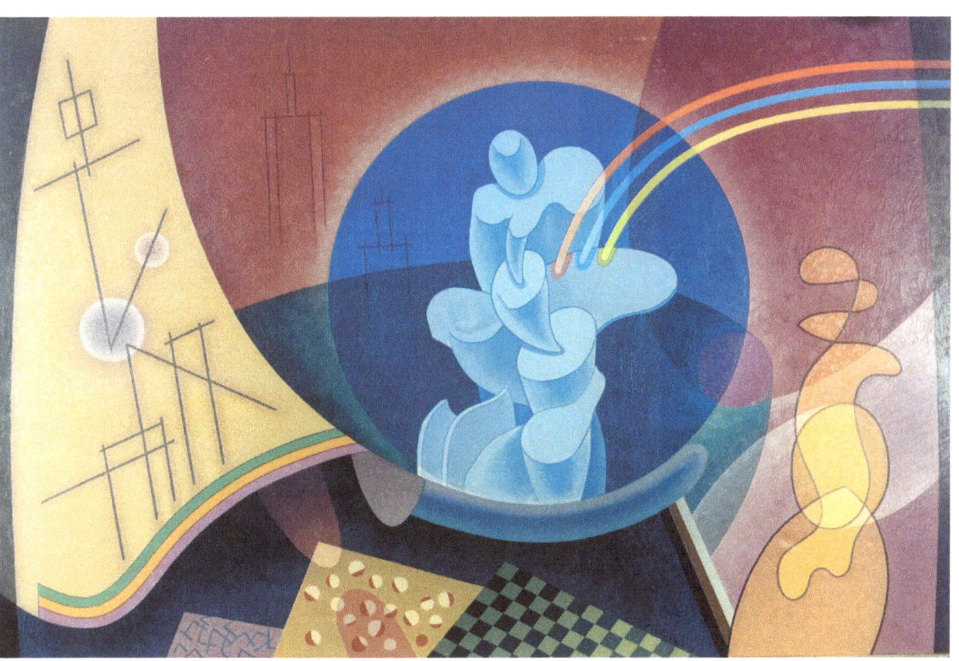

Art, Raymond Jonson, painting, Eastern New Mexico University, Portales.

Gene Kloss Born, 1903, Oakland, California; died, 1996, Taos, New Mexico. Studied at the University of California, Berkeley. Bought a two dollar book on etching, taught herself. She and her husband, the poet Phillips Kloss, came to Taos in 1925. The landscape and the people of New Mexico became her subject matter. Elected to the National Academy of Design. Noted especially for her etchings. For the first Public Works of Art Project, did nine aquatint etchings, 270 prints. For the WPA Art Project under Russell Vernon Hunter, did oils and watercolors as well as etchings.

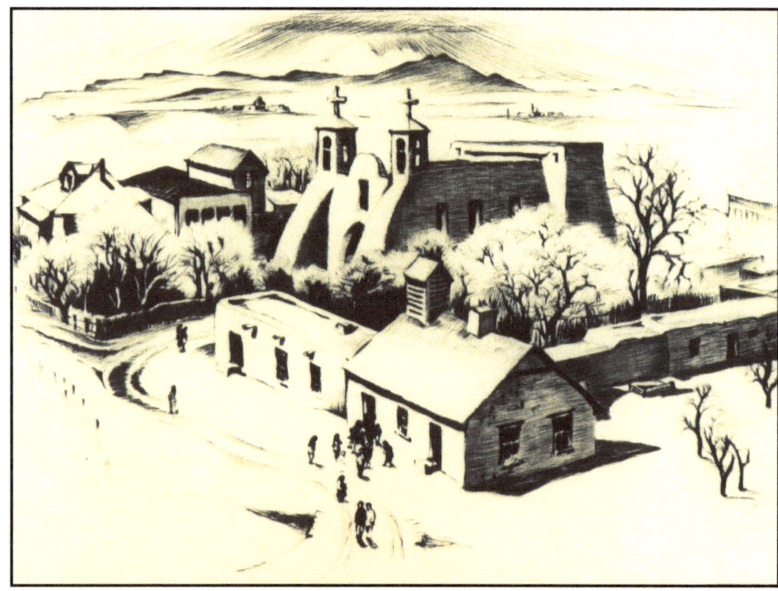

New Mexican Village, Gene Kloss, etching, Clayton High School, Clayton.

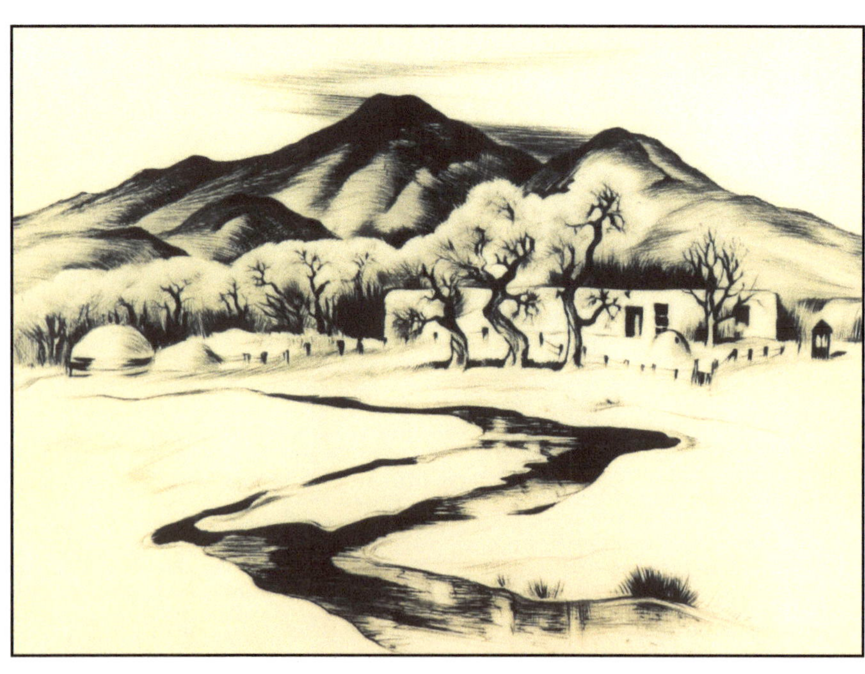

Ranchito, New Mexico, Gene Kloss, etching, WPA Museum, Clayton Public Schools, Clayton.

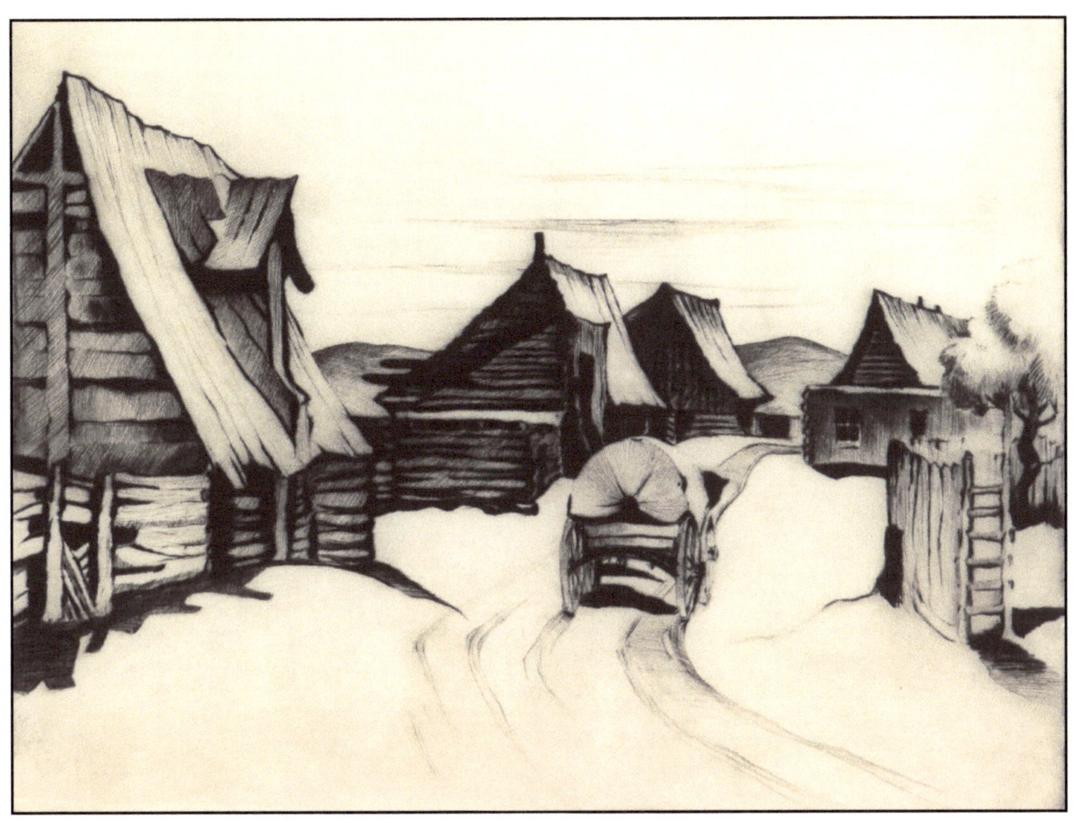

New Mexico Mountain Town, Gene Kloss, etching, WPA Museum, Clayton Public Schools, Clayton.

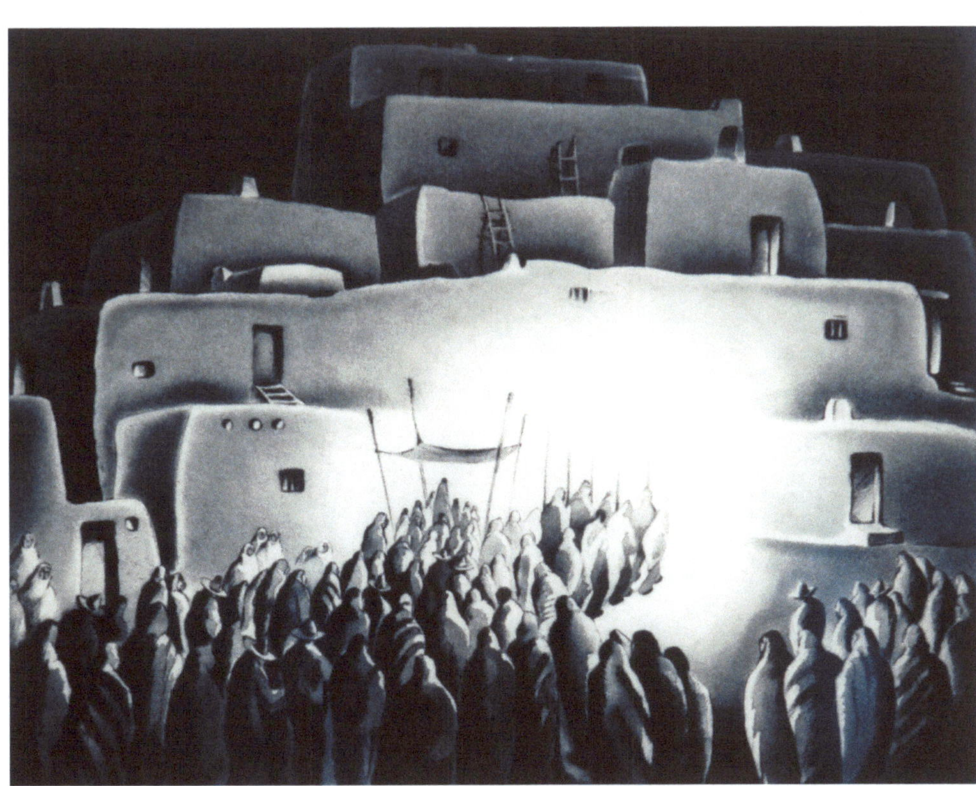

Christmas Eve, Taos Pueblo, Gene Kloss, etching, Melrose High School Library, Melrose; National Park Service Regional Office, Santa Fe. Photograph courtesy of National Park Service.

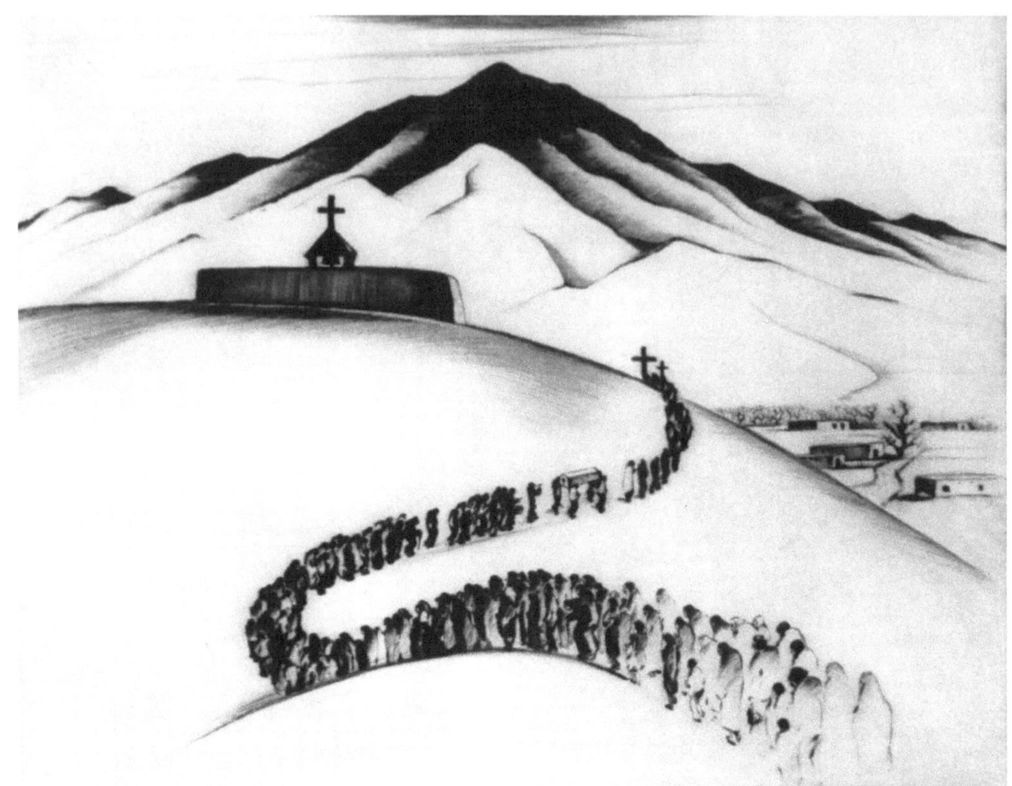

Penitente Good Friday, Gene Kloss, etching, National Park Service Regional Office, Santa Fe, and other sites.

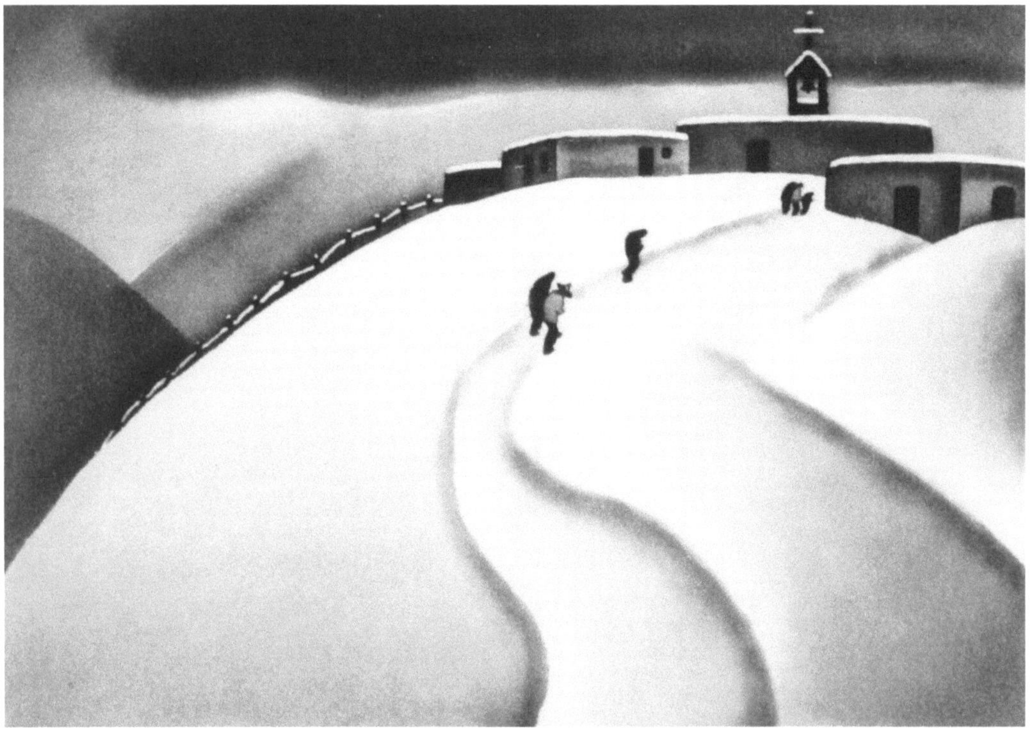

Winter Mass, Gene Kloss, etching, National Park Service Regional Office, Santa Fe.

The Sanctuary, Chimayo, Gene Kloss, etching, National Park Service Regional Office, Santa Fe, and other sites.

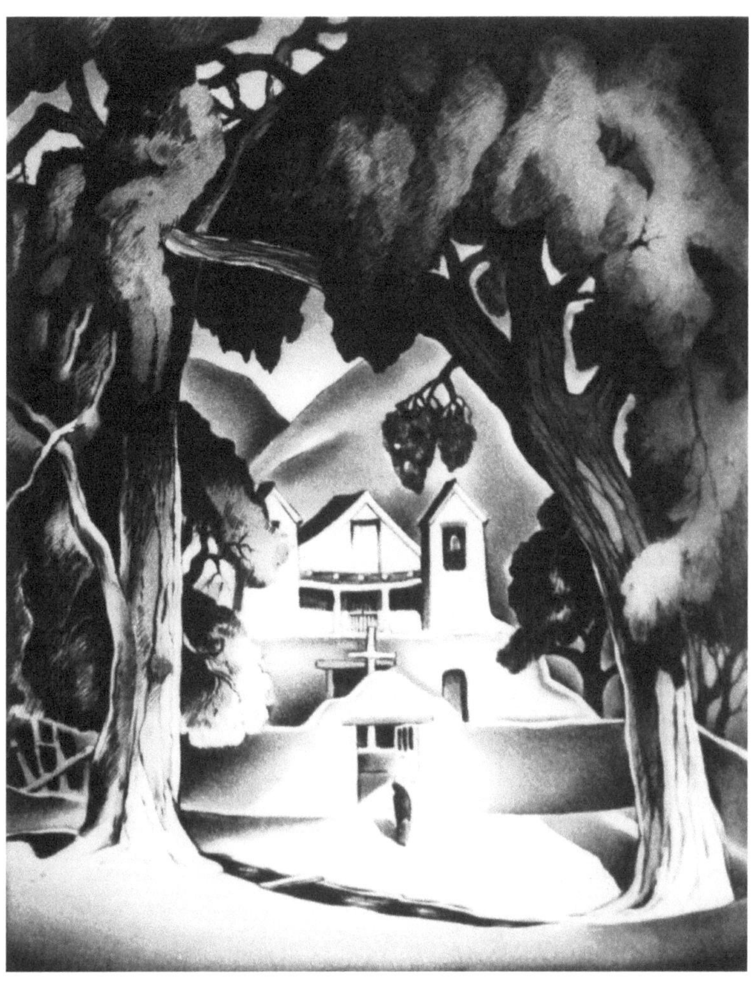

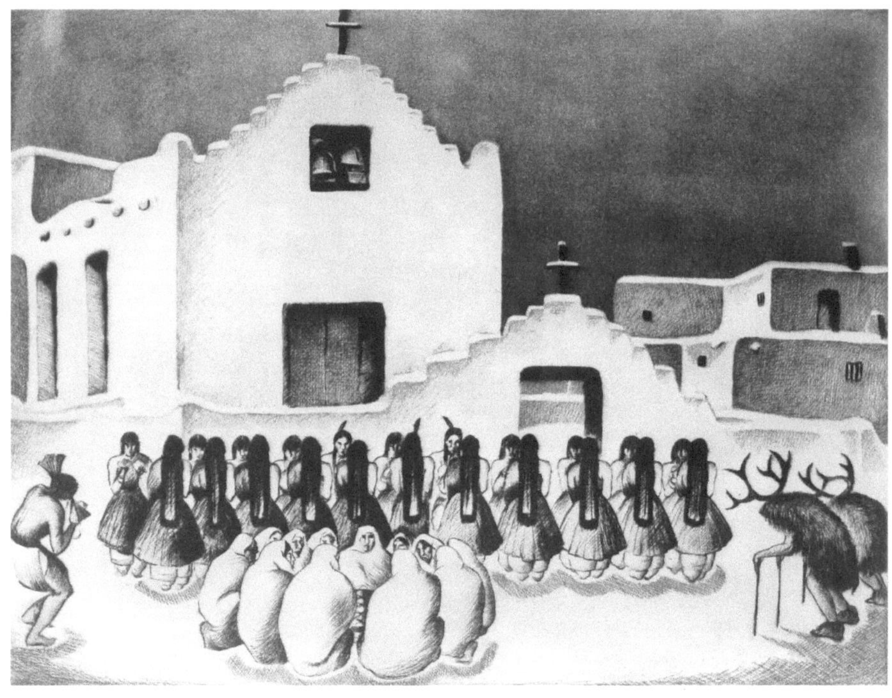

Indian Ceremony, Gene Kloss, etching, WPA Photo Collection #5432, New Mexico State Records and Archives, Santa Fe.

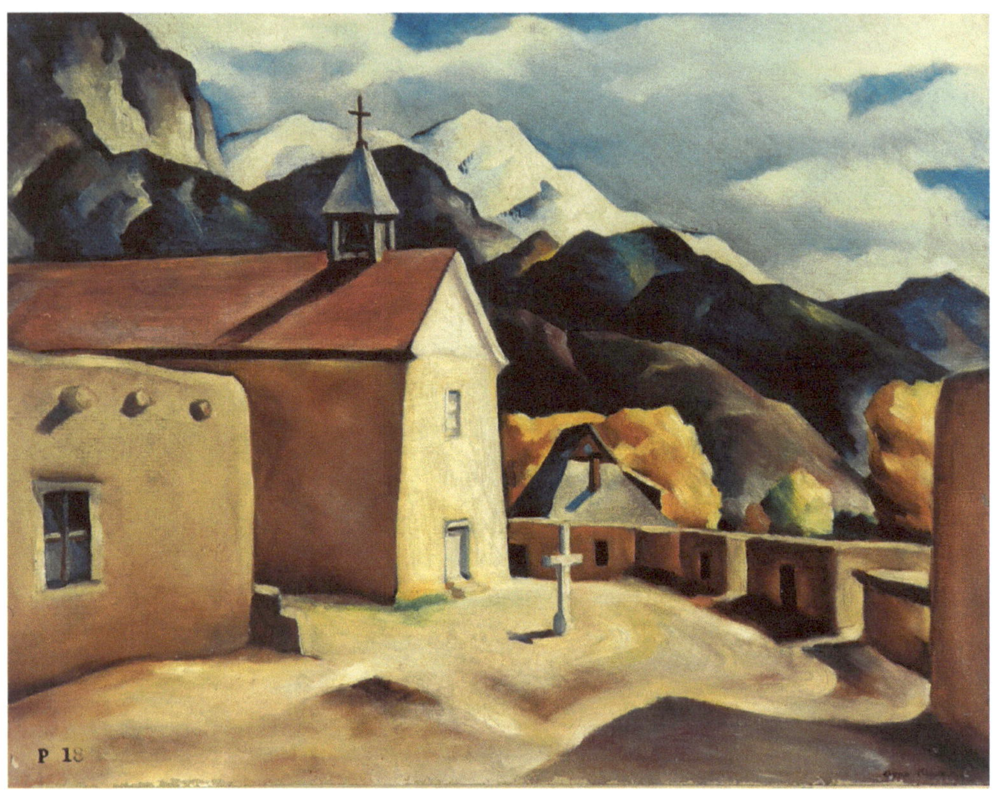

Church at Trampas, Gene Kloss, painting, Melrose High School Library, Melrose.

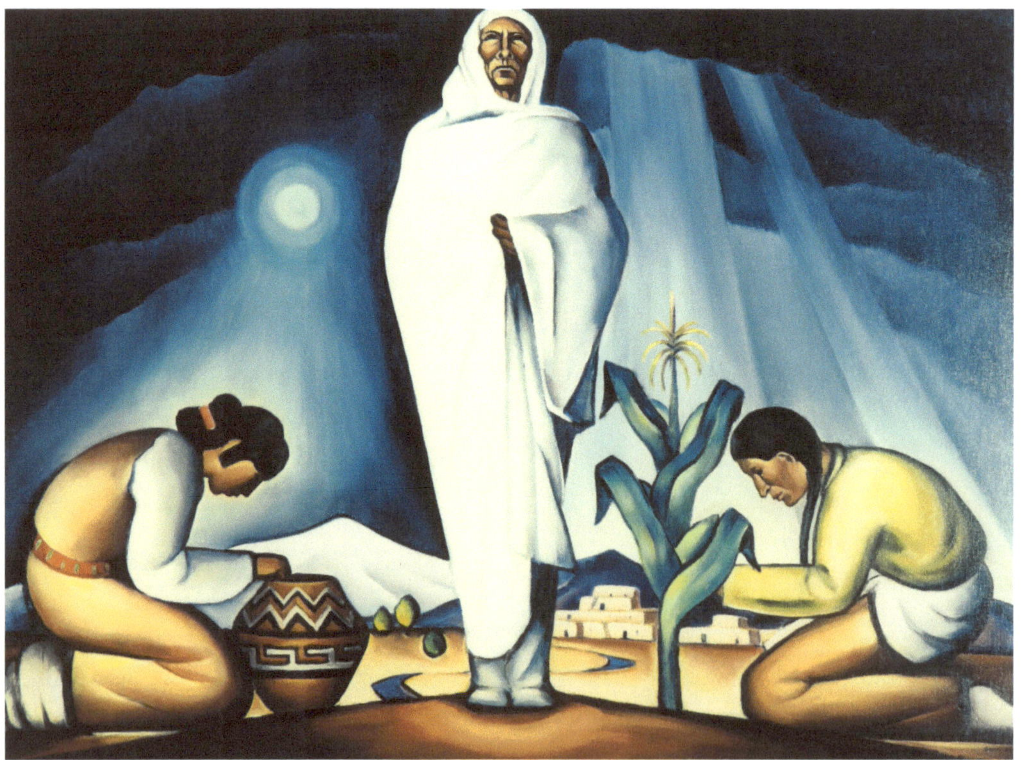

Rain Priest, Gene Kloss, painting, Albuquerque Museum, Albuquerque.

Paul Lantz Born, 1908, Stromberg, Nebraska; died, 1998, Phoenix, Arizona. Lived and painted in New Mexico from 1930 to 1939.

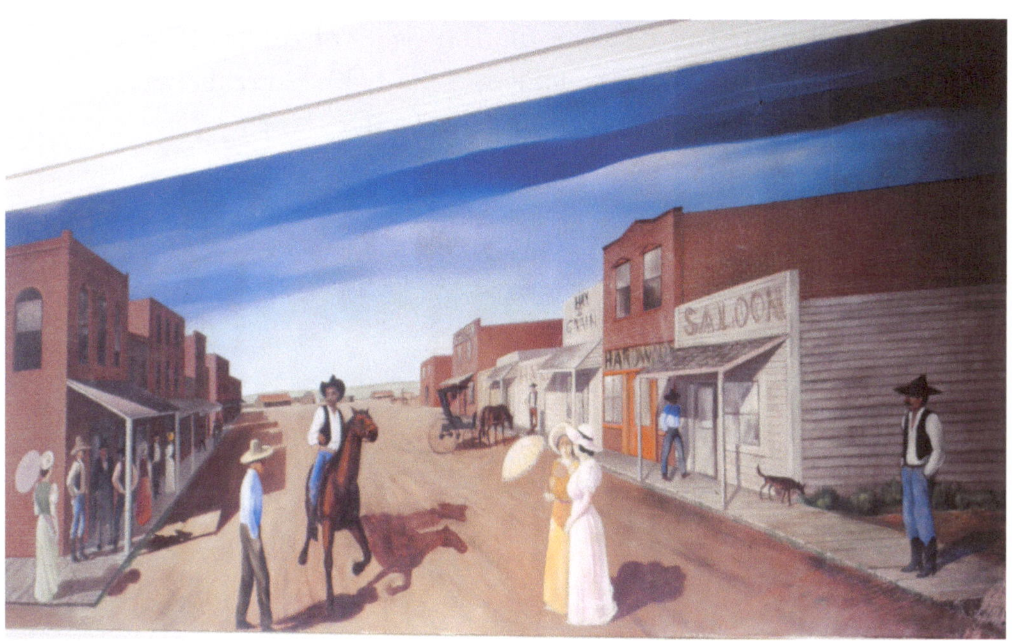

Clovis Main Street, Paul Lantz, mural, Eldon Smith Architect Office (formerly U.S. Post Office), Clovis.

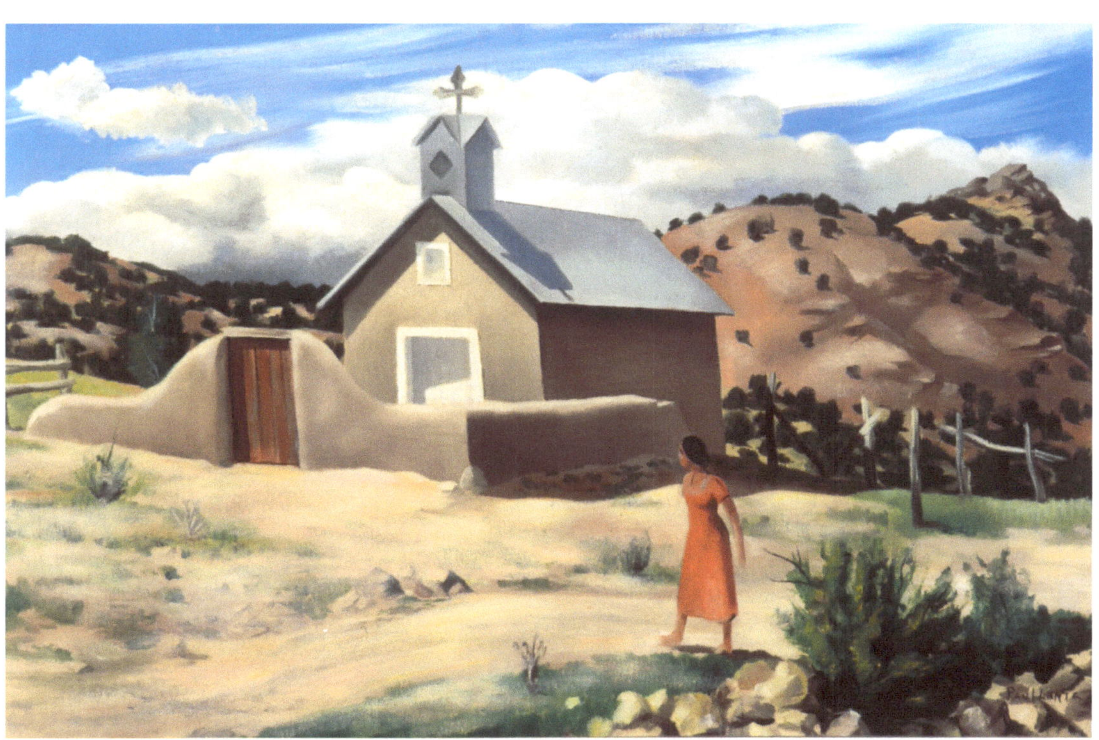

Church in the Rio Grande Valley, Paul Lantz, painting, McKinley County Courthouse, Gallup.

Tom Lea Born, 1907, El Paso, Texas; died, 2001, El Paso, Texas. Studied at the Art Institute, Chicago, and in Europe. Worked on murals in Italy, 1930. Came to Santa Fe in 1933. Studied Southwestern history and worked part time at the Laboratory of Anthropology. Did murals throughout the Southwest in the 1930s. After the war, achieved recognition as an illustrator of books and a writer.

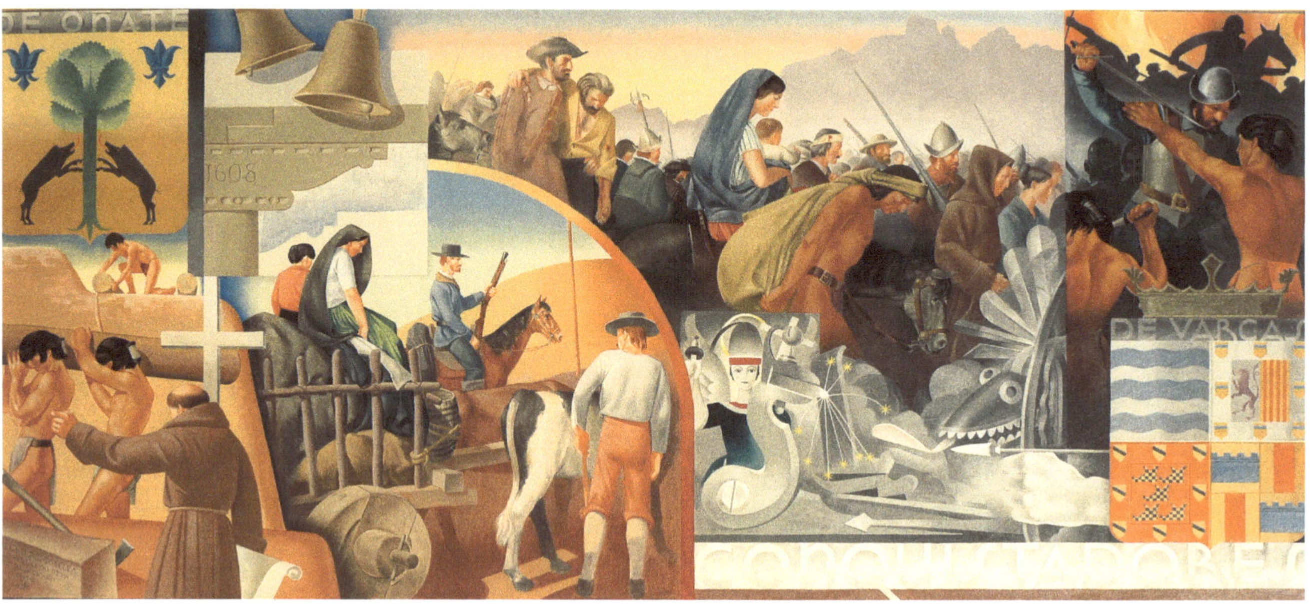

Conquistadors, Tom Lea, painting, New Mexico State University Library, Las Cruces. (Documents the Spanish conflicts.)

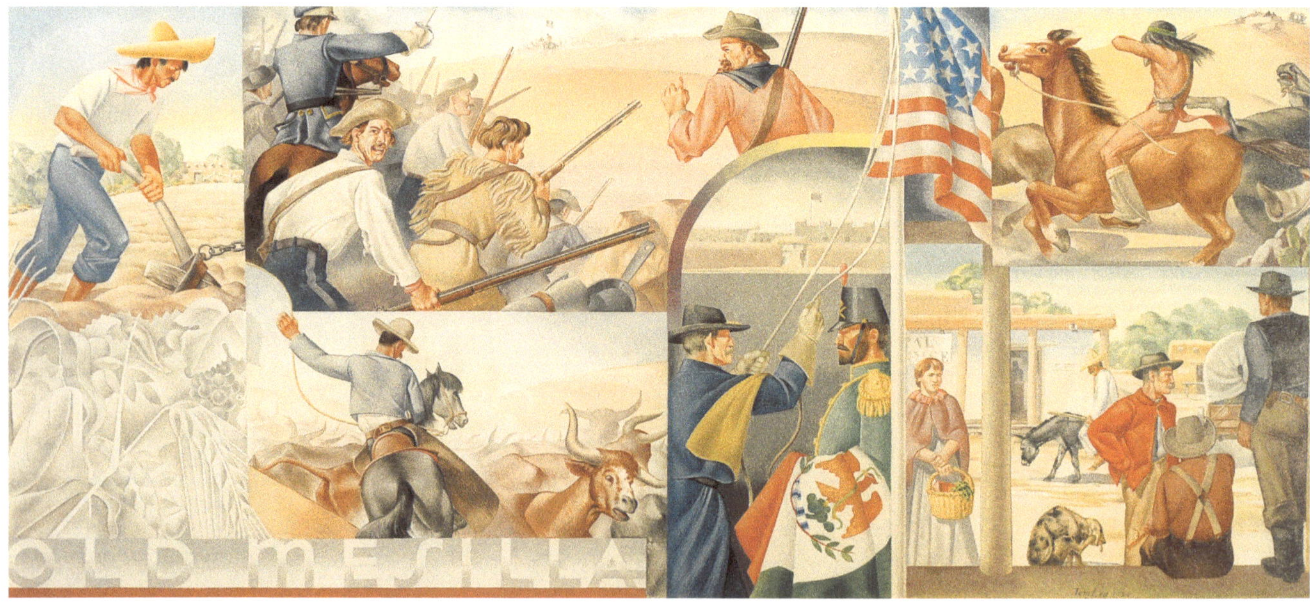

La Mesilla, Tom Lea, painting, New Mexico State University Library, Las Cruces.
(Documents farming and cattle raising, scenes from the Mexican War, Apache raids, Mesilla becoming part of the U.S.)

John Ward Lockwood Born, 1894, Atchison, Kansas; died, 1963, Taos, New Mexico. Studied at the University of Kansas, Pennsylvania Academy of Fine Arts, in Paris, and later with Andrew Dasburg before moving to New Mexico in 1926. Active in the Taos art community. Taught at the University of New Mexico, also at the University of Texas. Painted four frescoes in the old Taos Courthouse: Avarice Breeds Crime, Justice Begets Content, Obedience Casts Out Fear, and Superfluous Laws Oppress. (Also see Fresco Quartet.)

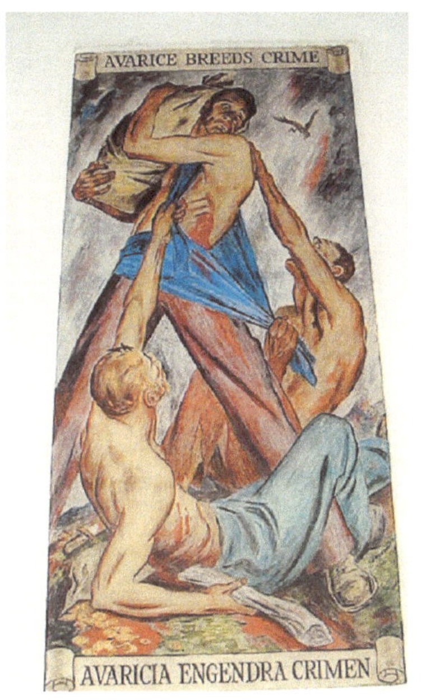

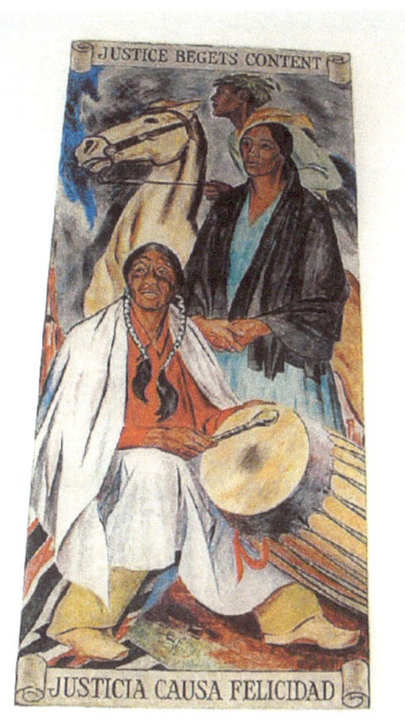

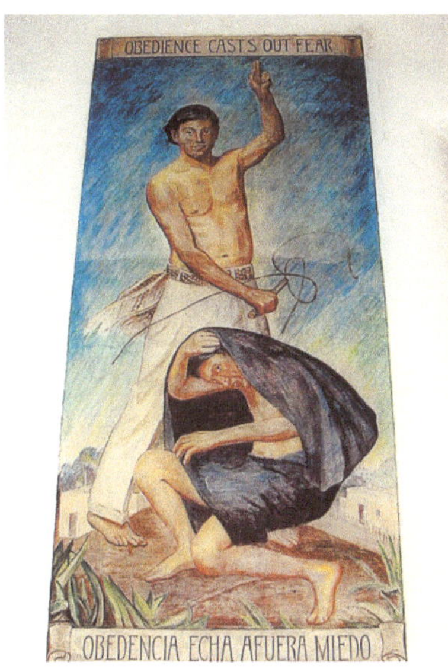

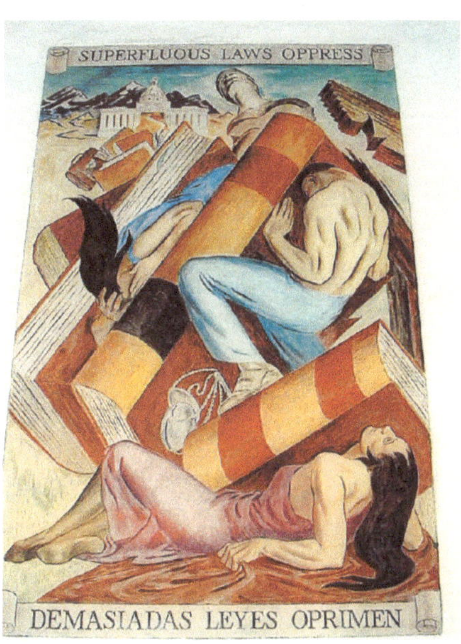

William Lumpkins Born, 1909, on Rabbit Ears Ranch near Clayton, New Mexico; died, 2000, Santa Fe, New Mexico. He left Rabbit Ears to study art, anthropology, and journalism at the University of New Mexico, Albuquerque. "Unless you have two or three oil wells," he commented, "you don't want to ranch." In 1935, when he heard the WPA was hiring in Santa Fe, he showed a portfolio of watercolors to Gustave Bauman, supervisor of the Public Works of Art Project. Bauman took a quick look. "Yes, you are an artist," he said, "Now go home and paint for us." Lived and worked in Santa Fe. Received many awards, among them, Santa Fe's first Arts Recognition Award and the Governor's Award for Excellence in Architecture and Painting. He comments on the Village paintings: "I just wanted to put in three cultures. . . . I was painting abstract at the time–I started painting abstract in 1930. The village is still there, pretty intact [the Spanish village, in a valley over from Penasco]. I wanted to represent the region through my WPA paintings so others could see the unique beauty of the area."

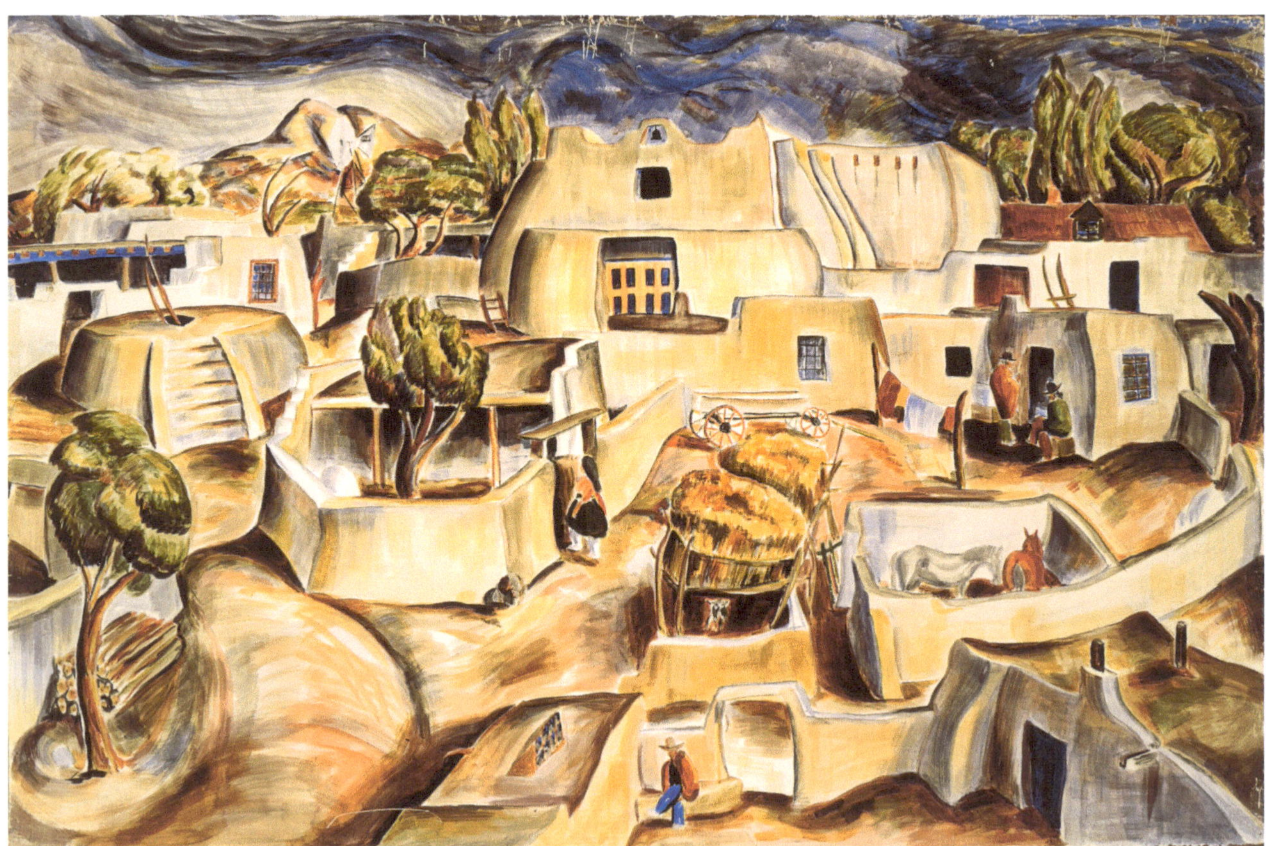

Indian Village, William Lumpkins, painting, Museum of Fine Arts, Santa Fe. Photograph courtesy of the Museum.

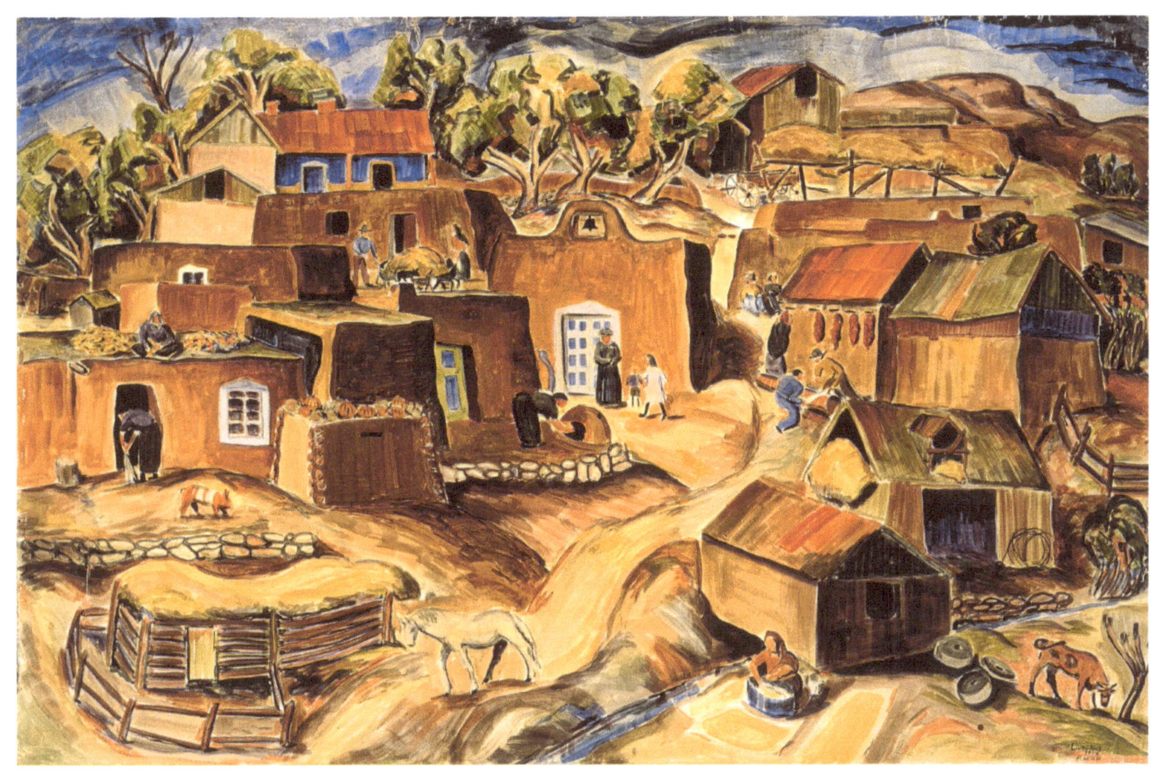

Spanish Village, William Lumpkins, painting, Museum of Fine Arts, Santa Fe. Photograph courtesy of the Museum.

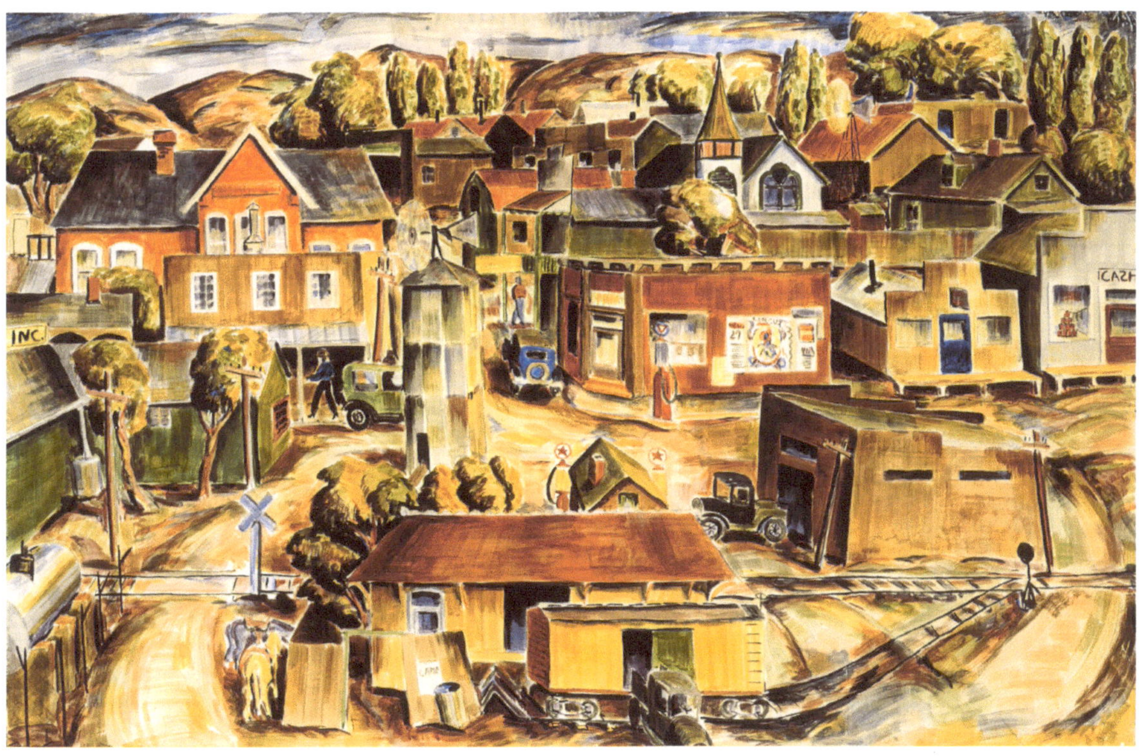

Anglo Village, William Lumpkins, painting. Museum of Fine Arts, Santa Fe. Photograph courtesy of the Museum.

Julian Martinez Born, 1879, San Ildefonso Pueblo; died, 1943, San Ildefonso Pueblo, New Mexico. Worked on restoration of prehistoric pots for Dr. Edgar Hewett, Director of the School of American Research, Santa Fe. He married Maria Montoya, later known as Maria Martinez. Together, as master potters, they developed the famous San Ildefonso black pottery.

Maria Martinez Born, 1886, San Ildefonso Pueblo; died, 1980, San Ildefonso Pueblo. Maria Poveka Montoya went to Saint Catherine's Indian School in Santa Fe, then back to the Pueblo for further study. At seventeen, she married Julian Martinez. Both she and Julian worked at the School of American Research, Santa Fe. Their work with the director Dr. Hewett on the Puye Canyon excavations of prehistoric potsherds was a major influence on the development of their special pottery. Asked to replicate the old pottery, they began making the "new old pots" for which they became internationally famous.

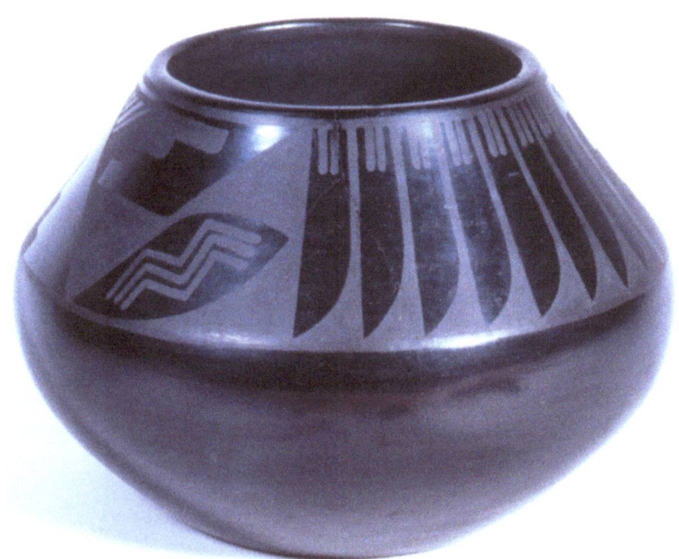

Black Pot, Julian and Maria Martinez, pottery, National Park Service, Santa Fe. Photograph courtesy of the National Park Service (SWRO 292).

Polychrome Jar, Julian and Maria Martinez, pottery, National Park Service, Santa Fe. Photograph courtesy of the National Park Service (SWRO 298).

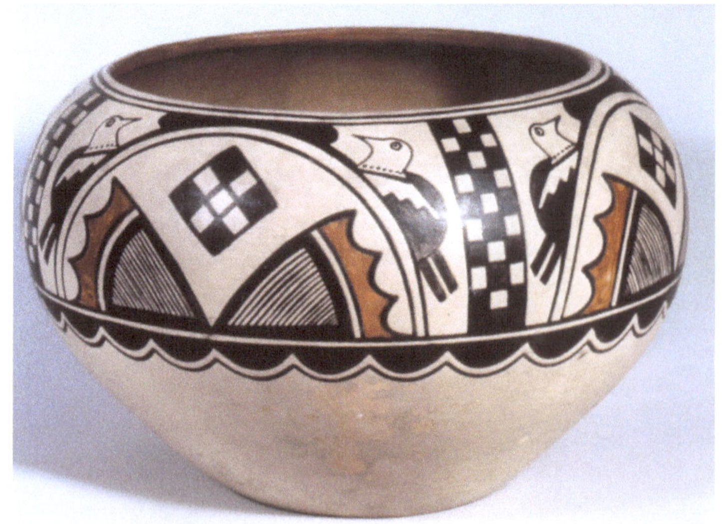

Ila McAfee (Turner) Born, 1897, near Gunnison, Colorado; died, 1995, Pueblo, Colorado. Studied in Los Angeles; later, in Chicago and New York. Moved to Taos in 1928. Lived there for sixty-five years before going back to Colorado. Noted for her paintings of animals.

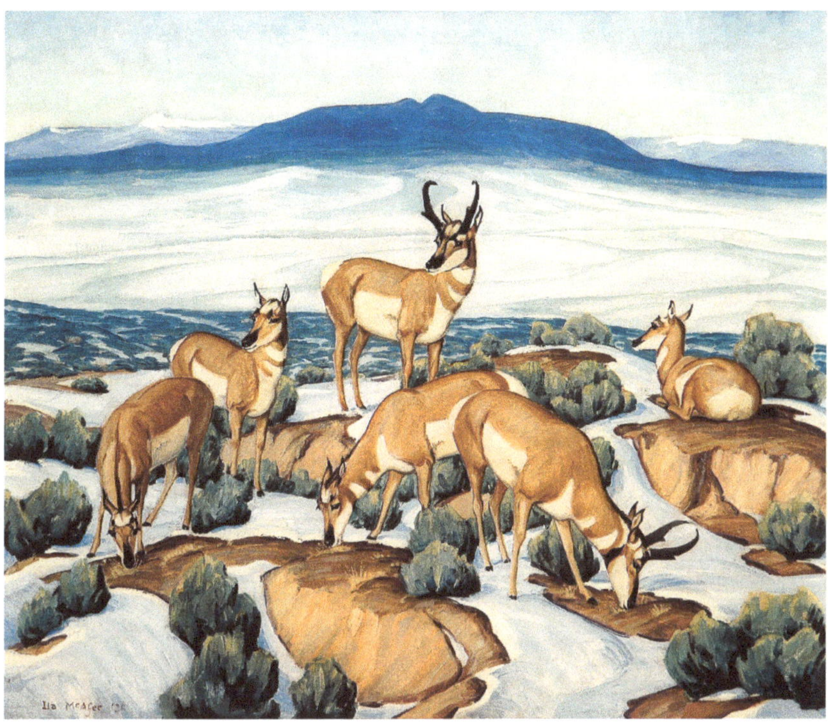

Antelope, Ila McAfee (Turner), painting, Albuquerque Museum, Albuquerque.

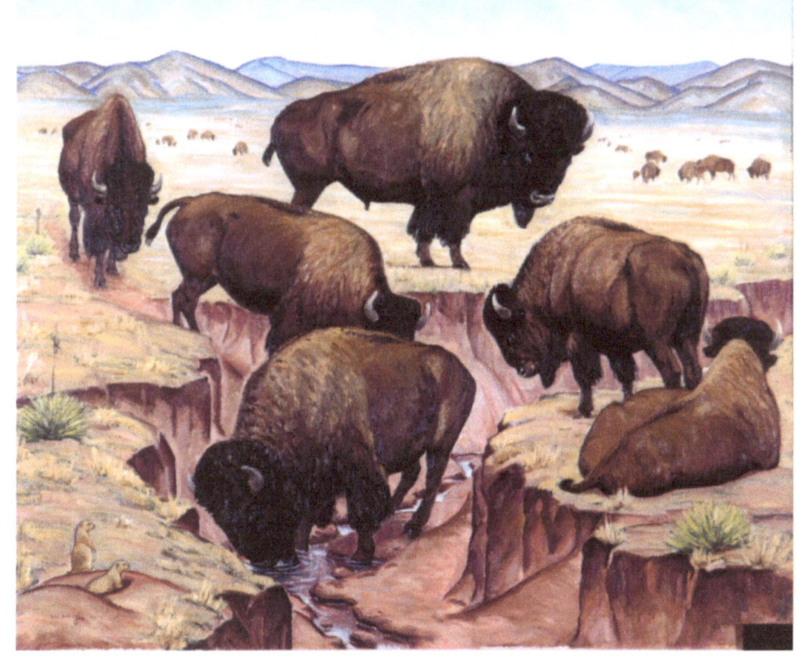

Bison, Ila McAfee (Turner), painting, Bernalillo City/County Courthouse, Albuquerque.

Ben Carlton Mead Born, 1902, Bay City, Texas; died, 1986, California. Studied at the Art Institute of Chicago. Became a major illustrator of western themes. Illustrated books of the folklorist J. Frank Dobie. Noted for his close attention to historical accuracy.

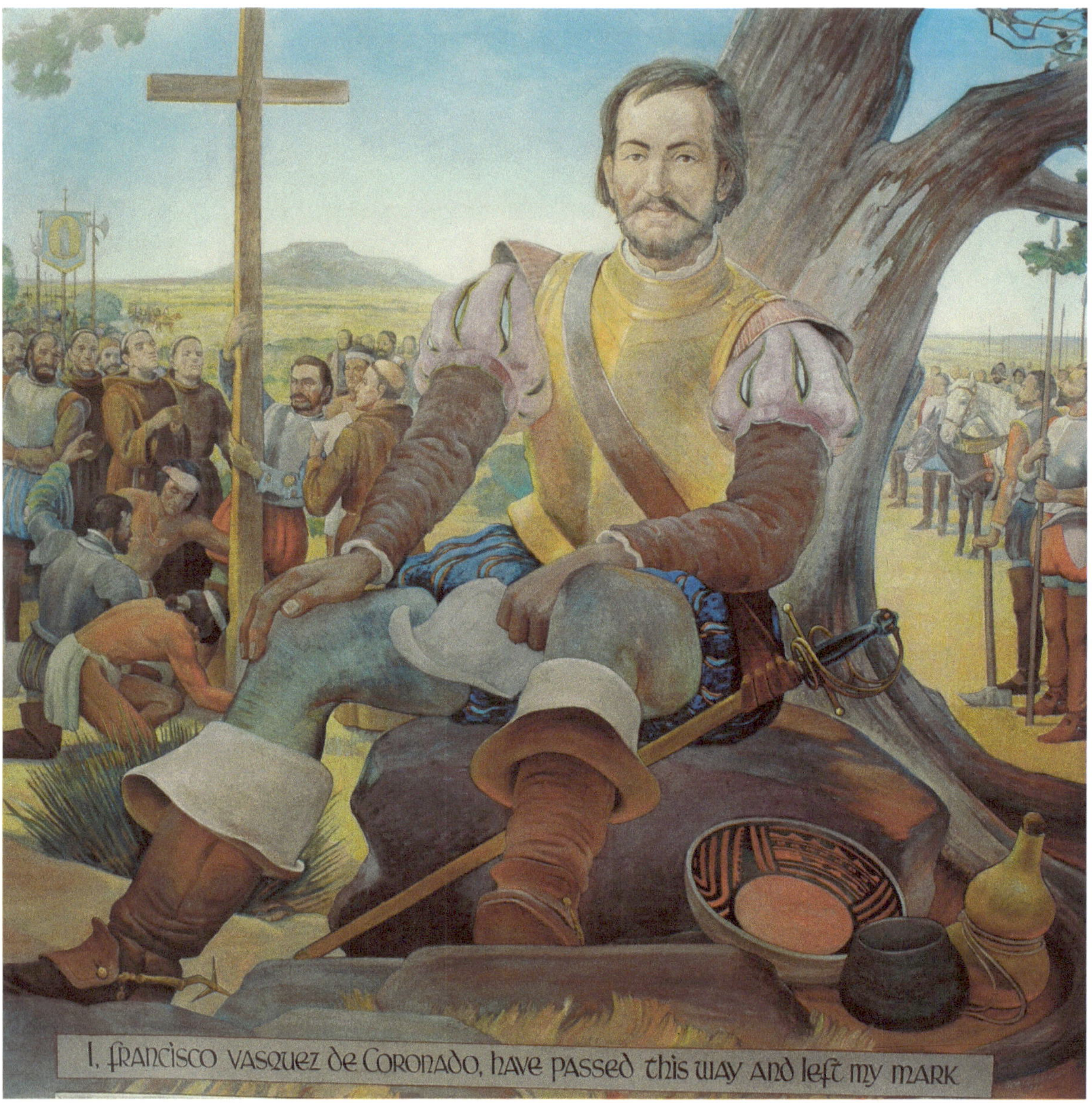

I, Franciso Vasquez de Coronado Have Passed This Way and Left My Mark,
Ben Carlton Mead, mural, Quay County Courthouse, Tucumcari.

Dorothy Morang Born, 1906, Bridgeton, Maine; died, 1995, Santa Fe, New Mexico. Trained as a pianist at the New England Conservatory of Music. Moved to Santa Fe in 1939. Self-taught as a painter. Became active in New Deal projects in both easel painting and as a teacher of music.

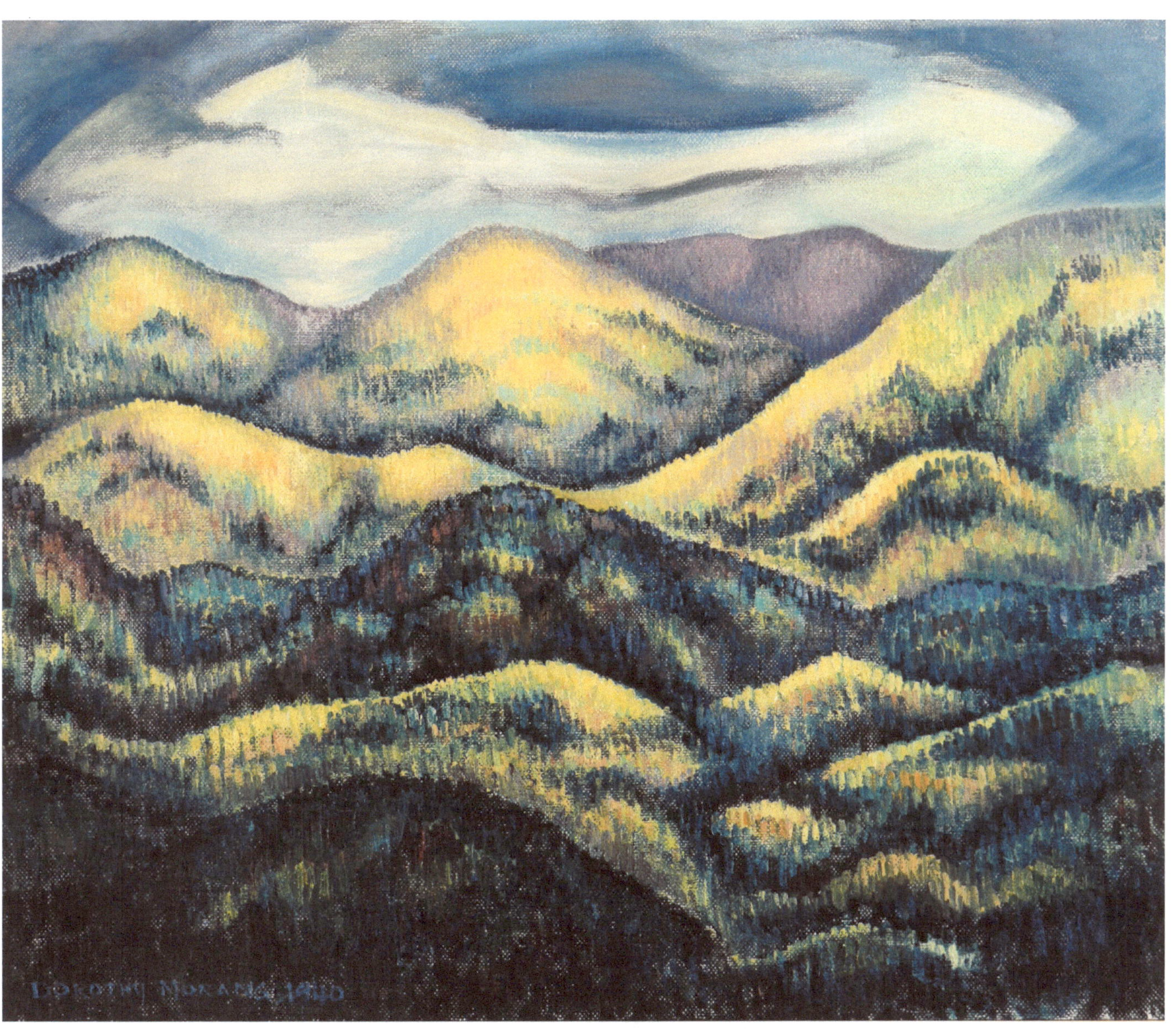

Aspen on the Sangre de Christo, Dorothy Morang, painting, University of New Mexico Fine Arts Museum, Albuquerque.

James Stovall Morris Born, 1902, Marshall, Missouri; died, 1973. Studied at the Cincinnati Art Academy, the Pennsylvania Academy of Fine Arts. Visited Santa Fe in the late 1920s and met John Sloan who arranged a scholarship for him at the Art Students League in New York City. He returned to New Mexico with his friend Charles Barrows during the Depression and worked on New Deal projects, including the Portfolio of Spanish Colonial Design in New Mexico. He settled in Santa Fe and continued his career as an artist.

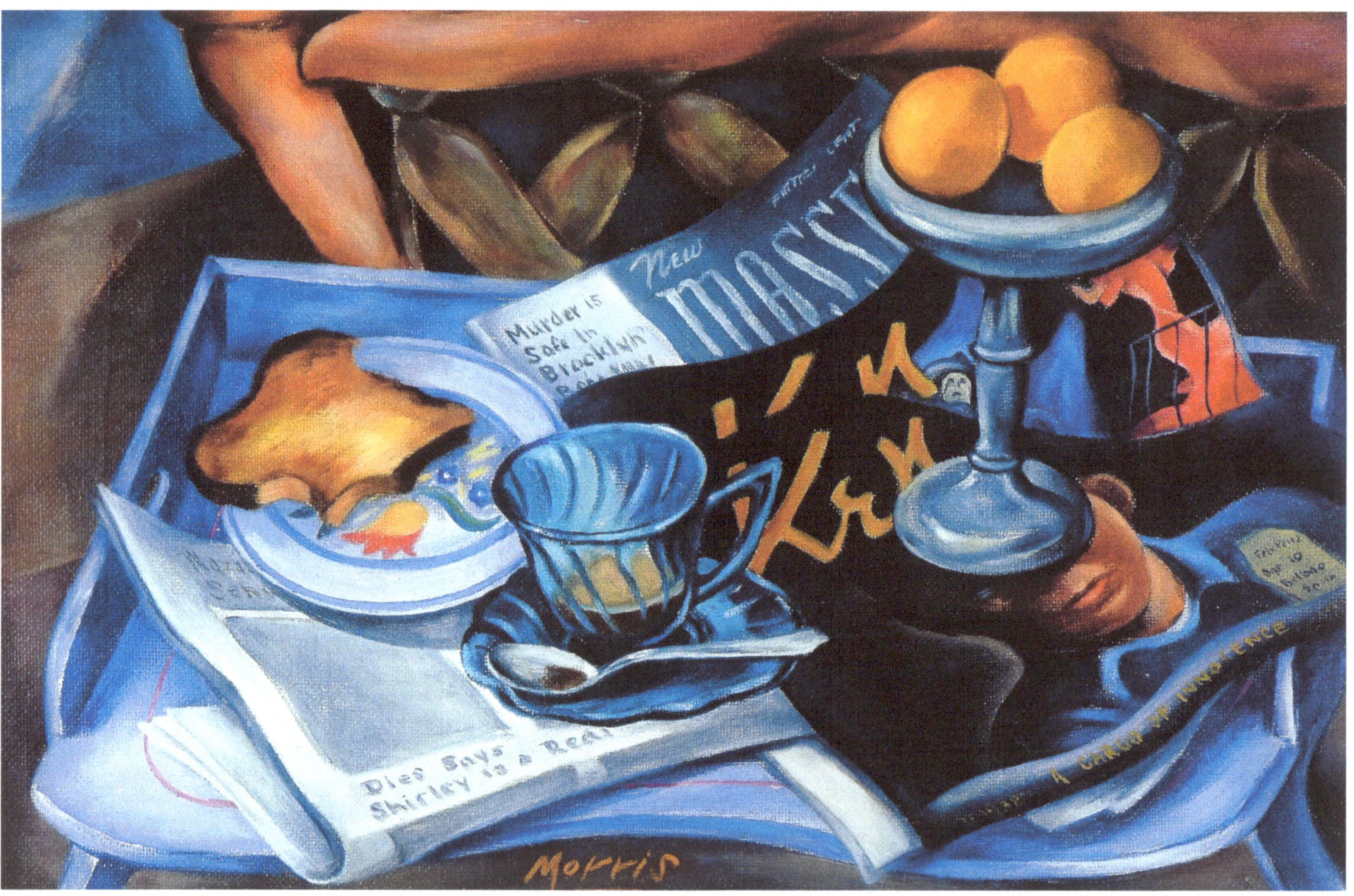

Breakfast Trays, James Morris, painting, University of New Mexico Fine Arts Museum, Albuquerque. Photograph courtesy of the Museum (82.184).

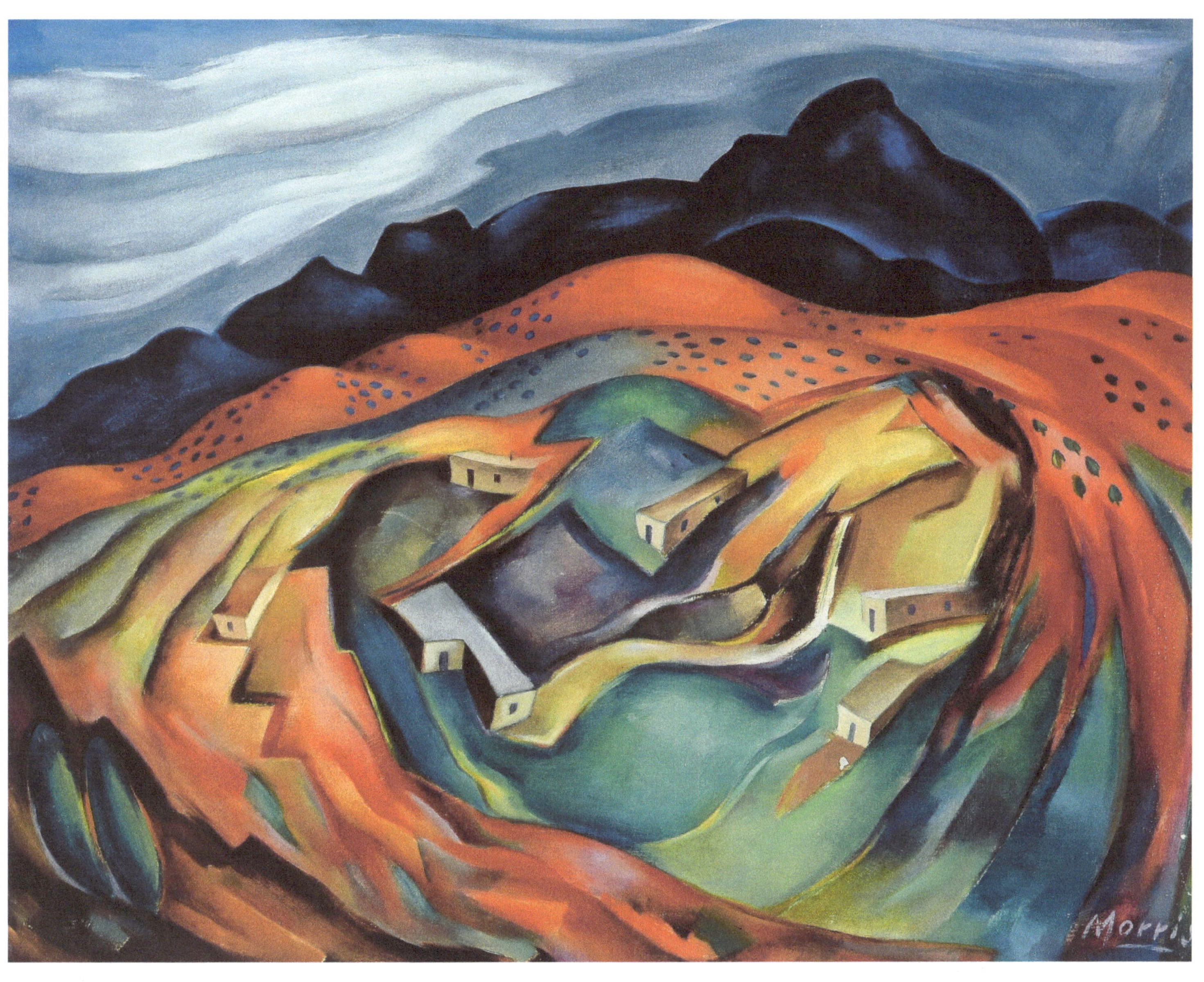

Mountain Village, James Morris, painting, University of New Mexico Fine Arts Museum, Albuquerque. Photograph courtesy of the Museum (XO.85).

Lloyd Moylan Born, 1893, St. Paul, Minnesota; died, 1963, Santa Fe, New Mexico. Studied at the Minneapolis Art Institute, Art Students League, New York. Became a full time resident of New Mexico in 1939. Traveled to Mexico where he learned techniques of mural painting which he continued to develop under the WPA art program.

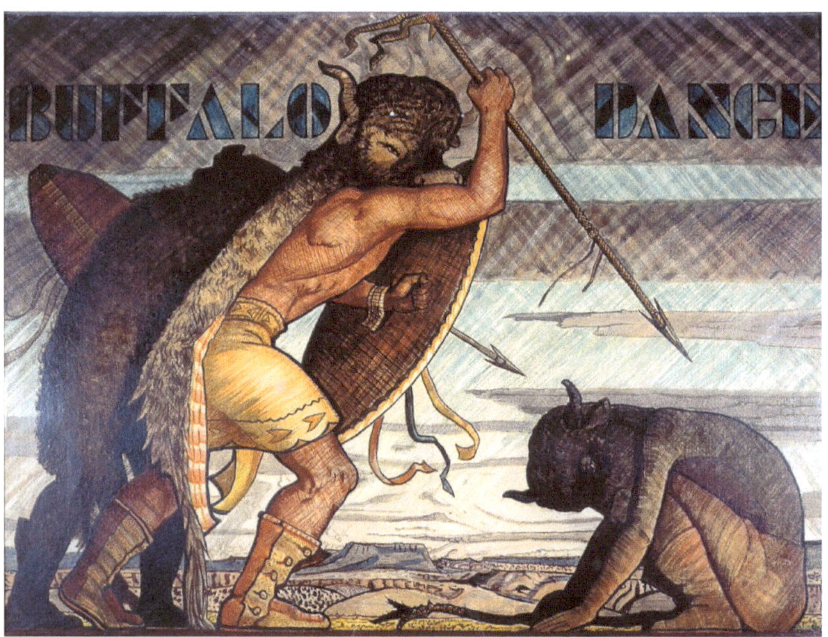

Buffalo Dance, Lloyd Moylan, painting, Kirtland Officers Club, Albuquerque.

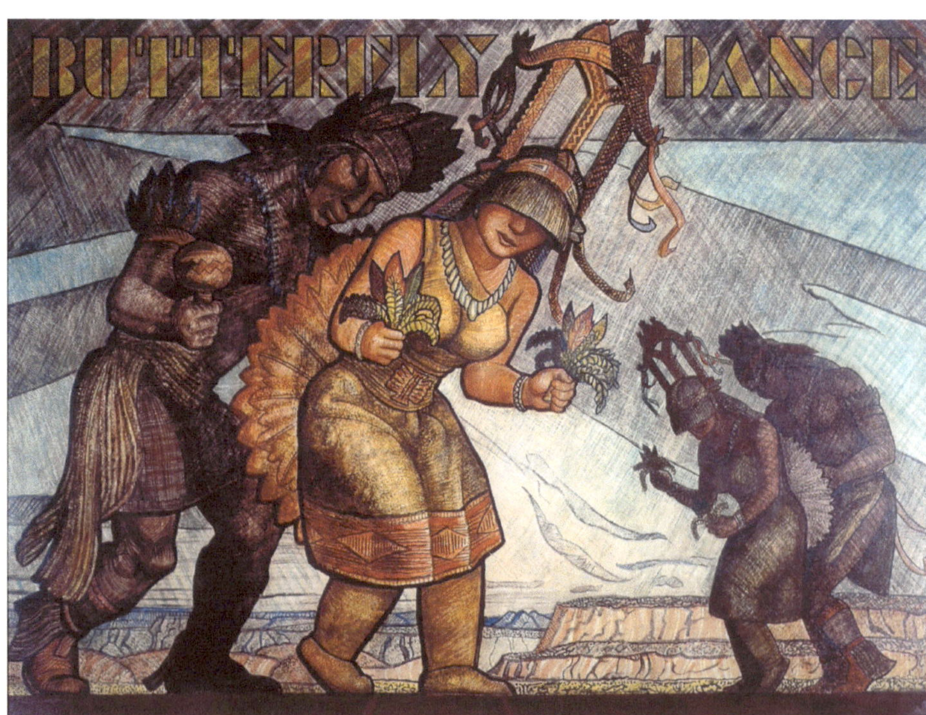

Butterfly Dance, Lloyd Moylan, painting, Kirtland Officers Club, Albuquerque.

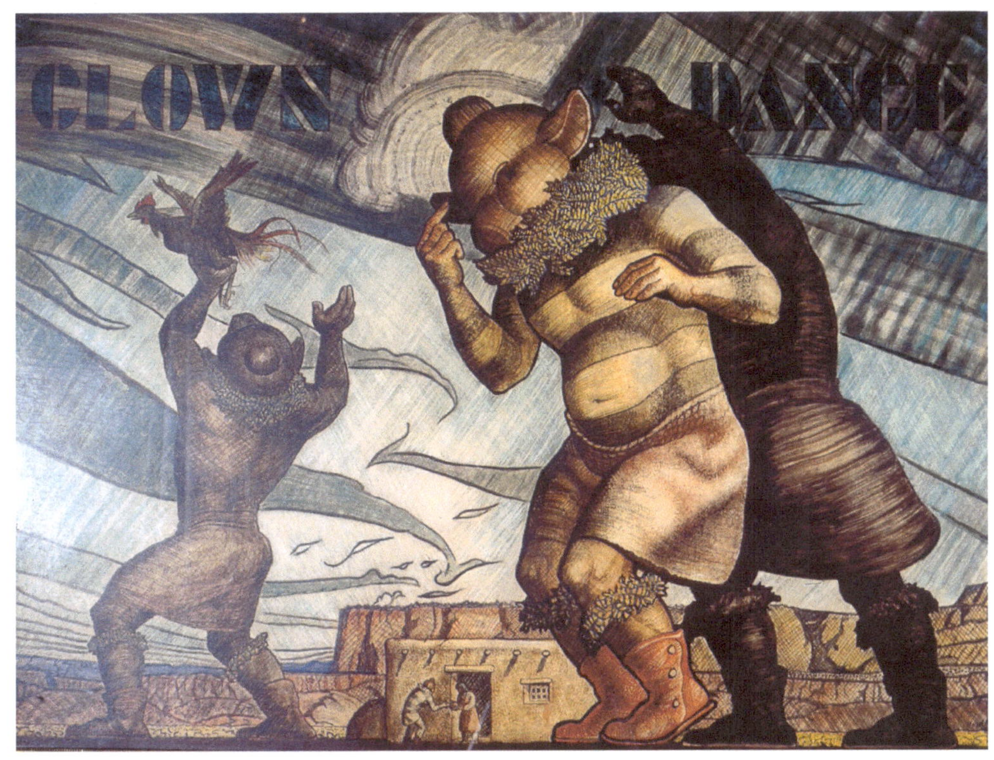

Clown Dance, Lloyd Moylan, painting, Kirtland Officers Club, Albuquerque.

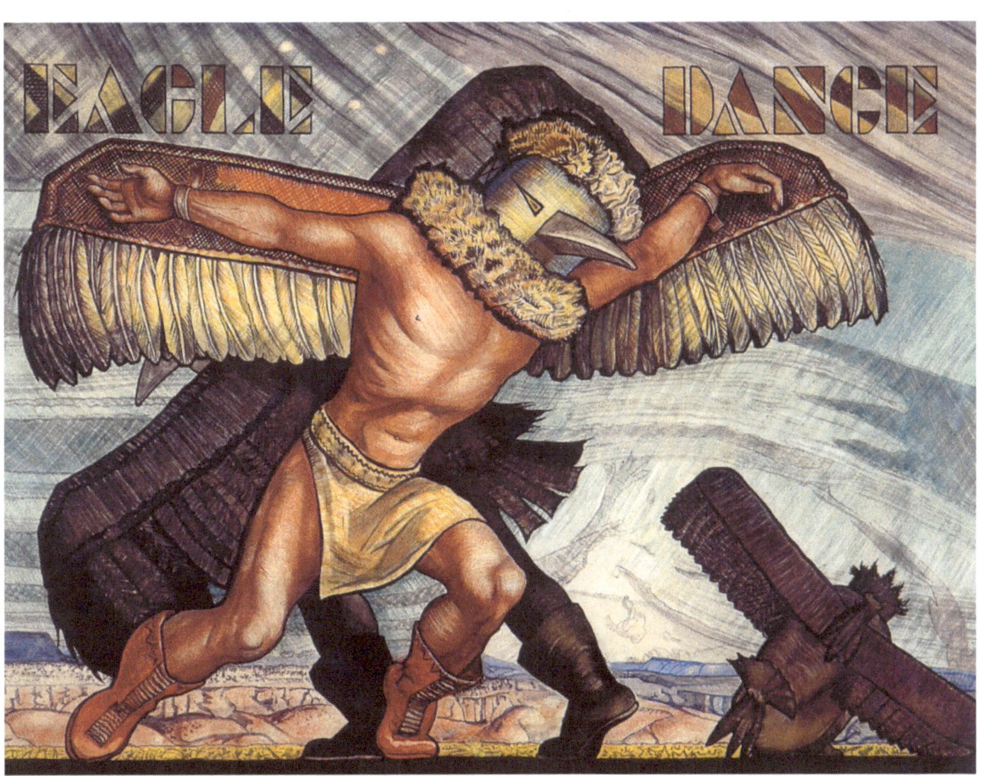

Eagle Dance, Lloyd Moylan, painting, Kirtland Officers Club, Albuquerque.

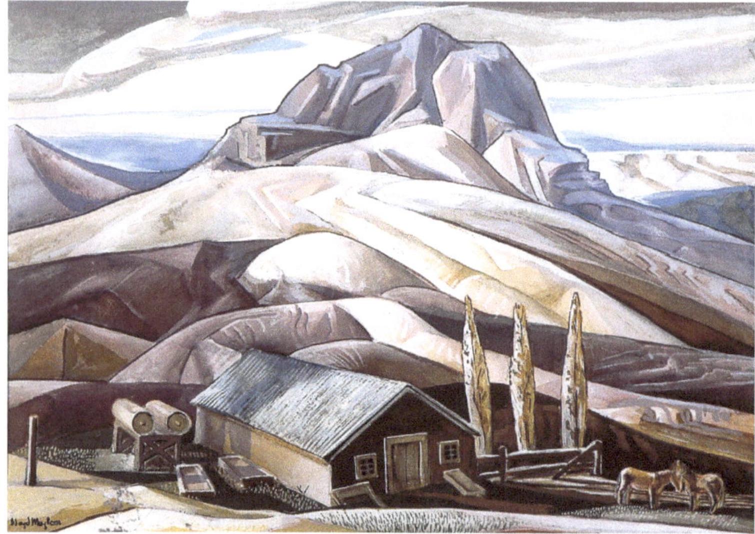

Storage Barn, Lloyd Moylan, painting, McKinley County Courthouse, Gallup.

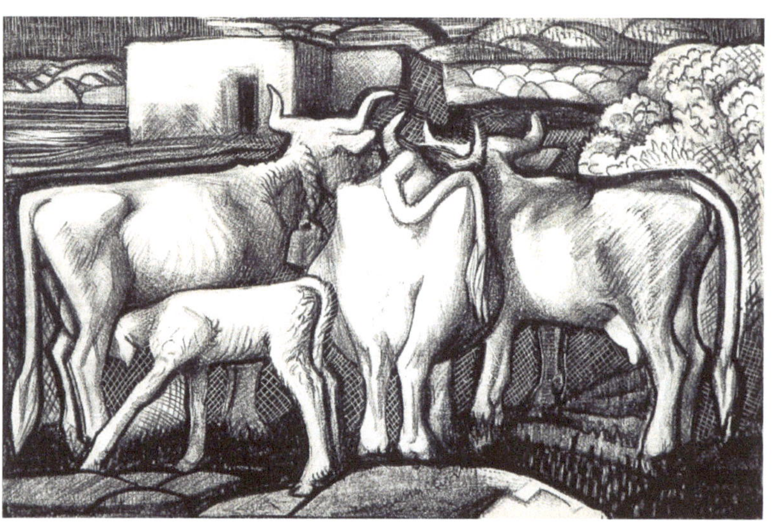

Dinner, Lloyd Moylan, litho print, McKinley County Courthouse, Gallup.

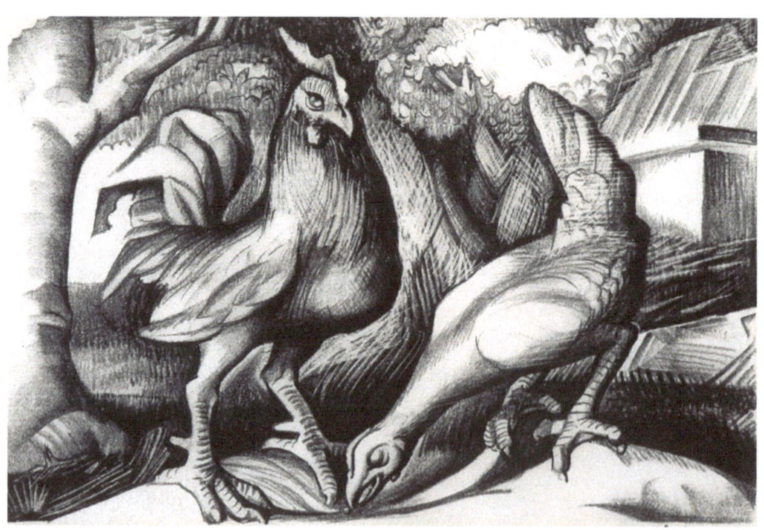

The Bread Winner, Lloyd Moylan, litho print, McKinley County Courthouse, Gallup.

Eulogia Naranjo

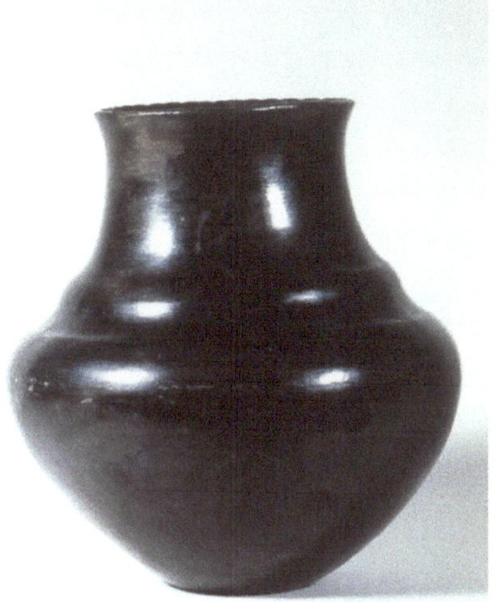

Blackware Jar, Eulogia Naranjo, pottery, National Park Service, Santa Fe. Photograph courtesy of the National Park Service (SRO 349).

Willard Nash Born, 1898, Philadelphia, Pennsylvania; died, 1943, Albuquerque, New Mexico. Studied art in Detroit. Moved to New Mexico in 1920. Studied with Andrew Dasburg and was a founding member of the group called Los Cinco Pintores. Became known as a Santa Fe modernist. Taught art for a time in California.

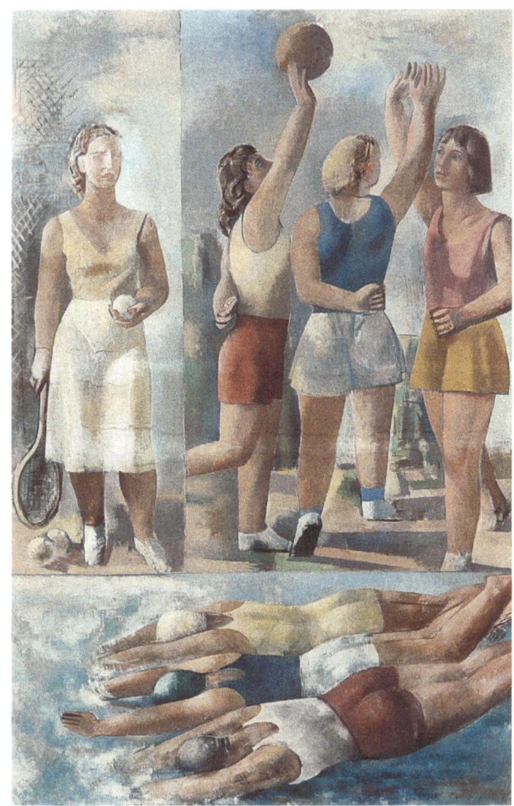

Untitled, Willard Nash, one of a series of athletic paintings, University of New Mexico Fine Arts Museum, Albuquerque.

Helmuth Naumer Born, 1907, Reutilingen, Germany; died, 1989, Santa Fe, New Mexico. Traveled around the world before settling in New Mexico. In 1927 lived with the Santo Domingo Indians. Settled in Santa Fe a year or two later. Landscape and people of New Mexico became his lifelong subject.

San Ildefonso, Helmuth Naumer, pastel painting, Bandelier National Monument Archives, Bandelier.

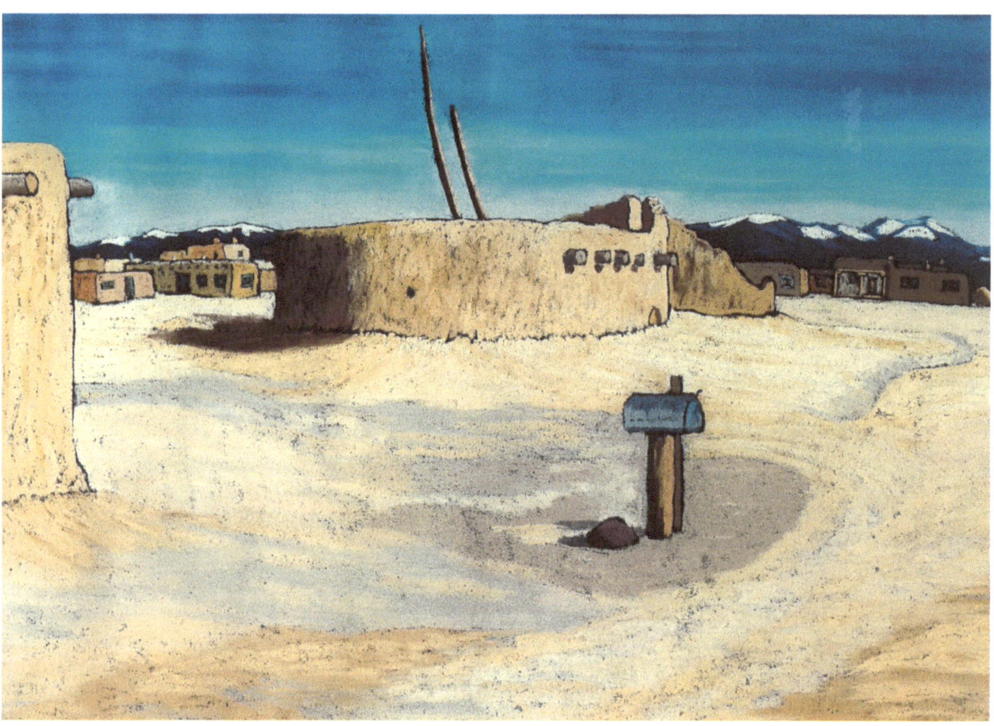

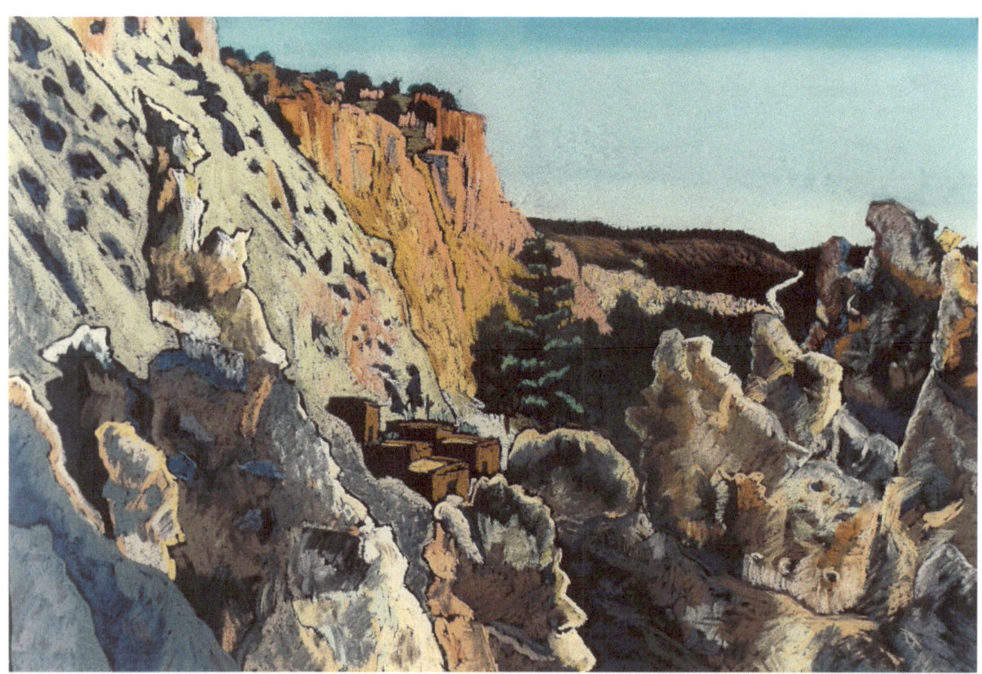

Ruins, Helmuth Naumer, pastel painting, Bandelier National Monument Archives, Bandelier.

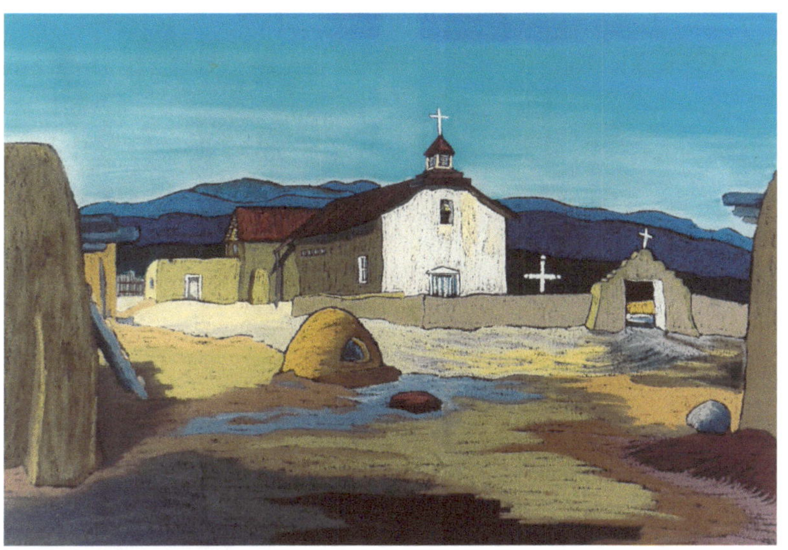

Picuris Pueblo, Helmuth Naumer, pastel painting, Bandelier National Monument Archives, Bandelier.

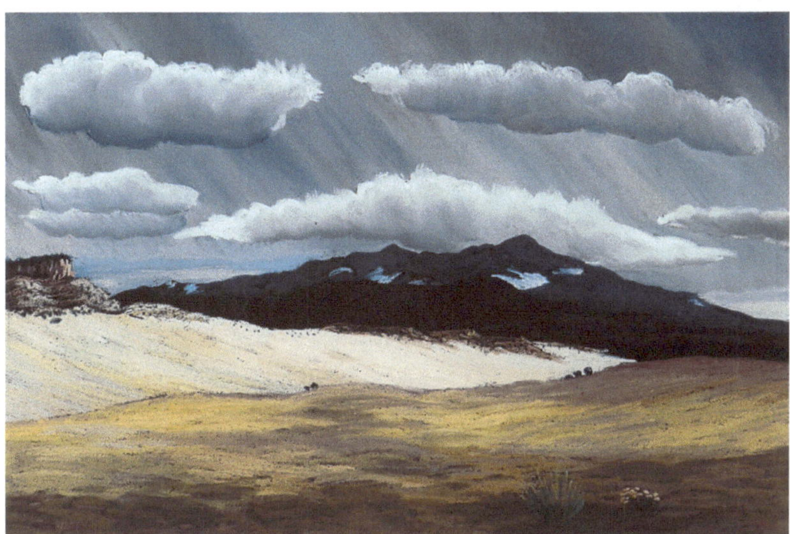

Mount Taylor, Helmuth Naumer, pastel painting, Clayton High School, Clayton.

Canoncito, Helmuth Naumer, pastel painting, Clayton High School, Clayton.

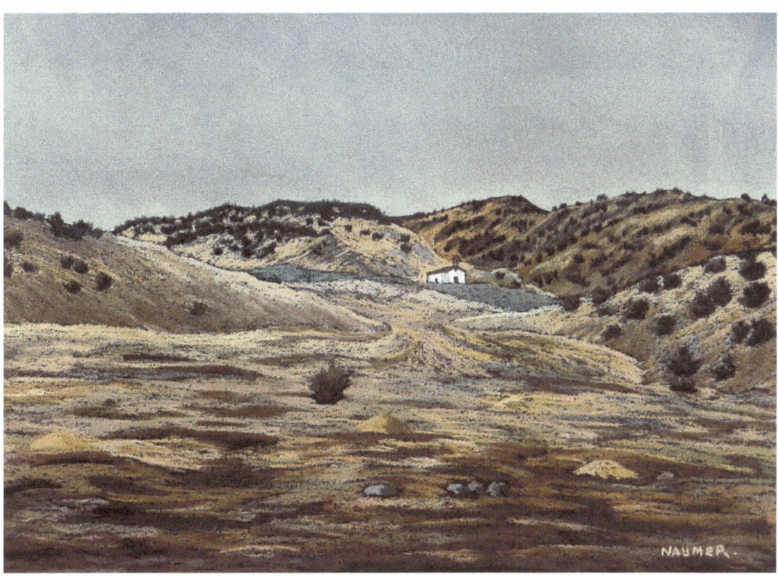

B. J. O. Nordfeldt Born, 1878, Tullstorp, Sweden; died, 1955, Henderson, Texas. Came to the U.S. in 1891. Studied at the Art Institute, Chicago; later in Europe. In 1919 settled in Santa Fe where he lived for the next twenty years. Taught, painted portraits, and made a series of lithographs that were sent to the public schools.

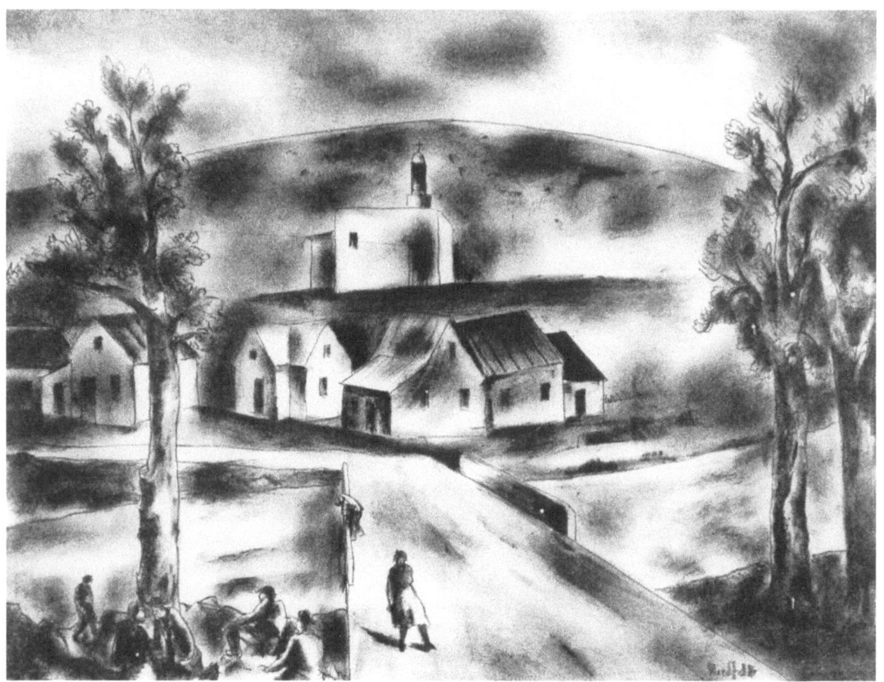

Tres Ritos, B. J. O. Nordfeldt, lithograph, National Park Service Regional Office, Santa Fe, and other sites.

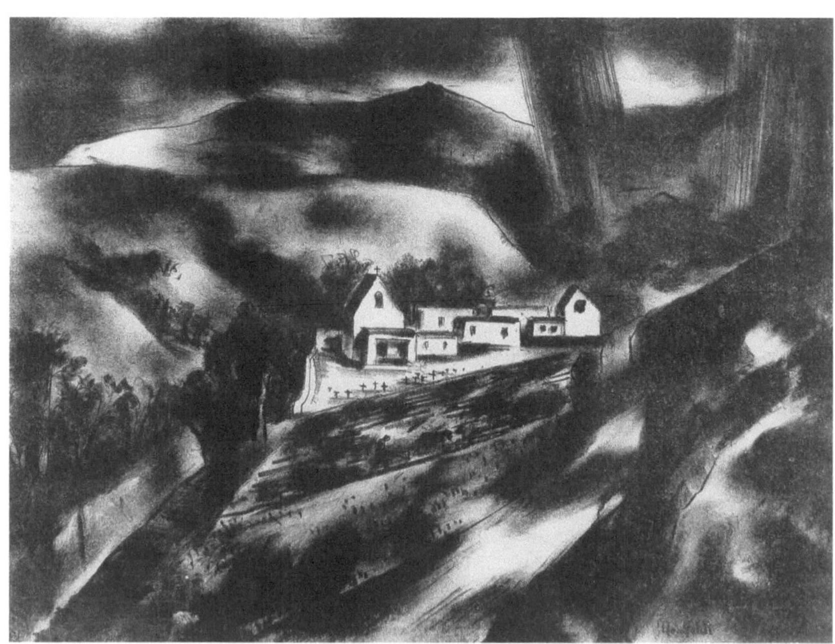

Rio en Medio, B. J. O. Nordfeldt, lithograph, Clayton High School, Clayton, and other sites.

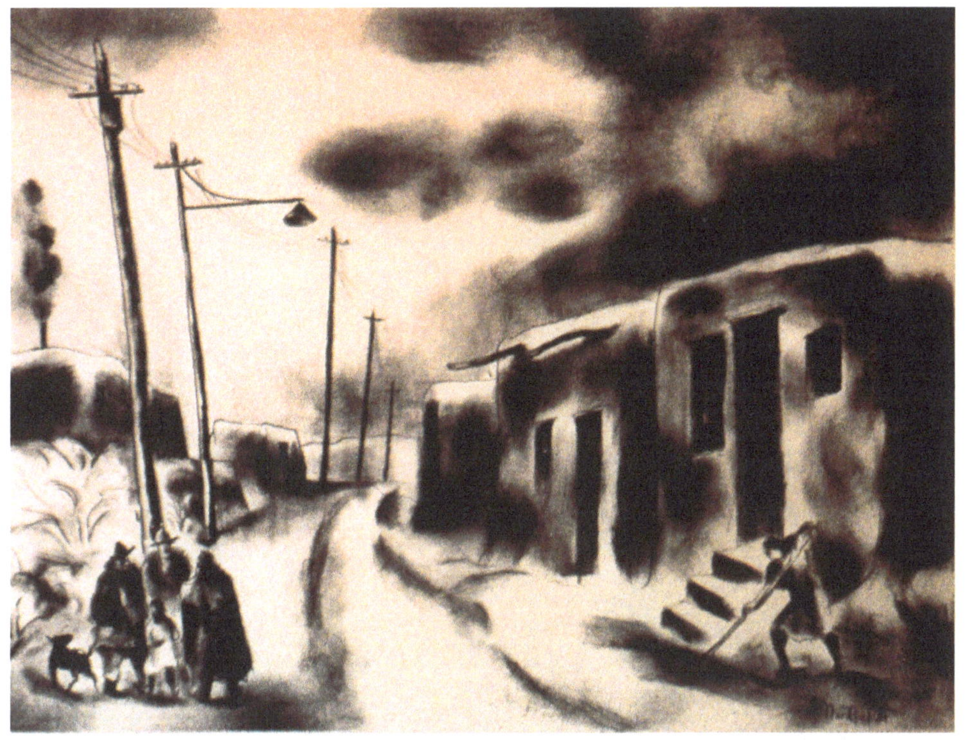

Canyon Road, B. J. O. Nordfeldt, lithograph, National Park Service Regional Office, Santa Fe, and other sites.

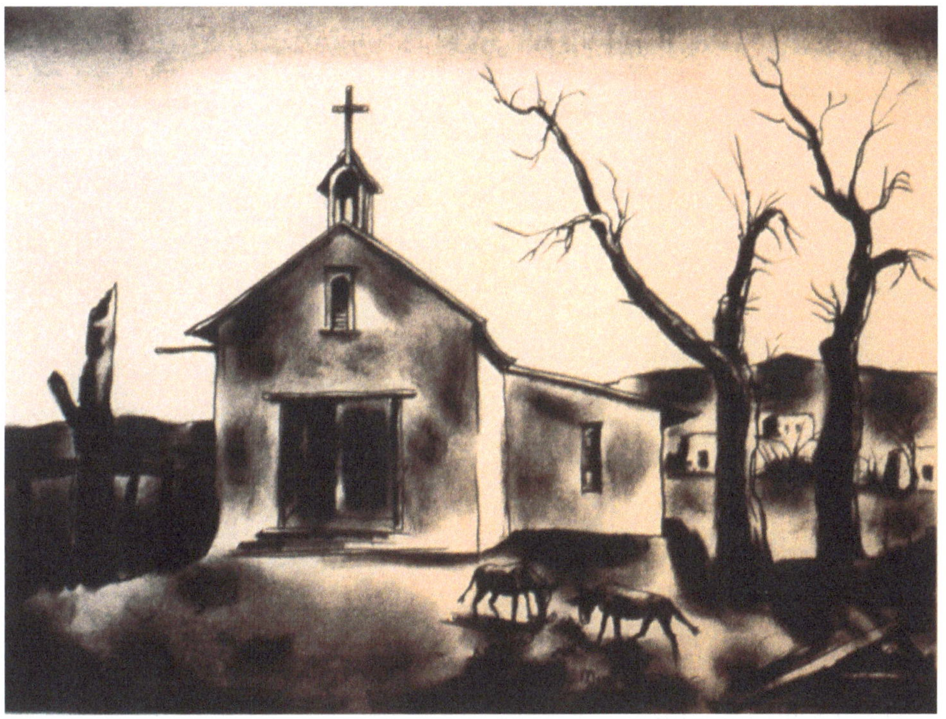

Morada, Santa Cruz, B. J. O. Nordfeldt, lithograph, National Park Service Regional Office, Santa Fe, and other sites.
Photograph courtesy of the National Park Service (C13919, SWRO 368).

Max Ortiz (Dates unknown) Born in Pena Blanca, New Mexico. He was a painter and weaver and taught weaving on Spanish looms at the Melrose Art Center as a part of the Federal Art Program.

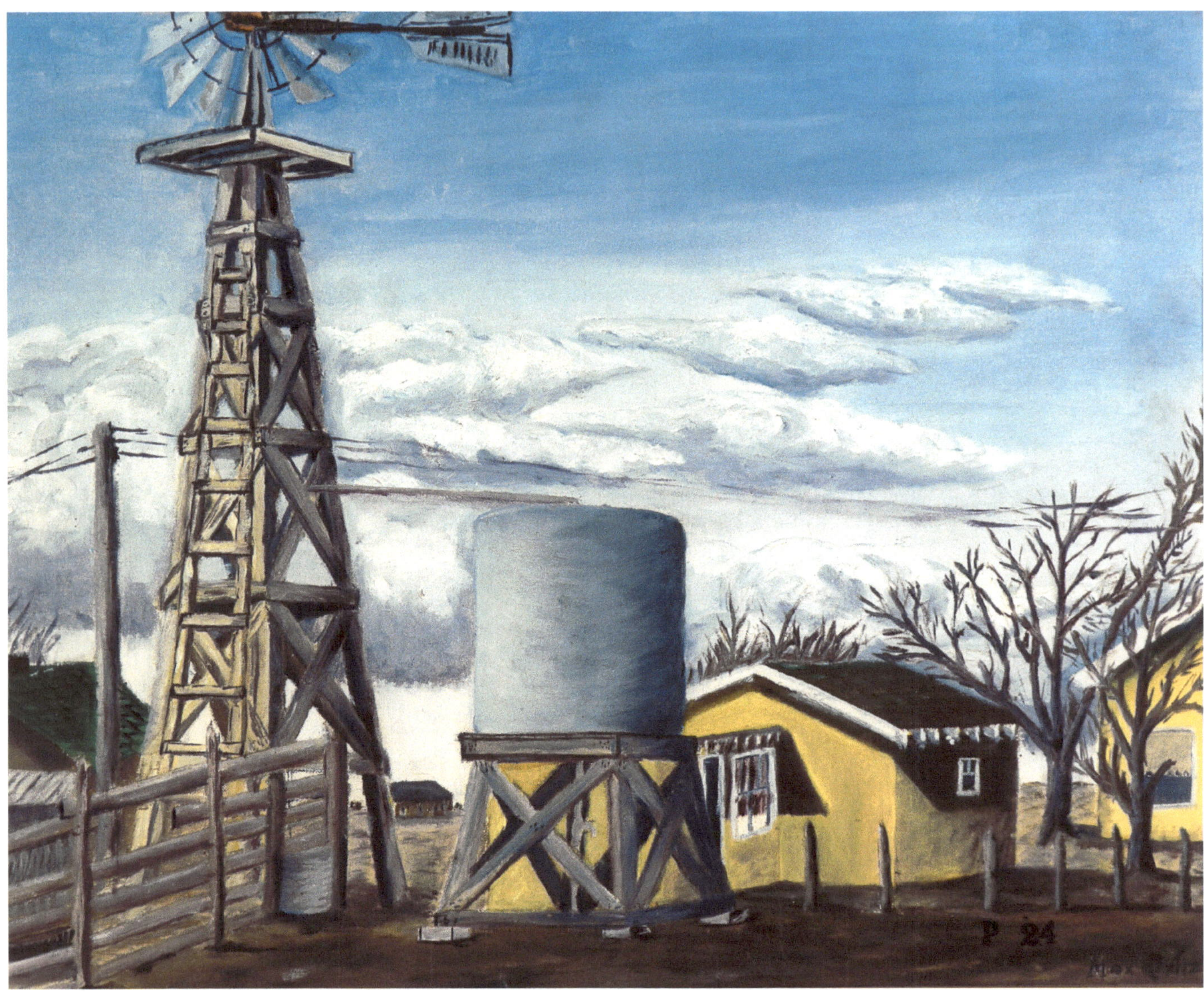

Windmill, Max Ortiz, painting, Melrose High School, Melrose.

Sheldon Parsons Born, 1866, Rochester, New York; died, 1943, Albuquerque, New Mexico. Studied at the Academy of Design, New York. Began a successful career as a portrait artist until ill health and his wife's death brought him west. Came to Santa Fe in 1913 to recover from tuberculosis, stayed on to continue an active career as an artist.

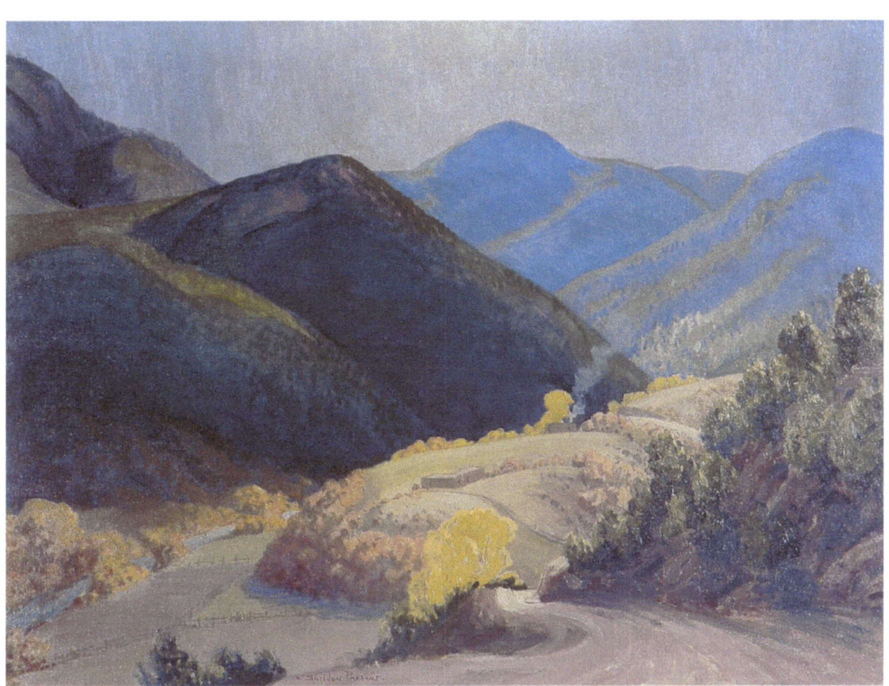

Chupadero, Sheldon Parsons, painting, New Mexico School for the Deaf, Santa Fe.

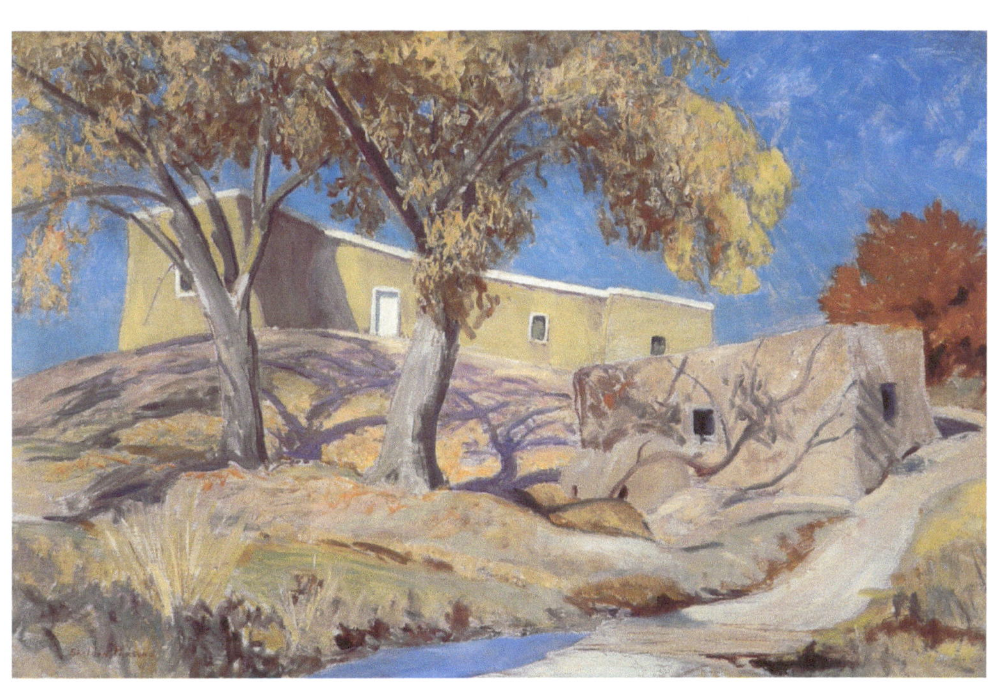

Casa on the Hill, Sheldon Parsons, painting, McKinley County Courthouse, Gallup.

Bert Phillips Born, 1868, Hudson, New York; died, 1956, San Diego, California. Studied at the National Academy of Design and the Art Students League, New York; Academie Julian, Paris. Came to New Mexico in 1898 with Ernest Blumenschein on a painting expedition. They bought a team and wagon and started south. When their wagon broke down, so the story goes, they went down to Taos to have it fixed and stayed on. Phillips became a founding member of the Taos Society of Artists, lived in Taos for the next sixty years. Painted two of the frescoes in the old Taos Courthouse: The Shadow of Crime and Sufficient Law Protects. (Also see Fresco Quartet.)

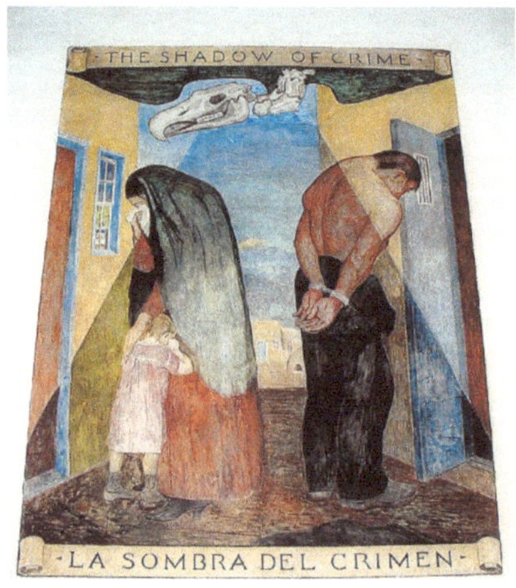

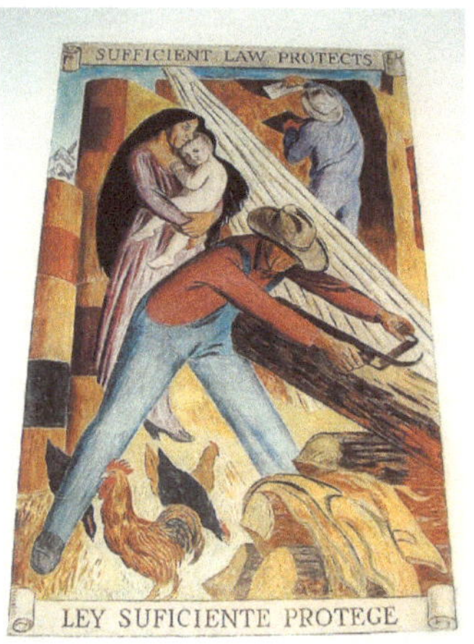

Agapina Quintana

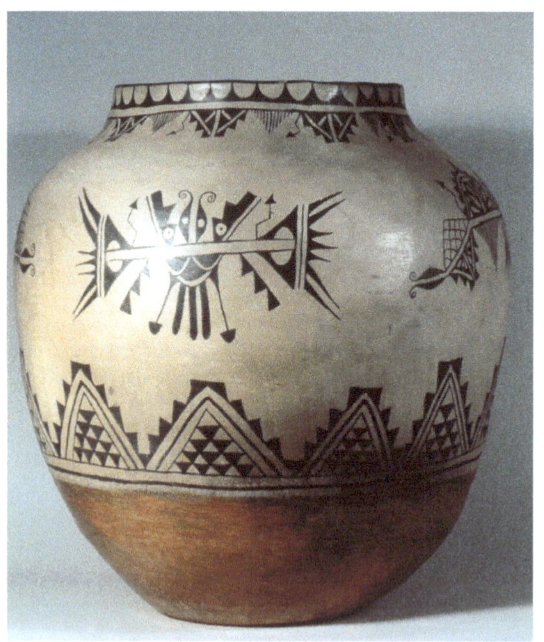

Storage Jar, Agapina Quintana, pottery,
National Park Service Regional Office, Santa Fe.
Photograph courtesy of the National Park Service (C13876, SWRO 305).

Eliseo Jose Rodriguez Born, 1915, Santa Fe, New Mexico. Studied at the Santa Fe Art School where he painted for three years. One of a group of New Mexican artists who painted murals for the Texas Centennial. He and his family have become internationally known for reviving the traditional craft of straw inlay mosaic work. For the New Deal, worked on the Portfolio of Spanish Colonial Design in New Mexico and other portfolios for the Laboratory of Anthropology. Assisted Louie Ewing in developing the silk screen process, new at that time, for the WPA.

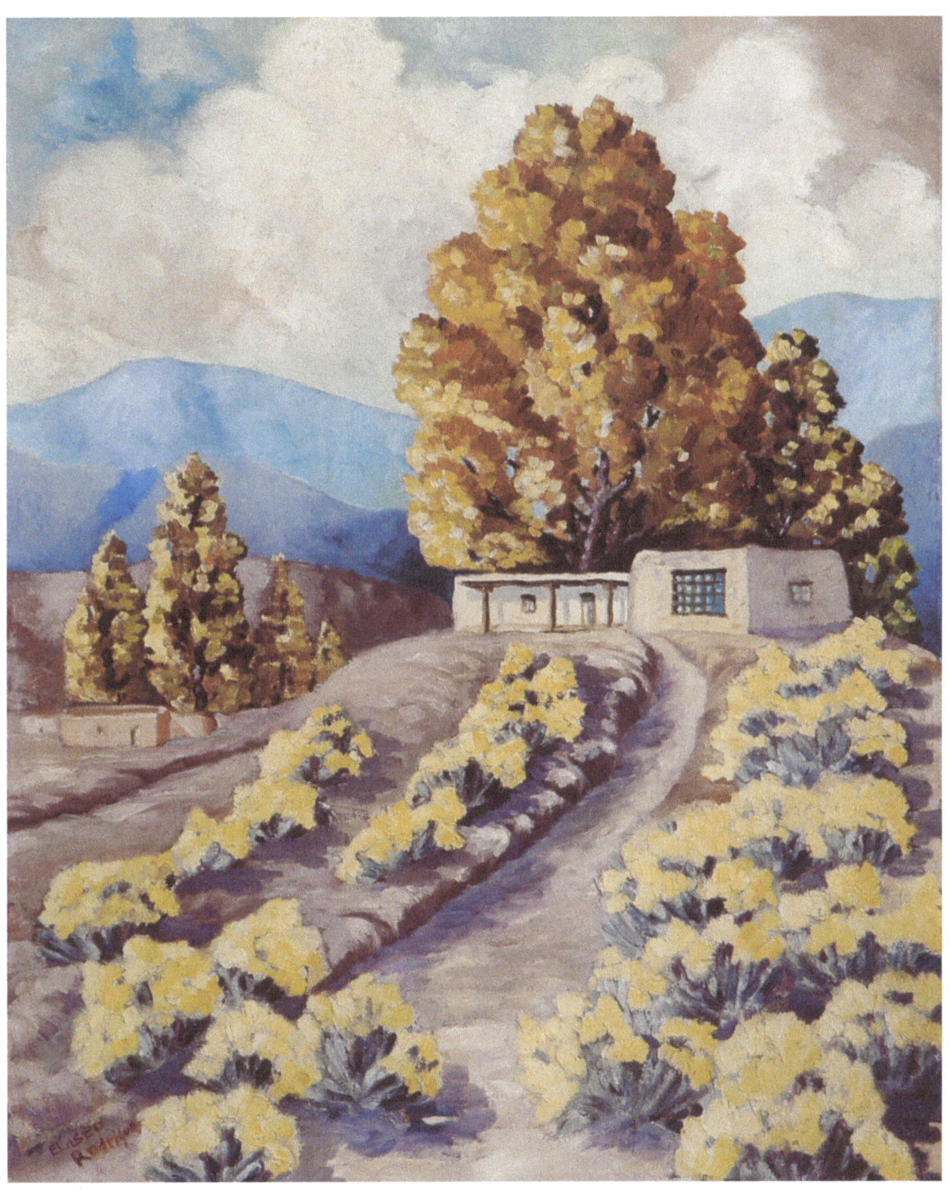

El Otonio, Eliseo Rodriguez, painting, Superintendents's office, Dexter Public Schools, Dexter.

Olive Rush Born, 1873, Fairmont, Indiana; died, 1966, Santa Fe, New Mexico. Studied at the Art Students League, New York; Howard Pyle School of Illustration, Delaware; Millar Class for Painters, Paris; Corcoran School of Art, Washington, D.C. Came to Santa Fe in 1920 and lived there for most of her lengthy career as an artist.

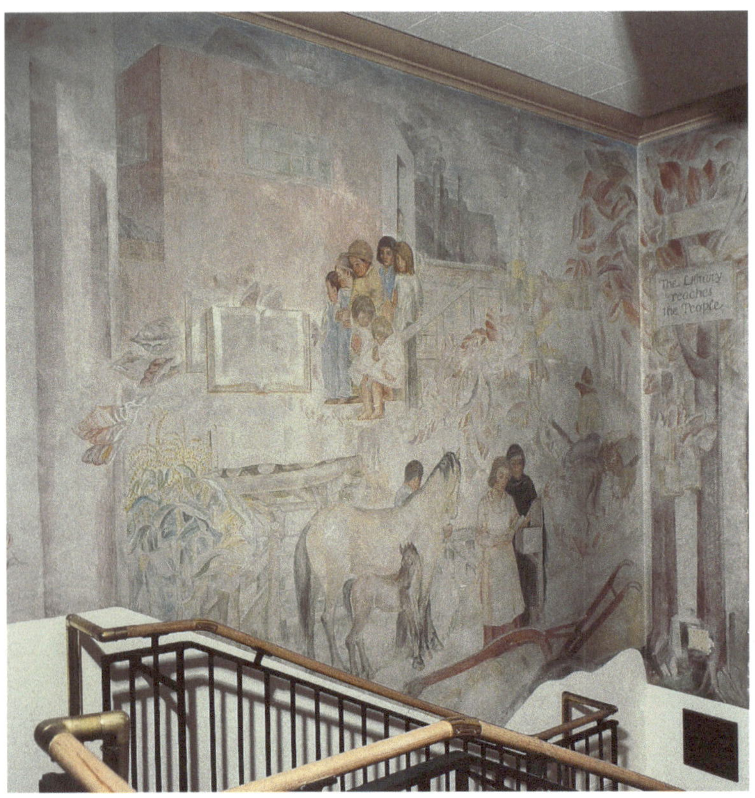

The Library Reaches the People, Olive Rush, fresco, Fray Anjelico Chavez History Library, Museum of New Mexico, Santa Fe.

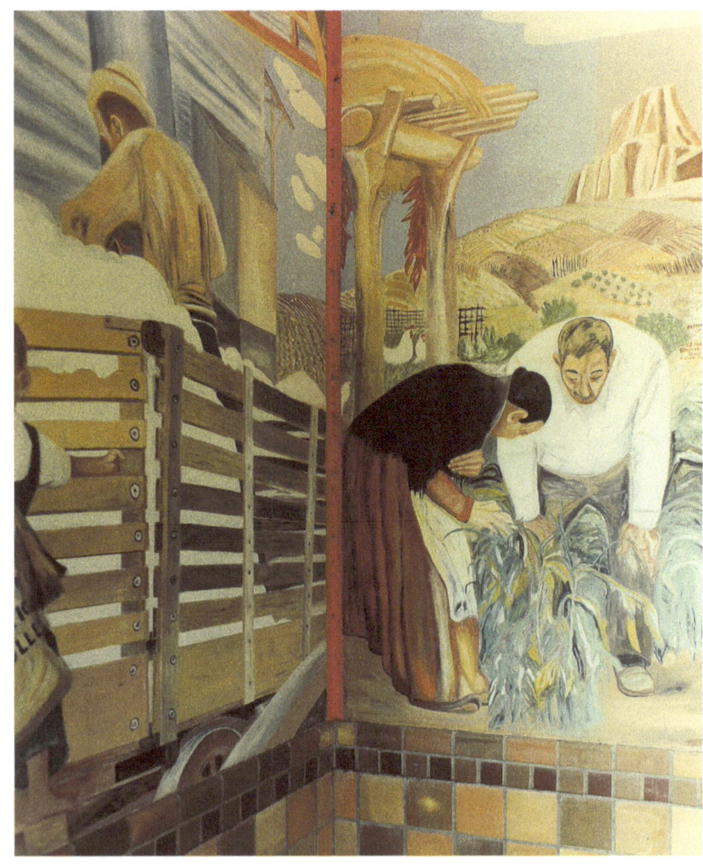

Untitled, Olive Rush, fresco, New Mexico State University, Biology Building, Las Cruces.

Juan Sanchez Born, 1901, Rio Pueblo, New Mexico; died, 1969, Raton, New Mexico. Spanish carver who worked in the Santero tradition. In 1936 employed by the Federal Art Project to create traditional carvings.

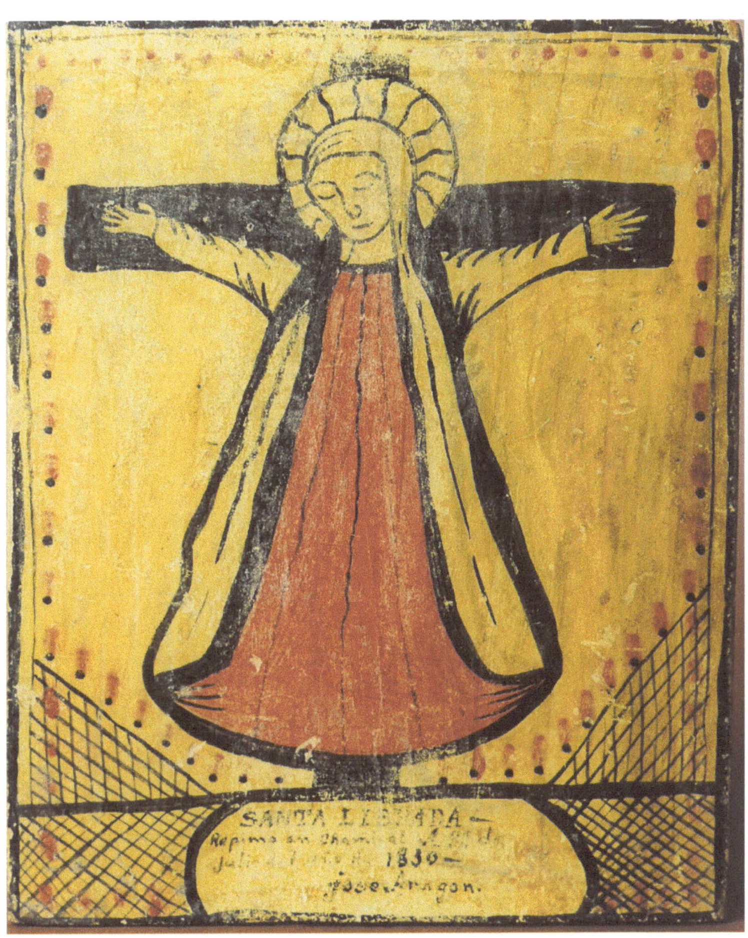

Santa Libhada, Juan Sanchez, retablo, Museum of International Folk Art, Santa Fe.

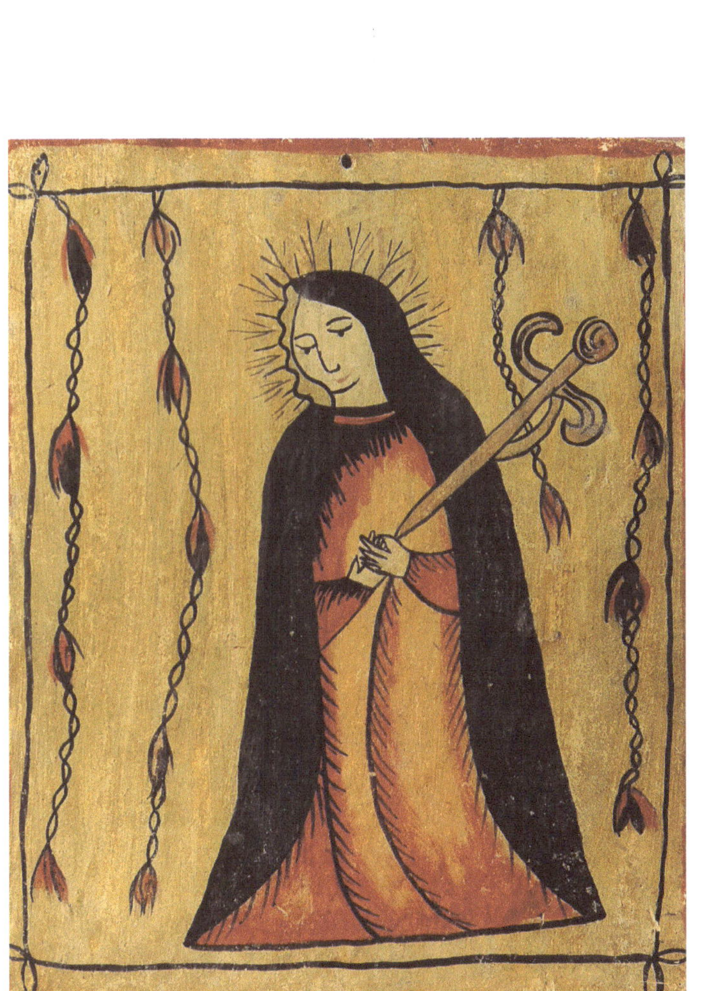

Our Lady of Sorrows, Juan Sanchez, retablo, Museum of International Folk Art, Santa Fe.

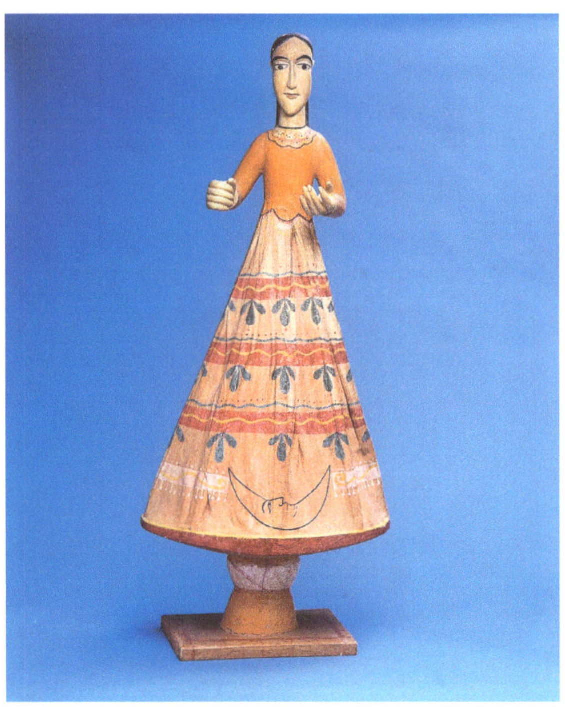

Immaculada Concepcion, Juan Sanchez, santo,
Palace of the Governors Museum, Santa Fe.
Photograph courtesy of the Museum (10751/45, D12).

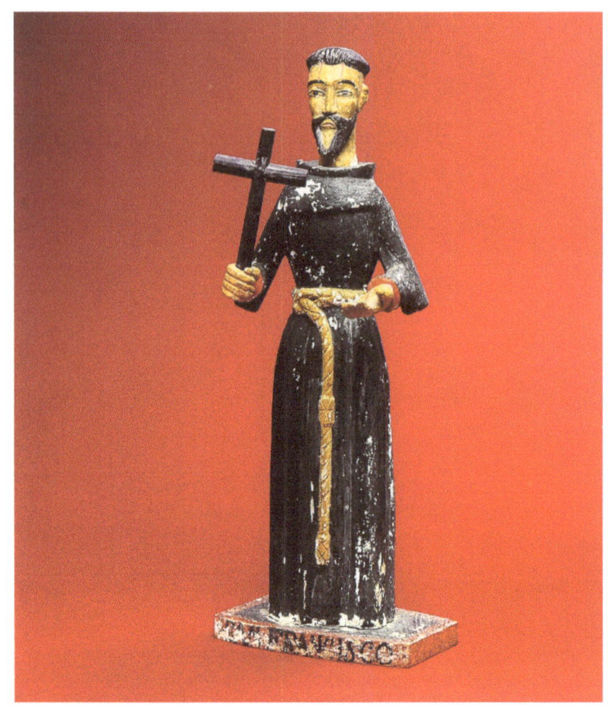

San Francisco, Juan Sanchez, bulto,
Palace of the Governors Museum, Santa Fe.
Photograph courtesy of the Museum (11385/45, D13).

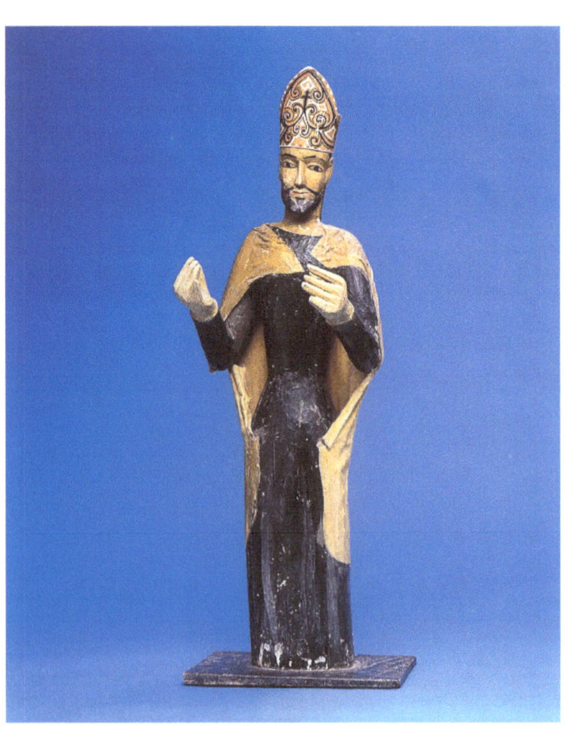

San Juan, Juan Sanchez, bulto,
Palace of the Governors Museum, Santa Fe.
Photograph courtesy of the Museum (10052/45, D14).

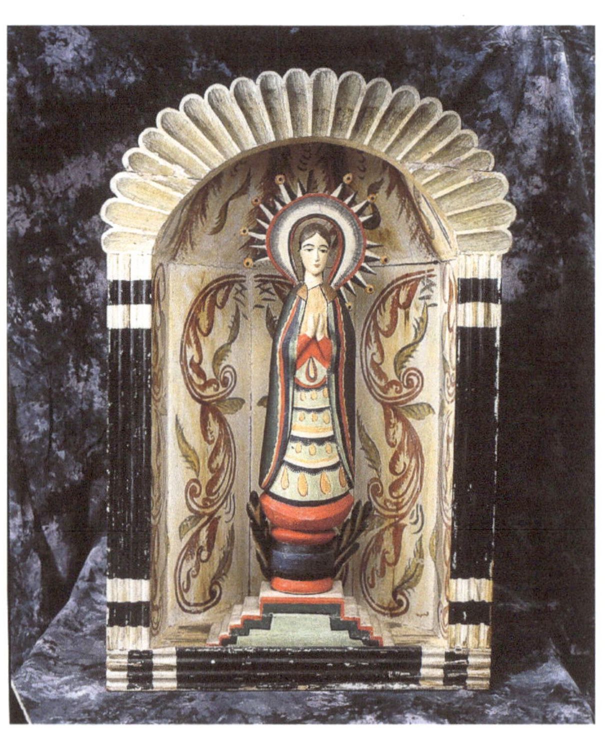

Nuestra Senora de la Luz, Juan Sanchez, bulto,
Palace of the Governors Museum, Santa Fe.
Photograph courtesy of the Museum (10752/45, D15).

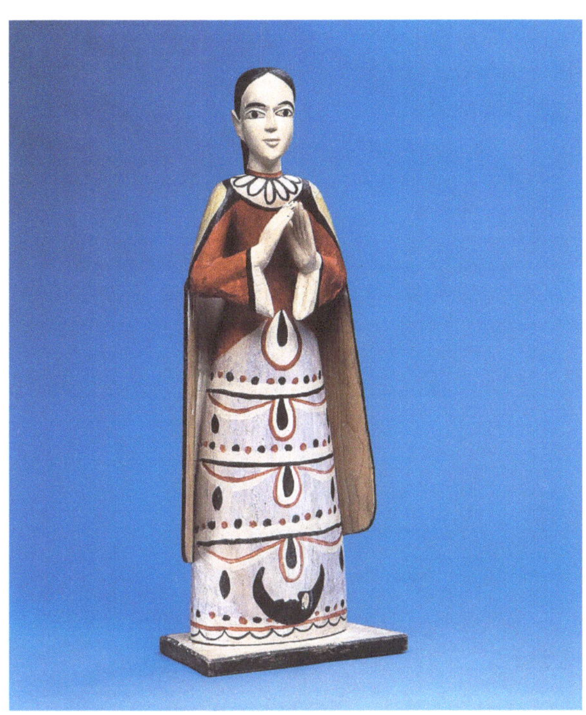

Nuestra Senora de la Purisima Concepcion, Juan Sanchez, bulto, Palace of the Governors Museum, Santa Fe. Photograph courtesy of the Museum (10749/45, D16).

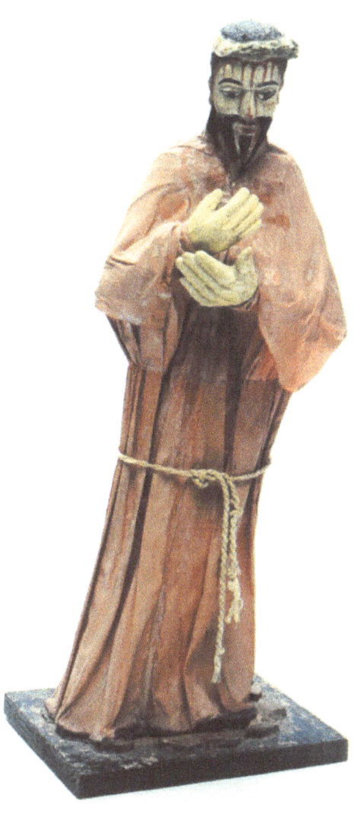

Jesus Nazareno, Juan Sanchez, bulto, Palace of the Governors Museum, Santa Fe. Photograph courtesy of the Museum (10748/45, D17).

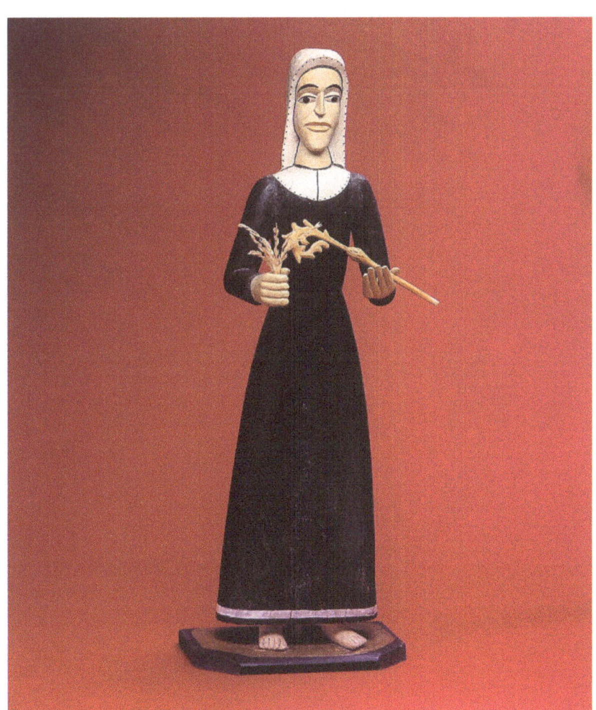

Santa Fertrudes, Juan Sanchez, bulto, Palace of the Governors Museum, Santa Fe. Photograph courtesy of the Museum (10750/45, D18).

Howard Behling Schleeter Born, 1903, Buffalo, New York; died, 1976, Placitas, New Mexico. Studied at the Albright Art School. Came to New Mexico in 1929. Worked in various media. In the 1930s developed a technique of pigment application that gave his work a raised mosaic appearance.

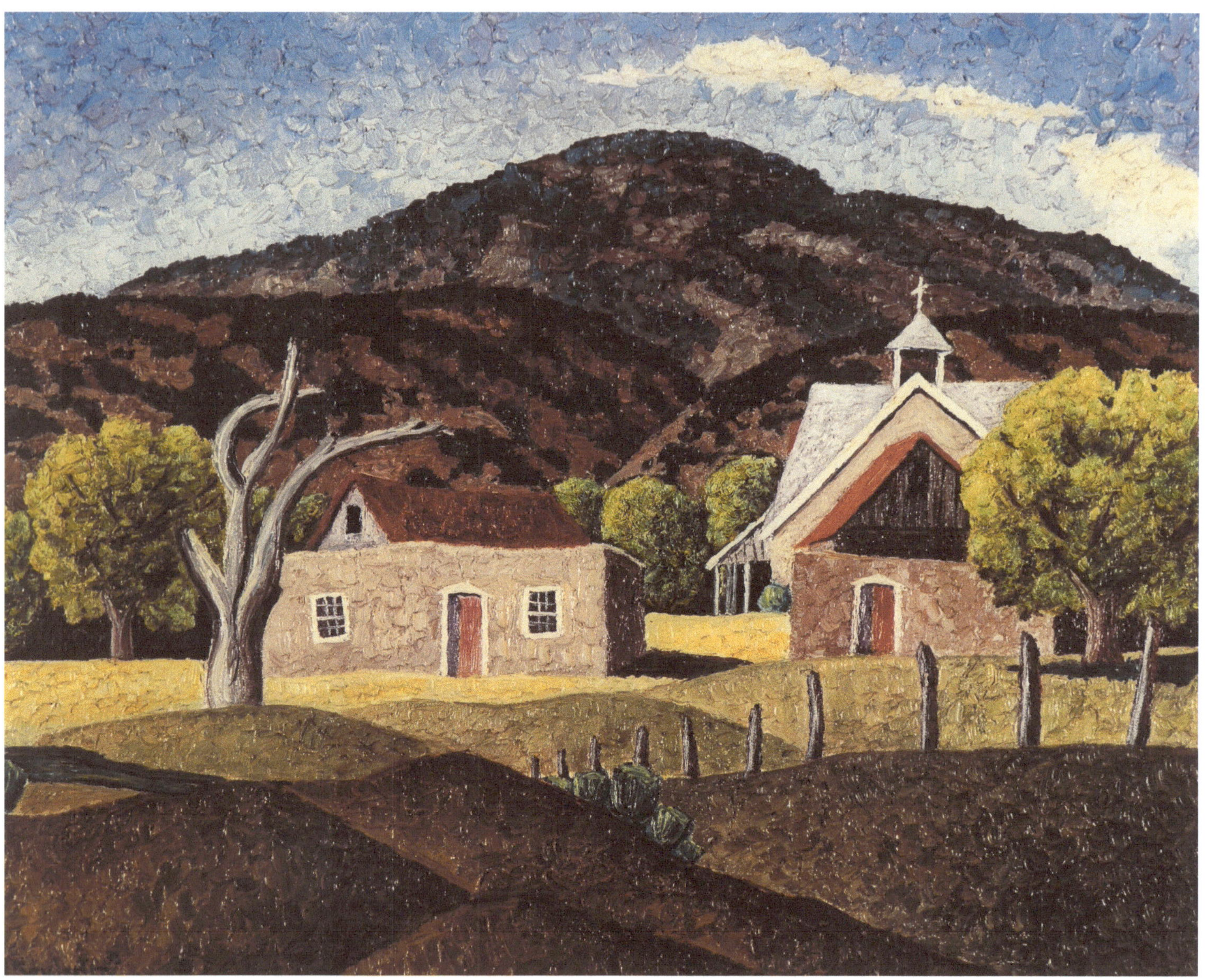

The Dead Tree, Howard Behling Schleeter, painting, Clayton High School, Clayton.

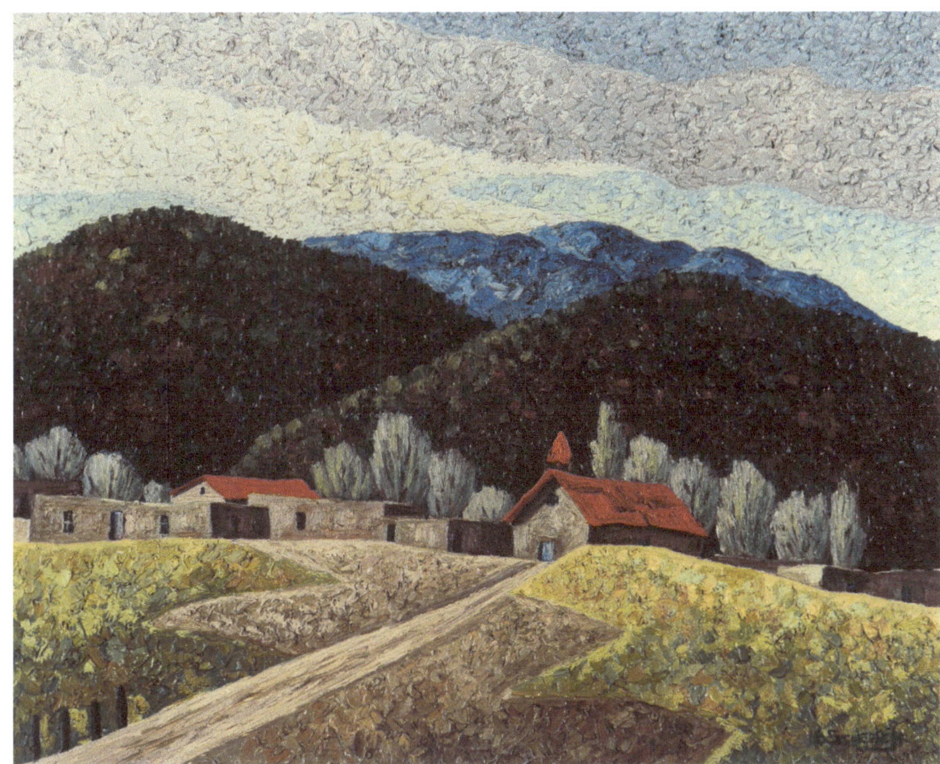

The Red Church,
Howard Behling Schleeter, painting,
Clayton High School, Clayton.

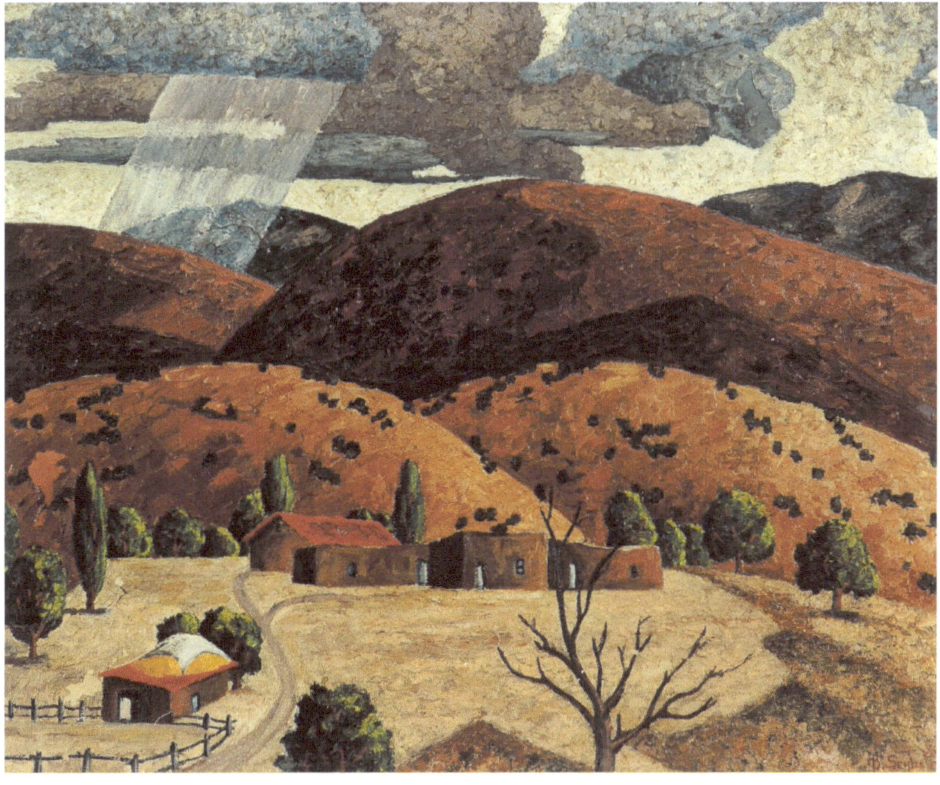

Rain, Howard Behling Schleeter, painting, Melrose High School, Melrose.

Eugenie Shonnard Born 1886, Yonkers, New York; died, 1978, Santa Fe, New Mexico. Studied at New York School of Applied Design for Women, with the noted Czechoslovakian painter Alphonse Mucha. Went to Paris to study sculpture, first under Rodin at the Grande Chaumiére, then under his student Emile Bourdelle. In 1914, returned to New York on the last steamer leaving France. Studied at the Art Students League. Came to Santa Fe after an active art career in New York. Did the terra cotta outdoor fountain, Carrie Tingley Hospital, Hot Springs (now the New Mexico Veterans Center, Truth or Consequences), under the first New Deal Art Program. Continued to live and work in New Mexico, exhibited nationally. She believed New Deal art programs were "very valuable" for artists and for the public. "Well, I think," she said, "at least they made people think in terms of sculpture, brought to their minds that there is such a thing [as art], and it is valuable."

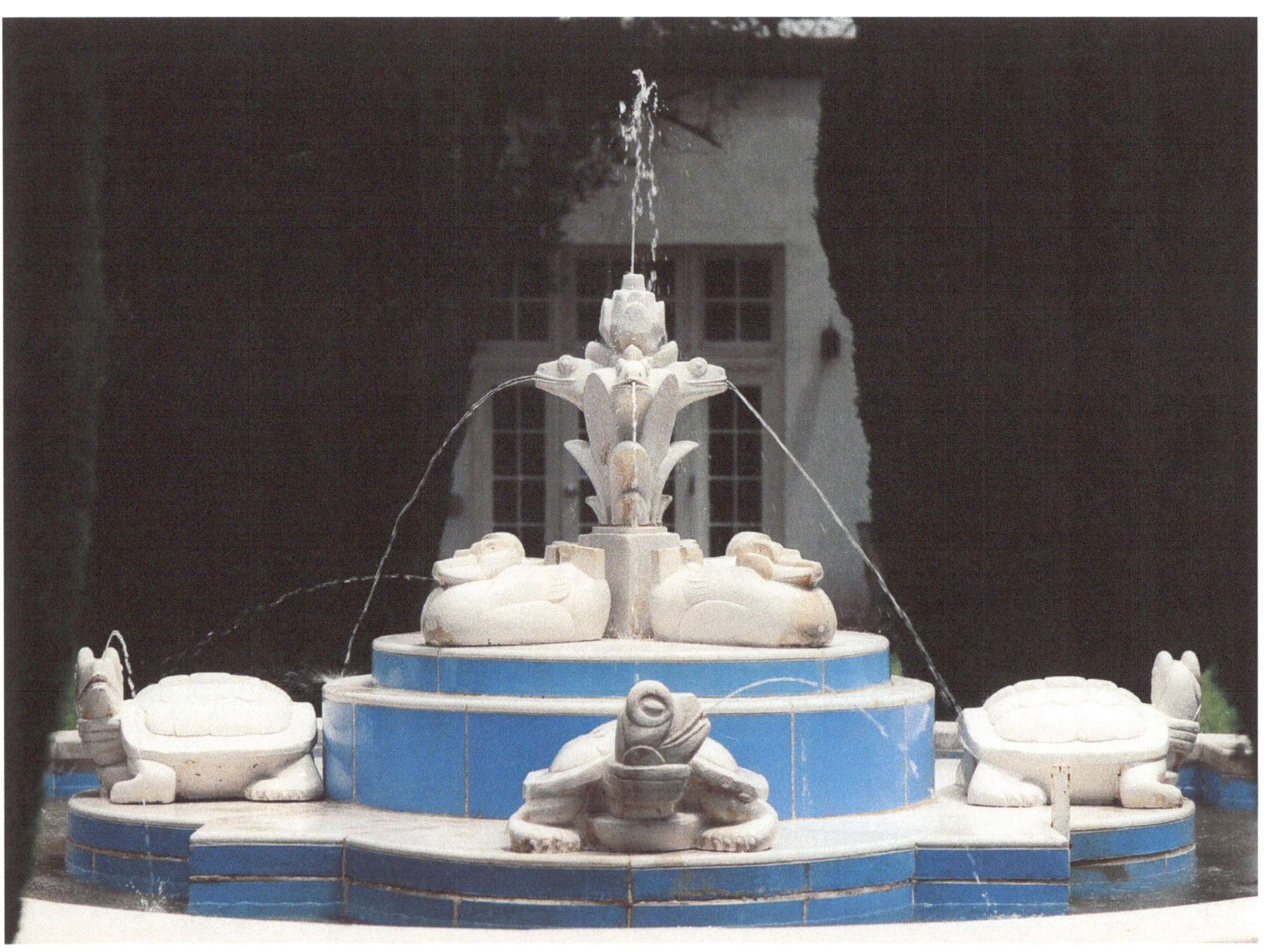

Turtle Fountain, Eugenie Shonnard, sculptured fountain, New Mexico Veterans Center, Truth or Consequences.

Will Shuster Born, 1893, Philadelphia, Pennsylvania; died, 1969, Santa Fe, New Mexico. Studied at the Drexel Institute, Philadelphia; later in Santa Fe with John Sloan. Came to New Mexico in 1920 to recover from tuberculosis, lived in Santa Fe for the rest of his life. One of the five painters who called themselves Los Cinco Pintores. In 1925 he and the artist Gustave Baumann created Zozobra, Old Man Gloom, the famous puppet burned each year at the Santa Fe Fiesta. Shuster said of his frescoes in the Museum of Fine Arts patio in Santa Fe: "They are pure fresco. . . . I studied it, but not with an experienced hand. I blundered my way into it. I experimented in my studio."

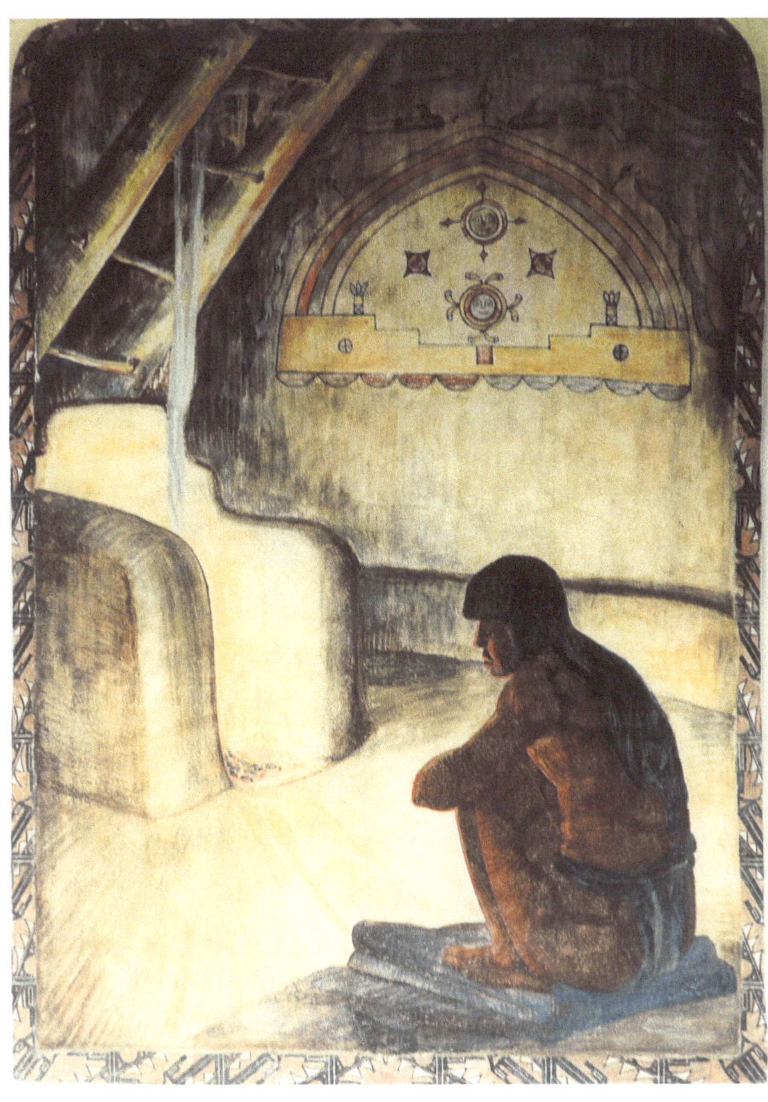

Voices of the Earth, Will Shuster, fresco, Museum of Fine Arts patio, Santa Fe.

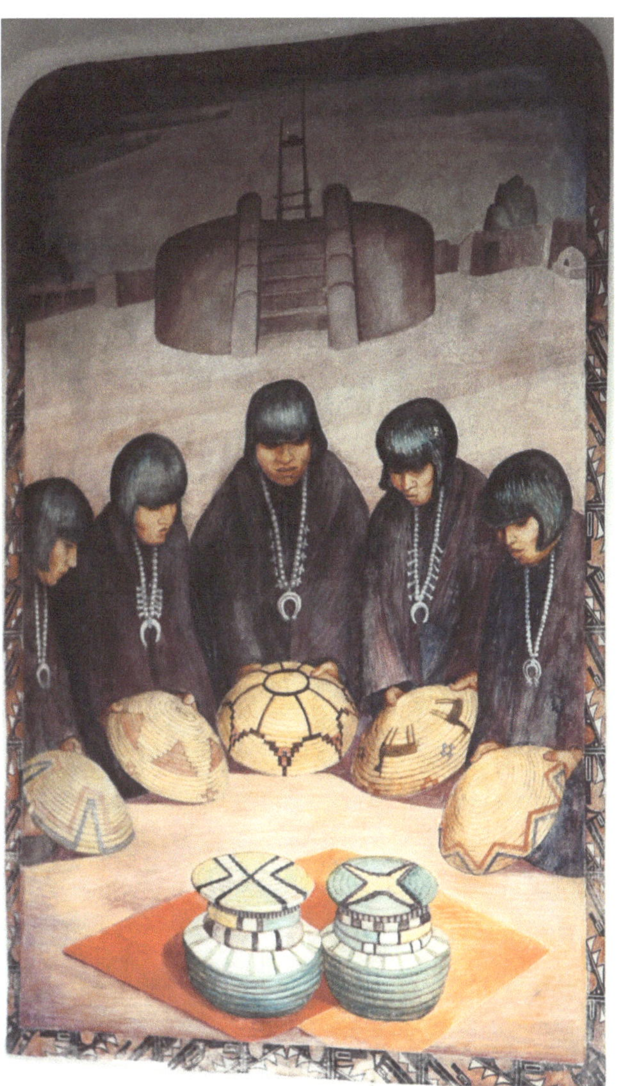

Voices of the Sipophe, Will Shuster, fresco, Museum of Fine Arts patio, Santa Fe.

Walter Ufer Born, 1876, Louisville, Kentucky; died, 1936, Taos, New Mexico. Received his early art training from his father, an engraver of gunstocks. Studied for many years in Germany and at the Chicago Art Institute. Came to Taos in 1915, was elected to the Taos Society of Artists, had an active career as a painter of Southwest scenes.

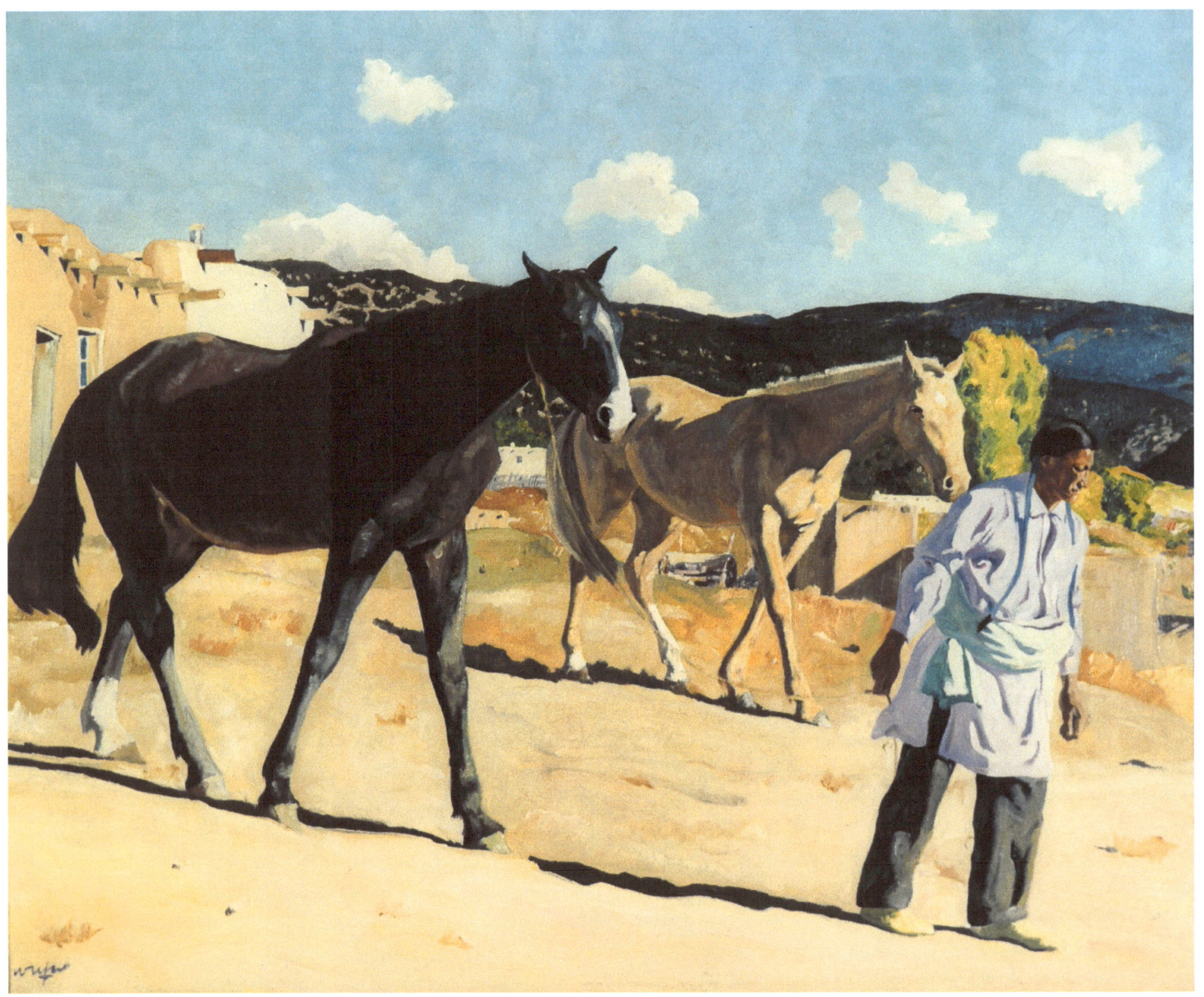

Blaze and Buckskin, Walter Ufer, painting, University of New Mexico Fine Arts Museum, Albuquerque.

Theodore Van Soelen Born, 1890, St. Paul, Minnesota; died, 1964, Santa Fe, New Mexico. Studied at the Institute of Arts and Science, St. Paul; the Pennsylvania Academy of Arts; and Europe. Moved to New Mexico for his health in 1916. Worked for a time as a painter-illustrator in Albuquerque. Moved to San Isidro trading post, finally to Santa Fe and Tesuque. For the WPA post office mural, the Portales News commented on his search for authentic materials: "The artist photographed sand hills and prairie and took back to his studio a car load of bear grass and other flora to be sure that his painting would accurately portray the Roosevelt County landscape."

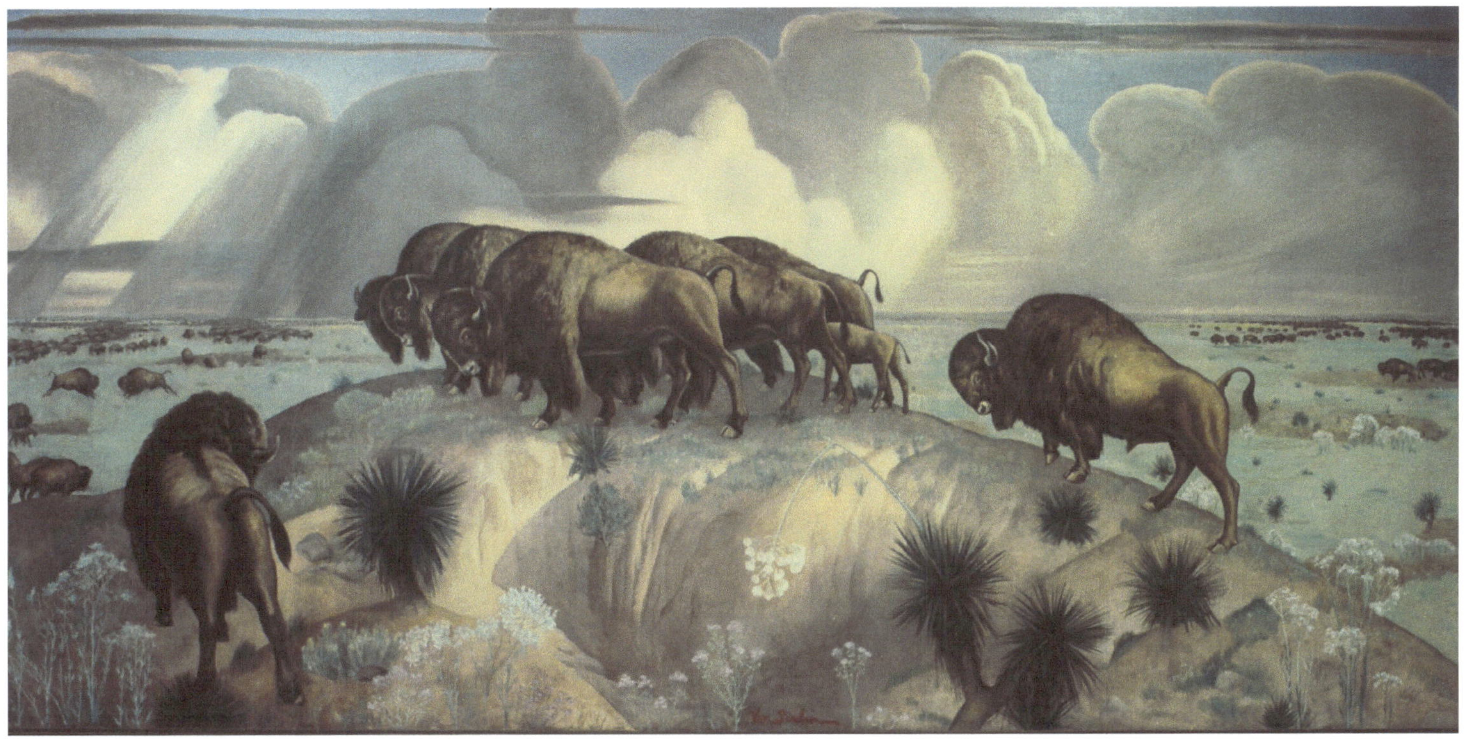

Buffalo Range, Theodore Van Soelen, mural, U.S. Post Office, Portales

Pablita Velarde Born, 1918, Santa Clara Pueblo, New Mexico. Studied at Saint Catherine's Indian School, then with Dorothy Dunn at the U.S. Indian School in Santa Fe. In 1939 at the age of nineteen she signed on with the WPA and worked at Bandelier National Monument. Under the supervision of the Park Service, she produced a large number of paintings. Her work there was the beginning of a highly successful art career.

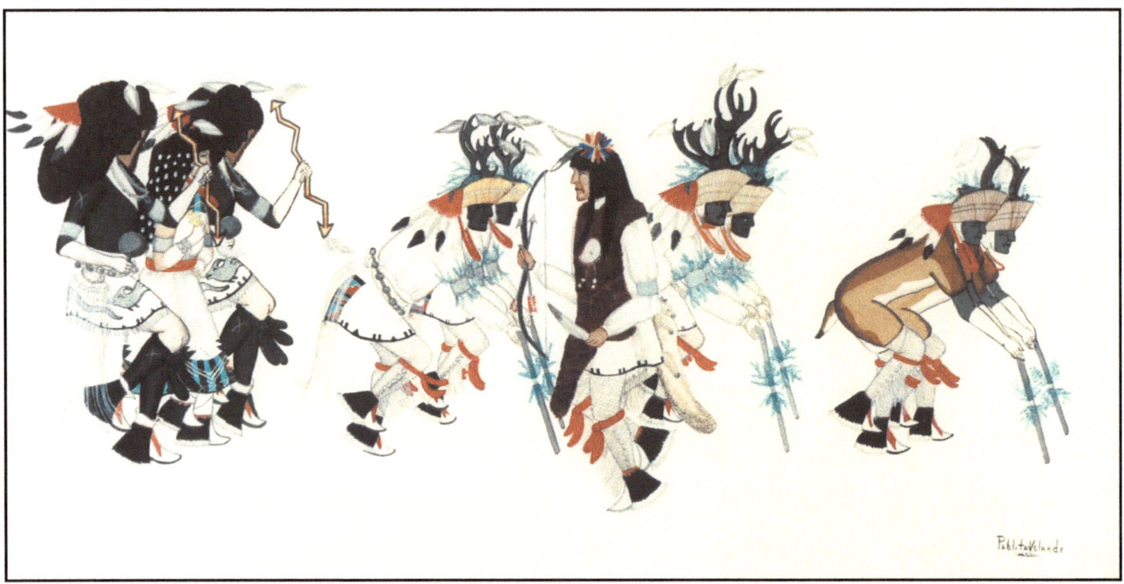

Deer Dancers, Pablita Velarde, watercolor, Bandelier National Monument Archives.

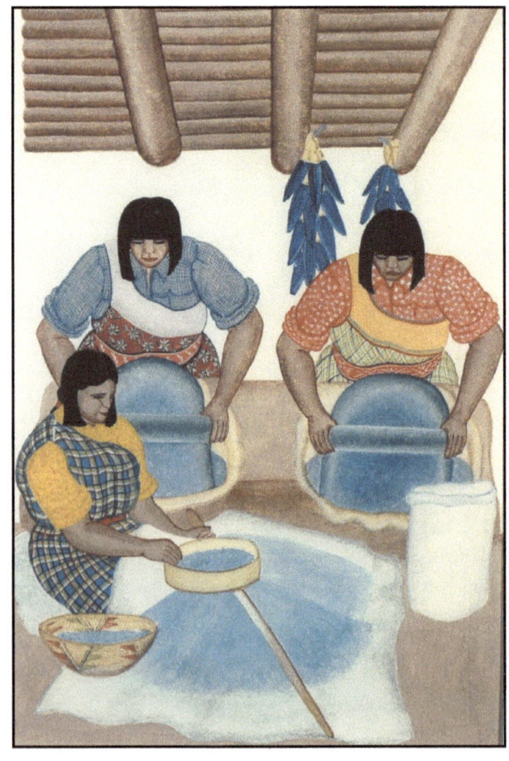

Grinding Blue Corn, Pablita Velarde, watercolor, Bandelier National Monument Archives.

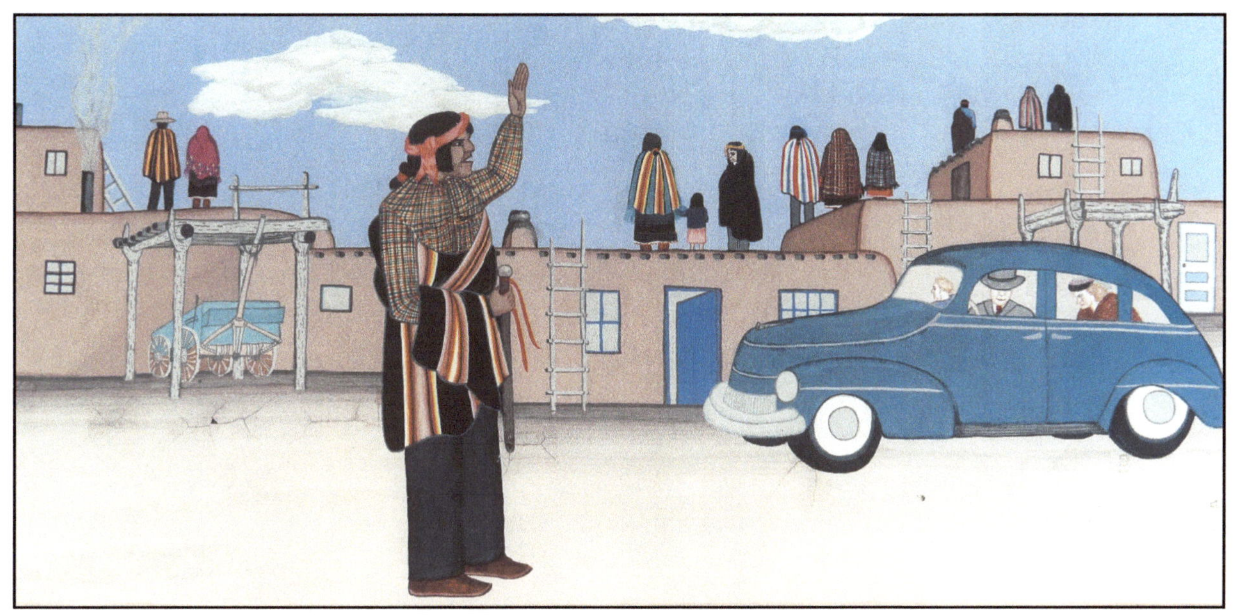

Governor Greets the Tourists, Pablita Velarde, watercolor, Bandelier National Monument Archives.

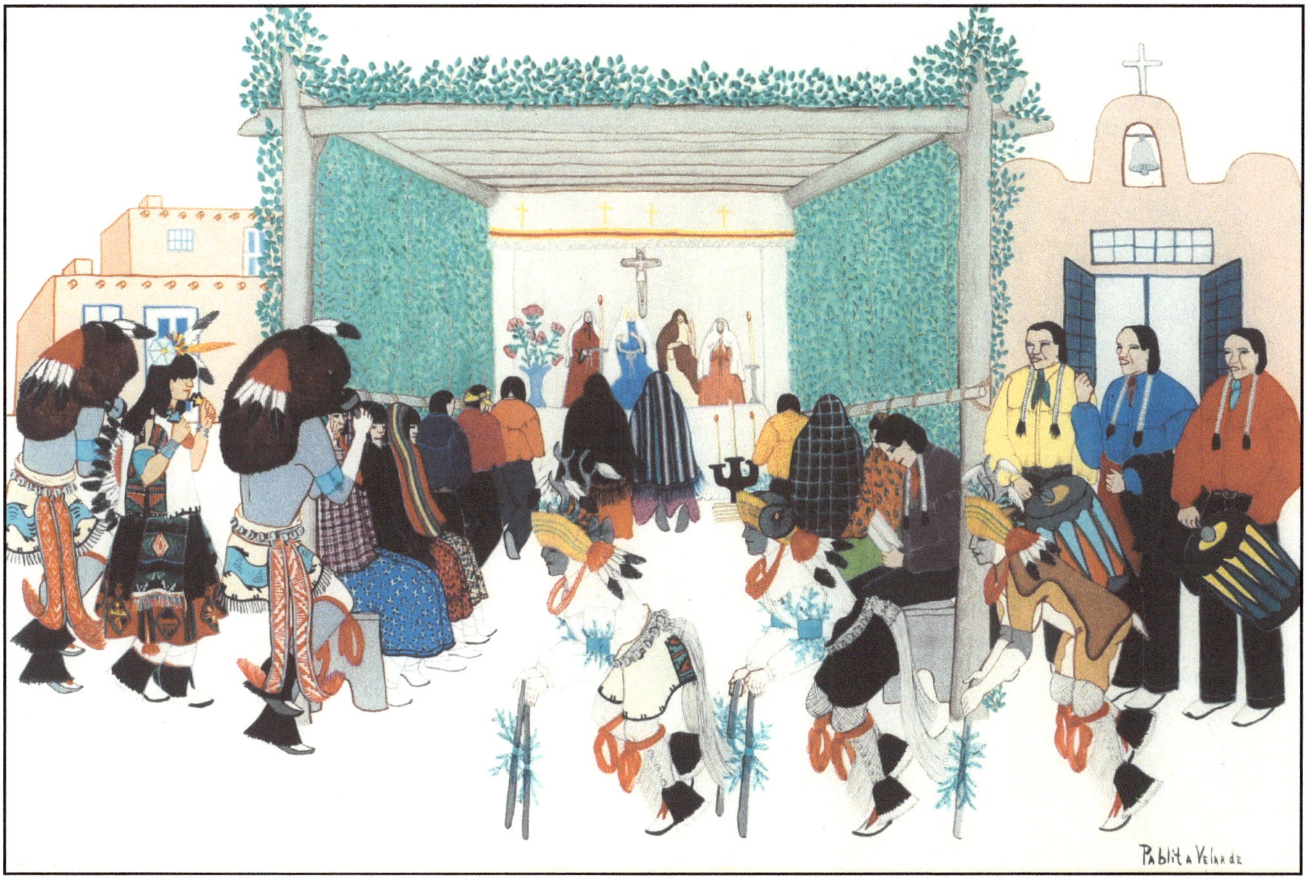

Ceremony, Pablita Velarde, watercolor, Bandelier National Monument Archives.

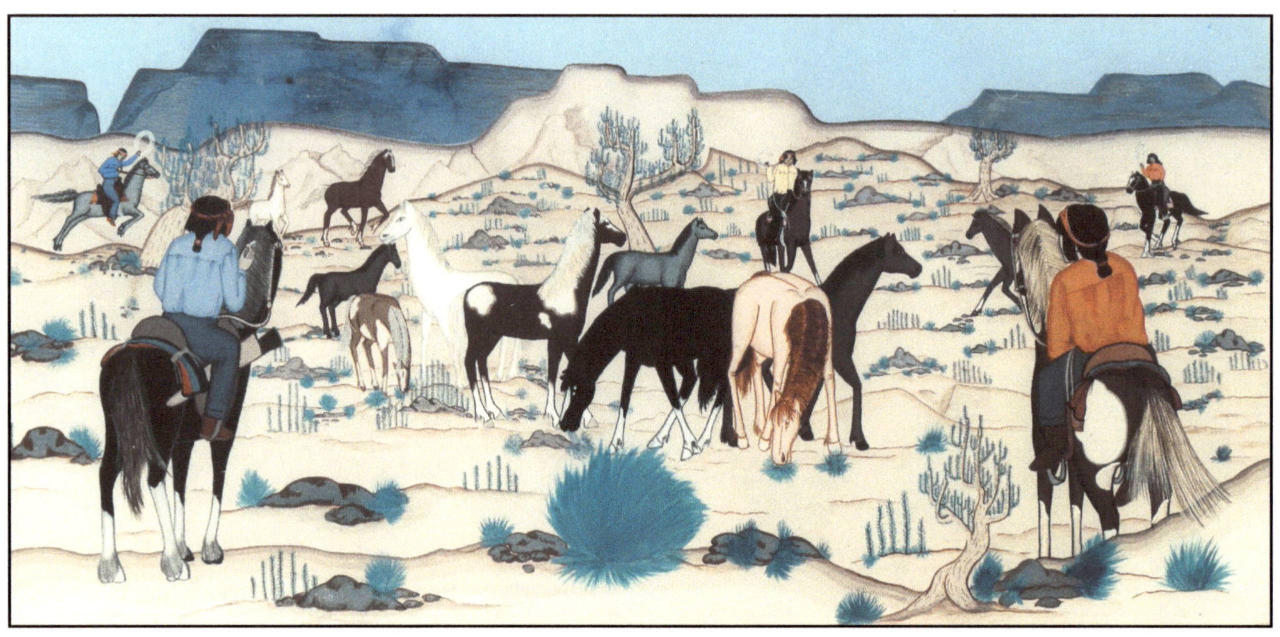

Round Up Horses, Pablita Velarde, watercolor, Bandelier National Monument Archives.

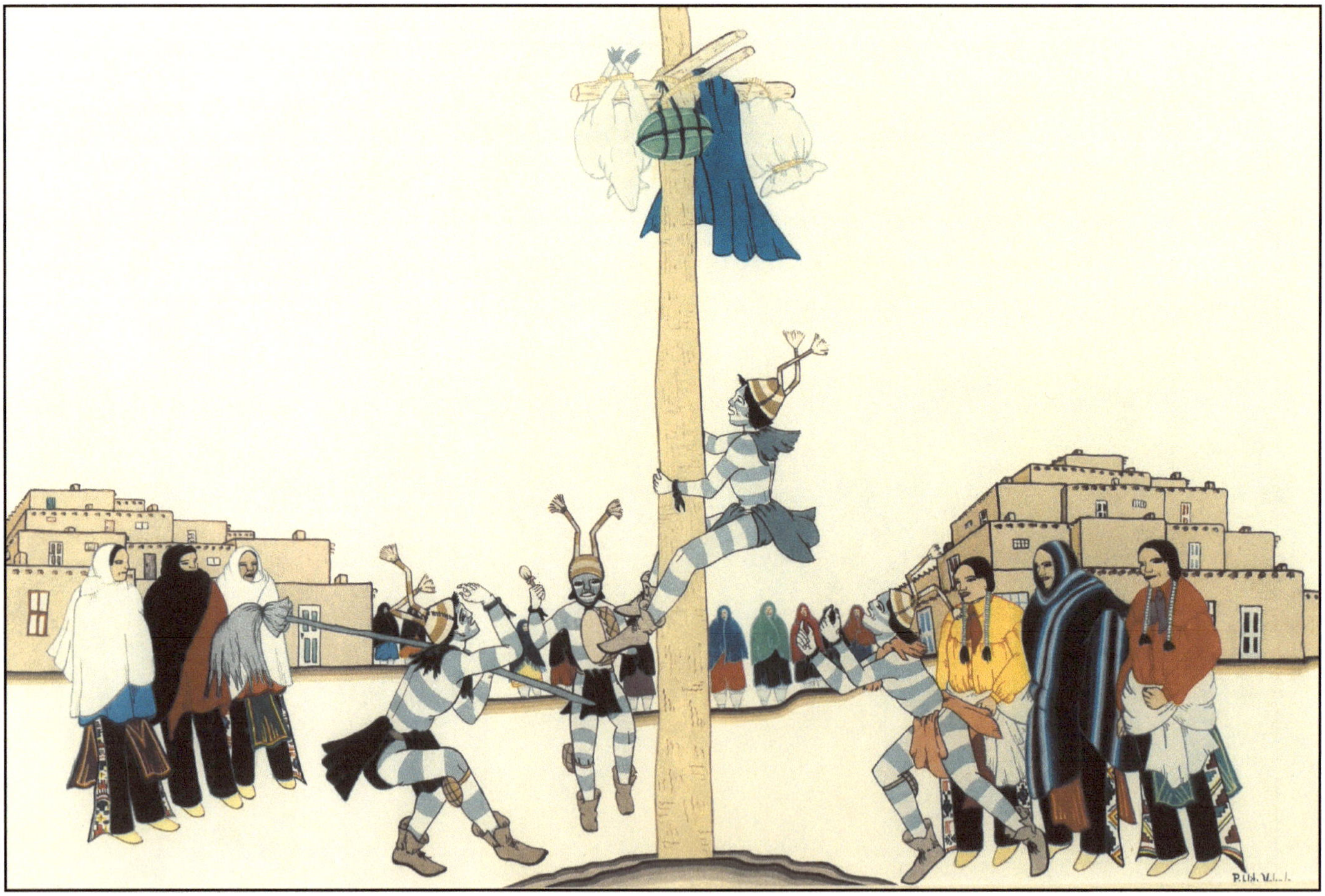

Pole Climb, Pablita Velarde, watercolor, Banderlier National Monument Archives.

Stuart Walker Born, 1888; died, 1940. Lived in Albuquerque. Worked with his friend, the artist Brooks Willis, to create murals in the Bernalillo Courthouse. Employed by the Public Works of Art Project to do watercolor sketches for the U.S. Forest Service. Showed art works in the New York World's Fair and in San Francisco.

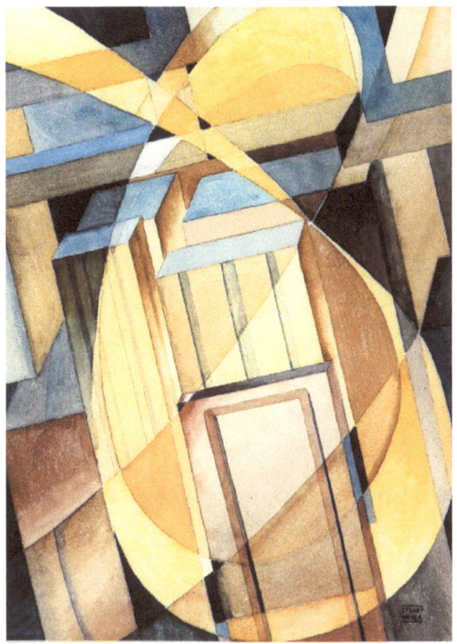

Abstract, Stuart Walker, painting, Golden Library, Eastern New Mexico University, Portales.

William Warder Born, 1920, Mora, New Mexico; died, 1999, Albuquerque, New Mexico. Studied at the University of New Mexico, and privately with New Mexican artists, Berninghaus, Bisttram, Dasburg, and Chapman. Started the University of New Mexico's Artist-in-Residence Program.

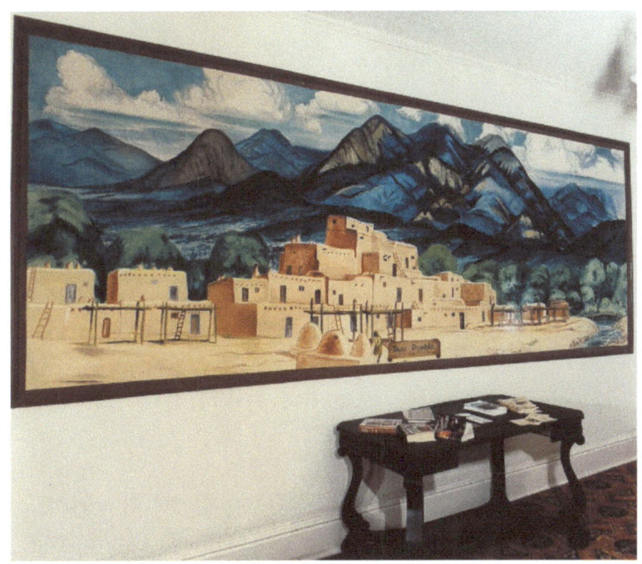

Taos Pueblo, William Warder, mural, El Portal Hotel, Raton.

Harold West Born, 1902, Honey Grove, Texas; died, 1968, Santa Fe, New Mexico. "No one encouraged me other than just my family," he said. "So I painted my first oil painting and I won first prize at the county fair." Studied under Russell Vernon Hunter; otherwise, self-taught. Settled in New Mexico in 1920. He praised the WPA: "It was a wonderful thing, helped me make a living, stayed home and painted."

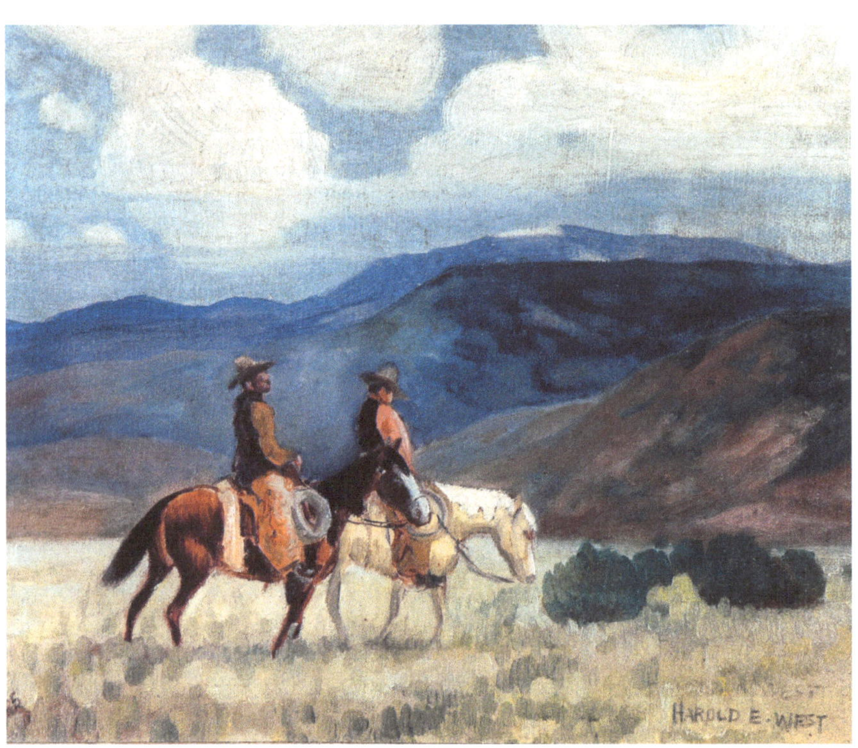

Bored Cowboys, Harold West, painting, Melrose High School, Melrose.

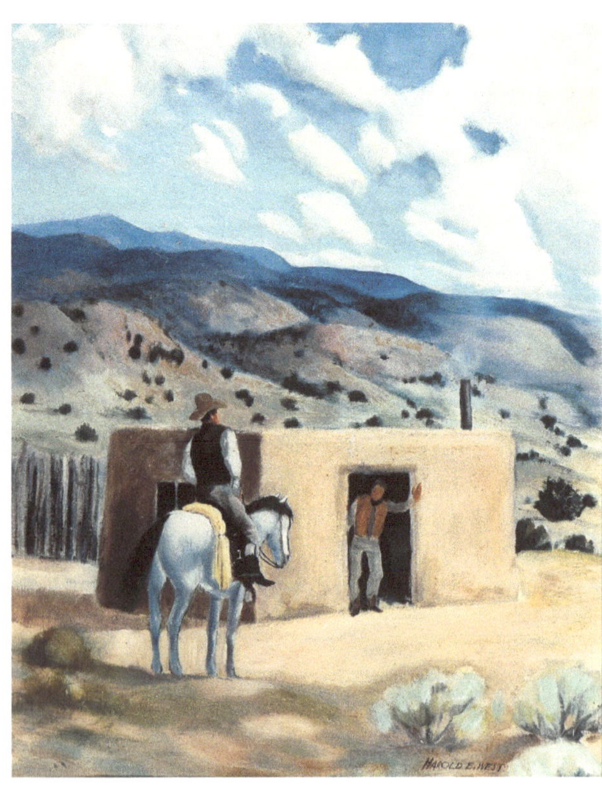

Get Down, Come On In, Harold West, painting, Clayton High School, Clayton.

Brooks Willis Born, 1903, Farmington, New Mexico; died, 1981, Santa Fe, New Mexico. Studied painting in Paris. When World War I interrupted his studies, he joined the American Volunteers Ambulance Corps. Returned to New Mexico, became the Executive Director of the Harwood Foundation, Taos; later, taught in the Art Department of the University of New Mexico. Left New Mexico in the early 1940s to work in California, returned after retirement and continued to paint.

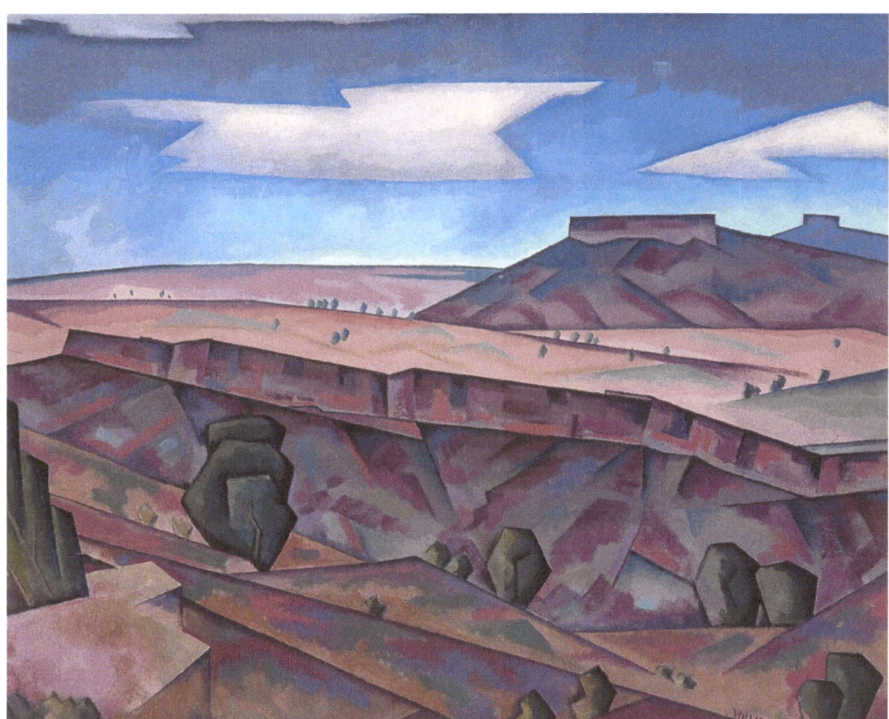

Desert, Brooks Willis, painting, McKinley County Courthouse, Gallup.

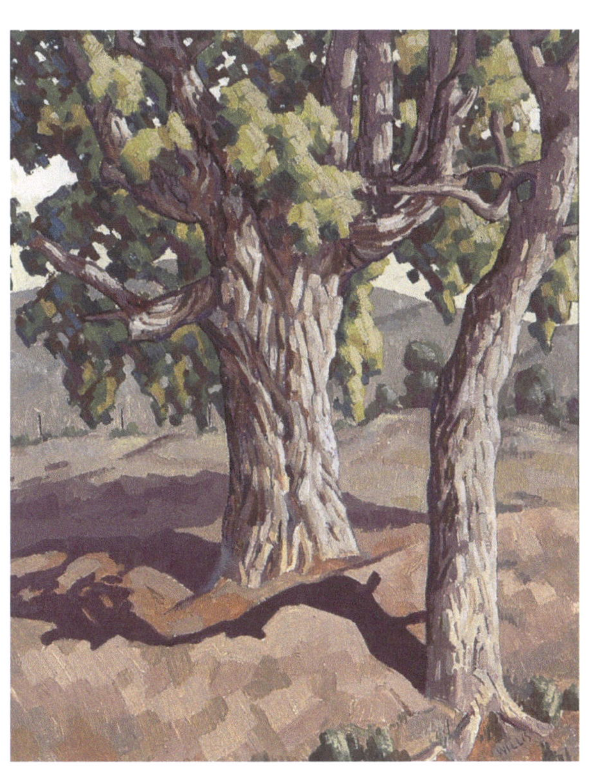

Cottonwoods, Brooks Willis, painting, McKinley County Courthouse, Gallup.

J. R. Willis Born, 1876, Sylvania, Georgia; died, 1960, Albuquerque, New Mexico. Began his career as a political cartoonist during the Spanish American War. About 1908 went to New York to study art. Traveled to California where he was a pioneer in the development of animated cartoons for movies. Came to New Mexico in 1917, booked as a vaudeville artist at a theater in Gallup. When the owner died of influenza, Willis bought the theater and settled there. Became well known for his paintings of aspens, also noted for realistic portraits of Arizona and New Mexico Indians and for photography of western scenes.

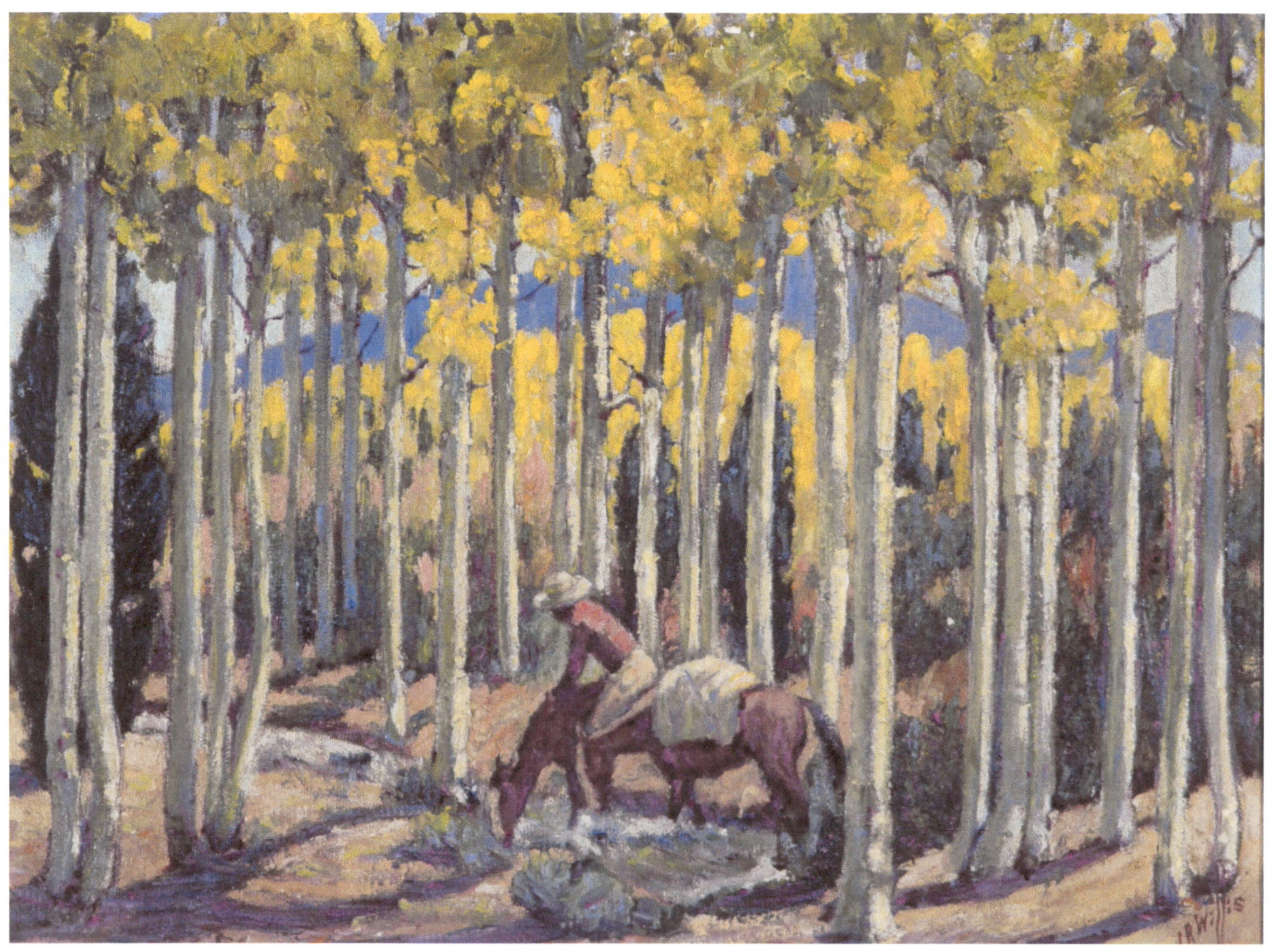

Untitled (Aspens), J. R. Willis, painting, Alamogordo Women's Club, Alamogordo

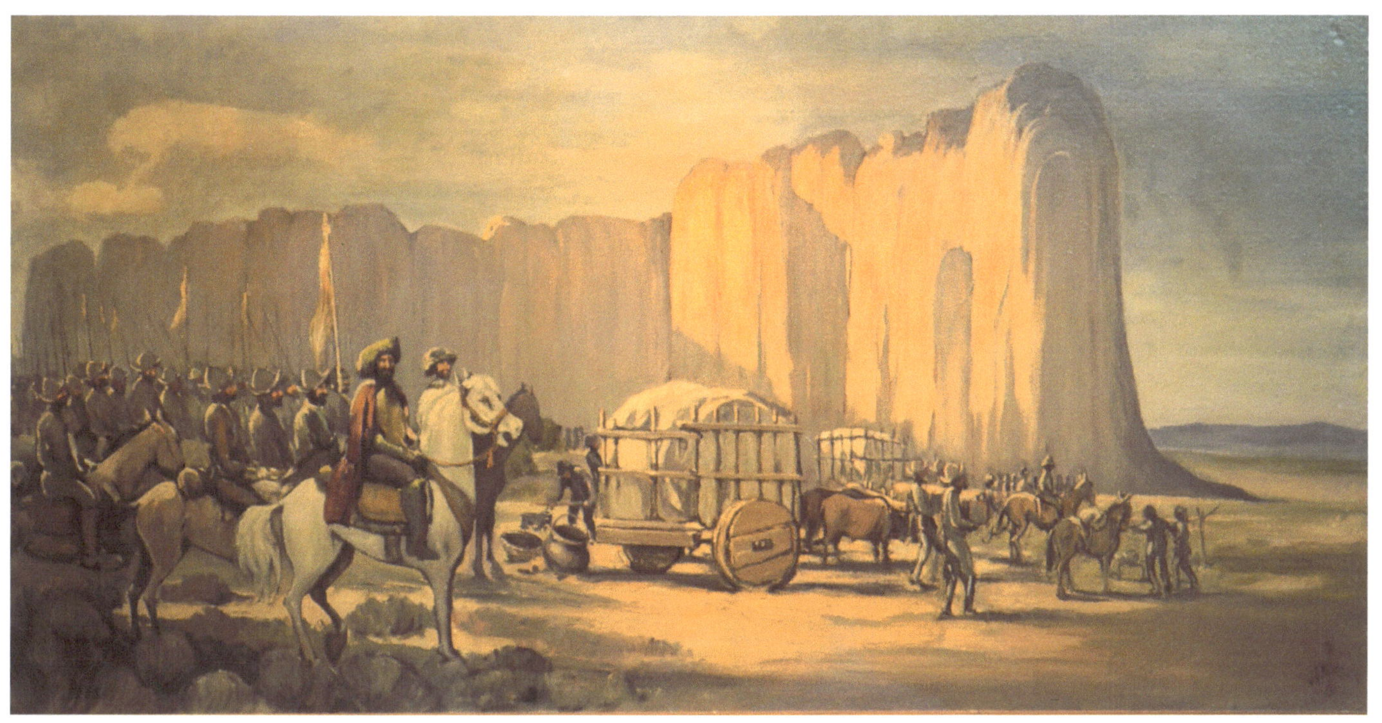

Conquistadors at El Morro Rock, J. R. Willis, mural size painting, Gallup High School Library, Gallup.

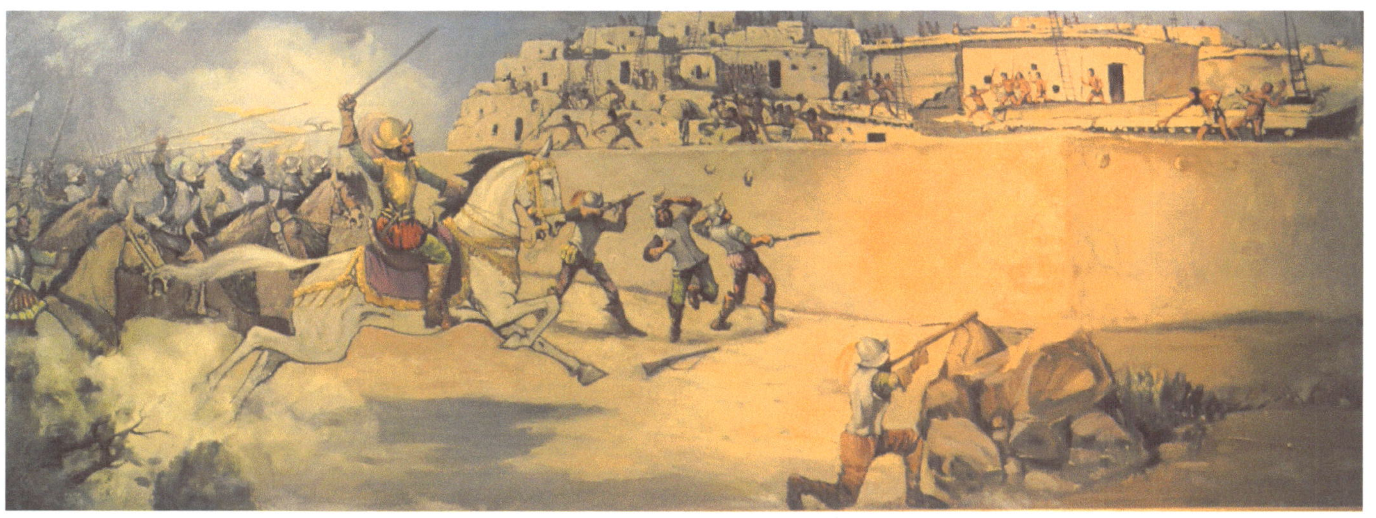

Conquistadors Attack a Pueblo, J. R. Willis, mural size painting, Gallup High School Library, Gallup.

Anna Keener Wilton Born, 1895, Colorado; died, 1982, Santa Fe, New Mexico. Studied art at various institutions, among them the Chicago Art Institute, California College of Arts and Crafts, and the University of New Mexico. Inspired by both Indian and Hispanic art. Taught art throughout New Mexico, became head of the art department, Eastern New Mexico University, Portales. Director of the New Deal Art Center, Gallup, during the Depression.

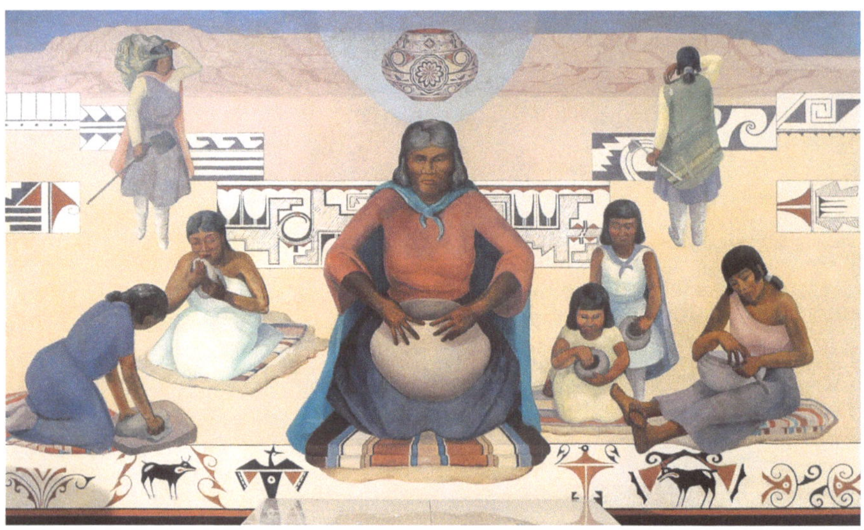

Zuni Indian Pottery Women, Anna Keener Wilton, mural, McKinley County Courthouse, Gallup

Biographical notes are taken from the following sources: Treasures on New Mexico Trails, edited and compiled by Kathryn A. Flynn, Sunstone Press, 1995; Van Deren Coke, Taos and Santa Fe: The Artist's Environment: 1882-1942, Albuquerque. The University of New Mexico Press, 1963; Sandra D'Emilio, "The New Deal Was a Great Deal: Federal Patronage and Mural Painting in New Mexico, 1933 to 1943," an unpublished essay; Interviews with Artists conducted by Sylvia Loomis for the Archives of American Art, 1964; Interviews with Artists conducted by Kathryn A. Flynn for the Office of the Secretary of State, 1992-1994, and later as Executive Director of the National New Deal Preservation Association, Incorporated.

The photographs in this book, unless otherwise noted, were taken by Pat Berrett in cooperation with the New Mexico Chapter of the National New Deal Preservation Association, Incorporated, a private non-profit organization focusing on the preservation of New Deal creations nationwide.

The Artist's Voice: Gene Kloss, Eliseo Rodriguez, Pablita Velarde

In the early 1960s and again in the 1990s, artists who worked in New Deal art programs were asked in state-sponsored interviews to talk about their experiences. These interviews, conducted by Sylvia Loomis and Kathryn A. Flynn, give us as personal account of that time as we are likely to have.

I have selected from these interviews the stories of three artists in their own words, Gene Kloss, Eliseo Rodriguez, and Pablita Velarde.

I chose them because they express in clear and vivid language what the New Deal meant to them. I chose them also because they represent the cultural diversity of the art projects. The Taos artist Gene Kloss comments: "What was interesting about the project was the fact they stressed the regional idea. That here was a country so different . . . it had very decided characteristics in its three peoples, the Indian, the Hispanic, and the Anglo, the Indian prevailing."

Gene Kloss

Gene Kloss was born in Oakland, California in 1903. She attended the University of California, graduated with honors in art in 1924, and after taking a few courses at the California School of Fine Arts in San Francisco, concluded her formal education and began working on her own. She was married when she left school, and almost immediately, in 1925, she and her husband Phillips Kloss made their first trip to Taos, New Mexico. For many years, because of work and family, they commuted between Taos and California. But from the beginning Taos was her artistic vantage point, and they finally settled there permanently.

She worked on the first New Deal program, the Public Works of Art Project, and later for Russell Vernon Hunter on the WPA Art Project. Because she was an etcher and could make many copies, her work was widely distributed. "She did those beautiful little prints," the Regional Director Jesse Nusbaum said, "we ordered those by the hundreds."

In June, 1964, she talked with Sylvia Loomis for the Archives of American Art. The following comments are excerpts from the Loomis interview in which Mrs. Kloss tells us about her life as an artist and about the New Deal art programs in which she participated.

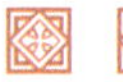  

The teacher of my anatomy and life class [at the University of California] was Perham Nahl . . . and the last semester at the university, he gave a seminar in etching. I had seen in his back office this big old hundred year old Star Wheel Press and it fascinated me. . . . He described the technique to me very conversationally. . . . So I messed up my mother's kitchen from one end to the other, and I thought I'd better get a little book, which I did the next day on campus. Two dollars. How To Make an Etching. So I went home and made an etching. Mr. Nahl had me print it. He inked and I turned the wheel. He looked at me and said, "If this is your first etching, you

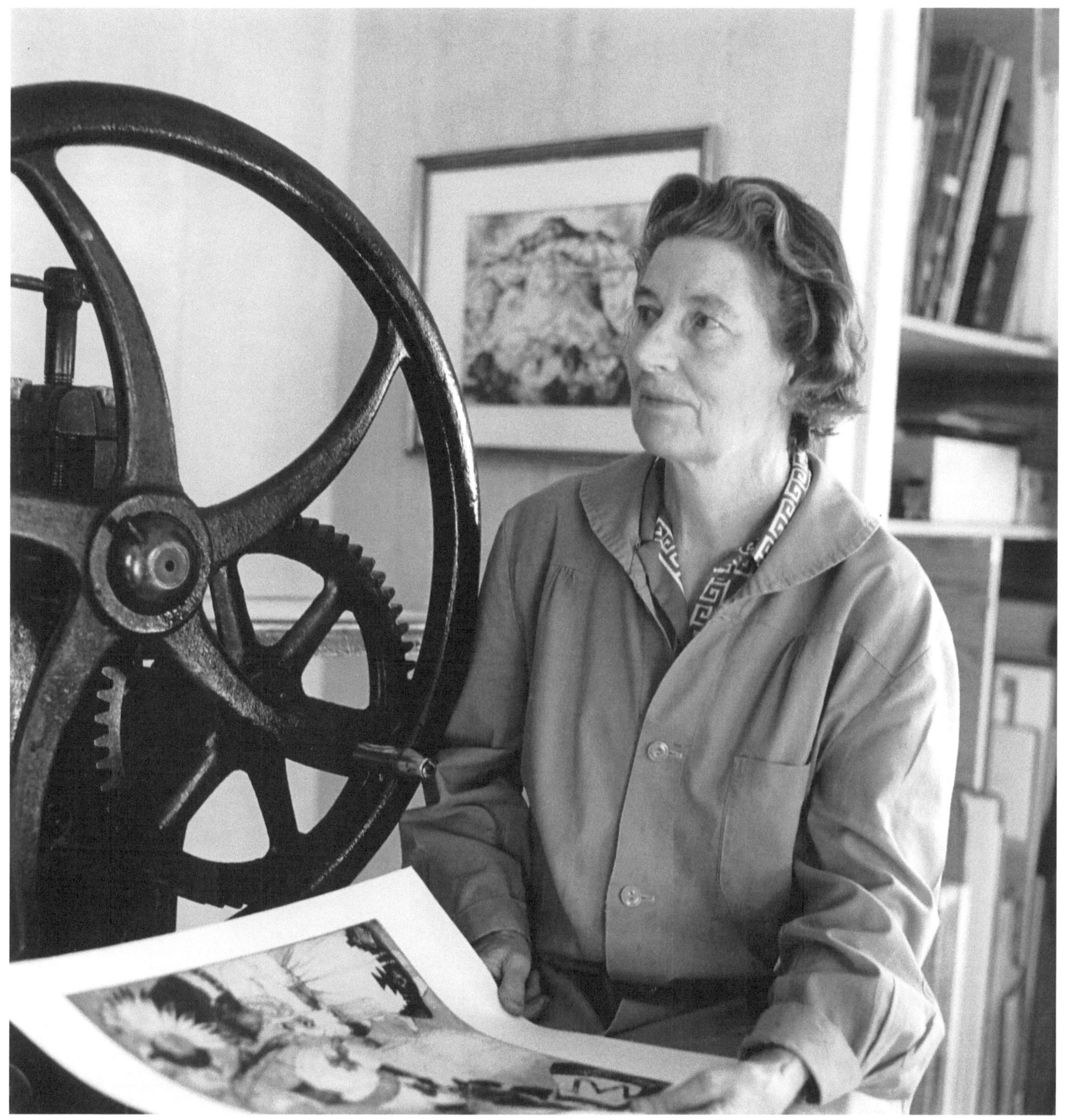

Gene Kloss (Photograph by Dick Spas)

are going to be an etcher." That's all I needed and that's all I got from him. It's been years of experience and working ever since.

My husband is a writer and poet and we have worked together in the intervening years. We started out on a trip that year, 1925. And we came to Taos, camped up in Taos Canyon for two weeks and in that time I did innumerable paintings and drawings and etchings. I even took my little press with me. We bought a sack of concrete and set it up on a stump in the woods and I printed my plates there.

We returned to California, and I had an exhibition in San Francisco and others, and it has been just that ever since, working, studying and exhibiting. Enough sales through the years to continue work, buy materials and live on.

[For the Public Works of Art Project] I decided to do aquatints on nine different subjects. For example, I did three of the pueblos. It was exciting because I got to do larger plates. I did thirty of each plate which came to at least 270 prints.

I had just recently become interested in aquatint. I had Mr. Lumston's book, an Englishman, on the art of etching and he describes various techniques in that, and the aquatint sounded very interesting to me. He describes Dame Laura Knight getting an ordinary deal box, stretching some muslin across the top, putting her plate in the bottom, and putting on an aquatint ground in rosin. I thought if Dame Laura Knight could do it, I could do it. So I went to the local grocery store and got an apple box, went to Penny's and got some muslin and stretched it over the top.

I put my polished copper plate in the bottom of this box, and I was down on my knees, pounding the top of it to let the rosin sift through the muslin onto the plate, when there was a knock on the door. Opened it and there was my neighbor Joe Sun Hawk and his six year old boy.

He looked at the box and he said, "This looks like a ceremony. We should have a song. Have you a tom-tom?" I said, "No. But we have a gourd rattle." So he rattled the rattle and sang an Indian song while I pounded the aquatint. I daresay that was the only aquatint ground laid to the tune of an Indian song.

I did a sketch from the window showing the distance and the big mountains with the snow ground and dark sky. A very simple subject and shortly after that, while we were at that same place, the Project started. Well, I was given the opportunity to experiment with this medium, and I had just acquired a new press so I could do large plates.

I had had this press that belonged to a company near Taos. . . . They had gone off to Spain and were selling this press for one hundred dollars. So I bought it. It was one of the original group made by the Sturgis Company in Chicago. . . . Joseph Pennell had one. There are six more. In his books he says that's the best press ever made. Better than anything you can get in Europe.

[For the WPA art project under Russell Vernon Hunter] I did three or four etchings with a larger edition of fifty each. Then I did paintings in oil and in watercolor. I don't remember how many.

They [prints and paintings] went to galleries, museums. Lots of them went to Washington for the offices. Years later visiting at Mesa Verde . . . they told us at the museum . . . that the guide tours were over and you could just ride around and we couldn't go through any of the ruins. Well behind the man who was talking was one of my etchings that I had done on the Project. So I introduced myself, which I wouldn't have done ordinarily, and said I just wanted to draw and I wouldn't walk off with any parts of the ruins. So he said it would be all right if I went over a rope or under a fence.

Our ideas, our religion are things we talk about, but there is little to depict as subject matter in art. Where they [Indians] have their ceremonies at dawn, at dusk, at dark, in firelight, outdoors, and it is very dramatic and very meaningful.

I just have recollections of very great enthusiasm, of gratitude [for New Deal art projects]. . . . There were a few artists who didn't work, who didn't share in a conscientious return for good treatment, but that's true anywhere.

And a few of them were a little stubborn about accepting the regional idea. I remember the courthouse murals. . . . They drew straws, and Victor Higgins got first place, and he insisted on doing Moses the Lawgiver because it was a courthouse. They said that this wasn't regional. And that was the only argument I remember they had. Otherwise things seemed to be most harmonious. But he had his way. He did Moses the Lawgiver, and the others did local subject matter.

I think it [New Deal art projects] stimulated an interest in art. Because people in outlying places who had never seen anything had murals in their post office and received some of the easel pictures or prints to hang in their schools and in public buildings. I think it is one thing that started the public interest in art.

Well, personally I would repeat that it [the New Deal] was a very pronounced help to me in my career because the government subsidy alone gave it dignity and importance.

Eliseo Rodriguez

Eliseo Rodriguez was born in Santa Fe in 1915 near Cristo Rey Church. "My family owned a lot of property there," Mr. Rodriguez said. "We had little money, but we had sheep, goats and a lot of vegetables." He got his start as an artist early, at 14, when he got a scholarship to the Santa Fe Art School. In 1935, when he was 20, he married, and he and his wife Paula built a house near Cristo Rey Church where they still live.

His first experience with the WPA came a year later. He got a job helping to dig a sewer line along the Santa Fe River and, also, to mix cement for the rock wall area that still stands today. When he heard about the Federal Art Project, he went right over and applied.

In August, 1999, Kathryn A. Flynn talked with Eliseo Rodriguez about his work as a WPA artist. The following account, taken from Mrs. Flynn's interview, is what he had to say about the WPA and its importance to him as an artist.

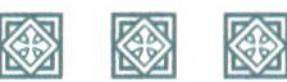

When I took my craft work, paintings on glass, carvings, and tin work, in for sale at the Native Market, Eleanor Bedell, the store manager, told me she couldn't buy any more items, but maybe I should go meet Russell Vernon Hunter, who was in charge of the Federal Art Project. He was located on West San Francisco across from the Dendahl Store.

He [Mr. Hunter] told me that before I could get into the WPA/FAP program, I would have to go to the County Courthouse and apply for relief or welfare. If approved, we would be given coupons, about $5 a month value, for food. That would establish that we were approved and entitled to be put to work on the Federal Art Project.

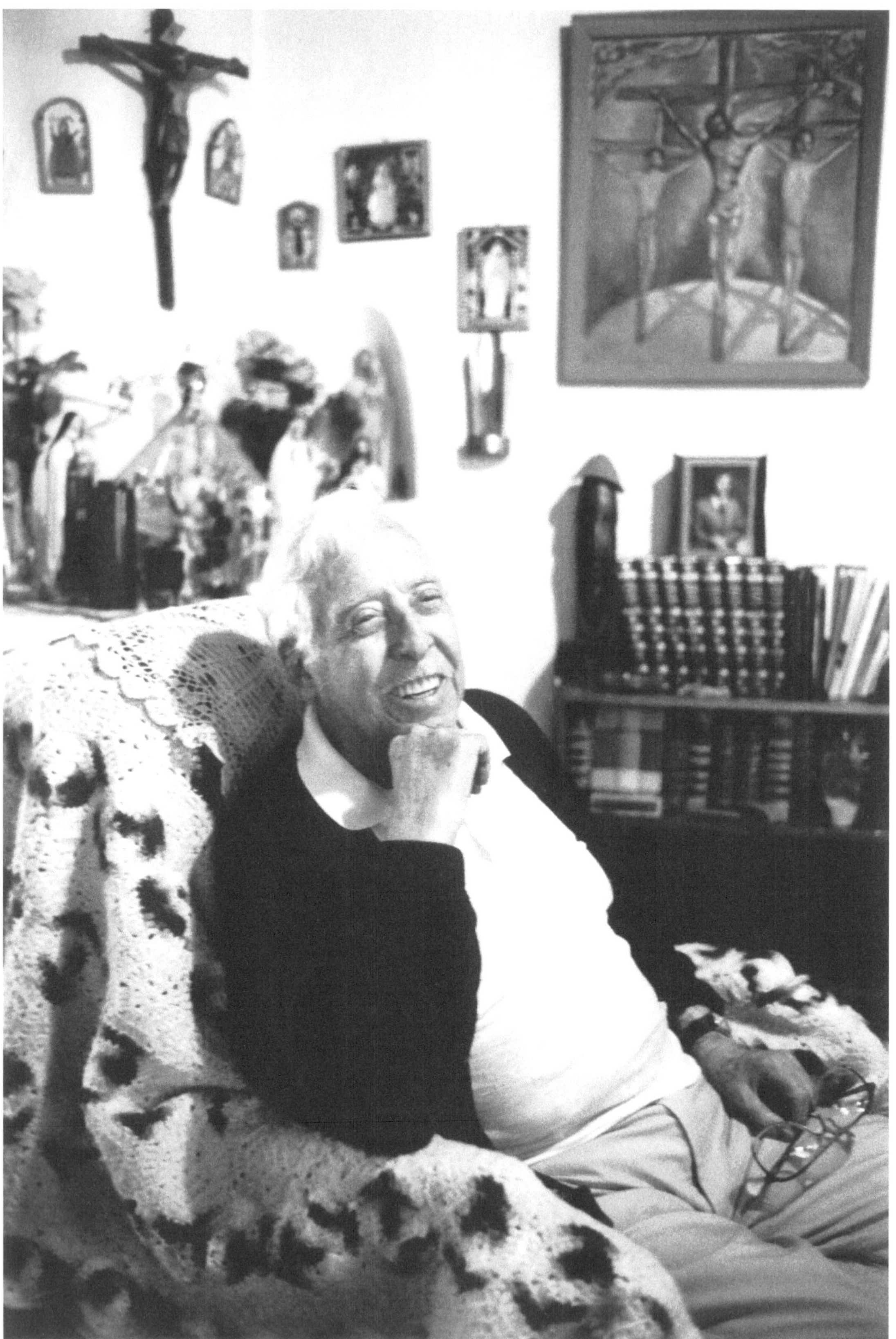

Eliseo Rodriguez (Photograph by Tony O'Brien)

[After being approved] I went back to Mr. Hunter. He gave me all kinds of materials to work with, canvasses, paint, watercolors, everything. I was excited and felt like I was in business. I didn't know which to do first, but I was always willing to do anything I was asked to do. I was willing to be versatile. Some people weren't, but I did paintings on canvas, on glass, watercolors. I was willing to try anything.

I helped Paul Lantz do a mural for the Texas Centennial and I worked on a mural with Howard Schleeter. Schleeter and I worked in space provided in the New Mexico State Capitol.

Louie Ewing and I worked on a mosaic tile creation for a fountain at Carrie Tingley Hospital for Crippled Children in Hot Springs in his studio next door to my house. He and I also worked on a Portfolio of Navajo Rug Designs for the Laboratory of Anthropology. That was silk screening.

The Laboratory of Anthropology selected some of their best blankets, and we copied the designs. I don't remember how many. We did reproductions that were 4' x 2' and we drew them to scale and then reduced them to print. We tried to make our colors as close as possible to the real rug dyes. We would build the screen frame, put the design on a film, cut it and then run a squeegy over it. We even developed our own squeegee.

Some hated having to do the [Spanish Colonial Design] Portfolio, which didn't require much creativity or artistic ability. They would make a plate of a rendering by E. Boyd, distribute them to all of us, along with an originally painted one to use as a guide for all of us to follow. This was sometimes a problem because the watercolors they provided didn't always match the colors used in the original. In the end, I heard the lack of uniformity created a problem for the Washington acceptance of the project.

E. Boyd asked me if I would be interested in experimenting in a different media. She said that this form of straw art [straw mosaic work] originated in Africa, was picked up by the Moors in Spain and brought by the Spanish to New Mexico. It was tacky, messy and tedious work. Like I said, I was willing to try anything so I tried doing the straw inlay applique work and enjoyed doing it and wanted to keep it going as a form of art that was dying out.

[I'm not doing it] as much as I was because I'm 84 years old. It's frustrating because I want to be producing or working in my garden, but I can't do those things anymore.

Paula and I have been doing the inlay work for 64 years, and we now have nine family members involved in doing it. It helps all of them with their needed income. Beyond them, there are 20 or 30 others doing this form of art. Paula has a large straw inlaid cross in the State Capitol. We both have things all over the country, and I have a piece in Berlin.

[I made] $75 dollars a month. We were paid by the month, and since we didn't have a family yet that took care of our grocery needs for a month. You turned in your work once or twice a week or once or twice a month depending on how fast you worked.

There were some artists who lived well from 1915 to 1933, and then when everything changed economically, they found it very hard to swallow their pride and accept relief so they could get on the Art Project. Proud or not proud, you still had to eat.

We had wonderful times together. We shared our meager amounts of food to get through the month, particularly with the Ewings, who lived next door to us. They were married the month before us. Also, we had wonderful Saturday night potluck parties at the home of Alfred and Dorothy Morang, Hal West, Jim Morris, Olive Rush and others. We ate and talked and did drawings together. Georgia O'Keeffe once told me she liked my work. She was not on any of the WPA projects though.

There weren't a whole lot of Spanish people working in the Project though. We weren't just assistants. Although in some cases, we were considered helpers. To me, a little disaster brings people together. This did, and we all got along. It was the same in the army. I was the only Hispanic in my group, but who cared!

I think we appreciated everything more then. We saved for special things, like going out to a restaurant for dinner, and the meal tasted so good. Now we take it for granted.

The FAP did more for me than if I had gone to college. It gave me so many possibilities, but some others didn't want to partake of those possibilities. It was a great advantage because it gave one an opportunity to build one's self if you wanted to. This opportunity came about as the result of one man, President Franklin Delano Roosevelt, who was like the father of our nation, like our own father who wouldn't let his own children starve to death. He worked it out so we could build up our country.

Pablita Velarde

Pablita Velarde was born on Santa Clara Pueblo in 1918. "My grandmother delivered me," she says. "My Indian name is Tse Twan, Golden Dawn." When she was very young, her mother died and left four little girls for her father to take care of.

Velarde was five years old when her father sent his daughters to Saint Catherine's Indian School. She spoke no English, she reports, and though the nuns were kind, she was lonely and cried a lot. When she was old enough for the sixth grade, her father made a fortunate choice. He sent her to the Santa Fe Indian School.

At first she didn't like it. "It was so military," she complained. "They marched us in all directions, to school, to eat, to buildings." But it was there that she met Dorothy Dunn. Dunn opened The Studio. "I went in for that," Velarde says. "She was the only art teacher in my career. [She] kind of started me. I couldn't do anything else with my life."

Pablita Velarde was 19 years old when she signed on for the WPA project in 1939. She worked at Bandelier National Park under the supervision of the National Park Service. It was the opportunity that enabled her to sustain the artistic ambitions she had developed under Dorothy Dunn at the Indian School.

In May, 1994, Kathryn A. Flynn talked with her about her work at Bandelier, her life there and the importance of the WPA in Velarde's distinguished career. The following account in Velarde's words is what came out of that discussion.

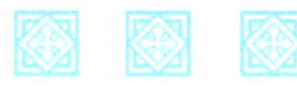

[My WPA work was] at Bandelier National Park under the supervision of the National Park Service. When they had money, they came and got me, and when they didn't, they took me home. I

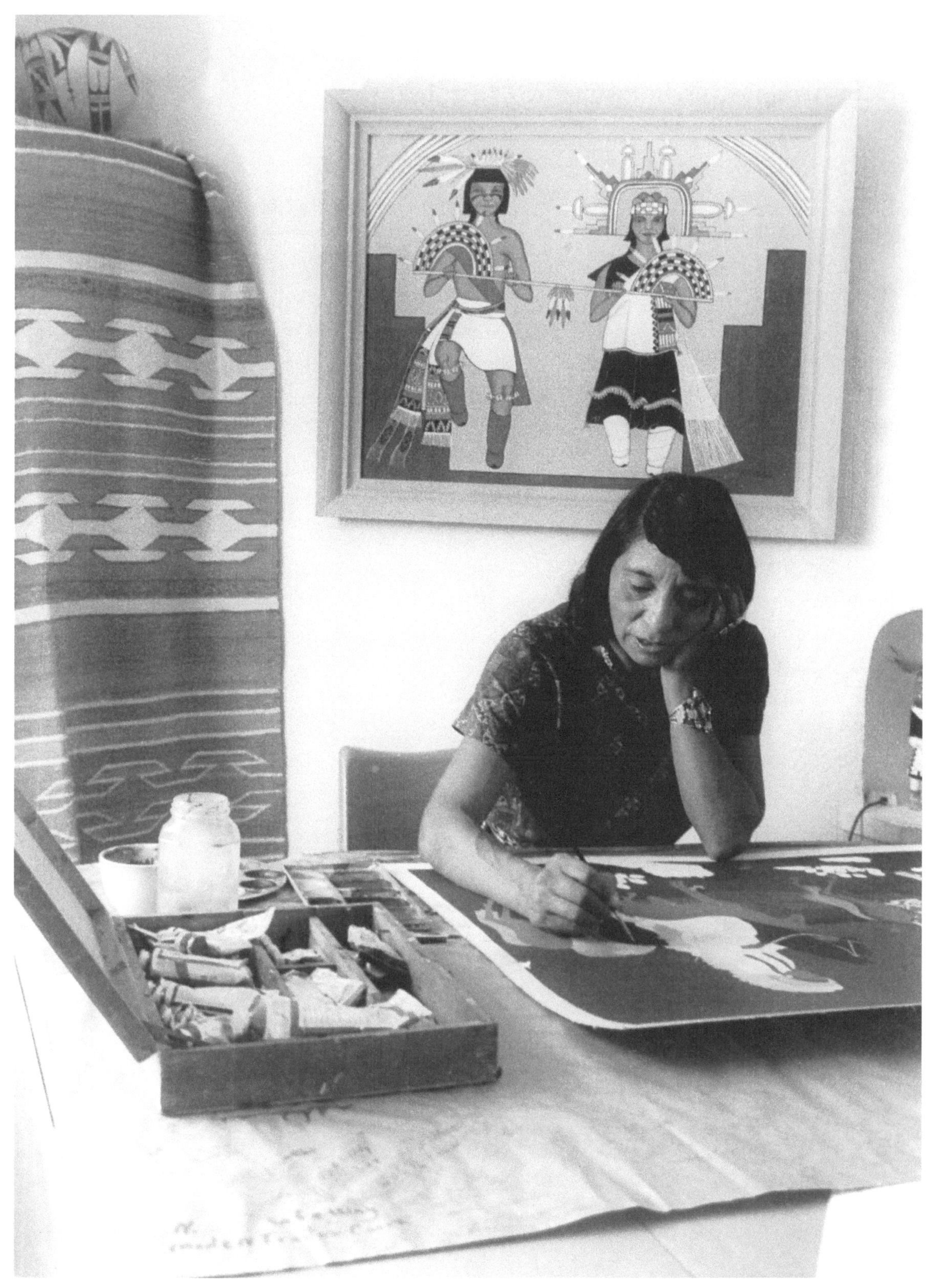

Pablita Velarde
(Photograph Courtesy of the Museum of New Mexico. Negative #174201)

did about eighty paintings depicting pueblo life, scenes like seasonal dances, government officials, native foods, clothing of different pueblos.

I stayed with the custodian's family. In their garage. I ate my meals with them. I paid for my food, but not rent. I was able to take home my savings and then spend it.

I enjoyed it. It was a good experience for my children too. The last two or three trips I went to Bandelier, I took my kids. They put us up in a cowboy's cabin, and we fed ourselves. We made a list of supplies we needed and gave the ranger money for our groceries when he went to Santa Fe. We always did this when we were snowbound. We went hiking and fishing in the streams. Never caught any fish, but the kids just pretended like it was something to do.

When we lived in the cowboy cabin, squirrels came up to the window to feed, and deer came into the barn to eat hay. The rangers had a donkey named Pasquelita but we called him Pesky. There were all kinds of animals.

Dale King, the park ranger who was the boss, wanted the museum to have an historical layout. How the pueblos were governed, how medical needs were met, how each pueblo might dress. So I did a lot of research. I painted little figures, little stages in order of government. I painted clothing, fixed their hair, dressed them up in their typical pueblo dress. Like Keres wear red boots, people up north mostly white boots, calico dress or manta, which are made by themselves. They only wear black mantas when they are showing the pueblo's true belief.

Most all pueblo women wore Indian style dresses that they made. Hardly any wore bought dresses because none had money. I was the only woman making money during the Depression so everyone hated me because I had money.

I painted most of the pueblos in New Mexico. I included the Keres in the southern part of the Rio Grande area. For the Taos pueblo, I showed the men with their blankets on their hips and their skinny braids. The Santa Clara men I painted in blue jeans for dress occasions with blue or other color shirts and the women in their calico mantas.

Custodian Dale King took me shopping in Santa Fe, and when I ran out of brushes, paint, easels, he would get me more. The government paid for my supplies and my salary. It was pretty good.

I was paid by the day, $5.00, and paid every two weeks. Checks, which I cashed any place in Espanola. I was known as Herman's daughter, and they would go after my poor old dad if the check didn't work out good. I never had a bad check. That way I got lucky.

My dad was a farmer and raised every vegetable that was edible. He raised beans and traded them for staples at the store. The Indians never gave us money for trade. They would bring us a bucket of corn for a bucket of milk. We had cows and didn't have pasteurized milk but let them use it the way it was.

I was inspired by the time I did the research and the paintings. I didn't want to leave my paintings at Bandelier, but [I] had to since they paid me for them. Because of getting this money, I was able to build my own home on the pueblo.

[When that job was over,] I was married with two little brats so I was stuck for about five years taking care of my family. But once I got them in school, I was able to go back to my artwork. Of course, that chased my husband away because he didn't like all the dirt and related messes. But after the divorce, I went back to my normal stage and did my painting.

After eighty years I am still at it, taking breaks now and then and creating my dolls for my paintings. In the [19]50s my dolls weren't popular so I put them on the back burner and kept the paintings rolling. But now the dolls are popular so I may have to put the paintings on the back burner.

Actually, now, I do what I want to do. I don't rush anything and if I want to do dolls, I do them. If I want to paint, I paint.

I think about [my paintings] a long time, and I know in my head when I start what I want in the end to look like. Sometimes I even dream about it and try to remember all the things that flash in my head. I develop a mental picture of what kind of illustration I want to do. Like when I do story paintings.

Not many [story paintings] lately. It's one of those things that has dried out on me. Sometimes the urge to paint dries out on me, and sometimes the dolls don't interest me enough to go back to work on them.

My sisters worked on WPA too. Two older and one younger. The Park Service hired my older sister, Legoria, to make pottery, and they took a tape of her making pottery. I don't know if they still have it or not. My younger sister is still alive, but we're both old. I am in my eighties; she is in her seventies.

My daughter, Helen Hardin, became a painter and my son, Herbert, a sculptor. They weren't always watching me though. The rangers watched after them till I found a babysitter. Before that the kids got into the museum and with a long stick, poked and peeled the skin off a mounted rattlesnake display. The rangers had to watch them more closely after that.

[When I started,] people probably thought I was crazy. Being in the early days, women were just supposed to be a housewife, raise babies, clean house and stuff like that. Women never thought of being a rebel like me. Only men painted. I broke that taboo. Women never built houses. Men did that. I broke that taboo too. I said, "I am not a man, but I am going to build my house with my Park Service money." And I did.

About two years ago [the Park Service] brought out all my paintings and had a reception. The ranger called and just said they were trying to get the WPA artists back to Bandelier. After I got there, I found out they were honoring me. They gave me a wooden plaque and had dignitaries there from Santa Fe and Washington. I was surprised. It was a nice honor.

[Before the WPA] people weren't educated about Indian art as art. They wanted landscapes and flower pictures. Things like that. Indian paintings just didn't go in their taste. It was hard to start back in the [19]30s and make a living as an artist. That is why I took many mediocre jobs. To survive.

It made me feel kind of important to be chosen by the government to do artwork in the brand new [Park Service] Museum. After that job my paintings started to sell. Before that I couldn't sell much for more than 50 cents to a $1.00. Later things sold for $50 to a $100, the highest.

The National Park Service put more self-esteem in my personality so I pushed myself to do things that were unheard of by Indian women. I got to be very pushy.

Acknowledgments

One of the pleasures of completing a book is to remember with gratitude the friends and researchers who have offered invaluable help along the way.

I want to thank my friend Dale Doepke who read this manuscript many times and whose general comments and particular criticisms made it better. I want to thank Professor Paul Christianson, Professor Charles Muscatine, and Professor John Wirth. They offered sensitive and careful readings. Their suggestions were especially helpful in defining the rich context of New Mexican art. I also want to thank my friends Flora and Sidney Biddle for attentive readings.

In regard to professional assistance, Kathryn A. Flynn, Executive Director of the National New Deal Preservation Association, Incorporated, was invaluable. Her book, Treasures on New Mexico Trails, was an essential source. She did research on the locations of New Deal art in the towns and villages of New Mexico, and, as I have noted earlier, she interviewed New Deals artists for the state and the National New Deal Preservation Association, Incorporated. I am very appreciative of the cooperation of the Association, a private, non-profit organization, that provided many of the photographs for this publication. Copies of these fine photographs by Pat Berrett of Albuquerque can be purchased through this organization. The actual sites of all the New Deal public art can be referenced in Treasures on New Mexico Trails.

David Witt, executive director of the Harwood Museum, Taos, generously took time to show the Harwood Collection of Patrocinio Barela's sculpture and helped us photograph important pieces. The Harwood Museum is the major depository of Barela sculpture, and David Witt is himself an authority on Barela.

Barbara B. Stanislawski is the Museum Curator for the National Park Service in Santa Fe. She furnished us with beautiful photographs taken by the Park Service. I gratefully thank her for her time and generosity.

Laura Holt, Librarian at the Laboratory of Anthropology, Museum of Indian Arts & Culture, generously offered assistance in gathering information on the personal histories of Indian artists.

Peter Mattair read the first draft of this manuscript and offered reassuring encouragement. He also turned out to be the best copy editor west of the Mississippi. Sharon Snyder is a bibliographical super-sleuth who found articles and books on almost every New Deal artist whose work is included.

I also want to thank James Clois Smith Jr., who enthusiastically supported the New Deal project for Sunstone Press, and Vicki Ahl, Sunstone's excellent graphics designer. Brenda Meeks and Annie Chee Ming Chau were the facilitators who provided aid and comfort whenever needed.

Further References to Artists Whose Work is Illustrated

KENNETH ADAMS (1897-1966)

Adams, Kenneth M., with Ruth W. Dick (Ed.). Kenneth M. Adams, N.A., 1897-1966. Albuquerque, NM: Western Art Gallery, 1972.

Cassidy, Ina Sizer. "Art and Artists of New Mexico: Art as a Goodwill Ambassador." New Mexico Magazine, June 1944, p. 22.

Coke, Van Deren. Kenneth M. Adams: A Retrospective Exhibition. Albuquerque: University of New Mexico Press, 1964.

JOZEF BAKOS (1891-1977)

Cassidy, Ina Sizer. "Art and Artists of New Mexico." New Mexico Magazine, February 1932, p. 18.

Jozef Bakos:An Early Modernist (exhibition catalog). Santa Fe: Museum of Fine Arts, 1988.

Robertson, Edna, Los Cinco Pintores. Santa Fe: The Museum of New Mexico, 1975.

PATROCINIO BARELA (1900-1964)

Barela, Patrocinio (compiled and published by Mildred Tolbert, Wendell B. Anderson, Judson Crews). Patrocinio Barela: Taos wood carver. Taos, NM: Tolbert, Anderson, Crews, 1955.

Crews, Mildred. "Sculptor in Wood." New Mexico Magazine, March 1963, p.17.

Gonzales, Edward, and David L. Witt. Spirit Ascendant—The Art and Life of Patrocinio Barela. Santa Fe: Red Crane Press, 2001.

Nunn, Tey Marianna. Sin Nombre: Hispana & Hispano Artists of the New Deal Era. Albuquerque: University of New Mexico Press, 2001.

WAYNE ERIC BARGER (1909–1952)

Bulow, Ernie. "Depression Art NotWallpaper." The Gallup Independent, January 18, 1990.

HOWARD BARTON (1907–1992)

Flynn, Kathryn A. [Ed.]. Treasures on New Mexico Trails: Discover New Deal Art & Architecture. Santa Fe: Sunstone Press, 1995.

HARRISON BEGAY (1917–)

Corley, George Andrew. "Navajo Artist Links Old and New." The Denver Post, March 30, 1947.

LeViness, W. Thetford. "Denver Art Show Focuses on Santa Fe's Artist Begay." Santa Fe News, October 31, 1952.

Ripp, Bart. "11 IndianPainters Created aTreasure at Maisel's." The Albuquerque Tribune, February 1, 1988.

CHARLES BERNINGHAUS (1905–1988)

Flynn, Kathryn A. [Ed.]. Treasures on New Mexico Trails: Discover New Deal Art & Architecture. Santa Fe: Sunstone Press, 1995.

Luhan, Mabel Dodge. Taos & Its Artists. New York: Duell, Sloan and Pearce 1947.

Porter, Dean A.,Teresa Hayes Ebie, and Suzan Campbell. Taos Artists and Their Patrons 1898–1950. South Bend: University of Notre Dame for The Snite Museum of Art, 1999.

OSCAR BERNINGHAUS (1874–1952)

Bickerstaff. Pioneer Artists of Taos, pp. 85-98

Cassidy, Ina Sizer. "Art and Artists of New Mexico." New Mexico Magazine, January 1933, p. 28.

Sanders, Gordon E. Oscar E. Berninghaus, Taos, New Mexico: Master Painter of American Indians and the Frontier West. Taos: Taos Heritage Publishing Co., 1985.

EMIL BISTRAM (1895–1976)

Cassidy, Ina Sizer. "Art and Artists of New Mexico." New Mexico Magazine, September 1934, p. 17.

Coke, Van Deren. Taos and Santa Fe–the Artist's Environment 1882–1942. Albuquerque: University of New Mexico Press for Amon Carter Museum of Western Art, 1963.

Gibson, Arrell Morgan. The Santa Fe and Taos Colonies: Age of the Muses, 1900–1942. Norman: University of Oklahoma Press, 1983.

Udall, Sharyn Rohlfsen. Modernist Painting in New Mexico, 1913–1935. Albuquerque: University of New Mexico Press, 1984.

Witt, David. Emil James Bisttram. Taos: Harwood Foundation, 1983.

LA VERNE NELSON BLACK (1887–1938)

Flynn, Kathryn A. [Ed.]. Treasures on New Mexico Trails: Discover New Deal Art & Architecture. Santa Fe: Sunstone Press, 1995.

Harmsen, Dorothy. Harmsen's Western Americana. Flagstaff: Northland Press, 1971.

Lucas, David J. "Not Too Long Ago–Paintings of the West by LaVerne Nelson Black." Exhibit Brochure for the Collection of the Valley National Bank of Arizona, 1970.

E. BOYD (1903–1974)

Boyd, E. Popular Arts of New Mexico. Santa Fe: Museum of New Mexico Press, 1974.

Cassidy, Ina Sizer. "Art and Artists of New Mexico: E. Boyd, painter." New Mexico Magazine, August 1938, p. 28.

Chavez, Fray Angelico. "E. Boyd." New Mexico Magazine, January 1975, p. 43.

Nunn, Tey Marianna. Sin Nombre: Hispana & Hispano Artists of the New Deal Era. Albuquerque: University of New Mexico Press, 2001.

PEDRO LOPEZ CERVANTEZ (1914–1987)

Flynn, Kathryn A. [Ed.]. Treasures on New Mexico Trails: Discover New Deal Art & Architecture. Santa Fe: Sunstone Press, 1995.

Lopez, Ruth. "The Role of Hispanic Artists in the WPA." Santa Fe New Mexican, October 23, 1998, p. 8.

Nunn, Tey Marianna. Sin Nombre: Hispana & Hispano Artists of the New Deal Era. Albuquerque: University of New Mexico Press, 2001.

MANVILLE CHAPMAN (1903–1978)

Cassidy, Ina Sizer. "Art and Artists of New Mexico: Blazed Trails." New Mexico Magazine, June 1935, p. 20.

Flynn, Kathryn A. [Ed.]. Treasures on New Mexico Trails: Discover New Deal Art & Architecture. Santa Fe: Sunstone Press, 1995.

Ladd, Joan. "Noted Muralist's Work 'rediscovered' inCity." Raton Daily Range, October 25, 1979.

REGINA TATUM COOKE (1902–1988)

Cassidy, Ina Sizer. "Art and Artists of New Mexico: Painter of Old Houses." New Mexico Magazine, June 1942, p. 22.

Nelson, Mary Carroll. The Legendary Artists of Taos. New York: Watson-Guptill, 1980.

ILDEBERTO "EDDIE" DELGADO (1883–1973)

"Eddie Delgado–Creative Artisan." The Santa Fe Scene, March 8, 1958.

Nunn, Tey Marianna. Sin Nombre: Hispana & Hispano Artists of the New Deal Era. Albuquerque: University of New Mexico Press, 2001.

Smith, Craig. "Dixon'sTinwork isExpressive and Practical." The Santa Fe New Mexican, October 8, 1999.

FREMONT ELLIS (1897–1985)

"Fremont Ellis." El Palacio, 28, 1930, p 16–17.

Nelson, M. "Impression of Fremont Ellis." New Mexico Magazine, March 1978, p. 36.

Warren, J. "Fremont Ellis: Always a Ray ofSunlight." New Mexico Magazine, July 1984, p. 28.

LOUIE EWING (1908–1983)

Campbell, Suzan. "Louie Ewing." Southwest Art, August 1990, p. 122.

"Louie Ewing, Silk-Screen Pioneer." Santa Fe Reporter, January 4, 1984.

"Well-Known Pioneer Artist Dies at Home." Santa Fe New Mexican, December 22, 1983.

JOSEPH FLECK (1893–1977)

Coke, Van Deren. Taos and Santa Fe–the Artist's Environment 1882–1942. Albuquerque: University of New Mexico Press for Amon Carter Museum of Western Art, 1963.

Fleck, Joseph A. Joseph A. Fleck, an Early Taos Painter. Santa Fe: Museum of New Mexico Press, 1985.

PAUL FLYING EAGLE GOODBEAR (1913–1954)

New Mexico Historical Review, Vol XXXVI, October 1961, No. 4, p. 257.

A.L. GROLL (1866–1952)

Cline, Lynn. "A Cold Can of Beans and aPickle." The Santa Fe New Mexican, September 4, 1998, p 382.

Flynn, Kathryn A. [Ed.]. Treasures on New Mexico Trails: Discover New Deal Art & Architecture. Santa Fe: Sunstone Press, 1995.

Porter, Dean A.,Teresa Hayes Ebie, and Suzan Campbell. Taos Artists and Their Patrons 1898–1950. South Bend: University of Notre Dame for The Snite Museum of Art, 1999.

LELA GUTIERREZ (1895–1969)

Flynn, Kathryn A. [Ed.]. Treasures on New Mexico Trails: Discover New Deal Art & Architecture. Santa Fe: Sunstone Press, 1995.

WILLIAM PENHALLOW HENDERSON (1877–1943)

Breeskin, Adelyn D. William Penhallow Henderson, 1877–1943: An Artist of Santa Fe. Washington, D.C.: Smithsonian Institution Press, 1978.

Cassidy, Ina Sizer. "Art and Artists of New Mexico." New Mexico Magazine, March 1932, p. 24.

Feldman, Sandra K. William Penhallow Henderson, The Early Years: 1901–1916. New York: Hirschl & Adler Galleries, 1982.

William Penhallow Henderson:MasterColorist of Santa Fe (exhibition catalog). Phoenix: Phoenix Art Museum, 1984.

ERNEST MARTIN HENNINGS (1886–1956)

Cassidy, Ina Sizer. "Art and Artists of New Mexico." New Mexico Magazine, February 1933, p. 27.

E. Martin Hennings: Paintings & Works on Paper from Europe & Taos. Santa Fe: Gerald Peters Gallery, 1991.

Fisher, Reginald. "E. Martin Hennings, Artist of Taos." El Palacio, August 1946.

VELINO SHIJE HERRERA (1902–1973)

Cline, Lynn. "Indian Artists as Illustrators of Children's Books Part of Winter Antiquities Show." Santa Fe New Mexican, December 26, 1997, p. 48.

Dunn, Dorothy. American Indian Painting of the Southwest and Plains Areas. Albuquerque: University of New Mexico Press, 1968.

Snodgrass, Jeanne O. American Indian Painters–A Biographical Directory. New York: Museum of the American Indian, 1968.

"Velino Herrera." New Mexico Magazine, July 1931, p. 19.

VICTOR HIGGINS (1884–1949)

Bickerstaff. Pioneer Artists of Taos, p. 175.

Cassidy, Ina Sizer. "Art and Artists of New Mexico." New Mexico Magazine, December 1932, p. 22.

Nelson, Mary Carroll. "Victor Higgins: Creative Explorer." American Artist, January 1978.

Porter, Dean A. Victor Higgins: an American Master. Salt Lake City: Peregrine Smith Books, 1991.

NILS HOGNER (1893–1970)

Chang, Richard. "Chamber Music Festival Celebrates 1997." Santa Fe New Mexican, November 24, 1996, p. B1.

Flynn, Kathryn A. [Ed.]. Treasures on New Mexico Trails: Discover New Deal Art & Architecture. Santa Fe: Sunstone Press, 1995.

ALLAN HOUSER (1914–1994)

Houser and Haozous: a sculptural retrospective, September 10, 1983–May 1, 1984. Phoenix: The Museum for The Heard Museum, Phoenix, Arizona, Phoenix, 1983.

Monacelli, L. "Allan Houser–Putting Life into Sculpture." New Mexico Magazine, March 1983, p. 26.

Perlman, Barbara H. Allan Houser: (HA-O-ZOUS). Boston: David R. Godine, 1987.

ODON HULLENKREMER (1888–1978)

Cassidy, Ina Sizer. "Art and Artists of New Mexico: Odon Hullenkremer." New Mexico Magazine, April 1936, p. 21.

Kutnewsky, F. "Life Saving Artist." New Mexico Magazine, February 1961, p. 37.

RUSSELL VERNON HUNTER (1900–1955)

Branham, M. "Last Frontier on Canvas." New Mexico Magazine, October 1961, p. 24.

Cassidy, Ina Sizer. "Art and Artists of New Mexico: Vernon Hunter." New Mexico Magazine, January 1936, p. 24.

Russel Vernon Hunter, 1900–1955. Memorial Retrospective Exhibition. Santa Fe: Roswell Museum and Museum of New Mexico Art Gallery, 1955.

PETER HURD (1904–1984)

Cassidy, Ina Sizer. "Art and Artists of New Mexico: Peter Hurd." New Mexico Magazine, December 1955, p. 30.

Horgan, Paul. Peter Hurd: A Portrait Sketch fromLife. Austin: University of Texas Press for the Amon Carter Museum of Western Art, Fort Worth, 1965.

Metzger, Robert. My Land is the Southwest: Peter Hurd letters and journals by Peter Hurd, edited by Robert Metzger, with introduction by Paul Horgan. College Station: Texas A&M University Press, 1983.

JOHN JELLICO (1914–)

Flynn, Kathryn A. [Ed.]. Treasures on New Mexico Trails: Discover New Deal Art & Architecture. Santa Fe: Sunstone Press, 1995.

D. PAUL JONES (–1998)

Flynn, Kathryn A. [Ed.]. Treasures on New Mexico Trails: Discover New Deal Art & Architecture. Santa Fe: Sunstone Press, 1995.

RAYMOND JONSON (1891–1982)

Cassidy, Ina Sizer. "Raymond Jonson Gallery." New Mexico Magazine, March 1950, p. 24.

Garman, Ed, with foreword by Elaine de Kooning. The art of Raymond Jonson, Painter. Albuquerque: University of New Mexico Press, 1976.

McCauley, Elizabeth Anne. Raymond Jonson: The Early Years. Albuquerque: University Art Museum, University of New Mexico, 1980.

Nestor, S. "Enchanted by light." New Mexico Magazine, November 1979, p. 24.

GENE KLOSS (1903–1996)

Kloss, Gene, withText by Phillips Kloss. Gene Kloss Etchings. Santa Fe, NM: Sunstone Press, 2000.

Luhan, Mabel Dodge. Taos & Its Artists. New York: Duell, Sloan and Pearce, 1947.

Nelson, Mary Carroll. "Images of Taos Engraved in Artist's Work." New Mexico Magazine, December 1986, p. 26.

PAUL LANTZ (1908–1998)

Artists of 20th-Century New Mexico: The Museum of Fine Arts Collection. Santa Fe: Museum of Fine Arts Press, 1992.

Cassidy, Ina Sizer. "Art andArtists of New Mexico: Paul Lantz." New Mexico Magazine, November 1935, p. 26.

TOM LEA (1907–2001)

Hjerter, Kathleen G. (Comp.), with an introduction by William Weber Johnson.

The Art of Tom Lea. College Station: Texas A & M University Press, 1989.

Rodenberger, Lou. "Tom Lea–Interpreter of Southwestern Border Life." Southwest Heritage, Summer 1980, p. 2–5.

West, John O. "Tom Lea: artist in two mediums." Austin: Steck-Vaughn Co., 1967.

JOHN WARD LOCKWOOD (1894–1963)

Adams, D. "Taos–art mart." New Mexico Magazine, September 1964, p. 26.

Cassidy, Ina Sizer. "Art and Artists of New Mexico: Ward Lockwood." New Mexico Magazine, February 1933, p. 27.

Eldredge, Charles C. Ward Lockwood 1894–1963. Lawrence: University of Kansas Museum of Art, 1974.

Luhan, Mabel Dodge. Taos & Its Artists. New York: Duell, Sloan and Pearce, 1947.

WILLIAM LUMPKINS (1909–2000)

Clay, Rebecca. "Down-to-Earth Architect Builds a Solid Reputation." New Mexico Magazine, April 1989, p. 30–36.

Hall, Douglas Kent. "William Lumpkins–Collaborating with Color." El Palacio, September 1995, p. 38.

Kusel, Denise. "Death of William Lumpkins closes chapter of art history." Santa Fe New Mexican, March 22, 2000, p. B1.

JULIAN MARTINEZ (1879–1943)

"Art of the potters." New Mexico Magazine, July 1943, p. 14.

Cassidy, Ina Sizer. "Art and Artists of New Mexico." New Mexico Magazine, November 1933, p. 10.

Gridley, M. "Art Out of the Earth." New Mexico Magazine, November 1934, p. 7.

Hyde, Hazel. Maria Making Pottery. Santa Fe: Sunstone Press, 1973.

MARIA MARTINEZ (1886–1980)

Gilpin, L. "Potter of San Ildefonso." New Mexico Magazine, January–February 1974, p. 32.

Hyde, Hazel. Maria Making Pottery. Santa Fe: Sunstone Press, 1973.

Marriott, Alice. Maria, the Potter of San Ildefonso. Norman: University of Oklahoma Press, 1948.

Peterson, Susan. The Living Tradition of Mária Martínez. Tokyo: Kodansha International; New York: distributed through Harper & Row, 1977.

ILA McAFEE (TURNER) (1897–1995)

Cassidy, Ina Sizer. "Art and Artists of New Mexico: Ila McAfee, Painter of Horses." New Mexico Magazine, November 1943, p. 20.

Nelson, Mary Carroll. The Legendary Artists of Taos. New York: Watson-Guptill, 1980.

Van Cleve, Emily. "The MagicArt of Miniature Landscapes." Santa Fe New Mexican, August 15, 1997, p. 30.

BEN CARLTON MEAD (1902–1986)

Dykes, Jeff. Fifty Great Western Illustrators. Flagstaff: Northland Press, 1975.

Forrester-O'Brien, Esse. Art and Artists of Texas. Dallas: Tardy, 1935.

Mead, Ben Carlton. "Ben Mead and Matt Dillon," a letter to the editor. True West 21:1, September–October 1973.

DOROTHY MORANG (1906–1995)

Cline, Lynn. "Independent Spirits—Women Who Defied Tradition." Santa Fe New Mexican, June 14, 1996.

Dohme, Ralph. "New Mexican Profile—Dorothy Morang." Pasatiempo, Santa Fe New Mexican, July 18, 1965.

Lieu, Jocelyn. "Dorothy Morang: An Inspired Painter." Santa Fe Reporter, April 18, 1990.

JAMES STOVALL MORRIS (1902–1973)

"Exhibition at Charles-Fourth Gallery," Art News, May 1949.

"New York Debut at the Charles-Fourth Gallery," Art Digest, May 15, 1949.

"Pieces of Men," Time Magazine, January 15, 1951.

White, Jerry. "About the Arts." Santa Fe New Mexico, 31 January 1965, p.3.

LLOYD MOYLAN (1893–1963)

Cassidy, Ina Sizer. "Art and Artists of New Mexico: Lloyd Moylan." New Mexico Magazine, April 1937, p. 25.

Indyke, Dottie. "A Showcase of Early Arrivals on Art Scene I." Santa Fe New Mexican, May 13, 1994, p 19.

EULOGIO NARANJO

Flynn, Kathryn A. [Ed.]. Treasures on New Mexico Trails: Discover New Deal Art & Architecture. Santa Fe: Sunstone Press, 1995.

WILLARD NASH (1898–1943)

Cassidy, Ina Sizer. "Art and artists of New Mexico: Willard Nash." New Mexico Magazine, September 1935, p. 23.

McCloud, Kathleen. "Willard Nash painted his way into fabric of history." Santa Fe New Mexican, Apr 25, 1997.

Udall, Sharyn Rohlfsen. Modernist Painting in New Mexico, 1913-1935. Albuquerque:
University of New Mexico Press, 1984.

HELMUTH NAUMER (1907–1989)

Cassidy, Ina Sizer. "Art and Artists of New Mexico: Helmut Naumer, Pastelist." New Mexico Magazine, January 1940, p. 23.

Gwynn, John. "InPursuit of the Fleeting Effects of Sky." Pasatiempo, Santa Fe New Mexican, June 8, 1990, p. 8.

Gwynn, John, "Painter Naumer Dies at 82." Santa Fe New Mexican, June 19, 1990.

B.J.O. NORDFELDT (1878–1955)

Cassidy, Ina Sizer. "Art and Artists of New Mexico." New Mexico Magazine, October 1932, p. 24.

Coke, Van Deren. Nordfeldt, the Painter. Albuquerque: University of New Mexico Press, 1972.

Hunter, Sam. B. J. O. Nordfeldt: An American Expressionist. Pipersville, Pa.: Richard Stuart Gallery, 1984.

MAX ORTIZ

Nunn, Tey Marianna. Sin Nombre: Hispana & Hispano Artists of the New Deal Era. Albuquerque: University of New Mexico Press, 2001.

SHELDON PARSONS (1866–1943)

Cassidy, Ina Sizer. "Art and artists of New Mexico." New Mexico Magazine, September 1931, p. 27.

Coke, Van Deren. Taos and Santa Fe—the Artist's Environment 1882–1942. Albuquerque: University of New Mexico Press for Amon Carter Museum of Western Art, 1963.

BERT PHILLIPS (1868–1956)

Bickerstaff. Pioneer Artists of Taos, pp. 51-63.

Broder. Taos: A Painter's Dream. pp. 96-113.

Carr, L. "My neighbor is an Artist." New Mexico Magazine, December 1923, p. 14.

Nelson, Mary Carroll. "Bert Geer Phillips: Taos Romantic." American Artist, January 1978.

Schimmel, Julie and White, Robert R. Bert Geer Phillips and the Taos Art Colony. Albuquerque: University of New Mexico, 1994.

ELISEO JOSE RODRIGUEZ (1915–)

"Eliseo's Garden." Santa Fe New Mexican, August 24, 2001.

Nunn, Tey Marianna. Sin Nombre: Hispana & Hispano Artists of the New Deal Era. Albuquerque: University of New Mexico Press, 2001.

Padilla, Carmella. "Eliseo Rodriguez: El Sexto Pintor." El Palacio, Summer/Fall 2001, Vol 106, No. 1, p. 26.

OLIVE RUSH (1873–1966)

Cuba, Stanley L. Olive Rush: A Hoosier Artist in New Mexico. Muncie: Minnetrista Cultural Foundation, 1992.

Cassidy, Ina Sizer. "Art and Artists of New Mexico: State College Murals." New Mexico Magazine, August 1936, p. 27.

Cassidy, Ina Sizer. "Art and Artists of New Mexico: Olive Rush." New Mexico Magazine, May 1957, p. 29.

JUAN SANCHEZ (1901–1969)

Flynn, Kathryn A. [Ed.]. Treasures of New Mexico Trails—Discover New Deal Art & Architecture. Santa Fe: Sunstone Press, 1995.

Gibson, Arrell Morgan. The Santa Fe and Taos Colonies: Age of the Muses, 1900–1942. Norman: University of Oklahoma Press, 1983.

Nunn, Tey Marianna. Sin Nombre: Hispana & Hispano Artists of the New Deal Era. Albuquerque: University of New Mexico Press, 2001.

HOWARD BEHLING SCHLEETER (1903–1976)

Artists of 20th-Century New Mexico: The Museum of Fine Arts Collection. Santa Fe: Museum of Fine Arts Press, 1992.

Coke, Van Deren. Taos and Santa Fe—the Artist's Environment 1882-1942. Albuquerque: University of New Mexico Press for Amon Carter Museum of Western Art, 1963.

"Schleeter Back in Santa Fe." Santa Fe New Mexican, August 17, 1958, p. 29.

EUGENIE SHONNARD (1886–1978)

Cassidy, Ina Sizer. "Art and Artists of New Mexico: Eugenie Shonnard." New Mexico Magazine, March 1932, p. 24.

Cassidy, Ina Sizer. "The Eugenie Shonnard Retrospective Exhibition." New Mexico Magazine, July 1954, p. 32.

Coke, Van Deren. Taos and Santa Fe—the Artist's Environment 1882-1942. Albuquerque: University of New Mexico Press for Amon Carter Museum of Western Art, 1963.

WILL SHUSTER (1893–1969)

Cassidy, Ina Sizer. "Art andArtists of New Mexico." New Mexico Magazine, February 1932, p. 18.

Dispenza, Joseph and Turner, Louise, with introduction by Richard Bradford. Will Shuster: a Santa Fe legend. Santa Fe: Museum of New Mexico Press, 1989.

Hillerman, Tony. "Meet Dr. Frankenstein Shuster." New Mexico Magazine, August 1960, p. 24.

Robertson, Edna. Los Cinco Pintores. Santa Fe: Museum of New Mexico, 1975.

WALTER UFER (1876–1936)

Bickerstaff. Pioneer Artists of Taos, p. 113.

Cassidy, Ina Sizer. "Art and Artists of New Mexico." New Mexico Magazine, January 1933, p. 28.

Egri, Ted. "Walter Ufer: Passion and Talent." American Artist, January 1978. "The Santa Fe-Taos Art Colony: Walter Ufer." El Palacio, August 1916.

THEODORE VAN SOELEN (1890–1964)

Cassidy, Ina Sizer. "Art and Artists of New Mexico: Silver City Murals." New Mexico Magazine, June 1938, p. 29.

Cassidy, Ina Sizer. "Art and Artists of New Mexico: The Theodore Van Soelen Retrospective Exhibition." New Mexico Magazine, August 1960, p. 35.

Coke, Van Deren. Taos and Santa Fe—the Artist's Environment 1882-1942. Albuquerque: University of New Mexico Press for Amon Carter Museum of Western Art, 1963.

Museum of New Mexico. A Retrospective Exhibition of the Work of Van Soelen. Santa Fe: Museum of New Mexico, 1960.

PABLITA VELARDE (1918–)

"Pablita Velarde, Indian artist of the red earth country." New Mexico Magazine, December 1960, p. 11.

Ruch, Marcella J. Pablita Velarde: painting her people. Santa Fe: New Mexico Magazine, 2001.

Wilks, Flo. "Pablita." New Mexico Magazine, August 1976, p. 28.

STUART WALKER (1888–1940)

McCloud, Kathleen. "The Vision of Transcendental Painters." Santa Fe New Mexican, September 19, 1997.

Mecklenburg, Virginia M. The Patricia and Phillip Frost Collection: American Abstraction 1930–1945. Published for the National Museum of American Art by the Smithsonian Institution Press, (nd).

"Tribute to Painter Stuart Walker on Occasion of a Recent Exhibition." Raymond Jonson Papers (Roll RJ8: 5754), Archives of American Art, Smithsonian Institution, Washington, D.C., 1940.

WILLIAM WARDER (1920–1999)

Ferrendelli, Betta. "Raton Native Leaves Mark in Murals." Raton Range, August 28, 1990.

Jones, Donna. "Muralist Brings Shades of N.M. to School." Albuquerque Journal, May 29, 1990.

Randles, Slim. "Artist in the Schools is a Multicultural New Mexico Original." Albuquerque Journal, May 11, 1996.

HAROLD WEST (1902–1968)

"Hal West Gallery Is Homespun Hacienda." Santa Fe New Mexican, August 24, 1958, p. 25.

Ortiz y Davis, Madelynn. "Artist Hal West Likes Long Skirts." Santa Fe New Mexican, May 26, 1968.

Schaefer, Jack. "Hal West: A Personal Tribute." Santa Fe New Mexican, December 6, 1968, p. 1.

BROOKS WILLIS (1903–1981)

Cassidy, Ina Sizer. "Art and Artists of New Mexico: Brooks Willis." New Mexico Magazine, December 1938, p. 25.

Weideman, Paul. "Randall DaveyProtegé Ignored the Rules." Santa Fe New Mexican, July 14, 2000.

ANNA KEENER WILTON (1895–1982)

"Anna Keener Paints Variety of Styles." Santa Fe New Mexican, October 5, 1958.

"Anna Keener Show Slated in Duke City Next Sunday." Santa Fe New Mexican, September 20, 1964.

"Obituaries." Santa Fe New Mexican, June 27, 1982.

Index

Place names, unless otherwise indicated, are in New Mexico. Specific buildings or organizations that hold art works are listed directly and by town. Bold indicate illustrations including photos of artists or their works.

S

T

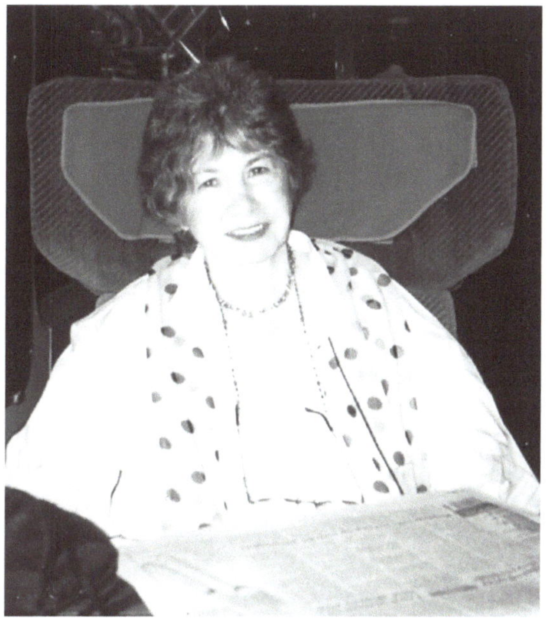

Jacqueline Hoefer's publications include *Imagining the Garden*, a book of poems; *Weather Songs*, three poems set to music by Lanham Deal; and critical essays on contemporary writers, among them, Samuel Beckett, Harold Pinter and Norman Mailer. Her last book was *Night in a White Wood, New and Selected Poems*, also published by Sunstone Press.

Mrs. Hoefer received a PhD in American literature from Washington University, St. Louis, Missouri, and in the early 1960s taught at the University of California, Berkeley, and at San Francisco State University. In 1967, she joined her husband Peter Hoefer in starting Hoefer Scientific Instruments, a San Francisco company specializing in producing instruments for biological research. After Peter Hoefer's death in 1987, she carried on as chief executive officer, until her retirement. She died in 2006.

www.ingramcontent.com/pod-product-compliance
Lightning Source LLC
LaVergne TN
LVHW070212110826
845147LV00003B/561
* 9 7 8 0 8 6 5 3 4 3 7 1 9 *